K. Sneaiedi

W 12 45

BELMONTE
DE LOS
CABALLEROS

BELMONTE
DE LOS
CABALLEROS

*Anthropology and History
in an Aragonese Community*

BY
CARMELO LISON-TOLOSANA

PRINCETON UNIVERSITY PRESS
PRINCETON, NEW JERSEY

Published by Princeton University Press,
41 William Street, Princeton, New Jersey 08540
In the United Kingdom:
Princeton University Press, Guildford, Surrey
Copyright © 1983 by Princeton University Press

First printing by Oxford University Press, 1966
First Princeton Paperback printing, 1983
LCC 82-48562
ISBN 0-691-09402-0
ISBN 0-691-02829-X pbk.

Printed in the United States of America
by Princeton University Press, Princeton, New Jersey

Reprinted by arrangement with Oxford University Press

To the Rev. D. Moisés García-Sanz
of Zaragoza

FOREWORD

THE READER has before him one of the finest ethnographies of the anthropological literature of southern Europe. One welcomes its reappearance almost two decades after its publication. This appraisal can be justified only by reference to what anthropology is and tries to do and, within that disciplinary purpose, what an ethnography is and tries to do.

Anthropology, very simply, seeks to contribute to our comprehensive understanding of human nature by documenting its diverse expressions. Nothing human is alien to anthropological inquiry, for everything human contributes to the understanding of the possibilities of that nature. Within that overarching purpose, it is the task of ethnography to document and communicate a comprehensive account of a given cultural tradition.

From the anthropological perspective—the very long term perspective of human evolution—we see cultures come and go with frequency. Documentation of those cultures—our archival function—is a crucial task. But documentation alone does not fulfill the anthropological purpose of communicating knowledge about actual life in other cultures. For this, literary sensibilities— a sharp eye and a good ear—are important. A fine ethnography, then, should be rich in corroborative detail for every observation made. It must be felicitous and resourceful in its uses of the devices of effective communication. It must avoid a heavy hand in relating its major points and in marshalling its corroborative detail. *Belmonte de los Caballeros* qualifies on all counts. It is a highly detailed and convincing account of life in an Aragonese agricultural town written with a fine hand by an observer with a finely attuned ear. It constitutes an invaluable resource on rural Spanish life.

Professor Lison has written, however, a special kind of ethnography. It is an ethnography, first, that is strong in its analysis of landholding, cash cropping, and rural social class and links effectively—for purposes of comparison—with the community

studies of the American sociological tradition. The book is a
baseline for any study of land tenure and rural stratification in
Spain and the Mediterranean. It is an ethnography, second, that
is exceptionally well integrated with the historical data. The per-
tinent local and provincial archives, civil and ecclesiastical, have
been read with great care and used in an extensive and fully
integrated manner throughout. This gives us both a sense of the
persistence over the centuries of certain structures and values—
the economic-political hierarchy, for example—as well as a sense
of the significant changes.

   This effective interweaving of history together with the use of
the very Spanish idea of life as the interaction of generations—
it is basic in the work of Marais and Ortega y Gasset—gives
illuminating dynamism to the account. We are shown the different historical experiences, different values, and different time
sense of the three generations—the declining generation of the
Civil War period passing out of power; the active, controlling
generation holding the center of the structures of power; and
the youthful generation emerging into power. This interaction
is related to the thematic account of the interaction between the
four strata of the town: the "braceros," the "jornaleros," the
"proprietarios," and the "pudientes." To these negotiations of
the categories of social and biological existence must be added
the author's full account of the interaction between officialdom
and official requirements and popular practice. He shows in
matters of juridical obligation and commitment to the law or in
matters of the fulfillment of Christian doctrine. Altogether, this
ethnography achieves in its detail and in its interweaving of
historical, generational, and class dynamics that quality of "de-
scriptive integration" which was the hallmark of the work of
E. E. Evans Pritchard, the great English anthropologist and one
of Lison's teachers at Oxford.

   There is advantage in the fact that this ethnography has been
written by a native son of the town and a Spaniard. This gives
him an awareness of the events of local life that add much corroborative detail—in the case studies of marriage and inheritance negotiations for example—and an intimate knowledge of
the nuances of cultural expression. Thus, many key terms of the
local idiom, in which repose so much daily preoccupation, receive
the fullest explanation and exemplification: *la campana, los pu-*

dientes, pobreza, trato, clase, familia, honradez, puntillo, verguenza, la gana, to mention a few. And the advantage to this ethnography of its having been written by a Spaniard lies in the use of certain concepts fully within the Spanish intellectual tradition. We have mentioned the idea of the "generation" but there is also the idea of the *vigencia,* the collective assumptions about the requirements and proprieties of social life. This latter idea easily embraces the complex but quite valid fact that such assumptions are not naturally compatible but are most often incompatible—at best complementary. These *vigencias* are in constant need of negotiation in ongoing social existence—a process the author captures effectively.

Spain's history of the last several hundred years has been one of governmental volatility and turbulence. The author sketches that turbulence and the ways it has affected life in the town. The turbulence has bred a certain cynicism and withdrawal from government and the rule of law or at least from the politicians and the bureaucratic regulations generated by the government bureaucracy. Lison makes a telling comparison between the civic commitment and the rule of law of the ancient Greek "polis"— the historical legacy of southern Europe—and the uncertainties of that commitment and rule in the modern pueblo. Allegiance to juridical obligation is weak, and the prevailing view of equity and civic obligation is personalistic. Lison suggests that the immediate cause of this individualism in civic matters lies in the inattentive socialization of the young; but in the longer term, the materials suggest that this withdrawal and cynicism is produced by the repeated imposition upon the town of intolerant state ideologies and authoritarian and totalitarian institutions. There is, however, considerable evidence, both historical and modern, in this ethnography of the town's capacity to manage its own affairs. The evidence argues for a return to more effective regional and local government as is characteristic of contemporary post-totalitarian Spain.

It is hard—perhaps impossible—to escape ideology in any thoughtful enterprise, even in writing ethnography. Yet if there is any work that might escape or, perhaps better, encompass the ideological struggles of the moment, it *is* ethnography. The question even arises whether ideological commitment is compatible with complete ethnography. Here we should keep in mind the time period in which this ethnography was written—in the late fifties and the early sixties. This was the heyday of the totalitarian regime that emerged victorious in the Spanish Civil War. In the face of such "intolerance" as was characteristic of the period, the author sought to produce an ethnography "tolerant" of all social and cultural facts and forces that had been at work in his community. Lison refers in his preface to a dictum of Bacon that may be a good "rule of law" for ethnography generally. Lison's purpose, like Bacon's, was "not to contradict and confute, nor to believe and take for granted . . . but to weigh and consider." The author has produced, in my view, a *compleat* ethnography, or one as closely approaching that ideal as may be possible for any anthropologist. Its commitment is to the documentation of all aspects of life in the Aragonese town and to the reader's understanding of what it is and what it was to have lived that life at its various levels, in its various classes, in its various generations and in its various time periods. May the reader have the time in this harried and clamorous age to do this book the justice of a careful reading.

James W. Fernandez
Professor of Anthropology
Princeton University
July 1982

PREFACE

THIS BOOK is the result of the material gathered during fieldwork carried out in Belmonte de los Caballeros between 1958 and 1960. It describes the life of the people in a small Aragonese community and attempts to capture the essential characteristics of the social structure and values which underlie it. These appear to be the result, or rather the expression, of a principle which organizes the life of the residents in terms of inferiority and superiority; a principle which both supposes and develops a strong individualism. The analysis of the forms of landed property, the stratification of the community, family relationships, the interplay of generations, the position of the residents before the law, religious experiences and practices and the system of values—the principal themes of study in the book—point to that conclusion.

I have taken care to stick to the facts, examining them from different angles; and, following a dictum of Bacon (Essay No. L) I present them here just as I saw them, 'not to contradict and confute; nor to believe and take for granted; nor to find talk and discourse; but to weigh and consider'.

Facts relating to one subject are not always confined to one specific chapter. The period 1931–36, for example, is examined from different perspectives in chapters II, VIII, XII and XIII. Some chapters support and explain others. In the analysis of family relationships and attitudes towards the law I have concentrated upon the negative aspects, that is on tensions and conflicts only mentioning in passing the positive ones. One could begin to read the book at chapter IX, but until one has read chapter XIII the real meaning of the behaviour of the people within the community cannot be fully understood. None the less I have preferred to follow a logical order in the exposition, describing the working of the institutions first and leaving to the last the values and attitudes which animate them. The name of the small town and surnames of people mentioned have been changed.

This book would not have been possible without the training I have received at the Institute of Social Anthropology, Oxford, and without the tuition and supervision of Dr R. G. Lienhardt, to whom I express my sincere gratitude.

I am much indebted to Mr R. D. F. Pring-Mill, who read through the typescript most carefully, for a good number of stylistic corrections and helpful suggestions. I would like also to express my thanks to Dr J. K. Campbell for his valuable comments and advice.

I am very pleased to be able to thank from these pages all the residents of Belmonte de los Caballeros, for the exceptional kindness which they have always shown me and for their co-operation in providing information. In particular I would like to mention personally the following, José, Ismael, Carlos and especially my parents María and Blas who, with their memories of bygone days, have often described to me the life of the small community during the first quarter of this century. My brother José has been at all times an excellent collaborator, keeping me in touch with what was going on in the town during my absences.

In the translation into English I have been helped by D. Carlos Fernández and by Mr Turner—my thanks to them. But in reality it has been Julia, my wife, who has done most of it and who has patiently copied and corrected the entire book. Her untiring efforts have made possible the presentation of this book in English. I express my deepest gratitude to her.

Finally many thanks also to the Board of Exeter College for awarding me the Alan Coltart Scholarship which helped me in the last months of writing this book.

C. L-T.

CONTENTS

LIST OF PLATES

MAPS

INTRODUCTION

'*A citadel-hill is suitable for oligarchy and monarchy, and a level site for democracy*' ARISTOTLE

'*Gradus autem plures sunt societatis hominum. Ut enim ab illa infinita discedatur, propior est eiusdem gentis, nationis, linguae, qua maxime homines coniuguntur; interius etiam est eiusdem esse civitatis*' CICERO

'*Sólo es prójimo el de la misma tribu*' UNAMUNO

ON THE MAIN road from Madrid to Barcelona, south east of the capital of Aragón, there is a small town of some 1300 people. It is situated in the heart of the middle Ebro valley, or more exactly on its smooth miocenic slopes.

To the north-east of the town's territorial boundaries (*término*) there extends a range of chalk mountains, white and sterile, with sharp pointed pinnacles rising occasionally to 300 metres. The lower slopes of these mountains dissolve into a great terrace of boulders and reddish soil where the vines, cereals, and almond trees grow. The final undulations of this dry, sunburnt and brick-red terrace are abruptly cut off by the road, which marks the division of two entirely distinct physical areas. On its right, towards the south-west, there stretches a broad plain broken up into a multitude of small green or yellow plots intersected with hundreds of veins injecting water everywhere. This is the irrigated land (*huerta*).

The district, like the rest of the Ebro Basin, has a mediterranean-continental climate, with severe winters, hot dry summers, and with maximum rainfalls at the beginning of the autumn and in the spring. The rains do not last long even during these periods; the rest of the year is invariably sunny and dry.

The mountains support only a poor growth of sparto-grass, low rosemary and thyme. The products of the terrace of red clayey soils depend on the scanty autumnal or spring rains. The *huerta*, rich in cereal, vegetables and fruits does not depend upon the rains, but is watered by a careful and thorough network of irrigation canals and ditches.

In a stubbornly dry climate the *huerta* is probably the best expression of the technical abilities of a people and their capacity to adapt themselves to their environment. The 668 hectares of irrigated land are divided into 1222 plots.[1] They are skilfully laid out and evenly watered, each with its ditch and its way of access, with dykes separating plot from plot. Large and small canals supply the water, which is rigidly controlled. These plots express, together with the nocturnal hours of waiting to take one's turn at watering and the tiresome buying of fertilizers in years of scarcity to improve the soil, several hundred years, generation after generation, of unceasing struggle between man and his environment.

*
*   *

The small town lines the road and forms an almost perfect rectangle. It is a 'Gassendorf' or a 'Strassendorf'. The pattern of houses seems to obey a clearly defined plan, being closely set together so that the town could be shut at night by means of two gates at either end of the main street. The houses outside this nucleus indicate the progressive growth of the town.

The road forms the main street and is bordered by white, three-storied houses with rectangular ground plans, with a slightly sloping roof covered with hurdles and ochre tiles. Several of these houses still preserve the loggia and the eaves, together with small wooden columns in the balconies and sun galleries, all of which are architectural forms deeply rooted in the small towns of the Ebro River valley, dating from the seventeenth and early eighteenth centuries and repeating the Aragonese-Renaissance style. These were rebuilt upon the ruins of former, humbler ones of two stories, similar to the present-day houses which form the streets parallel to or transversing the main street. The third group of dwellings is adapted to the unevenness

---

[1] These statistical data and those which follow are not to be taken with mathematical precision because, due to inheritance, new subdivisions continually appear.

A view of the hills and of the first terrace

End of the first terrace and beginning of the second terrace

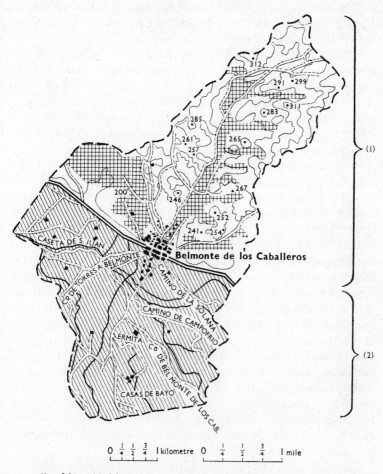

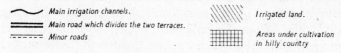

Map of the municipal district (término) of Belmonte de los Caballeros.

(1) *Hilly country and first terrace. Land without irrigation (cereals, and vines).*

(2) *Second terrace. Irrigated land or huerta (sugar-beet, cereals, vegetables and fruits).*

~~~~~~~~ *Main irrigation channels.*

▬▬▬▬▬ *Main road which divides the two terraces.*

-------- *Minor roads*

///// *Irrigated land.*

▦▦▦▦ *Areas under cultivation in hilly country*

Based on a map by the Instituto Geográfico y Catastral.

of the ground; people have hollowed out the earth and built their houses inside. These quarters are commonly called the caves. Twenty-five of the thirty-three caves are inhabited. I shall come back later to these divisions.

Some 175 of the 313 inhabited houses are buildings of two floors; about seventy have three floors, and the remainder have only one. Of the 313 houses, 210 are lived in by one family and 103 by two. It would be a mistake, however, taking these statistics alone, to draw conclusions about the necessity of building a larger number of houses, as other values come into play, as we shall see later.

In a three-storied house, the ground floor is composed of a hall, the kitchen, the scullery and a sitting room; the bedrooms are on the first floor and the granaries, formerly necessary for the storage of grain, form the attic. Almost all the three-storied houses line the main street. Those of two stories are of identical interior and exterior construction, but have no attics. Recently built houses consist of two floors without attics, which are no longer necessary. Wheat is no longer stored in the granary waiting for a possible buyer; it is brought to the silo of the National Wheat Syndicate. All the houses have a large yard with outbuildings such as barns and open sheds for agricultural tools, or for the tractor, carts and trailers; there are hen runs, pigsties (already considered unnecessary in new houses) and a well for getting water for domestic animals (hens, ducks, rabbits and perhaps cows, goats and pigeons). In many of the three-storied, main street houses there is a cellar as well where the wine is kept. It rarely forms part of the new buildings. The yard with its attached buildings is the expression of a domestic-agricultural economy.

Life is lived on the ground floor because it is cooler and more comfortable in summer and less exposed to the winds in wintertime. Awnings at the doors and blinds at the windows and balconies counteract the summer heat. During the summer the *patio*, the door of the house and the street are the scenes of social life. When the cold weather tightens its grip, the big kitchens with long benches round the hearth (fast disappearing now) and the café-bars are the gathering places.

There are many towns in Aragón built on a hill. In them it is easy to distinguish a late-medieval nucleus at the top, with the church tower and the ruins of an abbey or convent to which formerly the surrounding land if not the entire *término* belonged; or else a castle or a palace or an ancient manor house, almost always in ruins as well, formerly owned by the 'lord' who would have employed the majority of his neighbours to work his lands. The streets descend, slowly or abruptly, twisted, steep and narrow, from the nucleus. This type of town reflects a historic socio-economic structure the influence of which is still sometimes found today. In Belmonte de los Caballeros we encounter a form of habitat resulting from centrifugal forces which are quite different. It is situated in a broad, slightly sloping plain, along an ancient route, without any special strategic advantages. It is open to the four points of the compass. No house can claim the privileges of overlordship or boast a coat of arms. In fact there is no nucleus, unless it is the geometric centre of the town occupied by the parish church. This is significant in itself. Everything is uniform and equal, which indicates another aspect of social structure in the history of the town.

*
*   *

People asked me: 'Are you studying the history of the town?' and they added: 'This town has no history'. This is true, if by history they understand the lives of important men or famous deeds. In the documents which refer to the town, names are quoted of people without any significance, ordinary men and women who buy and sell their plots and who need to resort to the public notary for legalizing their affairs. There is no mention of *ricos-hombres*, *caballeros* or *infanzones* (ranks of Aragonese nobility), who possess large estates or who even live in the town. In 1542 the Portuguese G. Barreiros went on a journey to Rome. His work '*Corographia de algunos lugares*', printed in Coimbra in 1559, is the result of this pilgrimage. In it he writes: 'Belmonte (de los Caballeros) is a town . . . belonging to the Crown.'[1] A Dutchman, E. Cock, an archer in Philip II's Royal Guard, accompanied the monarch to the legislative 'Cortes' of the Kingdom of Aragón in the year 1585, and in his '*Anales del ochenta y cinco*', originally written in Latin, he

---

[1] *Viajes de Extranjeros por España y Portugal*, edited by J. García Mercadal, Vol. I (Madrid, 1952).

says: 'From there [Boltaña] after half a league one goes through another town called Belmonte, which is under the jurisdiction of the capital'.[1] The fact that the land here belonged to the Crown assumes that the overlordship of the town belonged directly to the King and that the residents were not subordinate to any other lord—as in fact the neighbouring towns were—and that the jurisdiction over the *término* was not held by one nobleman, but by an institution, that is to say the juries of the city, who were in the last resort the administrators and judges of the town. The plan of the town is thus living history.[2]

A popular tradition relates that in olden times the settlement called *Caballeros* was more than one kilometre from its present situation towards the southwest, around what is today the chapel of Our Lady of *Caballeros*.[3] Because of its proximity to the Ebro, floods from the river periodically damaged the houses in *Caballeros* and the stagnant waters were the cause of infection. This led to the foundation of a new settlement where the present town is situated. The name of the new town was lengthened to commemorate the event, and thus *Caballeros* came to be called *Belmonte de los Caballeros*.

In 1110 Alfonso I, *El Batallador*, 'The Battler', began to lay siege to the city after his victory over its Moorish king between Valtiera and Arguedas. During this time he made incursions into the lands of Fraga and Lérida, and probably after the surrender of the city in 1118 the town went to form part of the lands conquered by 'The Battler'.

Sixty-eight years later, on St. Stephen's day, 26 December 1186, Dominicus Arnaldus legalized *in Dei Nomine* a '*carta et auctoritate de venditione*' in which the owner Señora Dominga, widow of D. Domingo Mediela, sold '*ad vos Don Petro Sasse et ad vestram mulier donna Tota una nostra vinea quod nos habemus in termino de Caballeros*'.[4] So the first part of the tradition is true;

[1] *Ibid.*

[2] On 22 May 1806, Jorge de Llera obtained a Royal document in virtue of which he received the privilege of *infanzón*—the lowest title in the ranks of Aragonese nobility—erasing his name from the book of the commoners. He gained it after violent quarrels with the members of the Council which prove that he was considered no better than the rest. The privilege of *infanzón* implied exemption from payment of taxes. *Acta del Ayuntamiento*, 22 May 1806.

[3] Patroness of the town—25 March—together with Our Lady of the Assumption and San Roque—15 and 16 August.

[4] *Fondo del Pilar, alm.* IX, *Caj.* I, *leg.* n 35.

originally the name of the town was *Caballeros*. In two similar documents, one dated 6 February 1503 and the other 20 November of the same year, the name *Belmonte de los Caballeros* is found.[1] Events between 1186 and 1503, and the reason why the name of the town was lengthened, are not known. After 1550 the history of the town can be followed satisfactorily in the manuscripts of the parochial archives and the Minutes of the Council.

*
* *

Belmonte de los Caballeros has 1229 inhabitants.[2] The growth of the population can be followed accurately from 1689. In this year all 'the able persons', amounting to 241,[3] fulfil the Catholic paschal regulation. Children of both sexes who have not made their first communion are excluded from this census. In 1800 the number of 'capable' persons reaches 444.[4] In 1849 there are 600 souls.[5] A graph will indicate the subsequent demographic variations better.

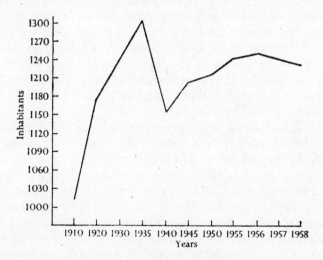

1 *Treudos de la Orden de San Juan de Jerusalén*, leg. 531, fols. 8 & 10, *Archivo Histórico Nacional*.

2 In 1958.   3 Vol. III of the *Archivo Parroquial*, fols. 378–80.

4 *Ibid.*, Vol. V, fols. 380–7.

5 P. Madoz: *Diccionario Geográfico-estadístico-histórico de España*, vol. XIII (Madrid, 1849).

The curve marks a continuous increase after 1910, which reaches its zenith in 1935. After that a brusque change is observed, due to the civil war, followed by a smooth rise until 1956, a year in which again a gradual decline in the population of the town can be traced.

The town lands cover 1717 hectares—1 hectare equals 2.471 acres. From these should be discounted (in terms of production) 68 hectares which include barren land and highways, 22 hectares upon which buildings have been erected, and 722 hectares of sparto-grass, thyme and poor pastures. The remaining 905 hectares are arable land, but 237 hectares of this area remain unirrigated, and here reaping depends on the rainfall and a good harvest only occurs every five or six years. The other 668 hectares of land are irrigated—*regadío*; here production is certain. Farming is the principal and generally almost the only source of revenue. A family composed of the parents and of two or three children needs to own a minimum of more than three hectares, the greater part *regadío*, to maintain the average standard of life peculiar to the community. If a similar family only owns two hectares, it needs to increase its revenue by other means, the most usual being 'to go for a day's work' (*ir al jornal*) whenever there is any possibility of doing so. In the second and sometimes in the first family one of the sons will emigrate, usually to the city, in search of work. The agricultural possessions of the father do not offer sufficient resources for both of them to follow the normal way of life.

This explains to a great extent[1] the fall of the population since 1956. Before 1936 the resources of the *término* were enough to satisfy the normal needs of its residents. The civil war broke the traditional mould of life in the community, offering in its turn new and broader outlooks in every sphere of living. The necessary acreage to provide the income needed by one family is greater today than before the civil war (1936). The consequences of this have been, on the one hand, the purchase or exploitation of arable lands outside the municipal district (see map) by the economically stronger families, and on the other, the emigration of either some of the economically weaker ones, those without

---

[1] The difference between deaths and births in the last ten years has been an increase of ten per annum.

ownership or the means of acquiring it, or else of one of the sons if the parents have some small possessions.

The descent of the line observed on the graph does not faithfully express this second fact, as emigration is practised in a restricted sense as well. More than a dozen men have got fixed jobs in the city where they go every day, returning home in the evening. For statistical purposes they are numbered among the residents, but if we bear in mind conditions of work in relation to the means offered by the *término*, they should be numbered among the absentees.

The following scheme indicates the present-day divisions by sex and legal status in the composition of the community:[1]

	Heads of family		*Vecinos*		*Domiciliados*		
	Males	Females	Males	Females	Males	Females	Total
Residents 'de facto'	303	59	121	44	629	600	1229
Absentees	8	1	3	1	25	17	42
Residents 'de jure'	311	60	124	45	654	617	1271

'*Vecinos*' are persons who have come of age or who are independent and who habitually reside in the *término*, being entered under this description in the council register. *Domiciliados* are persons under age or without the qualifications of the *vecino*. Entry on the Council register is achieved by two years effective residence in the town or by concession following petition after six months residence.

Official procedures, however, do not affect the popular estimation of new residents. If a new family establishes itself in the town it will very likely be called by the name of the town it came from, e.g. 'the Sevillanos' (those from Seville). The name will easily reach the third generation even though the second one has been born in the town. A family coming from a distant town, which they do not visit frequently, will be considered to have broken off its connexion and will be assimilated in Belmonte more easily and sooner than a family which comes from a neighbouring town, because in the latter case contact with relatives

---

[1] *Hoja del Ayuntamiento*, 1958. In the figures given above "heads of family" and *vecinos* also qualify as *domiciliados*.

and previous friends tends to be more frequent. An outsider—
forastero—who does not take an active part in social life will never
be properly considered as one of the town even if he has married
there and lived there several years. A *forastero*, even if he has been
fully accepted by the town, will never be allowed to criticize anything about it without being reminded of the defects of his own
town. If a resident who came from elsewhere holds an office in
the Council, public opinion will be hurt because 'there are plenty
of sons of the town who could fill the post as well as he or better';
besides, being an outsider—they say—'he cannot have the
same interest in the town as a son of the town'. If an outsider
owns land in the *término* his assimilation will be quicker because
his interests are there as well.

*
*   *

The town must be considered in relation to two wider units:
the State from which the Civil and Penal codes, the administrative law and the Spaniard's *Fuero* are derived; and the provincial
unit, with the Aragonese Statutory Appendix, its Civil Government and the Deputation. The town is the minor expression of
political segmentation: it is also a parish dependent on the
Archbishopric of the city. The Civil Government and the Archbishop are represented in the town by institutions which regulate,
at least officially, the public activities of the residents. These are
the Council, the Court of Justice, the Brotherhood of Farmers
and Stockbreeders, and the parish.

The Council is composed of the Mayor, who presides over it,
and six councillors. The mayor is the head of the municipal
administration, appointed by the Civil Governor of the Province. The post is unpaid and compulsory. It is the mayor's
concern, as representative of the Government, to enforce the
laws and government enactments, to keep order, to provide for
public and individual security, and to adopt upon his own
responsibility in exceptional cases the measures he judges to be
necessary. The concerns of the Council include the administration of its possessions, the approval of the budget and taxation,
the management of town planning, health, markets, electricity,
transport, education, culture and attendance at school, the
organization of urban and rural police and any particular work
or service which has as its aim the encouragement of municipal

interests and the general welfare of the community.[1] The
exercise of the mayor's authority is effected by a rural guard or
by the civil guard with its barracks in the town.

The Justice of the Peace presides over the town Court, in
which are held the 'Acts of Conciliation' or 'Judgements of
Agreement' and the 'Judgements of Default'. The hearing of
criminal cases exceeds the competence of the municipal court.
Its working will be discussed later.

The Brotherhood of Farmers and Stockbreeders is a body of
farmers, sheep owners and workers formed for the purpose of
co-ordinating and defending their interests. This body which is
obligatory and collects a membership fee in proportion to each
person's taxes, replaced the Agricultural Co-operative which
had been functioning at intervals since before 1800.[2]

The Brotherhood, with its elected President, supervises the
upkeep of the roads in the district; through it are obtained
fertilizers and credits at the lowest interest (2.75%). It also
represents the farming interests of the town before the Provincial
Board of Brotherhoods.

The *término* also constitutes a parish. Every individual is
baptized, receives first communion, is married and buried
according to the customary Roman Catholic rites. Civil marriage in the sense that the contracting parties go to the Council
to celebrate their nuptials, does not exist. The constable, as a
delegate, waits for the newly-married pair in the sacristy where
they sign a declaration. The signing of this document, in the
midst of the congratulations of the guests, has not the slightest
importance for those concerned. It is just one more signature,
one of the many requirements which are fulfilled at the celebration of a marriage, together with the bestowing of tips on the
waiting acolytes. Of course nobody knows or reads the contents
of the act, they merely sign where the constable indicates.
Divorce and subsequent remarriage are forbidden, but legal
separation of the consorts is permitted.

The parish achieves the highest outward expression of community life during the secular-religious festivals, the *fiestas* of the
town's religious patrons. The patrons themselves are not the
objects of special devotion, for other saints receive attention and

---

[1] Abella: *Régimen Local* (Madrid, 1956), third ed, Articles 59–121.
[2] *Acta del Ayuntamiento*, 28 August 1800.

prayers. There are few amusements during the week and one Sunday is the same as any other. But the *fiestas*, especially those of August 14th–18th, are a landmark in the course of each year. Trips to the city to buy clothes, newly whitened houses, newly painted rooms, clean fresh streets, bottles, cakes, garlands, flags and lights announce the proximity of the *fiestas*, always rich in matrimonial promise. One breathes *fiesta* in the atmosphere. People eat more and better, they drink a good deal, they shout, sing and dance day and night, and during these days everyone is different, less serious, more friendly. The youthful tone of the festival disguises a deeper reality: the festival is fundamentally an outburst of the community spirit bound up in traditional religious motives which penetrate the outer layers of family life and friendship. Dozens of people, whether children of the town who live outside it, or simply friends who have never lived there, come every year to celebrate it. Participation in the festival is not considered complete if a member of the family is absent; he or she will be inquired after by friends and be remembered several times aloud. Visits to sick relatives or friends are considered an obligation during this period. Visitors call upon their relatives or friends house by house and greet everybody in the street. At home the grandparents sit round their table, surrounded by all their children and grandchildren.

This re-affirmation of the bonds of family and friendship has at the same time a reverse side; the days of the festivals are most likely to revive any latent antagonism of town against town, though not of individual against individual. In an Act of the Council in 1883 it is written: 'to avoid any disorder which might arise during the days of the festivals, as a result of young people, it is provided that two members of the Council shall patrol the town each night'. Every year young men and, in smaller numbers, girls, come from the neighbouring towns to dance. Today the dancing goes on till after three o'clock in the morning. One night when some boys from Torres de Montearagón, tired of dancing, were making their way home, a rider on a mule appeared ringing a cattle bell, of the kind worn by the bulls which were to be fought the next day. At the same time shouts were heard: 'A bull has got away !' Next morning people commented with joy on how the boys from Torres had run across the fields, trying to hide and climbing trees. A few years ago some young people from Aldeanueva whipped a bull while fighting it. Suddenly the ring was invaded by young people from Belmonte armed with sticks; the men of Aldeanueva, beaten after little resistance, left the ring and ran home. Another incident occurred very recently when several boys went to dance at Torres. After a few minutes they realized they were the centre of an aggressive circle formed by people from Torres. Luckily some girls broke up the group, relieving the tension. The reason for the incident was that several days before both towns had played against each other in a football match. Torres lost the match, unjustly according to them, so they wanted to avenge themselves on the visitors, not one of whom had taken any part in the game, even as a spectator; it was enough to belong to the victorious town. On a number of occasions the people of Arcos have attempted to prevent the people of Belmonte from dancing at their festivals, and once the latter were stoned when on their way home at night.

Aldeanueva is situated on the opposite side of the mountains which border the northeast of the *término* of Belmonte. The towns are connected by a track of 6 kilometres which zigzags across the mountain. To some extent this prevents frequency of contact. There is a closer relationship between Belmonte and Arcos, 5 kilometres away along the main road, and with Torres, 3 kilometres away to the northwest. The artery which really links them, however, is the common canal from which water is taken to irrigate the fields. Regulation of the use of water, common interests in the obtaining of seeds and fertilizers and in the rise of agricultural prices, identical methods of cultivation—these three towns on the lefthand bank of the Ebro have much in common.

Fundamentally Belmonte orientates towards the city. The road which unites town and capital is one of the main traffic routes of the country. A regular bus service provides transport in either direction every two hours. Visits to the city are frequent. Men go to visit the banks, or to buy farming implements. Women go to buy clothes, materials and anything they consider necessary for the house. As well as these visits there are others for the purpose of a day spent in the city visiting friends or relations, a trip to the cinema, theatre, football matches or bullfights. If they have got time, they very rarely fail to visit Our

Lady of the 'Pillar', the patroness of Aragón, and seldom omit
to enter her cathedral if they pass near by. The capital is the
business and administrative centre, as well as the centre for legal
affairs, for fashion and entertainment. It is also the market town
and to some extent a religious centre, for it is considered remiss
if good Aragonese do not pray to the Virgin of the Pillar in her
cathedral every time they go to the city.

Finally there are half a dozen bank agents in the town, whose
activities are sometimes restricted for reasons I shall deal with
later, as well as insurance agents with increasing fields of action,
two cinemas each showing an average of three films a week,
three public bars and a tavern.

*

*   *

Until now I have said very little about the actual people who
compose the political unit (the Council, institutions, etc.), the
religious unit (the Parish), and the unity of agricultural interests (the Brotherhood, the environment). Yet what constitutes the *pueblo*, the community, is something more than the
institutions and the physical environment; it is something that,
presupposing them as a basis, affects them while it is affected
and conditioned by them. I refer to the body of traditions, conventions, opinions and beliefs, norms of conduct, relations and
pressures which set the patterns of community life. These compose the third aspect, the richest and most complex of all. The
physical environment is a *res data*; the institutions of the town
are something superimposed; the system of everyday relations is a
living reality.

A consideration of these three aspects of the life of the town
and their interaction is the aim of the following pages.

I

OWNERSHIP OF LAND: I

'Entre la cuidad y el campo hay más distancia que entre los más distintos climas' UNAMUNO

'La esteva, más que signo de poder, es símbolo de servidumbre' COSTA

'La tierra no es sólo espacio, sino tiempo' ORTEGA Y GASSET

A STRANGER to the town would be aware, after only a few chance conversations in the street, that the same topics come up again and again. Let us consider one of them.

I

As work in the fields absorbs the daylight hours of practically all the men over school age, it is only natural that every man's attention should be primarily taken up with the soil and the fields and that this should be reflected in their use of the language. This concern is revealed in the richness of a special vocabulary, while the abundance of characteristic colloquialisms indicate, if not true originality, a process of selection, adaptation and intepretation of words and phrases concerning tools, crops and country tasks. The value and yield of lands, the periodical rotation of tasks, the care of the soil, the selection of seed and fertilizer, arrangements for using the water in turn, methods of reaping, threshing, sowing, harvesting, etc., these make up the principal topics of daily conversation, whether it be on the way to and from the fields, at home, in the street, in the cafés or at evening gatherings. When a man has been on a journey the conversation invariably turns to the fields seen from the train and their cultivation, even apart from journeys with an agricultural purpose such as going to the cattle Fairs or Agricultural

Shows. The particular theme follows the rhythm of the soil, so that the work in the fields, seedtime, the beet harvest, sowing, threshing, the grape harvest, set the tone of conversation, each in its due season. On summer nights, when the pressure of work is greatest, one can observe an unceasing search for farmhands, mutual aid, and a sharing of tractors, mules and carts which are all brought in to get the reaping and threshing finished as soon as possible, even if it means working day and night, for the harvest is sacred, *sagrada*.

Every newly-married man's ambition is to possess his own fields. The parents' aim is to leave their children more land than they themselves inherited. With this end in view every ounce of energy is vital. Money is borrowed to buy a field, a tractor, a horse. There are fierce arguments over who has prior right to buy a certain field, with unpleasant consequences for the disputing families, who may never speak to each other again.

Fields are the most highly esteemed possessions. The history, agricultural properties and other details of each field are known; their ownership brings a feeling of respectable comfort, of a certain security with which to face the future. In any case if things don't go too well, if there is a serious illness in the family, one of them can be sold. But to have to sell them all is the greatest misfortune that can befall a man, and therefore they are only sold in extreme cases. A few years ago an old man committed suicide when he found out that his fields had been sequestered owing to his son's weak administration. He could not bear the disappearance of the fruit of his life's labours. The ownership of land binds the owner so closely to the soil that when things go badly or the property is not sufficient, he no longer has any reason for remaining in the town. He breaks away completely and goes to the city; this is considered a sad necessity.

This bond between man and the soil would be incorrectly interpreted if we saw in it any kind of mysticism or reverence on the man's part. He works hard because it is necessary, because it is the only way of getting his daily bread. 'Only fools work in the country', they say, 'only countrymen know what it is to work', to work in the open in winter and summer, by day and by night, without regular hours, putting up with the cold, the sun, and the dust of the threshing floor. City people are *señoritos* who know nothing about this and have no idea what it is to work. 'I'd like to give those fellows the hoe', people often say. When anyone complains of having too much work, if this is not agricultural, or when it is believed that someone does not work, they say: 'I'll give you the hoe'. Everyone's highest aim is not to have to work; 'if I had money I should throw away the hoe' is a common phrase. Note that they say 'throw away', not 'lay aside'. The hoe, which is not the most tiring tool to use, is a symbol for calloused hands, energetic work, speech that other people ridicule, rough manners, living in a small town, and being part of a low social class. They would like to throw all these things to the winds together with the hoe. It is the symbol of the *homo rusticus* and presupposes the existence of the *homo urbanus*, who ridicules the former, who in his turn criticizes, envies and tries to imitate the urban man. Frequently country people feel humiliated in the city, inferior to the city dweller with his fluent speech behind his little office window. 'We don't know how to approach people nor how to explain what we want', 'We can't mix with other people', 'We can't talk about anything except agriculture', are phrases which one keeps hearing. They believe that they have very little in common with the city dweller, with those who work in banks and offices, with lawyers, doctors and people who have studied, and when they have to deal with them they feel like 'a hen in a strange barnyard'.

This sense of inferiority, together with the toughness of the work in the country, the enviable comfort of those who 'live without working' in the city, the idea that everyone is exploiting the farmer and that the Government does not concern itself much with agriculture, weighs very heavily on their minds. If the schoolmaster tells them that their son 'would make a good student' they spare no effort or sacrifice so that he can study the *bachillerato* and get a position in the city or at least *no ser del campo* (not *be* of the country). The power and richness of the phrase, the bitter tone in which it is pronounced, reveal a world of differential social status. They do not say *no trabajar en el campo* (not to work in the country), '*no estar en el campo*' (not to be in the country), or '*no pertenecer al campo*' (not to belong to the country), but '*ser del campo*' (to *be* of the country). The verb *ser* differs from *estar* in that it refers to qualities essential to the person, that define him. *Ser* normally implies qualities from which the person cannot be separated, such as being a man, being a

woman, being Spanish, while *estar* indicates situations which
while they may sometimes affect the person essentially, cannot
be considered stable, as for example being ill. By saying '*ser del
campo*' or in aiming that a son '*no sea del campo*' (shall not be of
the country), they are assuming that the cultivation of the land
affects an individual's personality in such a way that this quality
can be expressed grammatically in the same way as being a man
or being a Spaniard.

So 'being of the country' marks an individual in such a way
that he will be recognized whatever the circumstances in which
he lives. His world, his conceptions, his habits and customs, his
speech and manners are different from those of people who do
not share his work in the fields. He cannot *alternar* ('alter'-nar,
mix) with them. 'May my son be something better than I have
been, may he not work like a donkey as I have', 'I would rather
my daughter married a cobbler than someone from the country', are phrases which centre around the same idea. This
desire, this anxiety to better oneself is reducing the rural population; there is a constant process of urbanization which began in
earnest at the end of the civil war. Geographically the city is
very near and it is ever present in thought.

II

The 'Deeds of Sale' of land, from the first one in 1186,
already mentioned, seem to indicate that the municipal district
has been divided since ancient times into a great number of
plots, this being the result of the absence of a *Señor* of the district
with jurisdiction over it. When fields are sold, their limits are
given with the names of the owners of the properties bordering
on them and the amount of money paid for them indicates
small divisions. In 1660, a French traveller journeying to France
from Madrid, found the road that connects the town to the city
very pleasant because of the numerous market gardens. He left
some notes in his diary: 'I left the city at about mid-day on the
18th, and went to spend the night at Lorena. Part of that road
is pleasant because of the market gardens which are seen *continuously* (my italics) in a broad valley, always watered by canals.
One passes over the little river by a bridge; and shortly

afterwards one comes upon the town of Belmonte (de los Caballeros); the rest of the road is a wilderness'.[1]

The 905 hectares of cultivable land are divided into 2,107 fields of an average area of 0·4295 hectares, their small size often making it very difficult to use machines. On the other hand, each one is a garden, as the aforementioned Frenchman found, carefully tended, exploited to the full. On the following table are the number of owners of land with the sum total of plots each owns within the *término* or municipal boundaries.

	Under 1 Ha.	From more than 1 to 3 Has.	From more than 3 to 5 Has.	From more than 5 to 10 Has.
Owners	128	132	28	29

	From more than 10 to 15 Has.	Over 15 Has.	103 Has.
Owners	8	5	1 Not a local man

The Minute of the Council of July 26th 1801, complains that half the property of the district is in the hands of people not living in the town. Some forty years ago the Council sold the last 103 hectares in the table to an outsider; this was salt land, full of pools, of doutful yield, thick with reeds and liable to periodic flooding from the river. There was no one in the town interested in it because the townspeople could not afford to buy in a block, drain the land, clean it, make dykes and wait for a number of years before getting any yield from it. Therefore the Council saw fit during an economic crisis to sell, even though to an outsider. The community criticized this decision so forcibly that the Council had to resign. Today the land held by the townspeople outside the limits of the municipal district exceeds 1,380 hectares which, added to the 802 hectares that they possess within the limits, makes a total of 2,182 hectares of cultivable land. This figure indicates that the land property has quintupled during the past hundred and fifty years, through patience and tenacity, and that once the townspeople succeeded in getting possession

[1] *Viajes de extranjeros por España y Portugal*, vol. II.

of the municipal lands—a stage which was completed roughly by the end of the nineteenth century—they embarked on a new economic expansion, spilling over the district limits.

In practise this second stage began in the years immediately following the end of the civil war, in 1939, when landowners from neighbouring towns came to offer their fields to the people of Belmonte, because they paid a better price for them; but it seems that this expansion has already reached its peak, because of the expense of buying and tilling fields at 15 and even 35 kilometres distance; besides, many of these fields cannot be irrigated and need to be rested for one or two years, and even then they do not pay unless it rains in the year that they are sown. They are always sown with wheat. The following figures show the approximate ownership of land both within the town limits and beyond.

	Under 1 Ha.	From 1 to 3 Has.	From more than 3 to 5 Has.	From more than 5 to 10 Has.
Owners	117	123	49	41

	From more than 10 to 15 Has.	More than 15	245 Has.	270 Has.	570 Has.
Owners	13	6	1	1	1

The total number of landowners in the first table was 330; in the above table there are 352, so 22 people who had no land inside the town limits have been able to acquire it outside during the last two decades. The National Institute of Land Settlement has made available advantageous conditions by which the tenants on an extensive estate in the district of Torres have become owners of the land they worked.

The second difference we notice on comparing the two tables is that while the total in the first two columns has diminished by twenty in the second table, the sum total in the other columns has increased by forty-two. Twenty-two new landowners have appeared, and forty-two of those included in the first table have managed to enlarge their property to reach or even surpass the minimum number of hectares necessary to achieve economic independence in the sense explained. The three landowners in the last columns of the table do not represent an immoderate

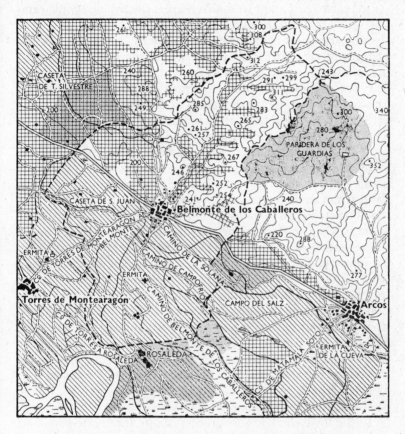

Municipal district of Belmonte and neighbouring districts. The stippled areas represent approximately the land owned by residents of Belmonte within neighbouring districts. They own some land in more distant districts not shown in this map.

0   ¼   ½   ¾   1 kilometre   0   ¼   ½   ¾   1 mile

Based on a map by the Instituto Geográfico y Catastral

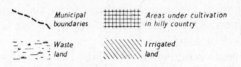

– – – – ⌐ Municipal
              boundaries

⌐·–·–·⌐ Waste
              land

╫╫╫╫╫ Areas under cultivation
              in hilly country

╲╲╲╲╲ Irrigated
              land

3

holding of land, since most of it is hill property outside the town
limits, where only about one quarter of the total area is cultivated each year; apart from this there is the risk that if the rainfall does not reach the necessary minimum there may be several
barren years and in this event it is only by having a moderate
margin of capital that they can sustain the loss of everything
including the wheat that is sown. Therefore the acquisition of
the new property has been to almost everyone's advantage; it
has not fallen only into the hands of the wealthiest.

Nor is the second table an exact indication of the distribution
of wealth; there are numerous other factors that must be taken
into account. As was said in the previous chapter, people included in the first two columns of the table need other resources
if they are to earn an annual living that is adequate, for the
land is not sufficient to supply this. At the same time, the 112
landowners in the remaining columns need extra labour at the
seasons when work is heaviest. From the second half of May to
the second week in August, and from November to the beginning
of January, the tasks which centre around reaping, threshing
and the sugar-beet crop require the combined efforts of several
people. At both these seasons there is a *tour de force* on the part of
some landowners to raise wages in order to get the farm-hands
they need, and also on the part of the smallholders, and labourers
who take advantage of the circumstances to ask for higher
wages and better working conditions. These five months of
abundant work, when in the evenings farmers go from door to
door in search of casual labourers, solve the problem of the
shortage of land in a number of families.

In the town there are six grocers' shops, three café-bars, and
a tavern, three carpenters' shops, a messenger who goes to the
city several times a day, two bakeries, four hairdressers, two
cinemas, a public telephone and a tobacconist. There is a post-
man, a constable, a tailor, a rural guard, shepherds and stone-
masons. In other words there are quite a number of other means
of supplementing the annual income from the land. A small
flour mill employs six regular workmen, while five families own
a small plaster factory.

Lastly several landowners who for various reasons cannot
administer all their lands, or sometimes simply parents who
wish to help their newly-married sons, go into partnership:

(a) *a medias*, i.e. by 'half shares' in some fields. The owner ploughs the first furrow and pays the taxes. The partner has to work the land. The cost of fertilizers and haulage, and later the yield are shared equally between the owner and the partner.

(b) When the land is divided *al tercio*, i.e. by thirds between the owner and the administrator, the latter only contributes his work. Two thirds of the profit go to the owner and one third to the administrator.

(c) When the division is *al quinto* (by fifths) which is usual in the case of hill land with an uncertain harvest, the terms of contract are the same as in the previous case but the owner only receives one fifth of the profit.

(d) *Arrendamiento*. Sometimes the owner lets his fields. The tenant grows what he wishes, pays the stipulated rent for the fields, and is entitled to the profit. This use of land is both the most desired and the most difficult to obtain since nobody wishes to let fields, and it only occurs in a limited number of cases, as a result, for instance, of the illness of the owner, or when a father lets land to his son.

(e) *Administrar por su cuenta* (Stewardship): a few people who do not reside in the town, or women who cannot supervise the work themselves, employ a steward to look after their land. The owners provide and pay for everything; the steward receives 10% of the profit, plus a daily wage for his work.

This is a sketch of the arrangements for using land, in actual fact there are as many methods as there are cases of sharing, especially when land is granted by parents to their children. One must also take into account individual ways of coming by a greater income, such as the buying and selling of alfalfa, straw, cattle, horses, the sale of milk from a handful of cows, or going to France to work for a few agricultural seasons, as has been popular during the last few years.

In this section I have aimed at showing the division of cultivable land within the town limits, and the ways in which it is shared, the interest in acquiring more land even beyond the district limits, the approximate share that falls to each family, and the additional resources available to those whose property does not provide the minimum income necessary for the standard of living in the town. Even so not all the families reach the average level which could be taken as representative of the town, yet they do not consider emigrating and there are even some[1] who have no land at all either of their own, or shared or rented, nor yet a regular job. They live on wages from casual work. These labourers and the larger landowners represent two extremes on a scale graded according to the possession of land.

III

The agricultural year begins on All Saints Day, 1 November; it has been the traditional custom on this day to rescind all contracts concerning rent, to suggest contracts with the same or new clauses, and for new tenants to begin to use the newly acquired fields. By this day, the plots have been prepared for sowing, and are therefore free to change hands if required. This date used to be preceded by another, St. Michael's Day, 29 September, on which farm-hands were hired for the year, the terms including eating and sleeping in their masters' house. After lunch, that is to say when most people would be in the café, the master would take his servant there and would invite him to have coffee and brandy. Everybody recognized the meaning of this. Since the civil war (1936) both these customs have disappeared, owing to the fact that the landowners, even those with large areas of land, have available mechanized means of cultivating their land—which they do not let out any more—so that it is no longer necessary for them to have permanent hired labourers.

About the beginning of November the harvesting of maize and cotton should be over, if any has been sown, for neither are important crops; both are grown for sale and maize is also grown as fodder for horses and other animals. Since horses and mules have been largely replaced by the tractor, much less maize is sown. In the hills wheat is sown according to the practice of *año y vez*, that is to say the land is left fallow one year or more and is sown the next. The hilltops are formed of concentrations of chalk, and the layer of workable soil covering it is normally superficial and insufficient for cultivation. Dry land plants

---

[1] Sixteen heads of families have no property, but only seven of them live in the town. This confirms that families without property tend to leave the town as indicated. Absent heads of families still enjoy the rights of *vecino* because they have not been absent for long enough to acquire them elsewhere—or simply because they are waiting to make sure that their new occupation is more promising than the work in the town. There are cases of people who have returned to the community.

abound there, such as rosemary, thyme and gorse, which the sheep graze of necessity when they cannot be on pasture in the irrigated land. Between the hills lie little valleys, called *vals*, where land suitable for tilling has been deposited to a greater depth; heavy soil which, when made fertile by suitable rain, produces wheat of higher quality than that harvested on the irrigated land. As one goes from the *vals* up the slopes the land becomes whiter. Before 1936 this part was not sown, but now wherever there is a workable minimum of surface soil the last square inch is used, if the field is near the town.

On the irrigated land only wheat is sown where before it alternated with alfalfa; up to the aforementioned date the seed used was from the harvest of the year before but nowadays it is brought from other parts where it is considered to be of higher quality. Only wheat is sown in the hilly land, and the average amount of wheat—and other cereal—sown on irrigated land and in the hills covers about two thirds of the total land. The work is not too hard at this time of the year: the labourers go out into the fields at about eight in the morning and if it is far from the town they have lunch there, and return home at about five in the afternoon. With a tractor it takes half a day to sow three acres of land, whereas it used to take three days with mules. The surviving draught animals are being replaced by the tractor.

Towards the middle of November the sugar-beet harvest begins. The beet has to be pulled up before the land can be used for sowing wheat; on the irrigated land the wheat sowing may go on up to the end of the first fortnight in January. Pulling up the beet one by one is man's work; the women sit by the heaps of beet, removing the earth and cutting off the leaves. The piles of cleaned beet are loaded on to carts or trailers which the tractors pull either to the town weighing-machine or to the factory in the city. The area of land sown with sugar-beet has been declared beforehand to the factory where it is to be sold, as the factory allows the growers fertilizers and chemical products, and also gives them a card stating the week in which they are to deliver the beet. The area of land declared as sown with beet has always exceeded the area actually dedicated to this crop, as this is the only means of acquiring more fertilizers in years of scarcity, and of obtaining more cards, that is to say, greater

opportunity to deliver the produce according to an established
rota. If one only has a few cards it is sometimes necessary to dig
up the beet and leave it in piles by the roadside, or in the yard,
because of the shortage of time for preparing the same land for
the wheat crop. This is also the cause of the interest in finishing
the beet harvest as soon as possible, and the necessity for employing labour from outside the family circle, for everyone tries
to finish the work of the beet harvest as soon as possible, and in
the same few days everyone's attention is turned towards the
preparation of the land and the sowing of the wheat, the maize
and cotton harvest, and the irrigation of the land already sown
with wheat.

Normally mutual aid is arranged among the members of the
family—in the widest sense of the word; in addition there is
collaboration among friends and neighbours. There are a few
labourers who work for the same masters, especially when they
are the big landowners. Working for someone with a greater
acreage of land implies having sure work for a larger number of
days. At this season when hands are required, wages rise, and
the labourers who have been out of work at other times now
demand their conditions of work and wages. It appears that
before the civil war the normal conversation between employer
and labourer about the latter's work would be as follows:

'Are you out of work?'
'Yes.'
'Do you wish to work for me?'
'Yes. What tool shall I take?'

Nowadays the conversation acquires a different tone:

'Are you out of work?'
'Yes.'
'Do you wish to work for me?'
'What at?'
'................'
'No, not at that,' or 'if you want me to, you'll have to give
me such and such a wage.'

Between master and labourer there is no relationship apart
from the economic one. In recent harvests an average of eleven

million kilos of sugar-beet has been sold, which implies an income of almost eleven million pesetas with which to celebrate Christmas and buy toys for the children at Epiphany, as is the custom in Spain. Before 1936 sugar-beet was the principal crop of the town; now there is a greater tendency to cultivate wheat because the sugar-beet requires more manual work, and consequently more labourers and higher expenditure on wages, besides being subject to attack by pests and diseases.

If agricultural work has not been slowed down by cold weather or snow, the beet harvest should have ended by the second half of January. In actual fact the intense, fast work takes place from about 10 November to 5 January, in normal weather conditions; if work continues with the sugar-beet after this date, it is done calmly without exhaustion or haste, for that land will not be sown with wheat. By the beginning of February the former beet fields are ploughed to prepare for the new sowing of beet, maize or cotton. This first task is called *romper* (to break). On the second of February, the feast of Candlemas, the water supply from the main canal is cut off so that the irrigation ditches can be cleaned. The bailiff from the Irrigation Syndicate directs operations. The cleaning and maintenance of the remaining canals is controlled by the Irrigation Syndicate of the town, to which an annual tax is paid. In this month the vines are pruned and the fruit trees are trimmed and planted; this is light work since the vineyards do not cover more than 15 hectares and fruit trees number under 3,500. From the second week in January until the end of March there is no urgent agricultural work; there is free time for the secondary tasks, for meeting in groups in the café, at home, at the carpenter's or simply on the corner of the street.

In March, the land which was ploughed in February is tilled for the second time. This second task is called *mantornar*. Immediately after this, the earth is levelled so that the land has a slight slope away from the watercourse to ensure that the whole lot receives its share of irrigation. If beet is to be sown the land is fertilized. Towards the end of March, when the land is really dry, until 15 April, the sugar-beet seed is sown. Where the earth is finest and has already been ploughed twice, potatoes for family consumption are sown; cane shelters are made near the land where vegetables are to be grown; lastly, at the end of the month, the vineyards are tilled and dug. Sometimes at this time and sometimes in May, alfalfa is sown where wheat has been sown earlier, so that when the wheat is reaped the alfalfa remains. Once the sowing of beet is over, the farmer is occupied with minor tasks: spreading 300 kgms. per hectare of nitrate, watering the beet crop every ten days, cutting and harvesting the alfalfa from the year before, spraying the beet with insecticide, weeding the wheat, ploughing the hill land ready for sowing wheat in November, and watering the lands which are to be used for maize or cotton.

The sowing of melons, French beans, tomatoes, sweet peppers, onions, cucumbers, etc., for family consumption, takes place at the beginning of May when the potato fields also require attention. About the middle of the month cotton and maize are sown and fertilized and the beet fields have their furrows ploughed and hoed to rid them of weeds. At the end of May the beet is thinned out, mainly by the women, so that only the strongest tufts of beet are left. The soil is spread with nitrate, wheat and beet crops are watered, the latter are again hoed free of weeds, and in the second week of June the reaping of early barley begins, if it has been sown. In the third week the wheat is ready for reaping, and by St. John's Day reaping and threshing are in full swing.

Machinery is used for reaping, and harvesters are used over great areas of hill land if the terrain allows. Threshing machines work from five in the morning till one o'clock, and from three in the afternoon until nine at night, so that they work fourteen hours a day in the sun and dust. The wheat is carted from the fields to the threshing floor either by tractors with trailers or carts only a day or two before threshing begins, in order to leave the sheaves as near as possible to the man who is feeding them into the machine, thus avoiding extra work and wages. This means that the carting must be done at just the right moment; it may be necessary to go for the wheat at three o'clock in the morning. If there is an abundant harvest the tractors work day and night, almost non-stop, the drivers, usually brothers or brothers-in-law, taking turns. In addition, once their own carting has been done, the driver and the tractor are repeatedly in demand to carry the crop of those who have no transport of their own, and thereby the tractor owners increase their own profit.

When the season is over in the locality, harvesters, tractors and machines are driven off to other provinces where the wheat harvest comes later.

At the very time when reaping and threshing are at their height there are other tasks which demand attention no less imperiously. Thus the sooner the wheatfields can be cleared, the sooner they can be ploughed and watered for sowing another kind of maize, and the sooner the maize is sown, the better the chances of a good harvest. At the same time it is necessary periodically to water the beet and alfalfa fields, cut and harvest the latter, and, if there is still time, attend to the weeds that have sprung up again among the beet, as they have among the maize, cotton, and vegetable crops. The potatoes are dug up and the land where they were is prepared for planting winter greens. The watering of beet, maize, cotton, alfalfa and vegetables is done every ten days, and as it is done by established turns, a good many residents have to water their fields by night, since once their town's watering turn has passed it is forbidden to irrigate.

This is the principal season in the year for agricultural work. Activity, coordination and collaboration in the work reach their peak. No family is self-sufficient: if they own little land they need someone else's machinery to reap, cart and thresh; if they possess more than three hectares they will not be able to do without hired labourers or mutual aid to cope with all the aforementioned tasks at the same time. Wages paid reach their peak as well. Because of the difficulty of finding labourers, people resort to mutual aid, especially at threshing time, and instead of paying money they give help in return for service. All these tasks make it imperative to call on others for their personal collaboration and their tools and machines.

While the sugar-beet is a plant that has only been in cultivation for a short time—not reaching back to the beginning of the century—wheat goes back into the agricultural tradition of the community. During the sixteenth, seventeenth and eighteenth centuries, tithes were paid mainly in wheat; wheat was also paid to the doctor, apothecary, secretary and teachers right into the nineteenth century, and a Council Act of 1800 mentions a communal granary where the wheat was stored. At the end of the first world war the price of wheat reached 0·71 pesetas per kgm., a price which was reduced to half in 1920; from then until 1936 the price gradually rose until by the end of the Republic it had reached an official minimum of 0·50 pesetas per kgm. But before this regulating law came into force there was an authorization for the importation of wheat, which caused fluctuation and a lowering of prices in the market. This was the cause of the difficulties in selling wheat and the increase in the acreage of land employed for sugar-beet in the years immediately prior to 1936. Cereal is today once more the principal crop, with more than two and a half million kgms. bringing some twelve million pesetas into the town, with which the people can buy new clothes and amuse themselves in the festivals of mid-August.

When threshing is over, and the festivals have come and gone, there is a period of anticlimax, during which the fields that have grown wheat are quietly levelled and field boundaries, verges, and irrigation ditches repaired. By September it is pleasant to gather fruit and vegetables in the evening as well as early cotton and maize. The grape harvest comes at the end of September and in the first week in October: in a few days all the grapes are gathered and pressed and wine is produced by traditional methods. The Act of Sale of 1186, already mentioned, refers to the sale of a vineyard; grapes as well as wheat were used to pay the tithes. On 4 October 1802, the Council received an order from the City Council to the effect that the wine produced in the town should all be sold to the city and its sale to other towns and villages was forbidden. According to Madoz,[1] wine was the principal product of the *término* during the first half of the last century. At present it does not even produce enough for its own needs.

September, when the wheat has been sold and the agricultural work is at its lightest, is the favourite month for weddings: all ten weddings which took place in 1959, for instance, occurred in this month. October is characterized by frequent visits to the city to attend the festivals there. In November the agricultural cycle begins anew.

The annual agricultural cycle imposes different rhythms of work according to the time of the year; they may be rhythms with a slow, medium or fast cadence. A period of work at a fast

---

[1] Madoz: *Diccionario Geográfico-estadístico-histórico de España*, vol. XIII (Madrid, 1847).

rhythm is termed by the residents a *campaña agrícola*. It centres fundamentally around the principal agricultural activities of the locality and is concerned with the crops of greatest economic importance. In the town, people speak of the *campaña* of reaping, of threshing, of sugar-beet, meaning the work relevant to each crop. A *campaña* represents the climax of the hard work of a season, and is followed by a transition period which settles down into a stage of quiet calm in the work of the fields. This is a period of anticlimax, which in its turn is followed by another period of transition leading up to another *campaña*.

The occupations concerned with cultivating the land impose a rhythmic cycle; certain tasks imply others. Sometimes these tasks, or at least some of them, all come at the same time, precipitating their rhythm and the value of time, work reaching fever pitch. Thus a *campaña* as well as marking a climax in the rhythm of work implies an increase in the value of time, translated partially into terms of higher wages; it is a time of the most active cooperation among members of the community and mutual dependence among the different sections, because the landowners need the labourers as much as the labourers need them. Twenty-four hours during a period of anti-climax is not the same time at all, life is more peaceful and people can 'kill time' in groups in the street or in the cafés. The former collaboration and subordination change into free communication, into individual autonomy. During a *campaña*, each day and each hour is absorbed by its allotted tasks, 'there isn't time for anything' they say; all activities not relevant to the agricultural cycle of the moment are set aside; for some this means not even attending Mass on Sundays or going to tavern and bars. During a period of anticlimax the church, café and bars are fuller, 'there is time for everything', people say, 'even for getting married'. We could summarize the foregoing in the following chart:

During the *campaña* of the sugar-beet, one can see that there is a lack of correlation between the work which takes first place in local life and the increase in visits to the bars and tavern, but one must take into account the Christmas feasts which go on until January 6th. The relationship is clear during the following anticlimax and the transitional period when work gradually increases in intensity until the *campaña* of the wheat, when visits to

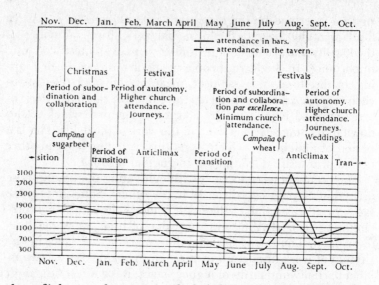

the café, bars and tavern reach their lowest level, corresponding to the period of the most intense work. The festival week in August, which comes immediately after the strenuous wheat harvest, brings an immediate anticlimax without the normal period of transition. This week is clearly reflected in the height of both curves; the festival in March does not influence the curves to such an extent because it is only for one day. Although September is the month of fewest tasks, there is a marked fall in both lines, due in part to the August festivals when the bars and tavern were frequented at all hours of the day and even kept open all night. Attendance at Sunday Mass is lowest during the periods of the most intense work, and highest during an anti-climax; it is lowest of all during the wheat harvest when work is at highest pressure. Holidays away from the town take place during the two periods of anticlimax on the graph: March and August-September. In March people normally go to the festivals in Valencia, and in the two summer months to San Sebastián and Barcelona. Pamplona, which is nearer than any of these three cities, has festivals of an extraordinary picturesqueness; everyone says that he would love to go there some year, but at the same time puts aside all possibility of attending them because they take place in the second week in July, at the time of the wheat harvest, when 'one can't leave the work'.

IV

It has been shown how the local agricultural year follows the cycle of the seasons, and that work is especially concentrated in a few weeks, when specific tasks have to be done. These are traditional activities and any variation depends on economic circumstances, the rise and fall of prices, changes in the market, etc., but whatever plant is cultivated the rhythm of the seasons must be followed. The cycle of the seasons, associated through hundreds of years with a certain crop, presents a fixed frame of time because it is repeated every year in its identical general characteristics. Every set of operations concerned with the cultivation of a particular crop appears in its cycle, year after year, with the same ecological time structure, leaving consistent impressions on the mind. So the residents have a collective consciousness of time, originating from and expressed in terms of *campañas* and other agricultural activities. A period of time known as *campaña* is a common frame of reference for popular thought; an anticlimax is a period of much less agricultural activity and therefore offers less reason for the conceptualizing of time. It is usual to hear phrases such as 'it happened at threshing time', or 'at sowing time', 'at reaping time', 'when the wheat was turning green', 'the wheat was already yellow when . . .': or 'when you could hear the rustle of the ears' referring to the sound of the wind moving the full ears of wheat, or 'as soon as the threshing is over we shall be off on our summer holiday' etc. Phrases like these suppose a frame of collective memory.

Not only are these phrases repeated in ordinary conversation but they were also often repeated in the Minutes of the Council, where one might have expected a greater precision. In January 1806, the Council decided that if the priest should fall ill 'at harvest time or seed time . . .' he should bring a substitute to say Mass; the Minute of June 15th, 1851, begins with 'It being harvest time . . .' Many other examples referring to seed time, reaping and threshing could be quoted and also references to 'the time of the grape harvest', mentioned for the last time in a Minute of October 1861. Today people still speak of the *campaña* of the grape harvest, although compared with that of wheat it is almost without content. But as it is a traditional phrase it is still sometimes used. The cultivation of the sugar-beet, on the other hand, which has developed recently and become as important as wheat, as a reference for the collective division of time differs from the latter in that there are no subdivisions into seedtime, growing, ripening and harvest; there is only the *campaña* of the sugar-beet which covers every aspect of its cultivation under one name. Moreover it is improbable that new subdivisions will arise, owing to the tendency among the younger people to refer to months and hours, according to the calendar and the clock, and not to agricultural work.

It has been said that the agricultural year begins on All Saints' Day, which is preceded by St Michael's Day, when arrangements were made between master and labourer, and that at Candlemas the water is cut off from the canal and the irrigation ditches are cleaned. These practices make us think of a division of time or of an agricultural cycle, expressed in religious terms. This is corroborated by a glance at old papers, or—to a lesser extent—by listening to ordinary conversation. Fairly frequently one hears such expressions as: 'by St John's Day', 'by St Michael's Day', 'by All Saints' Day', 'by the day of the Immaculate Conception' (8 December), 'by Candlemas', referring respectively to the periods of threshing, the beginning of the agricultural year, the sugar-beet and the cutting off of the water for irrigation. The names of the Saints' Days and religious festivals are, then, interchangeable with the agricultural tasks which coincide with them. At the same time these are dates used not only to mark the beginning and end of agricultural tasks, but are also extended to refer to different occupations and activities.

A Council paper dated 24 June 1802 reports the decision that the surgeon and the apothecary shall be admitted to the locality for two years, dating from 'St Michael's Day', and will be paid according to the price of wheat on St Michael's Day. Another paper dated 12 December 1803, stipulates that the miller, the shopkeeper and the baker are to pay their dues to the Council 'every year on St John's Day'. 'On St Michael's Day', according to the page dated 24 June 1804, 'the doctor is to begin to practise his profession'. We are told in the Minute of August 6 1804 that the innkeeper was obliged to supply wine to the town until 'the day of St Andrew the Apostle'; a house was let from St John's Day ...'—7 June 1885, 21 December 1889—etc.

There is an abundance of proverbs that bring the saints, the weather and the produce of the fields close together: 'if it rains by St Michael's Day the beet will swell more', an expression which is too recent, like the cultivation of the crop, to have found a rhymed form like the following:

> '*En llegando a San Antón*   'When we come to St Anton's
> *las nieblas a un rincón*'   Day
>   All the mist are swept away'

and also:

> '*Las tormentas por San Juan*   'Thunderstorms about St John's
> *quitan vino y no dan pan*'   Day
>   give no bread and wash wine away'

None of the saints' days or feast days mentioned come at a time of anticlimax; they are all symbols of periods of intense agricultural work. It is not a matter of there being two divisions of time, one religious and one agricultural; the expressions are interchangeable in the sense that the phrase 'by St John's Day' means by 'reaping time', by 'threshing time'. St John is a symbol for all the tasks of reaping and threshing; these tasks of primary importance in the life of the community are expressed in a religious context by a society traditionally christian. The result was and still is up to a point, a harmonious synthesis of religious beliefs, christian rites and agricultural occupations.

I have emphasized how a *campaña* deeply rooted in the past has afforded numerous shades of meaning and points of reference to the residents' conceptualization of time. However some of these points are losing their meaning today, owing to the use of new methods or to changes in the crops cultivated. Before 1936 groups of reapers would come to the town from other regions to reap the cereal crops by scythe. It was a long tough job and there are more written references to it than there are to threshing. Today reaping machines finish the task for the residents in a few days with a minimum of muscular effort; and so conversation centres around these reaping machines, the speed of carting the harvest, the tractors used for this job and the threshing. Little more than the name remains of the *campaña* of the grape harvest, together with the dusty old papers which refer to it again and again. Something has already been said about the lack of new divisions of time with reference to the sugar-beet *campaña*.

The religious aura which surrounded the agricultural tasks is also gradually disappearing. The month, the week, the day and the hour are replacing the ancient conventional divisions of time. The ecological conceptualization of time has the savour of a past which may be relatively recent in years, but which is technically very far away. It was conceived and expressed in terms of the experiences and occupations of a society different from the present one. Once these changed they rendered it unsuitable for adaptation to the present day. The town today consists of a group whose methods of agriculture have undergone technical and economic changes, which in their turn have replaced the framework of the rural and christian society of other days. The ecological and religious conception of time which used to predominate in the society now holds less significance.

On 5 October 1851, the members of the Council held a meeting to discuss what agricultural produce should be made taxable. According to the minutes this was a delicate problem, since 'most of the townspeople grew a little of everything for home consumption'. It was in other words, a family economy characterized by each household cultivating a limited amount of produce for themselves only. Nowadays the attitude towards the soil is very different; it is no longer a means of subsistence but rather a factor of production. The traditional general knowledge of methods of cultivation is being replaced by specialized knowledge, the farmer has acquired a technical and economic mentality. They have passed from the old system of growing for the family to the production of wheat, sugar-beet, alfalfa and cotton for the market. A few figures will emphasize more clearly the change that has taken place: before 1936 fertilizers were almost unknown; today almost 600,000 kgms. are used annually. As recently as 1941, there were only three tractors, employed in driving the threshing machines; ploughing was done with animals. There are now thirty-two tractors which are taking the place of animal labour. In 1941 there were 190 draught animals, but by 1960 their numbers had been reduced to ninety-six, which implies that a certain number of farmers must understand as much about machines, motors, and fuels as they do about the actual work in the fields. In 1936 there was only one car in the town; in 1959 the total number of cars, vans, and motorcycles had reached fifty-nine. Before the civil war every farmer kept back part of his wheat crop to use as seed; nowadays the selection of seed is considered of first importance, and in 1959 wheat from Egypt was sown which had been developed through the course of several harvests from grain found during an archaelogical excavation, and from which an abundant harvest was expected. At the same time as the quality of the Egyptian wheat and the relative power of German, French and English tractors are discussed, there are comments upon the advantage of the extensive growing of a single crop in other nations, as in North America, and its possible repercussion on national agriculture.

The popular concept of space has expanded in a way that could not have been imagined three decades ago, and the images of distance have undergone a transformation. International competition in the wheat and sugar market especially, which it is known cost less to produce in other countries, makes people foresee possible disruptions of their habitual agricultural cycle. In the summer of 1959, the possible admission of Spain into the Common Market was discussed with fear and scepticism. It was feared that if Spain were admitted, the government might, in agreement with the other Common Market countries, decide what crops should be grown in the area, and that they might be different from those cultivated hitherto, necessitating changes and adaptation to new methods.

As the concept of space formerly based on a limited rural ecology has been enlarged to cover an almost world-wide economy due to technical and economic developments, so the traditional conceptualization of time based on set patterns is disappearing before a new concept of time; and this not only because of a failure to adapt the former to the present focuses of interests but because time extends to centres of interest which are as yet still in the future. Time nowadays is not thought of as something stable, divided according to the tasks in the field that occupy the larger part of the day; daily work no longer provides an enduring framework for its conceptualization. The possibility of disruptions in the activities, crops and the agricultural cycle, seen from a technical and economic point of view and on a world scale, brings the future effectively into the present. The new frame and experience of time is making the old concepts, where the weight of tradition has kept them still alive, hollow, almost meaningless. The two concepts of time, the one belonging to the past and the other based on the possibilities of the future, can both be detected in the town. The characteristic that they have in common is to contend with each other over the present; but while the old concept of time is slowly falling back, the new one, although confusedly thought of, is gradually coming to the fore.

II

OWNERSHIP OF LAND: II

'*Tomar partido es no sólo renunciar a las razones de vuestros adversarios, sino también a las vuestras, abolir el diálogo, renunciar en suma, a la razón humana*' MACHADO

'*La pobreza no es la escasez de recursos pecuniarios para la vida, sino el estado de ánimo que tal escasez engendra; la pobreza es algo íntimo, y de aquí su fuerza*' UNAMUNO

IT HAS BEEN indicated in the previous pages how to an outsider the people of Belmonte appear as a united group, especially in opposition to other small communities. However within the actual structure of this united group lie internal tensions and conflicts. It will be seen how the ownership of land can under certain circumstances provoke violent antagonisms within the community, though on other occasions landownership can intensify the cohesion of the group.

I

Towards the end of January 1930 the defeated dictator Primo de Rivera left Spain. By failing to call a meeting of the 'Cortes' within three months of the General's fall, the king went against the Constitution. After eight years of dictatorship elections could be delayed no longer, as was proved by military uprisings and demonstrations by the numerous political parties then in existence. Elections of councillors were held on 12 April 1931, almost without disorder, and without Government pressure being brought in to sway the election. The resulting landslide passed even the most optimistic republican hopes: in the cities an unprecedented majority of republican councillors were elected; in the country monarchists predominated. The Captain-General of Madrid discovered that in the army sentiments were anti-monarchist up to the rank of Captain. On 14 April, different cities proclaimed the Republic, and while red flags and tri-colours were flown the King departed into exile. Once the Republic was established it directed its efforts towards the following aims: to separate the Army and the Church from politics, to carry out agrarian reforms, and to place teaching on a civil and secular basis. I shall only refer here to the religious and agrarian problems, which have a direct bearing on the town.

The Assembly prepared one law establishing divorce by mutual consent after two years of marriage, recognizing only civil marriage; and another declared that the Society of Jesus should be dissolved and its goods confiscated by the State. Paragraph 4 of Article 26 of the Constitution forbade the religious orders to teach; the State salaries of the clergy were withdrawn, and the corps of army chaplains was dissolved; the cemeteries were made secular, and Catholic funeral services were forbidden unless specially requested in the will of the deceased. The majority voted for all these articles of the Constitution, causing the withdrawal *en masse* of the Basque representatives and the resignation of the President of the Government and one of the ministers. In his first speech the new President declared on 13 October 1931 that 'Spain is no longer Catholic'. If we bear in mind the influence of religion in the social life of Spain, that traditionally the Church and State have always been united, and that a much greater number of pupils were educated in the schools run by religious orders than in State establishments, it is obvious that the impact on a large section of public opinion should have been one of shock. Apart from the purely legal side of the matter there was also an extremist element that understood more about direct action than about laws; they interpreted this in their own way and in four months burned down 170 churches. The Primate of Spain was dismissed because of his anti-Republican attitude. According to some these were 'victories', while according to others they were 'insupportable attacks on liberty'.

The agrarian reforms sought a solution to the old problem of the ownership of extensive property—*latifundio*—by one person.

The law of 1932 dispossessed with compensation the big land-owners in Andalucía, Extremadura, La Mancha, Toledo and Salamanca. The need for this law was probably felt more in Andalucía than elsewhere, since 3 per cent of the owners of vineyards in Jerez, for instance, owned 67 per cent, and 68 per cent of the lands of Cádiz were in the hands of owners of more than 250 hectares. The confiscated land became the property of the State; and the Constitutional Assembly debated the most practical way of distributing it, considering different solutions according to the political creeds of the various parties: 'The land for the man who tills it'; 'The land should belong to the State and the working of it to the Unions'; 'Family property'; 'Private property', etc., and the general inclination was towards the land being distributed either among collective associations or among private individual farmers. The municipalities were left to decide by a majority of votes which of the two possible methods of distribution was most suitable in each case.

In the decades preceding the advent of the Republic, life in the community followed its daily rhythm in a monotonous but peaceful way. The cultivation of the land kept the residents occupied; there were no wirelesses to put the people in contact with the outside world and normally no newspapers were received. Life was generally poor and hard, since fields were cultivated with the Roman plough and the use of fertilizers and the selection of seed were almost unknown. The community as such enjoyed tranquillity, unity and order; there were no signs of internal hostility. What is more, months before the rise of the Republic one of the men who was later to become leader of a political faction in the town, organized an excursion in which everyone who wanted could take part, independent of economic, religious or political differences; the last, in fact, hardly existed at all. Such a community excursion with such a group of people would have been inconceivable just one year later, but at that time popular opinion seemed indifferent to politics. Before Primo de Rivera's dictatorship of 1923–30, political speeches were made in the town now and then by representatives of the parties, but they never succeeded in arousing sufficient interest for a political party to be founded in the locality. 'When the Republic came', they remark, 'we didn't even know what it was'.

Land ownership was roughly distributed according to the first Table, p. 19, with the addition of lands cultivated by over fifty tenants on the aforementioned estate; there, that is to say at about 3 kilometres from the town, there was land available for anyone who wished to cultivate it. If a couple wanted to marry and had no land of their own they negotiated with the steward of the estate for the rent of an allotment. It seems that only a score of men with families were farm labourers, without land of their own or rented, who had no money nor the strength or pluck necessary to make rented land pay in those days. Because alongside the facilities for renting land went difficulties in getting the land to yield sufficiently, owing to the poor methods of cultivation and the difficulty in selling agricultural produce. Wheat, for example, the basic part of the annual income, was carted to the flour mills where the millers fixed the price; if the farmer needed money at harvest time, which was usually the case, he had to sell at the buyer's price. If he could manage without the money for the time being, he stored the grain in a granary in the hope of its fetching a higher price later. Once the minimum price for wheat had been officially fixed at the close of the Republican period there were cases in which the millers sent out receipts indicating that the wheat had been paid for at the official price, when in actual fact the payment had been less; but the seller could do nothing but accept and sign the receipt, because of the imperative need for money. For the farmer working rented land, or with few fields of his own, without horses and means of transport, the situation was even more difficult. It was still difficult for those who delayed the sale of wheat; they were really only varying the difficulties. And under these circumstances the labourers who lived only from their wages could not ask for higher pay. The number of economically discontented people was high.

Those who were better off, with more fields, tools, horses and means of transport faced the circumstances from a more comfortable position. They did not pay an adequate wage to the labourers they employed; they insisted on high interest on occasional loans. The office of mayor had circulated among a dozen well-to-do families for the past hundred years. In the church the pews were filled with these families, whereas generally speaking the poor were indifferent towards religious matters; if they attended church at all they only put in an appearance occasionally at *fiestas*. Nevertheless nobody interfered with anybody else because of their religious or political views. During a political speech in 1920, the speaker, who was an outsider, had to make a sudden departure without finishing his speech because he had dared to attack religion. The mayor forbade him to continue.

In short, when the political propaganda of the various parties touched the town there was no organized internal discord; political ideas, reduced to the most elementary concepts, had no effect on the life of the community. The discontent over the national agricultural drive extended to all income groups among the inhabitants, even though the consequences of the Government's failure in this respect were worst for the smallholder and the farmer of rented land. The wage-earning labourers, most of whom were new to the town, and therefore without the roots in the community of those who had lived for many generations in the same place, could have rented land, but they preferred to live on an uncertain wage. Finally, religious practices, generally speaking, were associated with those who were better off and enjoyed a greater degree of authority through having the local government in their hands.

The political parties in the city soon directed their attention towards the small towns, knowing that the lack of definite political ideas gave the first party to arrive a good chance of increasing its voting power. The speeches took place in a large hall, where a silent film was sometimes projected on Sundays, or in school rooms, or even in the open air in the market-place. Political placards were hung at street corners; there was a generous distribution of leaflets on party policy; a radio was installed in one of the bars, where the customers could follow the course of national events. *Pronunciamientos*, strikes, murders, the burning of the editorial offices of newspapers, of convents and churches throughout the country was the order of the day. So it was inevitable that, in the face of so much pressure from without, popular opinion should begin to take an interest and to take sides, in theory at least, with one or other party or ideology. The choice of party was nearly always determined by the religious or non-religious tradition of the family, by its economic position, as well as by private opinions about the actions and not only the ideas of the various parties.

The first political group that appeared could be called Liberal, corresponding to a national party already characterized as being for freethinkers and those with anticlerical leanings. In the town the followers of this group could be summed up in one word as anti-religious. They did not make life difficult for other members of the community and limited their activities to ensuring that their families did not take part in religious ceremonies. The acceptance of more extremist views came about, in part, through there being in the town a small number of people not native to the community who had married into it. So the Leftists appeared who, by their acts of aggression, were partly responsible for the later organization of Rightists. Whilst the Leftists were taking shape there was a gradual cleavage within the community between them and other residents who were as yet unorganized. The Leftists acquired headquarters where followers received assignments, held discussions, and prepared for action. They gained a foothold on the Council. At this stage opposition crystallized into the Rightist party with their own headquarters. But while the first group, consisting of about half the residents, was an active body, keen for change, with leaders and a programme, the second was characterized by its passivity, on the defensive against the attacks of the first and without a local leader.

If we consider the laws relating to the Church and religion that were voted by the Constituent Assembly we see that, in the first place, they were very similar to those in force in France, for instance, where they were not considered an insult to religion; and secondly that they provide no basis whatever for burning churches and convents, or for direct attacks on religious practices or on those observing them. Agrarian reform makes no mention of Aragón because of the better distribution of land there, and the absence of big landowners; besides, when we consider the problem from the point of view of the town, we have already seen that there were no big landowners and that there was a possibility of acquiring rented land. Nonetheless the principal objects open to attack by the Leftists were fundamentally religion and land ownership. Although active aggression began about the same time against both and increased correspondingly, it is better to analyse them separately.

One of the words most often heard on the wireless and in speeches and read in the papers was 'Liberty'. In the name of Liberty the Assembly legally limited the power of the Church; in the name of Liberty the extreme left wing illegally attacked and destroyed people associated with and property belonging to it. The town Council abolished certain processions on Feast days and the band, which was the traditional accompaniment to the High Mass on festival days, was forbidden to enter the church at the rear of the processions. It was made to wait outside for the congregation to emerge, and was then instructed to play the 'Hymn of Riego', the popular version of which was:

> 'If the priests and monks only knew
> the beating they are going to get,
> they would rush up into the choir
> and sing: Liberty, Liberty, Liberty'.

Another time the Leftists soaped the doorway and pavement so that the faithful on the way into church would slip and fall amid merriment on the part of the spectators; on a further occasion they broke the big watchman's rattle with which the acolytes used to announce the beginning of the Good Friday service at street corners.

The Rightists replied to this by accompanying the images of the Saints in the processions with pistols, and protecting the street corners with armed men. While one side announced that as the procession passed the canal they would throw the images of the patron saints of the town into the water, the other side did its best to make the procession more solemn than ever. The repeated insults in public to religion and to the Virgin of Caballeros, the Patroness of the town, shouted through the open windows of her shrine as well as to the faithful on their way to and from church, paved the way for the organization of Catholic Action in the town.

But all this is still only one side of the more complex issue that divided the community into two camps, because with a few exceptions the families that assiduously practised their religion were at the same time the ones who owned larger holdings of land. In reality their property amounted to very few hectares, as has been said, so that even a biased interpretation of the agrarian law would not have permitted the local Council to confiscate their land and divide it among the few labourers in the locality, who in their turn had not wished to rent land. But the Leftists, who by then had control of the Council and were in daily contact with similar bodies in the city, had to test their efficiency. A workmen's union was formed, such as had existed throughout the nation wherever the political circumstances had allowed since 1888; the union, keyed to politics, was one of the most efficient weapons in the hands of the party it represented.

In the town the union took the following form: a tavern in the market square was used as a labour exchange, membership of which was obligatory. If a farmer needed a labourer or labourers for work in his fields, he was not allowed to deal with them directly nor could they offer their services to anyone. They had to go to the exchange, give their names, and usually to wait there in the tavern until someone wanting farmhands that day employed the man or men whose names were at the top of the list. In a community where all complications are hated the measure could hardly have been more provocative: when we add to this the fact that the labour exchange was obligatory, a reason sufficient in itself to make people do their utmost to avoid it, and imposed by the other side, we find an organization that is doomed to failure from the start, as was the case. Those belonging to the Rightists were reluctant to register; there were moreover a few established bonds between some labourers and landowners for working according to personal agreements, beneficial to both; so naturally some labourers delayed joining the union. As the Leftists could not tolerate disobedience they decided to act. They declared a public holiday and prohibited work on that day. The Leftist supporters obeyed this order while most of the Rightists went out to work in the fields as usual. On the way they met pickets of union men who intimidated them into returning home; groups of women pickets did the same with women on their way to the fields. Some people decided to go home, but those who chose to resist were beaten up; one of them died later as a result of his wounds.

The Rightists, by now organized on the lines of a national party, considered that the situation had become unbearable; there were taunts directed at them and their families in the streets, insults to the women going to and from the church, arrogant threats of mass killings phrased in crude but expressive metaphors derived from the farm tools, and of course continual threats to dispossess them of their land. They gathered at their headquarters periodically to find a way to deal with the situation; one night, in the middle of the meeting, they were arrested by order of the Leftist mayor. They were released a few days later on conditions that they let a portion of their land; this condition was also imposed on others who were not at the meeting and had therefore not been taken prisoner. The theoretical distribution of the fields took place, but the plans were never carried out because of the outbreak of the civil war.

The brief account of these events leads up to the analysis of a wide range of inter-relationships, based chiefly on the ownership of land. The inter-relationship of such pairs as property and religion, property and social position, and all that involves the attitude of people towards politics, the law, authority and religion, will be dealt with later; what follows will be limited to comments of a general nature on the blocks or groups already referred to. Later, when touching on some of the aspects mentioned here, we shall see them in a wider context, where their significance can be more deeply appreciated.

II

In the history of the nation the period from 1931 to 1936 is characterized by repeated efforts radically to alter the structure of the country. Within the community this produced a violent struggle between the two groups over the attempted inversion of positions in the traditional hierarchy. Political party propaganda brought about the *mise en branle* of diffused forces, making hitherto uncommitted people conscious of belonging to a definite group. Even though they had no political ideas their choice of party was not accidental, but was governed by an existing reality: their hierarchical position in the community, measured in terms of the possession of land or their lack of it. Later conflicts therefore came about within a social structure that in its turn reflected the geographical environment.

The transition from a passive group to an active one developed quickly and spontaneously: each group centred round the most important and personal aspects, the ownership of land

or lack of it and the attitude towards religion. In practice, the
community was divided into two groups characterized and led
by two very actively antagonistic minorities, especially that of
the Left, and a mass of people definitely adhering to one or other
group, following the direction of its leaders. Dedication to the
cause and party consciousness broke former bonds of friendship
and kinship; there was a tendency to greet and be friendly
towards members of the same group, whilst systematically
avoiding the others. Quarrels, rivalry and hatred developed
out of these estrangements. Each group had its café, its meetings
and even its feastdays, religious on the one side and secular on
the other. During the strike already mentioned brothers
struggled against brothers and nephews struck uncles. The
Cause attracted the most generous and self-denying impulses,
overcoming other bonds that could have united those who had
taken different sides; they fought for the Cause, not on an
objective, impersonal plane, with mutual respect, but on a
level of personal, individual attacks; there was no attempt to
approach the problems objectively, to discuss matters in a
balanced way, and to reach a mutual understanding.

To discuss the problems and to arrive at an understanding
would have involved a recognition of the existence of the other
block with its rights and interests, an acceptance of the fact
that each group was a complement of the other. To both groups,
in particular that of the Left, this meant having dealings with
the very people they were bent on destroying and was therefore out of the question. As they saw it the other people with
their hated ideas and values had no right to exist. How could
one discuss matters calmly with such people? The only solution
possible therefore, was for one group to dominate the other by
direct action, that is by violence.

The aim of the attacks by the Leftist leaders was to destroy
the structure of the community, by making a radical break with
the past, overcoming each of its key points with values, practices
and ideas that were diametrically opposed to those previously
held. This disintegration of the social structure was begun in the
name of a new social myth, 'Liberty', by attacking the customs
and festivals that strengthened the bonds of union among the
residents. So, during the summer festivals, while some were
struggling to maintain the solemn, religious character of those

days in honour of the patron saints of the town, others were putting all their efforts into secular amusements, the hours of which were arranged to clash with the religious ceremonies.

In addition, new holidays of a secular character appeared for the working man; they had a republican flavour and the Rightists took no part in them. The Council, that is to say authority, passed from the Rightists to the Leftists. They, with the authority thus acquired, attempted to carry out a policy of protection of the worker without land of his own and of the smallholder, who began to occupy a place of primary importance in the locality. But the intention was not only to help the economically weak in order to minimize the difference between strata, but rather to invert the social structure so that those who formerly occupied the lower levels automatically passed into the higher ones, taking the places vacated by those who had occupied the highest position. In this respect the structure aimed at was the same as before, except that they were trying to turn upside down the socio-economic status of the individuals in each group.

The most direct way of destroying the existing socio-economic hierarchy, based principally on the possession of land, was to dispossess landowners of their fields and redistribute them among those who, through having none of their own, were on the very bottom rung of the hierarchy. That is precisely what they tried to do. In other words, a community in which religious ideas, or their content, penetrate into all social manifestations, changed into what was not only officially unreligious, but atheist; the religious festivals became secular; from a situation where members of the Council presided over all religious ceremonies there was a change to a condition where not only did they not attend them but actually prohibited them in part; the people who had occupied the lowest levels of society appeared at the top, so that a new social order was established setting forth ideas received from the city; the system of property was altered, at least in theory, breaking the basis for the difference of social groups and causing the inversion of the structure itself; the focus of political power changed hands, one group was dispossessed of, and the other endowed with, an efficient means for the achievement of its aims; as opposed to the slow, traditional ways of solving problems came ideas, and above all actions, that were direct, progressive and violent, with no intermediate stages, breaking and opposing the past. Among the Leftists women, traditionally sheltered in the home, came out into the street wearing party colours, forming groups like men and singing, shouting aggressively and dancing in great gangs during the festivals as if wishing to demonstrate that in the name of Liberty their habitual seclusion in the house had been relegated to the past. Not only is one dealing, therefore, with the inversion of status within the structure of society but with a radical change in the values which upheld it, following the injection into it of ideas and attitudes which were quite contrary to anything known before.

In a community where all behaviour has the entire community for its severe judge, the word 'Liberty', so widespread in national circles, appeared to be destined to clear the existing atmosphere of heavy social pressures. The system of attitudes and customs determines conduct in a most rigorous manner, as I shall explain later; the imposition of some of them is fairly weak, but others are considered as basic, and as such bring great pressure to bear on the individual. Some of the heaviest are those related to morals in a *lattissimo sensu*, but always bearing in mind that one is dealing with Catholic morals, which have a great influence on the whole range of attitudes and customs related to them. These pressures act as inhibiting factors, especially for those whose religious ideas are non-existent, deficient or shaky. The word 'Liberty' in its official and national acceptation, just because it was official, modern, and national, allowed people to break socially the weighty bonds of attitudes and customs that were considered antiquated. It is difficult to attack principles, attitudes, or social pressures, whatever they may be like, because one is dealing with impersonal, extra-individual realities; but it is easier to attack an organization which is thought to be the original source of those principles. The church attracted a good number of attacks. The church is the parish priest, the building in the market place, the hermitage out in the fields, the religious festivals and the processions of March, Holy Week and August, and the people who practise the cults. Moreover the most assiduous in the practice of religion, and therefore its chief defenders, were those who in general possessed the greater number of fields, more economic

means, greater power and prestige. So in this social upheaval
people found themselves involved in a double attack—against
property and against their religious ideas. The two objects of
attack became identified as the same, for any attempt to reverse
religious ideas and sentiments destroys the fundamental values
shared by those who are economically more powerful, and the
confiscation of land removes the basis of power and prestige
with which the practitioners of religion surround every religious
expression and cult.

In short, a national upheaval favoured a reaction—the pattern
of which followed the lines set by the structure of the community itself—against the structure of the community, against
strong social pressures, considered in part as arising from
religion, which was itself identified with the bigger landowners,
that is to say, with those who occupied the highest position in
the scale of prestige and power.

This upheaval represents an experimental period clearly displaying the essential characteristics in the structure of the town.
The economic, social and cultural crisis centres around religion
and the ownership of land, intimating that these are the
foundations on which the relations of the residents are chiefly
based. The destruction of the existing structure and its inversion, attempted with such vehemence and speed by one of the
groups, met with the most tenacious opposition from the other
group, which tried to prevent a change which for them implied
vital losses. The civil war reinforced in its essentials the old
structure that had been, to some extent, already adapted by
events towards a greater readiness for change. When the
Republic was proclaimed, the Constitution based on Weimar's
which was the most democratic in Europe, declared Spain to
be a democratic republic of the workers of all classes. In fact,
the most democratic democracy in Europe brought about the
creation of the most authoritarian and intransigent groups
known in five hundred years of the history of the town.

III

Finally, property is not always the cause of discord; sometimes it acts as a means of strengthening the unity of the group
in order to deal with problems of common interest against
another group foreign to the community. During the past five

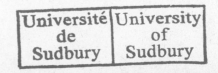

years the residents have managed, by arrangement with the directors of a sugar-beet factory, to install a weighing machine in the town for weighing sugar-beet and unloading it there without having to transport it to the factory. One of the residents who represents the interests of the town attends the operation of weighing, making a discount of so much per cent on the gross weight, according to the amount of earth still attached to the crop. People from neighbouring towns can also bring their sugar-beet to the municipal weighing machine if they want. The residents of Arcos considered themselves humiliated and after slight opposition acquired their own weighing machine. Once the civil war was over a delegation of the National Syndicate of Wheat was established in the town by government order, and there the people of Belmonte and neighbouring towns sell and unload the wheat they harvest. As latterly the granaries were found to be insufficient and unsuitable, the town, subsidised in part by the National Syndicate, built a single barn large enough to store all the wheat produced in the locality and in the surrounding towns. Although these towns can and in fact do unload their wheat there, they did not contribute in any way towards the cost of construction of the new granary and their help was not even sought. Once it was finished the inhabitants of Arcos once more considered that Belmonte had stolen a march on them, and managed to get the Government to install—through influence and for no real reason at all according to the people of Belmonte—a branch of the National Syndicate of Wheat in their town. They then planned to build their own granary. They wanted the economic help of some seventy of the inhabitants of Belmonte to subsidize it because they had lands within the *término* of Arcos. As they lived in Belmonte and brought home all their crops, they flatly refused to do so; they cycled to Arcos where they held a meeting of protest against the demand. When they returned there was a meeting of the Brotherhood of farmers, the Council, and other residents who owned no land in Arcos, and they decided to send a deputation to Madrid to try to settle the problem at the Ministry of Agriculture, because they considered that the planned granary was unnecessary. The deputation was sent. The matter has not yet been decided.

Recently Belmonte joined the surrounding small towns that

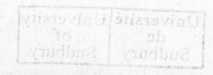

use the same canal to buy a waterfall that should increase the facilities for irrigating the land. These examples prove that whether within the town or outside it, the possession of land sometimes produces conflicts and sometimes reinforces the unity of the group; in other words, that much of social life, both within the community and outside it, is organized around the ownership of land.

III

STRATIFICATION: I

'*La vida es esencialmente un diálogo con el contorno*'. '*No hay vida sin interpretación del contorno*'.

'*Vivimos en función de nuestro contorno, el cual, a su vez, depende de nuestra sensibilidad*'.

'*El carácter de una sociedad dependerá del modo de valorarse a sí mismos los individuos que la formen*'. ORTEGA Y GASSET

THE PREDOMINANCE of agricultural topics in conversation introduced us to the analysis of the cycle of agricultural activities of primary importance in the life of the community. Expressions quoted revealed a whole range of differentiation and social distance. I also indicated the emotive character of the phrases which betrayed the sense of inferiority felt by the countryman towards the city dweller. The sacrifices made by parents to educate their children at a school in the city clearly showed the desire to improve their social position. The agricultural *campañas*, or periods of the most intense work, were considered sociologically as times of greater subordination and collaboration between individuals, indicating a marked social hierarchy.

The last chapter underlined how the amount of land owned by an individual affected his political ideas, religious practices, and the acquisition of power and prestige. The division between Right and Left, or traditionalists and progressives, followed closely the differentiation in economic power.

The size of landholdings, different sources of income, subordination, collaboration, power, prestige, social position, the desire (and efforts) to reach a higher social level, are all aspects which have arisen out of the central theme of property. These aspects will now be discussed, and besides completing and confirming this theme from a different point of view, they will explain essential characteristics of the social structure of Belmonte.

It would be easy to begin the analysis by way of the numerous linguistic expressions that reveal an elaborate system of social positions; but leaving them aside for the moment I shall take as a starting point the second half of the sixteenth century, to sketch briefly the historico-social structure of the community in relation to the theme.

I

The oldest papers in the parochial archives go back to 1557. The well-preserved pages are an inventory of births, marriages, and deaths. Greater sociological interest is afforded by the canonical visits of the bishops, who used to write reports in which they indicated to the parish priest how he should proceed in his ministry. By reading the two sources of information carefully it is possible to sketch in broad outline the life of the community, its stratification, customs, work and amusements. These data are completed by the Minutes of the Town Council which date back to 1798. I quote below four death notices, the commentary on which will introduce us to the theme of this chapter.

'On 17th September of the above mentioned year (1558) died Lorenza de Urgilles. Received the sacrament of the eucharist. Was buried in the cemetery. Made a will with Alonso Jiménez as executor. Left one hundred *sueldos* for her soul and for an anniversary service...'[1]

'On XVII of January (1563) died Miguel de Pueyo, manservant to Bartolomé Bailo. Died without confessing. Buried in the common grave (*fosal*) of the church'.[2]

'Sunday, day of Our Lady of August (Aug. 15th, 1563) died Guillén de la Brocada; received all the sacraments; made a will with Fr. Jerónimo Ibarz, deputy to the curate, as executor, in default of a notary. He directed that he be buried in the common grave and was buried in the church at the wish of his executors. Left three hundred *sueldos* for his soul, and for his burial, novena, and anniversary'.[3]

'On XXX of November 1563 died Ramón Moreno and died intestate. Four hundred *sueldos* authorized over his body. Taken for burial to the Monastery of San Lázaro in the city. The bells tolled a full peal...'.[4]

---

[1] Parish records, vol. I, fol. 3.   [2] Ibid., fol. 18.
[3] Ibid., fol. 19.   [4] Ibid., fol. 20, second side.

These entries have been copied in chronological order, but for purposes of analysis I shall begin with the second. The death notice of Miguel de Pueyo consists of twenty-three words in the original including the date. With regard to his profession he was a manservant in the service of Bartolomé Bailo. He died without receiving any sacrament whatever, and was buried in the *fosal* or common grave, where they buried those who lacked the means to purchase a grave in the cemetery or the church. The entry of course says nothing about his having made a will. A will is certainly made by Lorenza de Urgilles, who leaves 'one hundred *sueldos*' for her soul besides a further sum for an anniversary service. She received communion before dying and was buried in the cemetery, not in the common grave.

Guillén de la Brocada, whose name in itself seems to indicate a high social position, bequeathed for his soul three hundred *sueldos*, a novena and an anniversary service. He was obviously a rich man. 'He received all the sacraments'. Despite his expressed wish to be buried in the common grave, his executors did not consider this fitting and so (in consonance with his social position) paid for him to be buried not simply in the cemetery but in the church. That one paid for burial in the church is made plain from the pastoral visit of the Archbishop D. Andrés Sotos, for he directed: 'Item we command that those who have charge of the fabric and lighting (of the church) shall in no wise under pain of excommunication give or sell any perpetual sepulture nor chapel without our license or scriptis, or that of our Vicar General, in order that justice may be observed'.[1]

The last of the entries copied deals with Ramón Moreno, who died without making a will. It is probably for the same reason that he died without receiving the sacraments, perhaps suddenly; but of this the writer says nothing although he was under an obligation to record whether or not he received the last sacraments. In any case he was a rich man, since 400 *sueldos* were set aside for his soul. 'The bells tolled a full peal' and he was not even buried in the church in the town but taken to the 'Monastery of San Lázaro in the city'.

What so far seems simply a logical deduction from these records is ratified if we look through the death records in Vol. II.

[1] Pastoral visit of 26 April 1582, Parish records, vol. I, fol. 51–56.

The scribe explicitly draws attention to the relationship between wealth or poverty and burial. In the margin at the left-hand side of some of the entries, and in bigger letters, he writes: 'Pauper', and at the end of the entry: 'Buried in the common grave', as in the following entry which says:

> PAUPER. On the 21st day of December of 1673 died Felipe Guerrero. Received only the sacrament of Extreme Unction, as he fell from his mount and did not speak again. Buried in the common grave as a pauper.[1]

All through the pages one reads repeatedly: 'Buried him as a pauper.' Don Luis de Saranía, representing the Archbishop on his canonical visit, explains the meaning of the phrase when he writes: 'Item we command the V(icar) not to bury any person without receiving a guarantee of the fees of the Ordinary before two witnesses . . . unless he be a poor man, for him we order to be buried with great charity and without charging anything at all'.[2]

One can recognize at first glance the death record of a pauper, which does not normally exceed three lines. A pauper could not make a will to bequeath his effects, nor leave money for masses, novenas and anniversaries. As he could not pay for burial either he was interred in the common grave. The records quoted seem to indicate that burial in the common grave, in the cemetery, and in the church correspond to three categories of people, their classification into one or other of the three categories depending on their respective economic standing. For the common grave there is no payment—'buried him as a pauper'; we have seen that Lorenza de Urgilles, who was buried in the cemetery, left '100 *sueldos*' for her soul, and that Guillén de la Brocada was buried in the church, having left 300 *sueldos* for his soul besides a novena and anniversary service. Finally Ramón Moreno, over whose corpse 400 *sueldos* were ordered to be set aside, was interred in a monastery in the city. Without pretending that the amount of money expresses mathematically the social condition and corresponding burial, it is logical to deduce from the records a constant correlation between the

---

[1] Parish records, vol. II, fol. 264.
[2] Ibid., fol. 232–3; pastoral visit of 21 November 1615.

form of burial and the economic level of the person buried. In other words, the records prove the existence of distinct levels in the community and, what is also important, their graduated relationship to certain religious ceremonies.

The Council Minutes frequently refer to the stratification of the town. On 3 November 1799, the mayor called to the Town Hall by 'public proclamation, those inhabitants who have mules, carts and oxen'. That these constituted a stratum is proved by the Minute of June 1861 which says: 'That some fords in the district being in poor condition, according to complaints which (the mayor) had received from several *vecinos acomodados* (prosperous inhabitants), so that they were unable to pass with their carts . . . it was agreed that steps be taken to repair them'. In general the ownership of a cart, mules or oxen was a sign of being a 'prosperous inhabitant', a phrase equivalent even nowadays to a rich inhabitant; and wealth depended then and still depends basically on the number of acres of cultivable land possessed. At the same time it is worthwhile to observe that the complaints of the 'prosperous inhabitants' are promptly considered by the mayor, who himself was one of them. The following quotation (22 December 1861) indicates also that these prosperous inhabitants are the guardians of order in the community, for the mayor announced at the Council meeting: 'That he had received complaints from *vecinos bien acomodados* (very prosperous inhabitants) that the peace was disturbed by night by certain youths with clamour and noise on the occasion of their making the rounds. . . '.

In other contexts these same worthies are called the 'major contributors' (*mayores contribuyentes*), since on them fell the greater part of the municipal taxes, which are in direct ratio to the possession of movable and immovable property, that is, cultivable lands and houses. Thus the Minute of 14 April 1872, divides the inhabitants of the town 'with respect to the matter of contributions' into 'major contributors', 'medium contributors', 'tradesmen', and 'day labourers'. The function of the 'major contributors' in the life of the community is varied and active. They provide the greater part of the municipality's income, they pay the masters who teach in the schools, because they are the *pudientes*—rich and powerful.[1] They are summoned

[1] Minutes of the Council, 21 November 1872.

to the Town Hall to decide matters pertaining to (a) the town festivals, especially those of August;[1] (b) national political up-heavals in so far as they affect the town;[2] (c) internal order in the town and the creation of new municipal posts;[3] (d) the voting of municipal budgets and tolls;[4] (e) the building of bridges;[5] and regulation of irrigation works and sluices;[6] (f) they occupy the Council posts in a more or less periodic rotation. In a word, it is they who regulate the internal and external affairs of the community. They represent order and wield power. They are the few who can read and write, though they cannot always do that;[7] nevertheless they constitute a select group in the town in the matter of deportment, on which the Council relies on formal occasions. Thus the Minute of 21 May 1882, dealing with the programme of ceremonies for the reception of the Cardinal of the city, says: 'It was also agreed to invite the *personas más visibles* (the most "visible" or presentable persons) in the town to the reception'. Gracián, himself Aragonese and with an excellent knowledge of the local speech and customs, wrote: '. . . She does not see me, for I am small, and only those of good appearance are "visible"!' 'Still less will she "see" me', said the Student, 'for I am poor'[8]. The author opposes 'poor' to 'visible' since only the rich are 'visibles', and by the same token their behaviour is *bien visto* or 'well looked upon'.

The Council Minutes indicate another category of persons whom they call *profesores* (which means here professional men). They are the doctor, the two schoolmasters, the veterinary surgeon, the secretary of the Council and the chemist, to whom must be added the parish priest and the curate. They are dis-tinguished by their professions: they are not on the land nor are they 'sons of the town'. The inhabitants of the town must contribute, normally in wheat,[9] to the payment of the *conducta* or sum agreed upon by the Council for each *profesor* for the exercise of his profession. They for their part, in their capacity

---

[1] Ibid., 9 August 1857.   [2] Ibid., 1 October 1868.
[3] Ibid., 12 May 1869.   [4] Ibid., 14 September 1870.
[5] Ibid., 9 February 1862.   [6] Ibid., 14 May 1882.
[7] Ibid., 1 July 1804.
[8] B. Gracián: *El Criticón*, Colección Austral 1944, p. 193; Part II first published in Zaragoza in 1653.
[9] Minutes of the Council, 24 June 1804.

of 'special' residents, are not subject to this rule: 'the *profesores* are exempt from paying *conductas* one to another' but 'they are reciprocally obliged to one another in their respective professions'.[1] The title of 'profesores' by which they are distinguished leads one to suppose that they enjoyed the highest prestige in the town, but the papers are silent on this point.

With regard to the lower economic level of inhabitants the minutes also abound in references and different terms. Let us look at some examples. In 1856[2] the townspeople are working on the repair of a bridge; as they go to work on Sunday—which is expressly forbidden by the Council—the secretary who writes the Minute hastens to explain the reason: they work on Sunday only 'until the bells ring for high Mass, in order not to deprive the labouring class (*clase jornalera*) of a day's pay'. We are, then, dealing with a different stratum, with individuals or families owning no landed property or means of production, since their source of income is the daily wage, working for 'major contributors', or *pudientes*, or 'prosperous inhabitants', 'those who have mules, carts and oxen'. Together with the phrase 'labouring class' we find others with the same rich lexical significance. In the Minute of 30 June 1861 it is agreed that 'no resident of the needy class (*clase menesterosa*) shall go gleaning in anyone else's field'. That of 30 March 1862, speaks of the 'common masses (*la masa vulgar*) of this town'.

This pejorative phrase implies that the customs and habits of those who belong to this socio-economic level are not always in consonance with the traditional standards of the town that the 'prosperous inhabitants' strive to maintain. In a Minute of 31 January 1862, the members of the Council agree upon 'the procedure for keeping watch on a house where private gaming is carried on at night among the labouring class'. The 'prosperous inhabitants' and the Council—in practice the same group of people—represent the traditional values and customs of the town; the 'labouring class' forms the group of irresponsibles over whose conduct the former have to keep watch for the proper functioning of the community.

The Minutes of the early years of the last century make numerous references to another subdivision: '*los criados y*

---

[1] Ibid.   [2] Ibid., 3 December.

criadas'—the servants—i.e. labourers attached to the household and female domestic servants. Defining the duties and obligations of the doctor[1] the Council informs him that he is required to 'visit the sick morning and evening, including servants'; 'the apothecary must give all medicine to everyone, masters and servants, without any fee whatever'. When on 1 July of the same year the doctor and chemist sign the agreements they protest against the clause which includes the 'servants', wishing to be paid for attending them. The protest seems to show that the number of servants was considerable. The Council argued for their part that they 'could not depart from the obligations, agreements and conditions settled by the *Junta de Veintena* (an *ad hoc* committee of twenty) on St. John's day'.

The first reference to the group of inhabitants belonging neither to the 'major contributors' nor to the 'labouring class' is found in the Minute of 14 April 1872. They are called 'medium contributors' (*medianos contribuyentes*). This is the only direct allusion to them, and the only characteristic of the group to be glimpsed from the Minutes is that they come in between the other two more explicitly defined levels. From this date forward the papers speak clearly of 'three classes': '. . . there being present the contributors in the threefold number representing the classes in the town . . .'[2]; and '. . . the Council in association with nine contributors who represent the three classes . . .,'[3] or '. . . the contributors divided into three categories . . .'.[4] As servants paid no contribution at all but were regarded for the purpose as members of the master's family, the three classes or categories referred to in these last records comprise the 'major contributors', the 'medium contributors' and the 'labouring class'. The *Profesores* (professionals) are not 'sons of the town', nor do they contribute to the expenses of the community. They form a group apart.

In this brief historical sketch I have tried to outline the social stratification of the town in the past as an introduction to the presentday stratification, since this, in its essential characteristics, clearly shows the mark of the past four centuries. The following points need to be borne in mind:

[1] Ibid., 24 June 1804.   [2] Ibid., 29 April 1877.
[3] Ibid., 19 May 1881.   [4] Ibid., 1 April 1887.

1. Ownership of land is the fundamental criterion of stratification. It is natural that the Minutes should stress the contribution paid to the municipality rather than the actual number of fields possessed. One of the principal responsibilities of the Council was the collection of taxes, whence the Minutes give the lists of contributors with the amounts paid. The important point here is to see property as the direct cause of the contributions: the latter was proportional to the former.

2. An individual's social position is maintained with relative ease if he belongs to the group of 'major contributors'; social mobility is restricted for members of the 'medium contributors', and minimal for those in the 'labouring class'. Since the stratification is based primarily on ownership of land, ascent in the social scale will necessitate the acquisition of land or the enlargement of existing holdings. The normal means of acquisition are inheritance or purchase. The first keeps the individual within his category because, even if lands were divided among children, it was the rule to marry persons of the same category and these in turn brought with them inherited land. Purchase was extremely difficult because hardly any money was in circulation and barter or the exchange of services was the common form of payment. Even the *profesores* were paid not in money but in wheat. This is why it was so very difficult to ascend to the next level, particularly for the 'labouring class', lacking as they did the basic requirement for starting—land. The community, therefore, tended to be stabilized on its existing levels, with little mobility.

3. Throughout the documents we observe a marked emphasis on economic strata as such, with no political connotation whatever.

4. There is, however, a clear correlation between different economic categories and certain religious ceremonies.

5. The divisions to be observed from the documents quoted are as follows: (a) 'prosperous inhabitants' or 'major contributors' or 'the powerful ones' (*pudientes*) or 'owners of mules, carts and oxen'; (b) 'medium contributors'; (c) 'the labouring class' or 'needy class' or 'common mass'. Two subdivisions complete the picture: the 'professionals', standing in general apart from the life of the community and having little stability

in the town; and the 'servants', considered part of their masters' household.

6. The 'prosperous inhabitants' represent and guard the
town's traditional values; they look to and live by the past.
The conduct of the 'labouring class' is not always in accordance
with these traditions.

7. The 'major contributors' constitute the dynamic group in
the life of the community; they have a hand in all municipal
activities. The 'labouring class' is characterized by its passivity.
The 'medium contributors', forming a diffuse social layer,
never claimed the attention of the Minute writers; practically
nothing is said about them. The social classification is therefore
expressed in the dichotomy of rich and poor, those who command and those who obey, the *élite* and the masses.

8. Power and authority reside in the members of the Council,
and indirectly in the 'major contributors'. As council appointments were renewed every year, the 'major contributors'—the
only ones eligible as is proved by the Council regulations[1] and
by the constant recurrence of a couple of dozen surnames in the
Minutes—exercised power directly even though periodically.
However, by the end of the last century a tendency towards
democratization was already apparent. When the Council
dealt with taxes, the 'three classes' were represented.

9. The 'prosperous inhabitants' are those who are 'visible'
or *bien vistos*. Their education, behaviour and habits are the
model of 'what is correct'. They feel themselves responsible for
the proper ordering of the little community in everything concerned with the established rules of living. The 'labouring
class' is deprecatingly called 'the common (*vulgar*) mass of this
town'.

II

Although this study of social stratification turns exclusively
on the people living within a particular municipal boundary, it
is necessary again to refer to the regional and national dimensions which transcend the social life of the community. The *homo
rusticus-homo urbanus* dichotomy implies different occupations as

---

[1] Minutes of 29 December 1894; 20 January 1917; 15 January 1921; 4 May
1922 etc., according to which only the *Mayores contribuyentes* can be *compromisarios*.
Compromisarios are those who, being chosen (mostly by ballot) from the *mayores
contribuyentes*, held the right to vote on matters discussed in the Council.

the main criterion of differentiation. The man of the *pueblo* tills the soil, he belongs to the country, and 'being of the country' carries with it a whole train of socially pejorative qualifications. For, as has already been noted, this occupation is valued negatively in terms of prestige, education and style of living— i.e. tilling the soil assigns the individual *ipso facto* to an inferior social category. On a national scale the farmer occupies the lower rungs of the social ladder: very few occupations stand below this level. If then we look from this viewpoint at a small town surrounded by the fields which its inhabitants cultivate, we can say that it constitutes, as a whole, an occupational group of low social status.

Gracián, in *Crisis V*,[1] the title of which is significantly 'Square of the Mob and Yard of the Vulgar Herd', describes a market place where the people are chatting in small groups. He goes up to one of them and on hearing the tone of the conversation about national events he comments: 'Don't you see they're just four yokels from a village? . . . all they know about is sod-breaking' (*destripar terrones*; the literal meaning of the verb is to disembowel). The sarcasm leaves no room for doubt: it is for villagers to till the earth, not to hold opinions. Even today, 300 years later, if one suggests to a youth—who naturally has not read Gracián—the advantages that a change of occupation could bring, he will reply bitterly, 'Where can I go? Sodbreaking is all I can do'.

To be exact one must add a quantitative proviso to the above definition: not all the inhabitants of the town cultivate the land. There are marginal occupations. By these I mean the two ways of earning a living that have no connexion with agricultural tasks: that of the professional men and that of the shepherds. The professions of the first—priest, doctor, chemist, veterinary surgeon, secretary of the Council, schoolmasters and medical assistant—are regarded in the town as superior, but of this more later. The occupation of the second is considered inferior. The professionals do not depend on the land for their living. The shepherds own no land to live by. In neither of these two groups are there any natives of the town.

---

[1] Part II of *El Criticón*, pp. 181–91.

To complete the picture a further particular must be added, this time qualitative: some trades, such as that of undertaker, watercarrier and publican, imply a low social position. These, and other jobs that will be discussed later, are secondary occupations, to fall back on when farming work allows or to augment the scanty income from lands of small extent. In any case, those who divide their labour between the fields and secondary occupations regard themselves as fundamentally farmers and look on the other occupations as something additional. The fact of their being farmers measures *in modo recto* their social position in the community; the secondary occupation may give the measure *in modo obliquo* of the individual because a secondary occupation is a clear indication of the ownership of few fields, of insufficient resources and of time to spare for other jobs.

Other professions—shopkeeper, carpenter, butcher, blacksmith, miller and builder—are thought of as superior to the above mentioned. The volume of business is considerably greater and almost all of these do own some land. Landholding and trade combine to fix the position of each of them in his respective social stratum. Greater or lesser ability in the practice of his trade may determine personal prestige, which in turn gives the final touch to the social placing of the individual.

Hence the various perspectives from which occupation can be viewed: on a national scale, the country—*rus*—bestows its rusticity on the man who works there—*rusticus*. Within the community again the land performs its task of differentiation: those who are not rustics—in the pristine sense of the word— may occupy social positions superior or inferior to that of the farmer. A national criterion places the former, the professionals, in a superior position; the latter, the herdsmen, are classified in a low position by the values of the community itself, but both criterion and values derive from the relation of the individual to the soil. Other occupations, both secondary and those of greater importance, determine not the social stratum of the individual but his situation—*situs*—within it.

The town consists of a group of people who till the fields. These fields, the basis of rusticity, and of a low social position on the national scale, are at the same time the source of reputation and social esteem within the *término*. For while all are farmers, some are more so than others.

III

The data on the division of land shows seven groups of similar economic situation:

Number of hectares	Number of owners
Landless	16
With less than 1 hectare	117
From 1 to 3 hectares	123
From more than 3 to 5 hectares	49
From more than 5 to 10 hectares	41
From more than 10 to 15 hectares	13
With more than 15 hectares	9

These figures, are taken from the municipal land office files and are an 'official' version of property; they do not really reflect the actual state of affairs. It may happen that the head of a family or a proprietor owning less than one hectare of land may farm another hectare belonging to a proprietor who is entered among those owning over fifteen. So this hectare should be transferred to the group of the 117 proprietors with less than one hectare, and omitted from the last group in which nine people are enumerated; and the lessee, taking into account his annual income, should pass into the group immediately above.

The greatest difficulty comes with the division of land within the family on the marriage of sons, because the fathers frequently 'pass on' one or more fields to their sons by private agreements of which nothing is known to the land office. These private family divisions affect the above picture only in terms of numbers, since the social position of an individual is measured not only by the land he cultivates at the moment, which according to official computations is not his own, but by that which he will receive later by inheritance. Disregarding the flexibility of the figures in the second column, however, I shall attempt to outline the meaning of the division in the above table.

Five of the seven groups conform to a more or less arbitrary generic criterion of distinction; other figures for hectares could have been chosen to group the divisions in landholdings. The same cannot be said of the first group, those who own no property. I include in this group the *vecinos*, present or absent, who have neither land nor a fixed trade in the town. The distinction between those who own less than three hectares and more than three implies a fundamental criterion of differentiation: a property of over three hectares of cultivable land is regarded in the town as the minimum holding for the relative economic independence of a couple with two or three children under age. The owner of these plots does not need to go out to work for daily wages. Anybody who owns less does not attain the community's conventional standard of wealth. Once the amount is exceeded one may be more or less rich, according to the group, but these different groupings are of only relative importance compared with the division objectively considered as fundamental.

I call those with no landed property at all nor any fixed trade in the town *braceros* (manual labourers), a term indicating that they depend for their livelihood on their muscular strength. Some of these may be bound to one of the large landowners for whom they work in the periods of heightened activity. But with increasing mechanization such seasonal work is steadily growing shorter and fewer hands are required, which means that for seven months of the year it is difficult to find casual work in the fields. Some of them take advantage of the quiet periods to go away to work on large French farms. During the wheat and beet harvests the *braceros* are in great demand and they take advantage of these periods to raise the price of their labour considerably. Through most of the year they are normally paid 70 pesetas for a day's work; during the *campañas*, particularly that of wheat, a *bracero* can earn up to 145 pesetas a day.

During the rest of the year work is uncertain and the prospects of improving one's economic position are nil. This is why almost all the families in the town who were living in these conditions at the end of the civil war have emigrated during the last fifteen years. But the number of heads of families without property or fixed occupation has remained noticeably constant in the past decade because newcomers from poorer towns have acquired residential rights. The *braceros*, who in large part are not natives of the town, therefore represent the lowest economic level in the community, with very few chances of improving their situation in the course of a generation.

I refer to those whose landholdings are of less than one hectare as *peones*. Their property gives them a certain margin of security; on it they normally grow potatoes, beans, greens and fruit for home consumption, and so expenditure on vegetables is fairly low. They have a house with a yard in which they keep a few chickens, ducks, rabbits, and generally a pig, so that expenditure on protein foods is also slight. As work in their own fields takes up a small part of the year, they go out whenever they have the opportunity at any time of year and work for any proprietor, to earn day wages, or else they engage in secondary occupations. But even with what they earn from the small-holding and the yard and from wages it is difficult for them to reach the annual income regarded as minimal.

The families in this group feel more closely linked to the town, through their fields, houses and yards, than do those in the previous group. The parents do not emigrate. However, the sons may, or at least one of them, because the opportunities open to them in the town are practically nil. More than a dozen youths have secured steady jobs in the city, to which they travel daily. They prefer a modest but fixed wage to uncertain earnings for most of the year, even with high wages during two short seasons. Others wait to complete their military service before looking for a job elsewhere; a final group, with regular employment in other cities, where they have married and settled, have practically broken their ties with the town. In the majority of these cases the parents have either died in the town or still live there.

The *jornaleros* (occasional wage earners) represent the third level, those whose landholdings exceed one hectare but not three. They are not under any compulsion to earn daily wages, like the *braceros* and *peones*. The *jornaleros* work their land the greater part of the year, and when their own tasks allow and wage conditions are most favourable they offer their services as wage-earners. They enjoy a certain autonomy and some degree of choice as to when they work for wages. They are *jornaleros* in the sense that they are not bound to one master as the *braceros* sometimes are, nor are they *peones* in the sense of being ready to earn their wages working at any time in the fields of any proprietor, they go out to work when they judge the conditions to be best, and within a limited circle of personal connexions. Normally they cannot themselves cope with all the urgent work of their own fields during a harvest and to avoid paying high wages they help one another. In the last analysis the degree of autonomy and the width of choice in accepting employment are to some extent restricted by the fact that to achieve the community's standard of living they must of necessity earn a certain amount in wages during the year. Their independence is thus relative; they can choose in accordance with their own interests, but they must make a choice.

Besides the house and poultry many of them have acquired a limited number of farming implements: hoes, picks, shovels, scythes, ploughs, a horse and cart. Such implements are needed because most of their fields are devoted to the cultivation of wheat and beet. By those in this division the land is not regarded as the means of obtaining most of the main foods for home consumption, as it is by the *peones*, but as the means by which they obtain produce for sale. With the help of the extra wages the line which divides the community into two halves is frequently reached. But it is not crossed; the *jornaleros* remain just below the dividing line. By effort and sacrifice they could buy a few acres of land to establish themselves on the other side, but land is sold only in exceptional cases and even then others will probably offer more money than they can afford. The prospects therefore, are not at all promising for the sons. If each son receives one hectare of land, to which is added another hectare brought by his wife, he is simply back in the category of *jornaleros*. In the last five years eight young men whose parents belong to this group have taken courses at technical schools, largely subsidized by the State, to qualify as mechanics, electricians, etc.

The advantages of this group are reduced by dependence on economically superior groups. The *bracero* and the *peón* depend for their wages on those who have greater economic power; the same applies in the last instance, although less rigorously, to the *jornaleros*. But these latter depend in turn on those who exercise economic control in another respect: they have need of their tractors to till their lands, of their means of transport, and of their threshing machines. They occupy therefore an intermediate position, a situation of both master and labourer.

We find the next economic level, of those whose holdings are of more than three hectares but do not exceed five, markedly separate from the strata so far considered. I call these *propietarios*. They have achieved the indispensable minimum of land which will enable them to live in the style conceived of as worthy by the community, with no need to labour for others or for secondary occupations. On the contrary, they need the *braceros* or *peones* or *jornaleros* to assist them in the cultivation of their fields when the work is urgent. In economic terms they occupy an equivocal position: the number of hectares they own makes it uneconomic for them to buy a tractor, trailer and other accessories. Furthermore, it is not within the limits of rational production to have several horses with carts and wagons for the farm work. Faced with the mechanization that has taken place in the town in the last fifteen years they have chosen to keep one horse and cart for minor transport and to use tractors wherever possible. From their former position of being their own masters, owning all the means of production, they have come to depend in part on those who control the modern equipment.

This group is characterized by its stability. The mobility of the sons of a *propietario* family is restricted by the absence of any peremptory need for change and the lack of the economic resources needed to attain occupations with prestige. In the previous groups one finds an individual desire to master a given situation by personal effort; in this group the acquisition of wealth follows the more peaceful lines of inheritance. Personal efforts would lead to scarcely visible results. It is simply a matter of struggling to stay at the same level of independence. When the sons marry and inherit they remain comfortably installed in this group, *aurea mediocritas*. For this reason the parents do not think of giving their sons a career; they cannot indeed afford to send them to a university. However, if there are more than two sons one of them will probably try to find a job in the city, working in a bank for example.

The second characteristic of this group is that the *propietario* works his fields himself and only his fields. Thirdly his economic position marks the dividing line which separates the third and fifth groups, needing, although only for short periods, the labour of the one and the implements of the other. Lastly this *aurea mediocritas* is defined primarily by the individual's satisfaction at having achieved the conventional minimum of wealth: psychological criteria become as important as economic.

There now come two divisions which I shall consider under a single heading. As those in the second of these groups number only thirteen and do not in practice exercise functions clearly different from those in the first category, I group both under the term *pudientes*, literally 'potent' or 'those who are able'. '*The pudientes*' are so called in the town and they could hardly have chosen a richer or more expressive word to define them. '*Pudiente*' signifies powerful, rich, landed. For the moment I leave aside the first meaning.

These fifty-four families own more land than they can work with their own hands. They must, therefore, employ at regular intervals *braceros*, *peones* and *jornaleros* to look after their fields, and they are in a position to purchase tractors and all the implements which the use of a tractor involves. This is essential if the lands are to be economically cultivated. The use of machines naturally displaces a considerable number of hands and saves on wages.

Farming equipment represents in turn an important source of income. Tractors are hired out for tilling the ground, transporting beet and grain, and levelling the fields. In this respect tractor owners are mechanized *jornaleros* for those who require their assistance. They also hire out their services in other towns and districts where mechanization has not reached the same level, working the fields and especially threshing the crops if, in addition to the tractor, they have a thresher. Where it would be difficult to increase the family's revenue from the lands, which are inherited not purchased, mechanical equipment has come to augment the annual income considerably. The money goes into the bank.

This affluence promotes the desire for at least one of the sons to make the definitive leap, to leave the country behind and rise in the national scale of prestige. The son who is studying for the baccalaureate at a city school, or at the university or one of the military academies to become a professional man, not only confers prestige on his family but also proves the economic capacity of his parents. The lack or paucity of land may encourage emigration; so also does an abundance of it. The first type of emigration is an attempt to meet the most elementary necessities of life; the second reflects a quest for prestige and status, though there are of course other practical consequences for the brother or brothers who stay at home to cultivate the paternal fields. Yet both types are directly related to the ownership of land.

Finally there is the group consisting of those who own land exceeding fifteen hectares in extent. They are the '*ricos-ricos*' ('ever-so-rich') in popular parlance. By this reiterative term they are distinguished from the merely rich, the *pudientes*. Several of these families own not one tractor but two, not only a threshing machine but a combined-harvester as well, and combined-harvesters mean the disappearance of the threshing machines and with them a large number of hands and wages, precisely those which are the most highly paid. There is a correlation between mechanization and the diminution of the daily wages which are to a large extent the living of those in the first two divisions, and therefore between increased mechanization and increased emigration. These families have the means to buy the most up-to-date farming machines, which all the others need, for it is unquestionably more economical to cut and thresh a crop at the same time than to cut it, stook it, carry it to the threshing floor, and thresh it—all operations which require the payment of wages.

The *ricos-ricos* sometimes achieve a real *tour de force* by buying a field that is up for sale. The sums offered may considerably exceed the real price of the field, and they have been gradually raised until as much as three times the true value has been paid.

This small group shows fewer consistent homologies than the others. Some work their fields directly with their machines, others are present while work is in progress but take hardly any active part. Some have already reached a mature age and stand on the fringes of the institutional circles of the community, in contrast with the previous two groups whose members form the core of these circles. The operations of the *ricos-ricos* are limited to the able management of their capital, which in the last fifteen years they have put mainly into the extension of their properties inside and outside the *término* and into the mechanization of the means of production. It appears that at the present time some of them have reached the limit of agricultural expansion and tend to invest modest sums on the Stock Exchange.

Economic criteria have been used to classify the community into six groups each with its own possibilities, but these groups live side by side within the community. To what extent do they remain isolated and independent? How do they affect one another? What functions do they perform in local life? In what way does the economic structure affect the other institutional spheres? To answer these questions I shall begin with an analysis of the structure of power.

IV

Power is the individual's capacity, real or potential, for economic control by virtue of his membership of one of the six groups enumerated. Power lies not in the individual but in his economic position, with the qualification that between two *pudientes*, for example, one may exercise more power than the other by reason of personal prestige acquired by education, personal gifts, capacity for leadership, and so on. But these personal qualities affect the power derived from his economic position only accidently.

This power is exercised over the physical environment, over the means of production, in certain spheres of the behaviour of other individuals, and over community institutions.

The first type of power is exercised through property. The *braceros* are completely without it, that of the *peones* is insignificant. Membership of each of the remaining levels reflects the degree of power of the individuals, and the chances of acquiring greater power are conditioned by the opportunities for acquiring lands. As there is very little land available and what there is the *ricos-ricos* have the greatest chance of acquiring, it follows that, except in a few special cases, only the *ricos-ricos* have potential access to an increase of power.

As for the means of production, the second aspect of power, the *braceros* and *peones* can only reckon on the returns from their work, on their own hands. The *jornaleros* and *propietarios* have tools that have not changed since the days of the Romans, whose plough was still in use a few decades ago. The *pudientes*, and to a greater degree the *ricos-ricos*, own the most up-to-date means of production. These increase the volume of capital, bringing greater accessibility to wealth, and economic opportunities for renewing implements of all kinds. The chance to accumulate capital leads on the one hand to the increase of power in general and on the other to the concrete exercise of this power over certain actions of other individuals—by lending money and employing labour, which represents the third aspect of power.

Without the possession of lands, houses or liquid capital it is practically impossible to obtain credit from the banks. For a *bracero*, *peón*, or even a *jornalero* it is very difficult to borrow money. So, although the Farmers' Brotherhood has begun to solve this problem, in cases of urgent necessity they have had to resort to loans from families in the last two divisions. These have made their own conditions, demanding an excessive interest. But even apart from such sporadic cases, the exercise of power is manifested, positively or negatively, every day of the year. I refer in particular to the control over the working life of the *braceros* and *peones*, and in certain circumstances of the *jornaleros*, exercised partially by the *propietarios* and more fully by the *pudientes* and the *ricos-ricos*. In a peak period the first three groups impose their own conditions and rates of pay, but this period is very short and in slack periods, which extend over more than half the year, the *pudientes* and *ricos-ricos* impose their conditions of employment for the work available.

The *propietarios*, owing to their intermediate position, depend at peak periods on the *braceros*, *peones* and *jornaleros* for manpower and on the *pudientes* and *ricos-ricos* for mechanical assistance. Furthermore, they are at a disadvantage in the labour market because those in the upper categories can offer higher wages. This favours those in the first three groups, who do not lower their rates when they work for the *propietarios*. *Propietarios*, and more exactly, *pudientes* and *ricos-ricos* exercise negative control over the working life of the other three groups during a slack period since they normally have no need of them; the labour market is therefore practically in their hands. To sum up: *pudientes* and *ricos-ricos*, having at their disposal their own labour, the equipment for production, and the labour of those enumerated in the first three divisions, regulate in general the situation in the labour market and exercise real power over the *braceros*, *peones*, *jornaleros*, and *propietarios*.

All the foregoing may now be looked at from another point of view: that of the correlation between economic power and conditions of liberty. The latter cannot exist without a minimum of the former, and it is clear that initiative, authority, autonomy, control and economic security are attributes of the *pudientes* and *ricos-ricos*, even if in different degrees. Security and relative independence are the lot of the *propietarios*. A certain measure of economic security may be ascribed to the *jornaleros*. Dependence, insecurity and the habit of being ordered about could define conditions of life for the *braceros* and *peones*.

The ramifications of economic power are not yet exhausted since its influence extends to other spheres. The *pudientes* and *ricos-ricos* can manipulate economic sanctions, to evict a farmer or a tenant from a house, or threaten to resort in these cases to the courts with the consequent expenses; they can manipulate the selling and buying of fields and houses, and exercise the power of dismissal from employment. They are creditors not only in money but in the sense of giving references and information to the banks to enable those in the lower levels to secure a loan. They can quash fines or prison sentences in the town, and give favours and rewards—or not—in the most varied ways. One night, for instance, during the August festivals not long ago, a group of people disobeyed an order the mayor had issued some hours earlier. The offenders, belonging to the lower orders, were promptly summoned to the town hall and sentenced to spend the rest of the night in the municipal gaol. On hearing of the decision, one of those who enjoy great economic power interceded on behalf of the guilty because he was linked to one of them by a certain master-servant relationship. All were set at liberty. This brings us to consider another dimension of power, authority or political power.

Power in this second sense is inherent in political institutions which include the Town Council, the municipal court, and the Brotherhood of Farmers and Stockbreeders. The man who holds a political post exercises authority *de jure*. Who constitutes the ruling minority? To which economic group do those belong who through the political structure direct, up to a point, the public activities of the townsfolk? Is economic power translated into political power? We shall be able to follow this correlation more clearly if we regroup the six economic divisions into four. The economic power of the *braceros* and *peones* is minimal; henceforth the term *braceros* will include both. The *ricos-ricos* are on the

fringe of institutional organizations, and so will be included in
the category of *pudientes*. We shall be concerned, therefore, with
braceros, jornaleros, propietarios and *pudientes*.

Of the eight residents holding official positions—six on the
Council, one in the Court and one in the Brotherhood—
only two belong to the *propietario* group, and they do not possess
tractors. The remaining six are *pudientes*, and all own tractors.
Judging by the constancy of a couple of dozen surnames in the
Council Acts, for as long as they have been preserved, the
pudientes have always held Council posts. The rotation of political power is summarized concretely by a resident in this manner: 'If the family "L" assumes control, the family "M" relinquishes it. If the family "M" assumes control, the family
"L" relinquishes it'. 'L' and 'M' are the initials of two of the
large families predominant on the local Council in the last
twenty years. Although no important decisions are taken in
Council without reference to the Civil Governor, plans and
proposals, whether accepted or refused later by the provincial
authorities, always originate from the Council or from the
Brotherhood. In small matters the Council and the Brotherhood
enjoy wide powers; everything concerned with municipal taxes
(determining the amount and the objects taxable), the erection
of new buildings, water supply to the houses in the town, upkeep
of secondary roads and irrigation ditches, the sale of unculti-
vable community lands etc., is determined by the Council.

In 1959 a firm proposed to the Council the purchase of un-
cultivable common land for the building of a small factory. The
Council met in session to discuss the proposal. One of the councillors pointed out that if the *braceros* went to work at the factory
for a fixed wage throughout the year, they would not go back
to work in the fields for the *pudientes*. Where would the *pudientes*
find the labour they needed? Even so the building of the factory
was started though this shows how economic power, which in
this case was the prime motive, may control the working life of
the *braceros*. If we add that economic power is linked either
directly or indirectly to political power, the force of the control
exercised is much greater.

This is an important fact. It is true that not all *pudientes*
hold political appointments. To be elected one needs certain
qualities, personal prestige or the right friends. And not

all *pudientes* would accept an appointment. But it is also true, and has been so for at least 200 years, that the principal political functions have always been bestowed on those classified here as *pudientes*. This term, so deeply rooted in Aragón, expresses wonderfully well the social position of an individual. The only two *propietarios* who belong to the Council are plain councillors, not a position of the first importance. Furthermore, although not all *pudientes* get on the Council, no *bracero* or *jornalero* has at any time performed political functions of importance. These are reserved for the *pudientes*, or at least *propietarios*.

The Left's determination to achieve political power implied first that power was not in their hands and secondly that it was essential that it should be. Once it was attained they attacked the economic and religious powers and sought to subvert the structure of the community. The inversion of means and ends was curious and significant: instead of winning political power through economic pressure—which they knew they could not do—they found it necessary to force their way to an economic domination through political pressure.

Being a *pudiente* places the individual within reach of political influence and has done so for at least two centuries: the historical image of this group has been one of command. Not all the *pudientes* participate directly in decisions affecting the community as a whole, but as a group they do intervene indirectly, in the formation, development, detailing and channelling of any decision. A competent hint to a member of the Council normally leads at least to a discussion at a session. Before any important project is launched it must have the consent and support of the *pudientes*, of the 'major contributors', as the Minutes insist. It will be remembered that disapproval of a *fait accompli*, the sale of common lands, brought about the fall of the Council.

Attached to the Council are a number of committees whose members, almost always *pudientes*, have been selected by the Council itself. These organizations may be permanent, like the *Comisión de Beneficencia* (Poor-Relief Committee) which decides who should be granted assistance by the municipality, and the *Junta de Escuelas* (Schools Board); or temporary, such as the *Comisión de Festejos* (Entertainments Committee) entrusted with the organization of festivals. The temporary committees multiply and vanish throughout the year in accordance with the activity displayed by the Council. In all these cases the Council sheds a part of its authority and responsibility to the committee. Examples of the most recent committees are those formed for the building of a chapel (*ermita*) and for dealing with the supply of water to the houses in the town. On the latter problem a public meeting was held for the purpose of sounding public opinion. But such public meetings are characterized first by the small 'public' which attends them, and then by the fact that the 'public' hardly ever speaks up. Asked why they do not take any part in the discussion, they answer that they 'don't know how to speak in public'; the few who do speak are always the same ones.

Two points must be clear enough from what has been said. One is the mechanism of authority of the Council, which tries to lighten the weight of command and responsibility by subdividing it between committees. The other is the fact that the Council does not in reality duplicate or triplicate the channels through which authority is exercised. What does multiply is the number of people who are to bear the load, and as these belong to the same group, almost invariably the *pudientes*, the result is the division of authority, responsibility, and initiative among the members of a single segment of the population.

All this reveals the existence of nuclei of pressure which in general coincide with the *pudientes*, and to a lesser extent the *propietarios*, as well as the fact that the important decisions have been matured among wide circles before they are ratified and set in motion at Council meetings. Some exercise authority *de jure* and others vicariously; but as the *de jure* authority is periodically shifted round among the *pudientes*, and sometimes among the *propietarios*, there are grounds for the expressive metaphors of the townsfolk: 'it's always the same people in command', 'they're the same dogs in different collars', or for the ancient quotation from Gracián: 'This man threw . . . (the ball) . . . to that man, and that man to another, until it returned to the first, passing through a political circle, which is the most vicious—circulating always amongst the same people, without ever leaving their hands; all the rest were looking on for they could only watch the game . . . those who are in command and never let others touch the ball are always one and the same'.[1]

[1] Gracián, op. cit., Part II, p. 252.

Whether this 'source stratum' does in fact supply the individuals best qualified for the administrative functions they perform is questionable. The internal dynamism of the group, a more consistent education, greater efficiency and energy in facing and solving economic problems, and a certain experience acquired in positions of authority, would suggest that it does. They are more conscious of the problems of the community because these coincide with their own; or rather they have established a set of aspirations and values and a style of living which can be represented as applying to the town as a whole. No one else felt as they did the need to build a granary for the town, or new schools, or to supply running water to the houses. Yet although at first there was some silent opposition from those who did not appreciate the need on grounds of expense, the Council decided in favour of these projects. They are now approved by all; the granary and the schools are completed, the water supply almost so.

These men set the standard of living and seek to emulate in their aspirations and needs those whom they consider superior, the prosperous classes in the city. They help to some extent gradually to raise the average standard of living in the town. Telephones, bathrooms, and television are the latest innovations. But the lower strata not only cannot afford to imitate them but do not even feel the slightest necessity for a bathroom in the house, for example. If economic conditions improve, however, they hasten to copy the distinctive features of the superior groups.

I have not had occasion to refer to *braceros* and *jornaleros*, and little has been said of the *proprietarios*. Political power does not belong to the first two groups. Landed property of a certain size brings economic power, which in its turn opens the way to political power. Property, economic opportunity, and political institutions are closely inter-related and a given position in any one of these three orders implies a corresponding adjustment in the other two.

IV

STRATIFICATION: II

'*En el último fondo de nuestra persona llevamos, sin sospecharlo, un complicadísimo balance estimativo. No hay persona de nuestra contorno social que no esté en él inscrita con el logaritmo de su relación jerárquica con nosotros. Por lo visto, apenas sabemos de un prójimo, comienza tácitamente a funcionar la íntima oficina: sopesa el valor de aquél y decide si vale más, igual o menos que nuestra persona . . . entre los ingredientes que componen nuestro ser es ese sentimiento del nivel uno de los decisivos*'

ORTEGA Y GASSET

EXTERNAL and objective criteria, such as the distribution of property and the degree of real or potential economic and political power, may be used as an introduction to the study of social status. Another series of criteria, this time internal and subjective, are needed in order to analyse the behaviour, values and sentiments of each of the groups, as well as their attitudes towards one another.

I

Psychological interpretations allow us to animate and amplify the purely economic aspects of the hierarchy and to distinguish (a) the individual's awareness of the existence of hierarchical groups in the community, that is to say his judgment of them in terms of equality, superiority and inferiority; (b) knowledge of the position and social situation, and so the social status of others; (c) knowledge of the position, situation and status of himself. By 'social position' I mean the economic segment to which one belongs; 'social situation' is the niche or *situs* one occupies within the limits offered by one's own economic group. 'Position' is shared with others; the 'situation' is unique.

'Status' in the community is the sum of honourable positions which an individual or a family occupies in the total structure of the community.

Everyday speech proves over and over again that all the townsfolk are aware of the existence of distinct hierarchical levels and it also indicates what they think and feel about them. The distinctions are referred to by the generic name of 'classes', and people speak of the 'low class', the 'middle class' and the 'high class'. At other times they divide the population into 'poor people', '*peones*', '*jornaleros*'; 'middle class', '*pudientes*', and '*ricos-ricos*'. The fundamental principle of differentiation is always ownership of land. In classifying an individual they often use such phrases as these: 'that man hasn't a square inch of land', or 'that man hasn't got anywhere to fall dead in', meaning that he lacks possessions not only in land but of any kind. They define one another according to the number of acres they own, to which they add other forms of wealth such as money and farming equipment. 'He's got so many acres and a tractor' is a common reply to an enquiring stranger. Or again:'He belongs to a strong house', a phrase implying that someone comes from a very well known family with much land and modern agricultural machinery. When they refer to an individual in terms of family they always use the father's name: 'he's the son of ——', or 'his grandfather was ——'; very rarely is the mother's name mentioned. Economic and political power, the 'position', 'situation', and 'status', are recognized directly through the father or husband. 'That man is very clever', or 'he knows a lot', are expressions which when applied to holders of a university degree set them on a pinnacle of esteem and repute. Money obtained regularly from lands is a succedaneous criterion which embraces all kinds of wealth, and this rigidly measures the worth of a person in the saying: 'You're worth what you have', or in:

> 'When I had money
> they called me *Don* Tomás;
> now I have none
> they just call me Tomás'

'He's got more money than he weighs' is a way of describing rich outsiders whose income does not come from agriculture.

These phrases express part of the mental scheme of evaluation of others and the criteria on which they base themselves. If we amplify them in contexts of behaviour we shall obtain consistent results.

Property in land has been shown to have manifold sociological consequences: a person acquires as many degrees of esteem as the acres of land he possesses. Land measures social status and social status gives the measure of land. This is the fundamental principle of differentiation because power, in all its meanings, is a direct translation of the hectares of land owned. The reversible triad, property in land, economic power, and political power is, then, the primary basis for assessing social status. Let us examine closely the behaviour of families and individuals.

All children attend the same schools, where they meet and play with others of the same age. At this age games out of school are most often shared with children of the same neighbourhood, which already implies a certain restrictive circle of relationships. An angry mother may shout at her son, 'I don't want you to play with those children!', or 'you're not to play with the children from the caves!', when the child's companions are regarded as socially inferior. The youngsters tend to form their circles of friends from among those whose economic position is similar. Exceptions do however abound, and in almost all of the 'gangs' there will be one or more boys whose families by no means come up to the average economic position of the group.

If one of the boys wants to marry a girl whose social position is inferior, it is invariably the mother who assesses the situation. If she believes that the girl—or her family—is of patently lower social status there will be no wedding. Several persons have remained single for this reason, having lost their one chance of getting married. The father has little say in the matter; if the parents differ the mother has the last word. The father's attitude to the engagement of daughters is somewhat different, however; some have thrashed their daughters to make them break off a courtship with a boy of lower social position. But in one of these cases the couple succeeded in marrying because the mother changed her mind and naturally convinced the father. The mammas manipulate love affairs with great dexterity but not always with success. To make a son or daughter give up a proposed unsuitable marriage, they will use every form of persuasion. They repeatedly admonish the son or daughter to think what they are doing and promise them a plentiful inheritance if they will choose a more suitable partner; the boy or girl, they say, is 'a bad spender', is 'no good for work', and 'is a flirt' who will 'ruin the house'. If the boy persists they give him no money on Sundays and feast days so that he cannot take his sweetheart out, or they will not buy him clothes, or they will hide his best ones; they threaten to beat him (the girls they sometimes do beat), to 'throw him out of the house', or to separate them when they walk out together, and they repeat, 'if you marry her you'll go out of here with only the clothes you have on and you won't come back again'. Threats which have never been fulfilled, even when, as happens more frequently nowadays, the marriage has come off.

It is probably in marriage that friction between the different economic groups, or different levels of social status, is greatest. The problem is considerably more complicated than appears at first sight. Not only does the couple establish a new set of relationships, but the two respective families are involved; they may not take to each other very easily when their styles of living, their education and economic levels and points of view are different. A marriage that breaks the barriers gives rise to a series of relationships to which neither of the families has been accustomed. The new relationship begins coldly and usually ends by freezing. Then the families do not speak to one another and the married couple suffers the consequences. It is understandable that parents do all they can to prevent such situations arising. Two brothers began courting two girls. When one of them called upon his sweetheart's father to request his permission to see and talk to her at home, the father asked the young man: 'Does your father know about the affair?' The boy answered, 'No'. The girl's father said: 'Well, go back home, tell your father about it, and if he doesn't object, come back and we'll have a chat'. The father first wanted to be sure of the acquiescence of the suitor's family, because he suspected that they would object to his daughter on the grounds that she belonged to a family economically inferior. In the case of the other brother it was the opposite. This boy found himself involved with a girl whose family was economically slightly superior to his and her father refused him admission to the house several times.

Finally, values and family ties must be taken into account. Parents are respected and obeyed; emancipation comes after marriage. When the whole family exerts pressure for months on end it is hard for the individual to stand out against it. This explains why only a few achieve the proposed marriage in the face of such determined opposition. Recently, however, there have been cases of open rebellion, in which while the elder brother has yielded to family pressure, particularly his mother's, the younger has stubbornly resisted any sort of interference.

In spite of this basic endogamy of social position, the ideal in every marriage is to find a partner whose inheritance will enable one to rise to another economic group or, if one is already in it, to augment considerably one's own inheritance. Such pretensions conflict; thus, from a practical point of view, equality or an economic equilibrium of some kind generally has to be sought. This makes it possible to speak of an endogamy in economic 'situation'. A youth tried to court a girl. She showed no interest to begin with. He remarked to his friends, 'I don't know why she's such a fool. I've got 'x' more acres coming to me than she has'. Being a 'fool' means deprecating the 'situation' and 'social status' of the suitor when there is no positive reason, as there would have been had she expected to inherit more than he. According to him this was not the case, as later on he would inherit a few acres more than she would. He, in fact, was condescending in seeking her hand.

In the country towns of Aragón it is the custom to *rondar* the *mozas* (lasses) at night; the verb *rondar* means literally to make the rounds. To go out and *rondar* means singing *jotas* at particular points in the town or beneath the balcony of the 'lass' to whom the *jotas* are directed. The *jota*, the Aragonese regional song, is an octosyllabic quatrain of very varied theme:

La jota no es sólo jota	The *jota* is not just a *jota*
si es la jota de Aragón:	if it is the *jota* of Aragón:
es amor y es poesía,	it is love and it is poetry,
es patria y es religión.	it is the fatherland and it is religion.

On a nocturnal round *jotas* of amorous content naturally predominate. These range over all the emotional states of the singer; pains and doubts of love, insinuation, determination, scorn, etc. I give some which confirm and condense in popular form what has been expressed above:

No me quiere tu madre	Your mother does not like me
porque soy pobre . . .	because I am poor . . .

Or those beginning:

Tu madre a mi no quiere	Your mother does not like me
porque es pobre mi linaje . . .	because my lineage is poor . . .
Tu madre, porque soy pobre	Your mother, because I am poor
no quiere que venga a verte . . .	won't let me come and see you . . .

From the mouths of the girls the complaints acquire the same tones:

Anda diciendo tu madre	Your mother goes around saying
que una reina tu mereces,	that you deserve a queen,
y yo, como no soy reina,	and I, since I'm not a queen,
no quiero que me desprecie.	don't want her to despise me.

Of punishments and determination:

Mis padres porque te quiero	My parents, because I love you
me castigan con rigor;	punish me severely;
mucho puede la obediencia	obedience can do much
pero más puede el amor.	but love can do more.
Mi padre me tiene dicho	My father has told me
que me tiene que sacar	that he will have to put out
los ojos con que te miro;	the eyes with which I look at you;
y yo . . . que te he de mirar.	and I . . . Look at you I must.
Aunque me lleven atada	Even if they carry me bound
a la puerta de la iglesia	to the door of the church
no me tengo de casar	I just will not marry
con el que mi madre piensa	the one my mother thinks.

There are many *jotas* along these lines, which prompts one to consider the frequency of the situations to which they allude. The few quoted corroborate the points I have made; the interference of parents in the engagements of their children, the difficulty of marrying one of different social status, the chastisements sometimes inflicted by the father, and the preponderant part played by the mother in such relationships. Because although status is acquired principally through the man, the woman is its most jealous guardian. She always stands in her 'position', in her 'situation' and in her social status. At the August festivals the dance, lasting at least seven hours a day, is the most popular diversion. The youths prefer to choose their partners from among girls of the same position and status, but they do invite girls from any lower social stratum to dance as well. But a boy of low social status never dares to ask for a dance with a girl whose social status is markedly superior. Work in the fields imposes a sometimes continual contact between the most widely different social strata. The *pudiente* needs to call in the *braceros* and have dealings with them. After a few days of working in the same fields the separation of levels becomes blurred. This does not happen with the *pudiente* women because their contact with those of inferior status is more restricted.

A woman's occupation reveals the 'status' of her family. The daughters of *braceros* sometimes work as maids in the town and more often in the city; if they live in the town and are not in domestic service they earn daywages at certain tasks in the fields. Daughters and in some circumstances the wives of *jornaleros* work in their own fields when there is a lot to do. The daughters of the *propietarios* very seldom take part in farm work except at critical times such as threshing; those of the *pudientes* not even then. Some of these attend secondary schools in the city, play the piano, and acquire a veneer of general culture.

A third way in which the women express to a greater degree than the men a sense of social differentiation manifests itself in their perspicacious knowledge of the situation of other people. Some days before Christmas a charity campaign to help the poor is organized. They have all the details regarding these at their fingertips: if so-and-so has been out of work for so long, whether he owes money at the chemist's, if he cannot afford milk, if he needs a mattress, if the children lack proper winter clothing—these are details to which the men pay no attention. It requires real subtlety to place oneself in one's own situation *vis-a-vis* that of others. For any decision the women have to take in these circumstances they make comparisons with what is done in similar cases, not by those of the same 'position', but by those whose 'situation' and 'status' are the nearest that they can think of.

It is difficult to start a list of donations for charitable or religious purposes, particularly if the list is hung on the church door. The first question from the lady who is asked for help (it is always the women who determines the sum to be given), is 'how much did so-and-so give?'' This second person is the one regarded by the enquirer as of a 'status' closest to her own. The sum offered must therefore be the same or a little higher, 'to look better'. The arrangements for baptisms, first communions and weddings belong to the woman. For each of these rites a model is taken into account: what the family 'X' did, prepared and spent in the same circumstances. The family 'X' represents the closest in 'economic situation' and 'social status', and of course 'one cannot do less'. In the preparations for one wedding the father, taking advantage of a trip to the city, hired a coach to take the guests from the town to the city for the wedding breakfast. The coach—an unheard of thing—would have to make several journeys. The woman thought it humiliating to have only one coach and secured the three best in the garage. If the said family 'X' buys a tractor, a television set, an electric washing-machine, or lives in the centre of the town, goes to San Sebastián for their summer holidays, dresses the children in a particular way, sends a son to be educated in the city, etc., the families of equivalent situation and status must 'necessarily' do the same. This is valid for every stratum, taking into account that the symbols are not the same. The achievements of one's neighbour in social status are codes of conduct, categorical imperatives that call for immediate imitation by others. So strong is this compulsion, infused with a desire to excel the rest, that I know of no sphere in which it fails to act with full force.

II

If we were to divide the 905 hectares of cultivable land encompassed by the *término* (I omit the remainder for obvious reasons), among the 371 heads of families, we would get a landholding of 2·43 hectares for each individual head of a family. That would mean that the style of living of about a hundred and twenty heads of families would automatically be lowered, and that of some 250 would improve to some extent; but it would also mean that no inhabitant of the town would obtain the necessary annual income from the lands. As every proprietor would be able to work his own fields by himself, with no outside help, he could not use the spare time for the acquisition of other resources by means of casual wages. Furthermore, he could not invest the profits from the sale of farm produce in modern machinery for the better exploitation of the land. This hypothetical division would therefore entail a general retrogression to the Roman style of agriculture: less mechanization, lower efficiency, lower production, higher production costs, a considerable lowering of the average standard of living in general. It could not be defended on grounds of economic efficiency. Only by the emigration of surplus farm workers, with the consequent increase in land for those remaining, or by the stratification of the community, could it be made to work. Since the civil war particularly, these things have been happening to some extent as mutual cause and effect. Stratification, with the *pudientes* at the top, forces emigration on the disinherited. The latter on leaving have sold their houses and any small parcel of land they owned, which the former have bought up. Yet emigration poses problems of its own and requires an effort of adaptation that not everyone can manage. Some have returned to the town after being in the city. Those who stay behind or have returned have thus to face the fact of stratification.

In principle some relations between the different strata or levels described are essential. I have repeatedly alluded to the co-ordination and dependence demanded by the inequality of property, means of production, and functions assumed by the different groups. We have just seen, on the other hand, that marriage, which is the touchstone to the formation of consistent individual and family relationships, is inconceivable not only between persons of different 'position' but also between those of different 'situation'. Or, more expressly, the disappearance of one or more strata from the community would not affect the remaining ones with regard to the marriage market.

To what extent are the townsfolk conscious of the effects of stratification? One can observe a certain latent hostility between two extreme groups of 'rich' and 'poor', *pudientes* and *braceros*. Some of the *jornaleros* could be included among the poor, and some of the *propietarios* might go to swell the rich

group. But in general the *jornaleros* and *propietarios* are not involved in the criticisms of which I shall speak. Their intermediate position shields them.

The *braceros* are fully convinced that the worst work, the
hardest, is that of the fields. They know that workmen in the
city work eight hours a day and never on feast days, and have
an annual holiday. They themselves work from morning till
night, including some Sundays, and have no holidays. They
hear those who work in the city telling how they exert themselves as little as possible at their jobs if the employer is not
present; they cannot imitate them because their master is
always on hand and knows how much can be done in a working
day in each season and at each job. City workers have a fixed
wage with health and pensions insurance; farmworkers go from
one employer to another according to circumstances and the
work to be done, with no security of wages over the year and
without even knowing what insurance rights they can claim.
As for the rich, the farm workers only wish that they could be
made to live for a time on their own means so that they might
better appreciate the problems of the poor. When they are
urgently required for work during the *campañas* they sometimes
grumble that 'they ought to do it for themselves, that's what
they have the land for, and if not, everyone ought only to have
the land he can manage on his own'; or they reply with more
violent expressions: 'let them eat their land!' for example.
There is a great distance between their respective worlds and
problems and it manifests itself in disdain. It is as well to remember however that, in the circumstances mentioned in
Chapter II, words can be converted into deeds.

The rich or *pudientes* think that immediately after 1936 there
was still a chance for everyone to acquire ownership of a piece
of land or to obtain more. All those who before 1936 were tenant
farmers and had according to the *pudientes* 'the will to work and
were not content with wages alone', subsequently became proprietors. The poor ought to 'work harder, spend less and save
more'. The *pudientes* observe: 'Last Sunday X (a *bracero*) spent
more than I did in the bar'; 'I saw X (again a *bracero*) in the
Z—— (one of the best cinemas in the city), he was downstairs
(i.e. in the stalls, the most expensive seats) while I was upstairs
(the cheapest seats)'; 'X smokes Virginia tobacco and I smoke

black, and then they complain that they can't make a living';
'what's X's daughter doing, wasting her time at home? she
should go into service and earn some money, but they don't
like 'serving' anybody'. And so on.

There is a revealing word—*trato, tratar*. *Tratar* means to communicate or have dealings with another or others, to act well
or ill towards one's fellows, to look after them (well or badly), to
address them, politely or disrespectfully. When someone says
'*no se trata con X*', it indicates that he has nothing whatever
to do with the other person, to whom he does not even speak,
acting as if he did not exist. *Tratarse mucho con X* (to have a lot
to do with X) means to get on cordially in many ways. In
practice, to *tratar* with a person or family means seeing a lot of
them, visiting their home, asking and doing favours. They get
on, as they themselves say, 'as if we were kin'. This simile
denotes that they are in fact dealing with people outside the
family circle. The same applies to friends: one does not *tratar*
with a friend, one 'is' (*es*) a friend of the other and in friendship
the relations are more intimate and spontaneous than in *trato*.
To *tratar* with one another is to have social contact, that is,
keeping at the same time a certain social distance such as does
not separate kinsmen or close friends. The expression '*no me
trato con X*' is used also in a more restricted sense, meaning 'I
am not on sufficiently close terms with him to ask him this
favour'; which indicates that X is not within the circle of friends
or people with whom one normally has some dealings in the
fields, cafés, places of entertainments, etc. In such a case the
'distance' separates them too widely. What rules, therefore,
govern *trato*?

Economic groups in part mould the limits and form of *trato*.
Leisure hours, in the case of married men, are shared with
people of the same position; the groups of café cronies are the
most revealing. Each one 'knows what appertains to him',
whom he can have anything to do with, treat to or accept a beer
or a glass of brandy from. When anyone from an inferior
economic group butts in on a discussion in which only *pudientes*
are taking part, they remark 'he doesn't know where he belongs'. Very few will habitually sit at a table occupied by the
professionals because they know they 'don't belong there', that
they cannot mix with them. It is not fitting for a *pudiente* to

drink wine from the bottle (*porrón*) because the patrons of the tavern are ranked in the inferior group. He cannot mix either with them or the professionals because their worlds are quite distinct. To *tratar* and to mix imply a plane of equality, the same style of living. This in its turn determines the style of *trato*.

Trato also follows lines of neighbourhood. On summer evenings people sit at their doors to enjoy the coolness and chat. It is neighbours (*vecinos*) who make up these coteries. In general being a neighbour, i.e. living in a particular district (*barrio*), is in itself a sign of belonging to the same economic group. In certain cases where the 'situation' of one neighbour is markedly inferior to that of others who make up the group, this man will never sit with them; he may approach to ask a question but once answered he returns to his own door or to his group. The same applies to occupiers of neighbouring fields. If the 'situation' of both is similar they will probably treat each other more cordially than would be proper towards a field neighbour of inferior situation. In this latter case two people may be working in adjoining fields for a whole day or several days and exchange very few words. The *trato* in the first case stems from a working situation.

All these forms of *trato* may be influenced by personal motives of one kind or another; it may be possible, for instance, to enjoy cordial relations with a neighbour whose situation is inferior if only because he has an agreeable personality. In a discussion of sporting matters at the café anyone may take part freely, but this would not be thought proper in any other sort of conversation. The mayor has full access to the tables of the professionals by virtue of his office, but were he not holding this office he would not think it right to join them. From all this it follows that to the forms of *trato* based on economic considerations must be added others whose influence is at times greater. I refer to the social status of the person addressed, a social status that does not derive simply from wealth, as we have seen, but from other premises, the principal one being education.

A man who has received higher education enjoys the highest esteem and social status. The superior knowledge of anyone with a degree is recognised not only in his specific field of study but in all spheres of knowledge and activity. Persons with a career are more carefully and respectfully addressed, the title

'Don' being prefixed to their names. When they speak others listen. No townsman would take the liberty of arguing with them; on the contrary, they act politely and choose their words carefully. The priest is the person most highly respected, with the greatest authority and prestige. People seek his advice and guidance. A group of youths may be singing and shouting in the street, using dubious language. They are unlikely to be deterred by anyone and if reproached will retort: 'and what did you do when you were young?' But if they spot the priest in the distance they automatically proceed to behave with decorum.

Other reasons why a career implies superior status or social position are the comforts, style of living, manners and speech that go with it. In this aspect of the educated man the relation to wealth also appears. The doctor, chemist, veterinary surgeon, etc. are thought of as rich. Hence superior knowledge, enviable in itself, gives very tangible results in the popular view. A man who knows a lot earns a lot. This type of education means leaving the country behind and enjoying a considerable income, twin aspirations confused with the ideal. It is also appreciated that education is not invariably allied to wealth; for example, some time may elapse between leaving the university and finding a job, and often the job is not as well paid as was hoped. Those in these conditions they call '*don sin din(ero)* ('*Don* without mon(ey)').

Even before graduating a student enjoys a very high social status in the community. This manifests itself in his dress and the way he uses his time when at home during vacations. When the people come home from the fields in the evening they 'put themselves straight', that is, besides cleaning themselves up they change into clothes suitable for going out, sitting at the door, promenading, flirting, or visiting. The student's dress must be appropriate to his position the whole day, not just at night. To the mother of a student who did not worry about these standards of dress they said: 'how can you let your son dress like that, being a *señorito* (young gentleman)?' They assume too that in view of his condition he will only smoke Virginia tobacco, which is more elegant and expensive than black tobacco. He does not work in the fields even at harvest time when his father is hard put to find labour. While the whole family co-ordinates all its efforts to deal with the tiring work he will be reading the sports magazines; a student cannot work on the land; he is a young gentleman. His status is higher than that of his brothers and everyone respects and follows his opinions because 'he knows more'. If by reason of his personal and academic qualities people think him '*muy listo*' (very clever) he attains the pinnacle of prestige.

Another very effective measure of the social status of a university man or advanced student is the range of his matrimonial opportunities in the town. A *propietario*'s son with a degree from a university, military academy, etc. acquires together with his 'title' the right to marry the daughter of the most powerful of the *pudientes*. On the other hand, a girl who studies, even if she has no degree, is regarded by young men without such education, whatever their 'position' and 'status', which may be superior to those of the girl, as inaccessible. In fact she stays single or else marries a 'suitable' outsider.

It is hard to place the student in any one of these groups; lacking land, economic power and political power, he nevertheless reaches the height of popular prestige. On the other hand, unscrupulous business methods have raised some people to a high level of economic power. By increasing their wealth they have made an enviable economic situation for themselves, but although their way up has coincided with the one described as normal in this study, this 'situation' has not been accompanied by the equivalent political power and social status. On the contrary the community has criticized them sharply, because the means they employed offended against the values of the community.

Wealth is the principal but not the only criterion of stratification. It owes its importance to its far-reaching influence on all other spheres of thought and behaviour, although in intensity other criteria may ultimately be more important.

V

STRATIFICATION: III

'Tan absurdo como sería querer reformar el sistema de las órbitas siderales, o negarse a reconocer que el hombre tiene cabeza y pies; la tierra norte y sur; la pirámide cúspide y base, es ignorar la existencia de una contextura esencial a toda sociedad, consistente en un sistema jerárquico de funciones colectivas'. 'El impulso de entrenamiento hacia ciertos modelos que quede vivo en una sociedad será lo que ésta tenga verdaderamente de tal'.

ORTEGA Y GASSET

RENÉ ALLEAU in his analysis of the nature of symbols[1] develops as his principal thesis the advantage and even the necessity of distinguishing the concepts of 'symbol' and 'synthème'. The symbol, he says, is 'en partie concevable, en partie inconcevable', 'l'expression d'un lien entre l'humain et le divin'. The *synthème* on the contrary 'est fondé sur le compréhension de la signification qu'il transmet et sur le déchiffrement de l'enigme qu'il propose à des hommes qui, grâce à lui, peuvent communiquer entre eux'. 'L'essentiel de ce synthème demeure qu'il soit interprété aisément par tous grâce à une analyse immediate'. Affirming the same ideas he sums up his thesis: 'Le nom de 'symbole' doit être réservé aux signes reconnus comme sacrés par une Eglise ou par une tradition religieuse. Le nom de 'synthème' doit être réservé aux signes conventionnels par l'intérmediaire desquels un lien mutuel est établi par les hommes, soit entre eux, soit entre une idée et une chose ou une action, soit entre deux points de l'étendue, soit entre des moments de la durée, soit entre les choses sur lesquelles ils opèrent'. Finally, under the name of differentiating synthèmes,

---

[1] René Alleau: "De la nature des symboles", *Flammarion* (Paris, 1958). Pp. 23, 25-7, 35, 40.

he groups the 'signes conventionnels liant à un indice une relation de dépendance ou de distinction entre les membres d'une
famille, d'une tribu ou d'un groupe sociale'.

I

Up to now I have qualified the different groups or estates in
terms of property, power, group awareness and mutual contact,
endeavouring to portray the activities and relationships that are
repeated almost identically day after day. There is no doubt
that the style of living, amusements and ways of spending
money, of looking after the home, and of manners and speech,
reveal unmistakeable differences, pretensions, and satisfactions
peculiar to the various social strata. For furniture and dress, the
choice of wine or beer as the normal drink, spending Sunday
afternoon in the town or in the city, etc., are to a certain extent
indvidual decisions which accentuate one's own worth and personal tastes at the same time as they attract the attention of
others. With the quality and quantity of differentiating 'synthèmes' that distinguish a person or a family goes a corresponding feeling of superiority. In the effort to surpass other people,
what has been considered thus so far is not sufficient; to property
and power must be added numerous personal touches which
enhance one's respective 'position' and 'situation'.

The 'synthèmes' differentiating styles of living which we are
to consider are the following: the 'synthème' of localization
(district and house), the cyclic 'synthème' (programme of
amusements and travel), and the verbal, political, moral, religious and family 'synthèmes'.

In the Introduction there was a brief description of the town
which it will be useful to recall. I defined it as a 'street-town'
(*Strassendorf*), whose three-storey houses, in the Aragonese
renaissance style, stand along both sides of the main road. This
forms the High Street. In the other streets, at right angles to or
parallel with the High Street, the houses are almost always of
two storeys and have no balconies or bay-windows. The caves,
more comfortable dwellings than their name would suggest,
form the third of the divisions mentioned.

The high street is the main artery of the town. In the middle
of it there is a small square with the Town Hall and the parish

church. Near the church is the halt for buses to the city, and in the same street are most of the shops, the chemist, post office, telephone, the main cinema which is also a centre for various entertainments, two bars, a tavern, and almost all the agencies of banks and insurance companies. This street, the best lit by night, the widest and straightest, is the one chosen for evening strolls, flirting and meeting friends.

Yet this street is probably the least suitable of all for walking. Since it is in fact a main road, one of the principal ones in the country, the traffic is dense. Some 2,800 vehicles a day pass through the town, with the resulting noise and dust. The evening stroll, with the constant hooting of horns and the rumble of enormous lorries, the dusty glare of headlamps, and stepping on and off the pavements to avoid them, is tiresome. The national laws, which an effort has been made strictly to enforce in the town, have proved incapable of preventing strolling on the main road. Neither inconvenience, danger nor fines have had much effect. Although mothers spend the day admonishing their children, 'don't cross the road!', 'don't go out on the road!', not one of them would go to live in any of the other streets; on the contrary, everything possible is done to acquire a house in the high street, one of the greatest attractions of which is to hear all through the night the procession of heavy lorries which pass within three yards of the houses!

The high street is considered the most elegant; one cannot go out in it dressed just anyhow, especially women. When they go shopping in this street they change their clothes and do their hair; they never go to the door wearing an apron, even if they live in the street itself. Such rules do not hold in the other streets, where it is permissible to go about almost as freely as at home. For certain farming tasks female assistance is required. Girls who go to work in the fields at these times wear suitable clothes. Nevertheless, in this costume they will not even cross the high street; they prefer to go by roundabout ways to avoid it.

Whenever there is a chance one sells a house situated in any other street in order to buy one in the high street; no matter if the price is higher or the comforts fewer, as sometimes happens. The Council, or rather its appropriate Committee, has thought up all sorts of restrictions to prevent the town from continuing to expand longitudinally along this street, and grants facilities for building in other sectors. The results have been poor. Sometimes two families live in one house in this street when one of them could have a house of their own elsewhere. Occasionally the owner of a house in the high street goes to court to get his tenant out of it. The inheritance of a house on this street generally arouses violent disputes among the heirs. One family with a house in another sector inherited a house in the high street. After spending a considerable amount of money on modernizing it they moved in. Meanwhile one of the sons got married. The couple did not hesitate for a moment about living in the same house. When the first normal frictions arose the parents suggested that the newly-weds should go to live in the house they owned in the other street. The young people for their part dared to suggest that it would be more fitting for the parents to go back to the first house and allow them to stay on in the new house in the main street. Neither of the couples gave way.

Not all the parts of the main street are equally 'high class'. It stretches for nearly a kilometre, and it is not the same to live at the ends as to own a house towards the middle, near the church. One family which owned a house in the street paid an exaggerated price for another situated nearer to the centre. When it was hinted to the wife that the purchase had not been economically sound, she replied, 'that's where the rich people live and I shall have them for neighbours'; to have as neighbours those who enjoy a more distinguished social status, to be accepted by them in daily contact and in the evening gossip circles, makes one feel a member of the élite.

If we now ask who are the people that live in this street we shall get a simple answer: the *ricos-ricos*, the *pudientes*, and a fair number of the *propietarios*. The paucity of exceptions is surprising since, when the children of a family living in this street marry, they cannot all stay on in the same house. But taking into account the factors of time and social mobility it is probable that those who are on the upgrade aspire and eventually manage to live there. For those on the downgrade it is difficult for lack of means. Though one of the deepest and most cherished desires is to own fields and to add to their number, the determination to acquire a house in the principal street has been known to lead to the exchange of a field for a house. Obviously for such an exchange one has to be in possession of a large

number of fields, to be a *pudiente*. Hence as long as this street
continues to be regarded as a differentiating sign it will be predominantly the *pudientes* and *propietarios* who inhabit it. The inheritance of the houses will lead in part to the same result.

The exceptions to the correlation of social category and area
of residence are also due partly to inheritance. If a *pudiente* inherits a house in a street of lesser importance he will probably
live there at least for a time. One family living in its own house
in a less distinguished part of the town bought and rebuilt a
house in the high street, where it now lives, leaving the first one
uninhabited. At the beginning of the century houses began to
be built along the street, since this was one of the normal areas
of expansion for the town. With some few exceptions it is curious to observe how clearly these houses reveal the relationship
referred to above. Those families whose social position has been
maintained or improved continue to live in the houses built by
their parents or grandparents; several of those whose means
have declined have sold their houses, which have been bought
by people who are rising in the social scale. One of the consequences is that the purchase of houses in the main street has
affected principally, although not exclusively, its periphery and
not its geometrical centre, where the rich families with deeper
roots in the community live, whose forbears signed the minutes
of the Council. That is to say, the ownership of a house near
the centre is in a large number of cases the sign of an old *pudiente*
family; the acquisition of a house on the outskirts, although still
in the high street, reveals to a certain extent the rising economic
situation of the purchaser and the declining economic position
of the vendor.

The interior arrangements of the house are revealing. The
characteristic features of the homes of the *ricos-ricos* and *pudientes*
are: a modern dining room which also contains a writing table
and sometimes a piano, with family pictures and devotional
images on the walls and a chandelier or a lamp with several
bulbs. This room is only used when they have guests to a meal
or visitors considered socially superior. The standard aspired to
for the interior of the house, which several *pudientes* have already
achieved, includes a series of amenities regarded as necessary
by the *pudientes* and as somewhat fanciful by the *propietarios*.
Among them are: an electric washing machine and gas cooker,

refrigerator, up to now a private water tank to give running water in the house, a bathroom, electric razor, sewing machine, television set, gramophone, telephone, modern furniture and painted rooms, a full or part-time housemaid, apart from a car or at least a motor cycle, a tractor with the necessary farm implements, and in certain cases a harvester. These represent the ideal standard of living.

The standard for the *propietarios* and *jornaleros* is noticeably lower. The distinctive signs are negative 'synthemes' in relation to the *pudientes*: their rooms are adorned with fewer pictures and details, they lack the writing table, electric or gas cooker, washing machine (which obliges them to go regularly to the public wash house, which is not done for the *pudiente* women), the refrigerator, water tank, bathroom, television, gramophone, telephone, maidservant, car and tractor. As positive signs one may mention: a sewing machine, sometimes an electric shaver, a motor cycle, always a wireless set, a bicycle, cart, and a good selection of farming implements even if oldfashioned. Finally the interior of a cave offers less comfort and the signs that go with a low social status. The generic term in popular use, '*los de las cuevas*' or '*los que viven en las cuevas*' plainly designates the lowest level in the community. The aspirations of this group are confined to the acquisition of the positive signs typical of the group above.

II

The programme of amusements reflects interesting valuations and preferences. Personal taste has to be taken into account, of course, but my intention here is simply to delineate the content, forms and tone of the people's amusements, underlining the general and constant patterns. As the amusements recur in accordance with the rotation of days, weeks, seasons and festivals, they are noted under the heading of the cyclic signs of differentiation.

Amusements, except for the coteries of elderly people who gather round the fire on winter afternoons, accentuate the important role of the street. The groups that form in the doorways of the houses, bars, tavern and cinemas and on any street corner, are the nuclei of regular evening circles. I have already described the recruitment and composition of them in terms of position and social status, but a finishing touch may be added: strolling one summer night in the high street at nearly one o'clock, a youth commented on the animated chatter of a single remaining group comfortably seated near the centre of the town, saying, 'they won't get up till nine tomorrow morning but my hoe will be waiting for me at five'. In fact, staying up late in the middle of the summer, when work presses, indicates not having to work the next morning, being rich, and so is a differentiating sign: 'only the rich can afford that luxury', they grumble.

Habitual attendance at the tavern or the bar carries the imprint of a well-defined manner of living. I refer to the attendance of the married men. The tavern draws its 'regulars' from the lower ranks; they frequent the establishment after supper and for preference consume wine (*vino ordinario*) from a long-spouted bottle called a *porrón*. In the bar beer and brandy are drunk copiously, and if wine is drunk it is of good quality and always drunk from a glass. The habitués of the bar, again I refer to married men, belong to the remaining hierarchical levels. It is however customary to visit all the drinking establishments during the major festivals, especially in the morning after the solemn mass, without regard to social condition or rank. The same applies when guests are to be entertained. To have aperitifs at the bar after mass is also a distinctive sign because to rise late on Sundays, dress carefully, attend high mass, and finish the morning in the bar are features proper to people of wealth, with no haste or urgency of work. Men of advanced age, with no particular occupation on this morning, even if they are at the top of the social scale, are not accustomed to go to this mass but to an earlier one, because going to high mass is for '*señoritos*'. *Señorito* in this context implies adequate social position and age. It is also considered a luxury to be able to play cards in the café every day after lunch. This is a clear sign of time to spare and a certain economic independence.

No particular patterns regulate the comings and goings of the bachelors in the bars and tavern, but although they patronize all the establishments indifferently they show a marked preference for the bar as a meeting place. The bar is in the middle of the town and has television, and on Sunday evenings an orchestra for dancing. It should be noted here that the boys from the highest strata are least assiduous in attending this dance, not from purely personal choice but because the girls they 'ought' to dance with do not go. This is one of the few distinctions in the programme of youthful amusements, for in the quantity and quality of drinks, cigarettes, clothes, cinema going, trips to the city, etc., no difference can be observed in relation to economic levels. On the contrary, it is constantly remarked in the town that the amount spent in the bar and at the cinema, particularly by the married men, is higher among the less well-off than among the *pudientes*.

The bar and cinema are two good public stages for demonstrating one's capacity to pay, one's own economic power, which must be proved by anyone whose capacity is in doubt. Furthermore, from another point of view, it is important for the less prosperous strata to show a more-than-ordinary effort, a strong desire to enjoy all the town's amusements which is often beyond the range of what they can afford. This is not simply an imperious need for amusement but an undoubted right. If one Sunday they cannot afford to see a film, or if it is hinted to them that they might restrict their expenditure on amusements, they argue, 'Haven't we the right to enjoy ourselves? It is all we can do'. The ever-present theme of comparison with others will give us, elsewhere, the key to a possible interpretation.

At *fiestas* dancing goes on for at least seven hours a day; all other items in the festival programme are regarded as quite secondary to this. In the few sports contests, for example, it is rare for youths from the town to take part; they are content to be spectators. But after three in the morning, when the dancing ends, as also on other special days, they go out 'to do the rounds' (*rondar*). The 'round' (*ronda*) consists of singing *jotas* at the top of one's voice in the street, of roasting a rabbit or a lamb, drinking, yelling, gesticulating, and on the following day talking over the details and incidents of the previous night. These *rondas*, which today are more controlled, used to give rise to certain transgressions, punishable by law. But on one such *ronda* a boy was able to encourage his friends by boasting, 'Don't worry if anything happens. My father is mayor.': a further illustration of the relation between amusements and status.

With regard to the cinema three points are worth mentioning. There are a number of season-ticket holders who always pay for admission whether or not they attend the performance, and always occupy the same seats—the second half of the stalls: this is a reflection of their economic capacity. Secondly, the cinema is not unaffected by religious considerations. One Sunday the priest commented in church on the moral quality of a film to be shown and as a result several families returned their tickets. To which it must be added that the fullest houses have been those at films of a religious character. Finally a word on aesthetics. To judge by comments on films which people have just seen, the purely artistic character of a film often passes unnoticed. They focus their attention on the plot and enjoy the dramas.

Melodrama makes its greatest impact on women of the less prosperous levels. A *pudiente* lady told me with some annoyance that at the times when an unbearably bad drama was being broadcast the servant girl stopped working. The time for the radio serial brought the women rushing home from the public wash-house; others would wait until they had heard the broadcast before setting out. Visits to the theatre in the city, however, are rare except for some few *pudiente* families. The revue is a highly appreciated entertainment: a succession of plastic pictures in colour, rhythm and sound woven round a feeble easily-followed story. The scanty apparel of the girls provides sex appeal and the degree of concentration required is minimal.

Music in the form of concerts has no appreciable appeal. Some *pudientes* who had been invited to a concert remarked as they came out, 'we don't understand that music'. Nevertheless a few of the *pudientes* do include in their small collection of records some *zarzuelas* (light operas), in which dialogue and singing alternate, which they delight in listening to.

Football is possibly the greatest sporting attraction for all social classes. Matches take place at seasons when the work is not at all urgent and offer the chance of admiring internationally famous figures. To this must be added eagerness for the city team to win; and as a youth who was not a fan remarked, 'since everybody talks football and goes to see it, you can't help going to a match or two'.

Compared with football, bullfighting is a minority entertainment. Aesthetic enjoyment of the bullfight demands of the spectator a certain knowledge of the technicalities and a constant appreciation of detail. The bullring principally attracts the middle-aged or elderly *pudientes*. It is a sign of distinction to buy a season ticket for all or part of the bullfights held during the festivals in the city. The gift of a comfortable seat at a bullfight with a good programme connotes prestige and good taste in the donor; not only on account of the technical knowledge required but also because tickets are expensive, two conditions which only those in the strongest economic groups can be expected to manipulate to advantage. The same, *mutatis mutandis*, could be said of the few devotees of shooting.

In the programme of diversions it is probably travel outside the region and above all abroad, that counts highest as an external sign of differentiation. This is the necessary extra, the highest embellishment of a way of life. Anyone who regards himself as belonging to the upper groups must have spent at least one summer holiday in San Sebastián. On August mornings a fair number of residents from the town are to be found chatting on the *Concha* (the beach at San Sebastián), under the clock, right in the centre of the fashionable *plage*. It is unnecessary to stress that summering at the seaside is an expression of status and age. On his return from this resort one townsman remarked in explanation of his visit, 'it seemed wrong not to know San Sebastián'; in view of his position he considered the journey essential. Other cities to which visits are obligatory are Madrid, Barcelona, and to some extent Valencia. A man of mature age described the broadness of the streets in Barcelona, their good lay-out and straightness, in such abundant detail as to make me think he had spent a long time in the city. To my enquiry he replied in a low voice that he had never visited Barcelona but had read everything that had fallen into his hands about the Catalan capital, in order 'to be able to talk with those who had been there and to make them believe that *he* had too'.

III

I have already spoken of the sense of inferiority which their own mode of expression gives to many people. From it stems the effort that many of those in the highest categories make to improve their diction. Sometimes in conversation with those they regard as belonging to a superior cultural level, they interpolate words of which they do not properly understand the meaning. This careful selection of words causes them to speak slowly and to accompany the expressions of doubtful meaning with solemn gestures. It is characteristic of many of the *pudientes* already well advanced in years. As one descends the hierarchical scale, however, uneasiness over modes of expression decreases. Conversation is more facile and spontaneous; words are more frequently vehicles for feelings. These two attitudes towards expression undoubtedly influence the use of the language and the choice of words. For example, the number of words connoting sex, sexual intercourse and sexual organs, etc. and their use, is markedly greater among the poorer groups. Even the women of these strata use some of them freely. Among women of good position there is a strict taboo on their use. Furthermore the men of these low levels try to avoid them in conversation with women of superior social status, the professionals, and the priest, although they do not always succeed in doing so. On such occasions those who consider themselves well brought up take care to avoid words regarded as low, and only in moments of annoyance or violent reaction do they utter them.

These two aspects of the use of languages and the choice of words are a corollary of education and family upbringing. Well-to-do families watch carefully over their children's schooling and sometimes supplement it by private tuition, or send the child to a school in the city for three or four years. In these homes there are always a few books, and a daily paper is taken (62 families take them) as well as a monthly magazine, generally of a religious nature. Reading, therefore, is customary among them. This does not apply to humble families, among whom the period of schooling is shorter and less intensive, and the parents do not worry overmuch about it. They attend neither private classes nor schools in the city and there are no books, newspapers or magazines in their homes; the outlook is altogether different. Their contact with the outer world is minimal; the stock of ideas they have to play with limited. One summer evening a group of people of high standing were discussing the early possibility of travelling to the moon. There happened to be a *peón* with them. He argued obstinately against the opinion of all the rest: 'nobody has ever got to the moon and they never will'. He had no notion whatever of recent conquests of space. In 1941 the number of illiterates in the town was 25, all belonging to these families.

The Council papers clearly illustrate the difference in attitudes towards school education and teaching. On 10 March, 1872, the mayor accompanied by the appropriate committee visited the schools, for reasons explained in a Minute of the same day: 'for a very long time past, scant progress has been noted in all the subjects of teaching prescribed by the regulations'. On 12 May the same year they returned, now for the third time and observed that 'the advances made were imperceptible'. In their attempt to remedy the deficiencies of the teaching they permitted themselves to make 'an observation to the teachers that they should not be absent from the schools during the regulation hours'. On 4 August, still in the same year, they examined the boys and girls and were 'hardly satisfied'. On the following 25 September and 30 October they returned and the 'teachers were urged to work with greater ability so that more progress might be seen'. Neither these admonitions to the masters to fulfil their duties more rigorously nor the hint that they change their teaching methods produced the desired results. However the mayor and committee were determined to improve the standard of education and to investigate the causes of the poor functioning of the schools. So on 3 November they renewed the attack and inspected them for the ninth time. They then discovered the real reason, for the secretary wrote in the Minute that they noted 'the poor attendance of boys and girls, having observed the same on all their visits, and in consequence they summoned the parents in order to ascertain the cause, this proving to be apathy on their part'. The repeated and tenacious efforts of the mayor and of the committee to raise the cultural level of the children had been wrecked by the 'apathy' of the parents. The former, the '*élite*', regarded education as a necessity; not so the latter.

As for ideas on politics, national or international, the gulf between the two extremes is wide. I am not now referring to the division between political parties, in which the correlation with social class was patent enough as we have seen, but to knowledge of political events in national and international spheres. Newspapers are the only source of information apart from the radio, and we have seen how many and what class of families take them; with regard to the radio, people—especially at the lower levels—prefer to hear something more entertaining than news bulletins on political matters. Discussion of important political topics will thus be limited to families in the higher strata; a complete lack of political ideas exists in the lowest levels. A single example, which links together two distinct positions, will suffice here. One Sunday some American soldiers from the base in the city went into the tavern. They quickly struck up a dialogue more in gestures than in words with the regulars, whom they repeatedly invited to drink wine. The locals were delighted by the munificence of the Americans. A person of higher position remarked of the soldiers, 'they think they are the only ones with a couple of pounds to spend on wine . . .'. The first looked on the Americans as splendid and friendly visitors who deigned to share a jug of wine with them; the second saw in them the rich and arrogant foreign soldier.

IV

A moral sign of differentiation signifies, in the context employed here, not religious ideology or the justification of religious ideas—although some of the values accepted may be religious in origin—but actual conduct in so far as it adapts itself to or departs from the central values of the community. When a townsman acts in accordance with such values his conduct is just, good, moral. If in his behaviour he violates these rules he commits a sin against community life, he sins socially and public opinion is the judge. A social transgression may at the same time break religious or juridical rules, but we are not concerned with this here.

It is evident that the hierarchy of rank reflects a considerable proportion of the values of the community and that these are regarded as the desiderata to be aspired to. A person of the highest social status will possess the social virtues required by the system while another lower in the social scale will be lacking in a good part of them. In other words, high social position is a 'synthème' which demonstrates personal fulfilment of the values of the community. Low social condition will be synonymous with failure in the fulfilment of all or some of the values.

It follows, firstly, that the upper strata impose, at least in outline, their own tastes and ideas; the system of crucial values in the life of the community is theirs.[1] Adaptation to the rules of conduct which rest on these values will for them require less effort, whilst violation of them will be graver. Secondly, the lower segments of the community are partially on the fringe of the system of values because their personal realization of them is deficient. As a corollary public opinion should be less severe in its sanctions on offences against social morality committed by the lower categories, but intransigent and rigorous towards those committed by the higher levels, which is what the following examples show.

The Council's books record fifty-five cases of theft between 1945 and 1949. They are thefts of grapes, fruit, grass, and more rarely of a few kilograms of wheat, beet, or of a poplar tree. Almost invariably the hierarchical status of the thief is given as low. Public opinion regards these acts, by the correlation mentioned above, as 'matters of little importance'. However a *pudiente* was once seen taking a cauliflower from someone else's field. The affair was gossiped about, harshly criticized and termed 'scandalous'. The Farmers' Brotherhood agreed, during a slack period, that the townsfolk should go out and repair certain roads and threshing-floors on the outskirts of the town. Personal participation in such work is a moral obligation. Two *pudientes* owning machines and other tools failed to offer any help. They were severely criticized: 'they have no shame', '*they* don't have to go out and earn wages', people said. From words they passed to deeds and covered the offenders' doors with mud. Nobody worried if anybody in the lower levels shirked the work. Another good example: in the week preceding the August festivals a party of youths goes from door to door collecting money to supplement the Council grant for the celebrations. If the contribution of a *pudiente* does not accord with his means the young men take it upon themselves to divulge the amount and the donor's name. Certain aspects of immorality affect only the upper levels. For example if anyone takes advantage of economic difficulties through which a family is passing to buy up their house or fields, the purchase is thought to be immoral.

The same qualification may have either a favourable or pejorative connotation. For one person work may be an

---

[1] Cf. pp. 79 above.

essential condition of probity: to criticize a *peón* in public as idle, for instance, is equivalent to coming to blows with him; a *pudiente*, under the same circumstances would probably answer with satisfaction, 'how lucky I am not to have to work'.

The sense of shame and responsibility is consequently much more developed among the groups of high position than among those in the lower levels. The eyes of the community as a whole are on them; they are the 'most seen' of the Minutes, and criticism does not gloss over any of their infractions of the rules of conduct. And the behaviour of the lower groups is a matter of less importance, unless it takes on obviously scandalous features. The greater development of the sense of shame effectively predisposes, of course, against any kind of conduct not acceptable by the community; it intensifies the sense of responsibility. The other groups behave more freely, are less sensitive to social pressures. Drunkenness, theft, premarital pregnancies (although few), etc., all strongly condemned by the communal values, are understandably more prevalent among the lower groups.

There is another group of values of great importance. Their importance lies in their peculiarity, for they have nothing to do with the values so far described. I allude to moral (still in the sense defined above) and personal qualities.

By 'prestige' I refer to personal qualities of any kind which, in line with the values of the town, adorn an individual. 'Prestige' is acquired in the first place by the practice of the moral virtues: seriousness of manner in speech and action, prudence in the management of business matters, and avoidance of all possible dispute with others. All the required moral virtues are summed up in one word, honour (*honradez*), on which I shall comment in full later. To be called 'an honourable man' is the highest praise. 'Prestige' derived from integrity has no connexion with economic power; despite all the minutiae and the importance of all the differentiation signs noted, 'prestige', in this first meaning, works as a counterbalance, an egalitarian principle. At the same time it is necessary to stress its decisive importance as a culmination of social status. A grave offence against one of the virtues destroys a person's reputation for integrity for a long time, and if he holds a public appointment he

asks for dismissal or transference. The ruling *élite* does not tolerate reprehensible conduct.

The second meaning of the word 'prestige' refers to intellectual faculties, understood in a wide sense, always highly
regarded. This form of 'prestige' too is independent of any
economic stratification. Furthermore people observe acutely
this lack of relationship and remark with ill-concealed pleasure,
'he may be rich but he is not so clever'. 'Prestige', finally,
comes from age, above all when the conduct of the old man is
considered irreproachable. It is customary to address those who
fulfil these conditions as *Señor*, 'Señor Juan' for example. *Señor*,
or 'the renown of Señor' as Gracián[1] says, is a sign of prestige.
Those who do not fulfil the second condition are usually called
tío (uncle).

These differentiating signs not based on, but marginal to,
stratification explain and complement the definition of social
status suggested in earlier pages. Social status derives from the
sum of economic power, plus political power, plus education,
plus the aggregate of differentiating 'synthèmes' or signs based
on stratification, plus the sum of differentiating 'synthèmes' independent of stratification. As each person's category is defined
by the combination of these factors, social status can be thought
of as the principle which holds them together. Further, as each
or any one of these factors possesses an independence of its own,
it must be possible to descend in social status without any
diminution of economic power, or to progress economically
without attaining a higher social status. The discussion which
follows on whether religion and the family are factors which
contribute to social status will throw more light on this possibility of disfunctional correlation. But first it must be made
quite clear that what has been considered under the sign of
moral differentiation points to, on the one hand, the varying
intensity of the sense of morality and, on the other, underlines
the existence of non-stratifiable values in the definition of social
status. This exposition will of course be incomplete until such
concepts as shame and *honra* are analysed at length.

V

The historical notes which introduced the study of stratification indicated a longstanding correspondence between wealth

[1] Gracián, op. cit., p. 280.

and solemn religious practices. The close correlation between religion, wealth and political party was the theme of another chapter. To be a *propietario* or *pudiente* was to be a conservative in politics and a defender of religious values, which meant attending processions with a pistol in one's pocket. The onslaught on religion on a national scale during the republican period was fully echoed by the other segments of the townsfolk, who by their own direct attacks provoked a sharp intensification of religious observances on the part of the right-wing group, since the situation left no place for half-measures. These historical facts have had important consequences for religious conduct in the postwar period.

Just as during the Republic the press and radio, the defamatory libels, the coarse caricatures of the ecclesiastical hierarchy, the constant attacks and the burning of churches created a national atmosphere of anti-religious pressures and attitudes, so since the civil war the national atmosphere has radically changed direction through the same media. Religious observance has been encouraged by all possible means. The national situation finds its equivalent in the town. On 20 January 1934, the Archbishop decreed on his pastoral visit that 'to oppose the constant dechristianisation of the town the Priest shall intensify the catechism'[1]. At that time roughly 30 per cent. of the population attended mass on Sundays. Today, according to statistics, the annual average for attendance at Sunday mass is 55 per cent. and the percentage for paschal observance is, in round figures, 80 percent. The attitude towards religion has thus changed in direction and in intensity.

Apart from the new social conditions, which forbid any attack on religion, there are other motives which reinforce official pressure in regard to religious observance. These are a sign of belonging to the correct segment of the community, whose ideas and values triumphed in the war. Furthermore, as the upper sections of the community, who continue to go to church, are those who lay down the elegant and acceptable forms of conduct, religious practice is today socially correct. As we saw above, attendance at high Mass on Sunday, in the middle of the morning, indicates that you have no need to go

---

[1] Parish record, last volume, fols. 15–16.

out and earn wages, that you are a *señorito*, and able to spend a
few pesetas at the bar.

In the higher levels of the town it is necessary to distinguish
between those who have always been practising churchgoers
and who would perhaps practise with even greater intensity if
the social conditions were markedly opposed—they repeat
emphatically, 'we are some of the few who used to go to church
before the war', and those who, although they would not
apparently go to church from personal motives, nevertheless
comply with the ordinary obligations of piety because these
form one of the aspects of the style of living proper to their
economic position. The first group supplies the largest contingent to parish associations and thus has the highest degree of
participation in religious activities.

The importance of some of these associations for the development of community life can be seen in the following case. At a
meeting of one association there was a long discussion on the
desirability of creating a parish hall with a lecture room,
cinema and theatre, library, bar, games rooms and other
amenities for a parochial recreation centre. The project having
been approved in principle, a special meeting was called to
which were invited all the members of the Town Council, the
professionals, and persons of higher economic standing. As the
idea seemed a splendid one, a house in the centre of the town
was bought and demolished and the new edifice erected on the
site. There are two points to be noticed: first, the way in which
the innovation originated at the highest levels and how their
values, in this case primarily religious since parochial control of
entertainments was involved, and their outlook on life, the
necessity for a lecture room and library, imposed themselves on
the town; and second, the connexion between economic power
and religious values, since if the *pudientes*, or someone among
them, had not sponsored the construction, it would have been
impossible to obtain credit from the banks. The largest contributions too came from the same stratum.

Another aspect to be borne in mind is the minority character
of some of these associations. One of the religious guilds has
traditionally limited its membership to fifteen and the same
guild has been monopolized by a few families. Another association, this time of married women, shows every appearance of

being the one proper to women of the most elevated levels. In reality any married woman can belong to it and there are indeed two members whose social position is of the lowest. But these few exceptions must be qualified, because the members of inferior economic level do not pay the full monthly dues and their contribution to the meetings and decisions of the associa- is nil, as their points of view, ideas and capacity for self-expression differ from and are inferior to those of the main body of the members. They form no part of the active core. It is possible that other women would join the association if guided solely by personal religious motives, but as their economic position and style of living do not reach the right level they would feel uncomfortable at meetings. Then there is the age-gap. There is an identical association for young girls. On marrying not one of them joins the married women's associa- tion because they do not feel at home among the older women.[1]

These women organize the charity campaigns, the tombola during the festivals, represent the town at regional catholic meetings, look after the cleaning and decoration of altars, and directly second the projects initiated by the ecclesiastical hier- archy. They go to church every day, and always occupy their favourite seats; they may bring in a priest from outside to administer first communion solely to their own children, or invite several priests to solemnize a baptism or a wedding. Their funerals and anniversary services are of the most solemn pos- sible; in the former the priest accompanies the funeral procession right to the cemetery. In general a first-class funeral is the mark not only of the pious *élite* but of the economic power of the family, for it is another of the social forms that go with a definite style of living, and one with a history of over 400 years as we have seen. Finally, it is interesting to note that the religious *élite* feel a certain responsibility and obligation towards the needy, being time and again splendidly generous in their dona- tions. In consequence they provide the poor to some extent with a share of the communal wealth and through this personal

---

[1] The remaining sodalities and religious associations lack this mark of distinc- tion, but it is to be noted that the responsible posts in all of them are almost always held by the same women. The Brotherhood of young men is an exception; all members hold offices in turn by annual rotation.

contact reduce the social distance separating the two extremes of the hierarchy.

The religious conduct, attitudes and observances of the socially inferior groups indicate the reverse. They have a specific conception of religion on which I shall comment later; for the present I shall confine myself to the connexion between stratum and religion. Many of them observe only the rites of baptism, first communion, marriage, the last sacraments, and church burial. If there are missions in the parish they may attend one or other of the meetings. These people almost make up the number of those who do not observe Easter, though some may attend mass on Easter Day, New Year's Day, and the feast of the Immaculate Conception. Their participation in the religious life of the community during the rest of the year is nil, because even if they are not at work on Sundays they do not go to mass. They do not, however, directly impede the religious practices of their children if they wish to perform them and it appears that they prefer their children to have religious beliefs.

The anti-religious attitudes of these minor sections of the community take two different forms, one ideological and the other comparative. They affirm that they 'do not go to mass because the priests are those who are in command but do not practice what they preach'. They continue with the well-worn themes: 'nobody has come from hell. If they (who practice) are so afraid why aren't they better than they are?' This direct allusion to those at the highest levels—'they'—lays a finger on the wound. 'The rich go to mass but they exploit the workers'. They cite examples in which they have been passive protagonists: once they worked over the agreed hours for a landowner, 'one of those who go to mass on Sundays', and he refused to pay them for the extra work. On another occasion, at the end of the war, when there was a bread shortage, a *pudiente*, notorious for his religiosity, deducted from wages the price of the bread he had supplied for them to eat. Employers have on occasion sent their men to work on a Sunday without worrying whether or not they have had time to go to mass, etc.

In this way they identify superior status with religion; from the antagonism of interests it is very easy to slip into the antagonism of ideas, so easy that many in trying to explain the essential differences between the two political groups during the civil war told me 'some attacked the church and others defended it'. To these informants the political ideology was secondary, or rather confused with the religious. If political party and religious practice are identified with the economically powerful strata, the antagonistic, economically weak strata will be likely to reject not only the political ideas of the former but their religious attitudes too. More briefly, membership of a given social group will influence the attitude towards religion, whether positive or negative, of those included in it. As we have seen, attendance at Sunday mass may for some be a function of their way of life, rather than a result of religious conviction. Similarly in the groups less well endowed economically some people do not practice religion because it is not the custom among them: as they say, 'they know what behoves them', and it behoves them, obviously, not to go to church.

Political power too is harmoniously linked with certain religious practices. The mayor and corporation occupy the pews of honour in the church at high masses and to them the preacher addresses the first greeting of the sermon. Processions end with the Council accompanying the clergy. This harmony of powers shows itself also in the invitation to the parish priest to attend certain meetings of the Council. We have already seen that the Council was invited to the meeting which decided upon the creation of a parochial centre. This subject, rich in historical data, will be considered separately.

Finally, do religious practices contribute to the raising of the social status of those who practise them? The correlation between religion and standing is evident, but is the practice of religion a facet of the style of living or a new contribution which brings with it the increase of social status? More concretely, if two *pudientes* have the closest possible affinity in economic 'situation', but one is more devout than the other, will the devout one gain greater social status? In this case religion is neutral. Indeed the inverse might be thought to apply to men because the most pious are sometimes the object of irony. Indirectly it could help to adorn personal status since if a *pudiente*, for example, did not practise like the rest and attacked religion in earnest this would be violently out of keeping with his style of living and in present circumstances would injure his personal prestige. Some of the *propietarios* may serve as an indication in this respect: they never practise for personal reasons, nor do they attack religious principles, and neither their social status nor their personal prestige has suffered on this account.

VI

It was pointed out earlier that access to wealth is the direct consequence of the social condition of the family rather than the result of personal work and effort. The family, mainly in its nuclear sense, is the final sign of differentiation to be mentioned. The social position and status of the father are shared by his wife and children, the family providing in principle the back-bone which governs stratification.

We have seen how certain surnames which appear repeatedly in the old papers, especially in the Council Minutes, belong to present-day families who enjoy distinguished social rank now as then. Their houses in the centre of the High Street are a mark of antiquity. Their social status has been inherited. To refer to an individual by his patronymic indicates that he shares, or is thought to share, the characteristics, aptitudes or defects of the family (in the wide sense) to which he belongs. 'He is a Gutiérrez' means that the man referred to possesses the qualities relevant to that family. 'He's a Morales' indicates that here is an individual of no economic power, quarrelsome and illogical, features characteristic of his family. The real test for determining the specific contribution of the family to individual social status lies in the marriage of the children. Brothers live in the same house sheltered by the paternal social status. Once they marry, how long does the shadow of the family follow them? They cultivate a few fields which are not their own property and they lack money. By their economic power they should be regarded as standing on the lowest rungs of the social ladder, but they consider themselves as much *pudientes* or *propietarios* as their parents, and in any classificatory enquiry they are placed by others in the paternal position and status. Their present economic power does not count in this case. The shadow of the family reaches them in the first years of marriage.

After some years, when economic independence has been acquired by inheritance of land, the position and status of brothers may begin to diverge. In these cases the leader of the family (in its widest sense) is normally the one who has the greater economic power. This superior position has sometimes led to a breach with his economically inferior brothers. If in such a case the wealthier brother has scaled the economic heights by reprehensible means, his social status diminishes considerably because both actions are disapproved of by the values of the community. Economic power and social status stand in inverse ratio in this case.

Social mobility may operate in a downwards as well as an upwards direction: families may descend in position, in status, or in both. A grave illness suffered by the head of a family or by one of the members of the nuclear family may lead to the sale of part of the property to cover the expenses involved. Unlucky business ventures or faulty administration can have the same result. In these cases the people say that the family has 'come down in the world', literally 'come to less' (*ha llegado a menos* or *ha venido a menos*), emphasizing the comparison with the previous position. In the first case the correlation between economic power and social status is not direct: the fall in the first does not follow the loss or diminution of the second. When descent in the hierarchical system is due to extravagance the loss of status is more marked and criticized than the economic debilitation. The latter is commented on as a function of the former, in so far as the main reason for the decline is bound up with moral culpability. Adaptation to or rejection of values is the criterion which in this case accentuates the lowering of status.

The inheritance of position and social status through family ties presupposes that the social structure undergoes no essential changes through several generations. This was probably the case in the community in the historical period reviewed. However since the end of the civil war the economic structure has undergone fundamental changes. Hence the importance of this historical moment for the study of social mobility. Let us first look at its impact on the family.

When the war ended the *pudientes* and *propietarios* were more or less comfortably ensconced in their respective positions. This means that they did not feel themselves compelled to change their ideas and business methods. The pressure towards new adaptations in the economy had therefore to come from other spheres. A small number of *pudiente* families faced the critical opportunities for expansion by relying on pre-war economic attitudes. They did not buy more fields or rent them because the first called for money which they did not possess, and the second required mechanization for which in its turn capital expenditure was necessary. Bank facilities for the securing of credit did not help because of conservative economic attitudes: i.e. not to borrow money because one should never owe more than one has got (based on the popular proverb, 'He who buys without being able—to afford it—sells without wishing'), and should not ask the banks for credit because they seek information on the applicant's economic prospects and morals from other residents of the town. The family's economic situation would be humiliatingly discussed by others.

Failing to adapt themselves to the changing economic situation they found it impossible to maintain the level of living that pertained to them, because the costs of wages, seed and taxes had risen and continued to rise. Also the standard of living gradually rose for all groups, the most prosperous families setting the new standards. As they themselves had only the same resources as in pre-war years, they inevitably fell behind. The young sons of several of these conservative families attempted to face up to the demands of a time of economic expansion but were held back by their parents, whose ideas they could not succeed in changing. They could not supplement rents by means of secondary occupations nor go out and earn wages by working in the fields belonging to others because both tasks would lower their standing. A *pudiente* could not play the *jornalero*. The effect of these conservative attitudes has been first, the displacement of economic power of the families and secondly the loss of standing, affecting not the parents, if still living, but the sons, now in their thirties, who no longer play the part in the life of the community which their fathers did. In twenty-five years the loss of economic power by a family has been translated into a lowering of social status.

The majority of the families however kept in tune with the new economic rhythm. In general the sons who returned from the front either sought jobs away from the town if the family's economic resources were reduced, or confronted the economic situation with initiative. They bought land when the chance arose, or rented it within or outside the municipal boundaries.

9

They modernized their farming equipment even if it meant asking the banks for credit, and to their usual occupations added others such as the buying and selling of straw, alfalfa, maize, cattle, etc. They transacted their business at the right time and in a dozen years multiplied their economic power, an economic power which in some cases has already been transformed into political power. Also as success in business implies individual qualities such as a grasp of problems and the ability to make decisions, they have increased their personal prestige and the social status of their families.

VI

STRATIFICATION: IV

*' Donde mejor se nota la influencia de la tierra en el hombre es en
la influencia del hombre sobre la tierra'*
*' El progreso exige, junto a la capacidad de no ser hoy lo que ayer
se fue, la de conservar eso de ayer y acumularlo'*

ORTEGA Y GASSET

THE SOCIAL life of the town in 1960 bears little resemblance to that what it was at the beginning of the civil war in 1936. New ideas and customs have replaced the old ones. What principles can be observed in the disappearance of the old forms and the rising of the new ones? I distinguish between two groups of problems which arise from two related, but different, concepts: that of social change, and that of social development. All alterations in the social life of a community represent social change. The growth of and adaptation to social change and its attempted direction by the members of a community following their own ideas and attitudes, comprise social development. Social change and social development are closely inter-related in social reality; but the conceptual distinction between them permits alternative reference to each one as well as emphasis on the more relevant aspects of each of them, for the study of social mobility. The illustrations of economic change which follow, are simple numerical examples that indicate the points of contact between the economy and other social institutions, between economic change and social development.

I

Three years of civil war put an end to the Republicans' purpose of remodelling the structure of the country. At the end of the war it was necessary to tackle the arduous task of national reorganization. Industry and agriculture had suffered severe blows. The material and economic difficulties of reconstruction during the early post-war months were accentuated by the outbreak of the second World War. When the belligerent Axis powers encountered their first reverses, Spain found herself in an uncomfortable position. The situation was made worse by the Potsdam declaration of July 1945 by which Spain was disqualified from membership of the U. N. Ostracism was complete in 1946, when the organization demanded that all its members should recall their representatives from Madrid.

Added to these internal and external difficulties were lengthy droughts which considerably reduced the already deficient agricultural production. Import of food-stuffs was practically impossible because of the empty treasury—the Republican Government in exile was using part of the gold reserves of the Bank of Spain to live on—and because the international blockade was at its height. In view of the situation a definite economic transformation had to be brought about. This transformation in the agricultural economy ought to be emphasized, not only because more than half of the working population of the country were farming, but also because, as the blockade persisted, it was practically the only method of obtaining basic food-stuffs.

Government protection for agriculture took different forms. The principal means of increasing agricultural production—and as yet methods were not much better than those used in Roman times—was the provision of capital for investments in agriculture. This capital was made available to people in the form of credit advanced by the banks. They partially extended the facilities for loans, thus broadening the scope of agricultural opportunities. More than half of the total number of the heads of families benefited from these facilities. The volume of transactions and future prospects prompted six banks to open branches in the town.

The creation of the Brotherhood of Farmers and Stockbreeders was also part of the programme for a more efficient organization of agriculture. Membership was, and is, obligatory, and each member has to pay a subscription. The principal function of the Brotherhood is to gather together the farmers and labourers into a syndicate and to defend their interests. As was said above, selected seed and fertilizers are

distributed through this organization, which also supplies credit
facilities for this purpose at the low rate of interest of only 2·75
per cent. The rate of interest charged by the banks is roughly
8 per cent. The Brotherhood also forwarded to the town a loan
of half a million pesetas at the same nominal rate of 2·75 per
cent to be paid in four years. These advantageous loans were
advanced for the exclusive purpose of encouraging agriculture
and livestock breeding of every sort.

In Chapter II there is a reference to the difficulties faced by
the residents in marketing wheat during the middle period of
the Republican Government, and also to how the residents had
to undersell or hoard it. Under these circumstances incentives
for greater production were rendered useless. The new Government intervened and stabilized the market of this product, becoming the only buyer at a fixed price, favourable to the pro-
ducer. So a fixed income and a sure market gave guarantees to
the farmer. Further, a branch of the National Syndicate of
Wheat was opened in the town to receive the harvest and thus
avoid the costs of transport. The delivery of wheat made, payment could be collected at any one of the branches of the banks.
This change in the circumstances of the wheat market has been
of great importance, especially as the production of cereals is
the chief occupation in the town.

Finally it must be remembered that it was owing to the National Institute of Colonization that some fifty tenants who cultivated fields on a farm just outside the municipal district became proprietors of the same, buying the land they each worked
on terms it would be hard to improve upon.

These were the principal changes which the farmer encountered in the early post-war period; changes in the agricultural and economic structure in which he played no part. For
him they offered opportunities he could manipulate according to
his own judgment. What advantage did he take of them? The
question can be answered in terms of 'social development'.

Besides these external stimuli, there was a desire among the
people themselves for an improvement of agricultural methods.
Before the war the reapers and the mule-drawn harrows played
the chief part in the harvesting of the crop. Yet already they had
begun to use threshing machines, and several *pudientes* had
clubbed together to raise the necessary capital to buy one. In

fact, this process of mechanization was made difficult by unfavourable conditions in the wheat market and the shortage of capital. Post-war incentives by the Government simply helped a process already initiated to resume its march forward.

In Chapter I mention was made of the increase in the resources of the municipal *término* or boundaries, because of the buying and leasing of lands in other *términos*. To the 802 hectares which the residents possessed and cultivated within the *término* we have to add no less than 1380 hectares situated in other municipal districts, most of which was acquired after the war. As the prices paid for these were appreciably above the average, people came from the neighbouring towns to offer their lands for sale. Influenced by the stimulus to expand, lands were purchased or leased more than 35 kilometres from the town.

At the same time every care was taken to turn existing plots to the best economic advantage. Irrigation channels were diverted where suitable and every available strip or corner of land hitherto scorned was brought under cultivation. Moreover the quality of the lands was improved by the extensive use of fertilizers; scarcely used in the past, they came to be used at the rate of more than half a million kilogrammes per year. To this must be added the selection of seeds. Further to obtain the maximum yield of the land without exhausting it, they introduced new products into the rotation crop system, having in mind the potential market value.

In this period a definite impulse was given to the rationalization of agriculture by the modernization of tools. The following table (the figures have been taken from records of the Council) shows the extent of this.

	1935	1936–39	1955	1960
Draught animals	242	C	156	96
		I		
Carts with 2 and 4 wheels	?	V	148	126
		I		
Tractors (used in 1935 solely for working the threshing machine) ..	2	L	14	32
		W		
Trailers	0	A	8	16
		R		
Trucks, cars, motorcycles	3		29	68
Bank branches	0		4	6

The tractor is the pivot upon which all other technical changes and improvements in tools turn. Up-to-date machines worked by tractor, such as trailers, and ploughs, have replaced the old plough and all the other Roman tools. The tractor has made possible the cultivation of certain soils and the buying and leasing of land at some distance from the municipal *término*. Also it is in itself a very profitable investment, increasing the annual income of the owner, as it can be hired out to others. In order to buy a tractor the people frequently had to apply to the banks for credit and wait patiently for months with their names on the distribution lists as imports were restricted. Secondhand tractors were sometimes bought to avoid delay. Yet, in spite of the obvious advantages, interest in the mechanization of agricultural methods and instruments was, in practice, a far more complicated and involved process than one would expect from a rational concept of agricultural economy.

Nobody doubted the superiority of the tractor from the moment it was decided to use it. Indeed, there was almost a tractor cult, and riding on tractors down the main street on return from work became a mark of social distinction. With the purchase of a tractor not only did one gain social prestige but at the same time the means for developing a new way of life, and creating a new social structure. The tractor with all its accessories changed the conditions of work.

Firstly, it considerably reduced the number of draught animals, carts and Roman ploughs. This meant the need to acquire a driving licence, some knowledge of mechanics, and contacts with fuel stations; it also involved entering the world of banks, commercial negotiations, and letters of credit. This was partly the reason why branches of banks and insurance companies appeared in the town. Secondly, it had adverse effects on local craftsmen such as the farrier, saddler and carpenter, who found that either they had to widen the basis of their occupations or seek some other supplementary employment. The positive result of this was the opening of a workshop for the repair of the new tools.

The recasting of the occupational structure does not stop here. The groups of reapers who used to come to the town are no longer needed; corn-cutting machines drawn by mules are used less and less and the threshing machines yield in importance to the combined-harvesters. On the other hand the *campaña* of the cereal was the time when day-workers were especially needed to deal with the many various and urgent tasks; this demand increased their wages from 75 to 145 pesetas. As the combined-harvesters sweep away the day wages—the principal source of income for *peones* and *braceros*—it is not surprising that these people choose to leave the town.

The consequences of mechanization have been no less important in the sphere of labour relations. The labourers of whom the ancient records speak as constituting part of the family, sat down at the table of their masters for the last time in 1936. Mechanization has made them redundant for the greater part of the year. The old idea of work centring around the nuclear family is vanishing. The new economy no longer demands the possession of a cart, a couple of horses, the use of harrows, ploughing with mules etc. The neighbour's tractor can do all these tasks more easily. Collaboration and mutual dependence have replaced the old family autarchy. At the same time the owner of a tractor needs to offer the services of his machine to make up the money he paid for it and to make a profit. Everybody in his turn needs to organize himself in groups or syndicates to protect his rights, to obtain agricultural credits, fertilizers, seeds and machinery. Physical toil has been partly replaced not only by technical development but by organization, collaboration and interdependence, and also by tedious 'red tape'. The steady and amicable relationship between labourer and master has given way to the less friendly and more changeable relationship of employer and employee. The former was a family affair, the latter a purely economic one.

To sum up: the repercussion of technical development in production has affected the demand for and conditions of work; has changed the occupational structure, introducing new occupations and eliminating some traditional ones; has remodelled personal and family relationships in relation to work, strengthening mutual dependence as opposed to the family autonomy; and has in these ways introduced an increasingly elaborate organization.

II

On the national scale the post-war period was characterized by the creation of incentives and facilities to increase agricultural

production. This followed three main lines: indirect political regulation of capitalization and credits; regulation of the
market by the control of buying and selling opportunities; and
the guaranteeing of personal efforts by fixed prices for some
agricultural products. At the community level the situation was
also distinguished by three features: dissatisfaction with the pre-
war agricultural conditions, the possibilities of taking advantage
of the above opportunities, and a desire to expand, innovate,
and invest. If we also take into consideration the introduction of
new techniques and agricultural methods, what have been the
positive results after twenty years, and how have these affected
the community? The best way of answering the first question is
probably by the use of figures, though we must remember that
these are round; the sources are informants with a good memory,
papers of the municipality, and the account books of some families.

Economic growth in the town is shown, to some extent, by the
following comparative table.

	1936 (A)	1959 (B)	Increase in % from A to B
	kgs.	kgs.	
Total wheat production	700,000	2,000,000	285
Wheat production per *cahíz*[1] in irrigated land	1,000	1,500	150
Total sugarbeet production	11,000,000	11,000,000	—
	pts.	pts.	
Price per hectare of irrigated good land	6,000	200,000	3,333
Daily wage ordinary	8	70	875
Daily wage extra	12	145	1,200
Rent of good house in main street: per year	500	4,800	960
Rent of inferior house away from main street: per year	200	1,800	900

[1] The agrarian measurement used in the province of Zaragoza, equivalent to
38 ares and 140 milliares. The acre equals 40 ares and 47 centiares. The are equals
119.6 sq. yds. The hectare equals 2.471 acres.

But the cost of living has risen at the same time. This increase
can be estimated by comparing the price of some articles in July
1936 with the price of the same in the summer of 1959, in order

to obtain the index number.[1] The estimation is necessarily rough, not only because individual families have their own standards of expenditure, but chiefly because of the large gap between the two dates at which the data are compared and also because of the small number of articles being considered. Nevertheless, more approximate results can be obtained with the figures corresponding specifically to the town, when applied to the different hierarchical groups already outlined, than if we were to consider figures dealing with the index number of the national cost of living.

If we take a housewife with a husband and two children, whose daily purchases would normally consist of $1\frac{1}{2}$ kgs. of bread, $\frac{1}{2}$ kg of meat and 1 litre of milk, comparing prices in 1936 and 1959 we get an index number of 1,078 (base, July 1936 = 100). So the cost of the above-mentioned articles has risen about 11 times. A suit of a certain quality ordered in the city cost nearly 140 pesetas in 1936; a similar suit in 1959 cost roughly 1900 pesetas, (an increase of 13·57).

How are these figures related to the possibilities of mobility for the different groups, and what do they have in common with their equivalents of the pre-war period? What hierarchical re-adjustment has followed the economic development and what other factors of the life of the community have been in operation at the same time?

The *bracero* lacks property, is only included in the list of *vecinos* by his name, and his daily wage is his only source of income. Until 1936 the daily wage was fixed for labourers who con- tracted their services from year to year on St. Michael's Day. For those who, not being labourers, occasionally offered their services, the wage varied between 8 to 12 pesetas according to the work. The chances of gaining a daily wage in those days was slightly higher than now because modern mechanization was unknown, although the number of available *braceros* and *peones* was also greater; even so, the *campañas*, particularly that of wheat, required outsiders to cope with all the urgent tasks.

By 1959 the conditions of work had changed. A *bracero* could not get a daily wage the year round as a labourer-*criado-*

---

[1] Here I must mention my gratitude to Don Alberto Aráoz, Nuffield College, and Juan Martínez-Alier, St. Antony's College, Oxford, for their help with the prepara- tion of these figures.

attached to a family, because the labourer had been replaced by the machine, which was also a substitute for a great number of daily wages, so that the opportunity of earning them had diminished. During the off-seasons, February to May, the second half of August, September and October—for more than some six months in the year—daily work was not easy to find. During the *campañas*, which cover almost three months in the year, it was easy to earn the second type of daily wage (145 pesetas). From these figures we may infer that a *bracero* who takes on daily work of both types at every possible opportunity, still cannot earn 70 pesetas daily throughout the year.

Here is a table of the opportunities of employment as seen by a *bracero*.

From June to August he can earn:

	80 day wages	(145 pts. per day)		=	11,600 pts.
In September—					
	10 day wages	(70 pts. per day)		=	700 pts.
In October—					
	10 day wages	(70 pts. per day)		=	700 pts.
In November—					
	15 day wages	(70 pts. per day)		=	1,050 pts.
In December—					
	20 day wages	$\left\{ \begin{array}{l} \text{10 at 145 pts. per day} \\ \text{10 at 70 pts. per day} \end{array} \right.$		=	2,150 pts.
In January—					
	15 day wages	(70 pts. per day)		=	1,050 pts.
In February—					
	12 day wages	(70 pts. per day)		=	840 pts.
In March—					
	8 day wages	(70 pts. per day)		=	560 pts.
In April—					
	15 day wages	(70 pts. per day)		=	1,050 pts.
In May—					
	10 day wages	(70 pts. per day)		=	700 pts.
			Total		20,400 pts.

Consequently, the real wage of a *bracero* is an average of 56 pesetas a day (55·89) throughout the year. Of these 56 pesetas he spends a minimum of 40 pesetas daily for rent and basic food. Other essential articles—vegetables, fruit, wine, oil, sugar, fuel—whose cost for four persons nearly always exceeds the remaining 16 pesetas of the wage, still have to be accounted for, not to mention the expenditure in the bar, at the cinema, and on cigarettes and clothing.

In 1936 he spent about 40 per cent of his wages to buy 1½ kilogrammes of bread, ½ kilogramme of meat and a litre of milk; in 1959 these took about 50 per cent (49·28) of his actual wage. To get a suit he has to pay the equivalent of 27 days wages as opposed to 17 in 1936. Though the price of a normal day's wages has risen 9 times (8·75), the price of essential articles has risen about 11 times. In other words, the economic position of the *bracero* has deteriorated.

The lines of social development within the components of this group are therefore clear. The *bracero* could not contend with the rise in prices on his insecure daily wage. He had to seek steady employment independent of variations in the agricultural cycle, and this was not possible locally. The post-war economic structure led to emigration. Zaragoza and Barcelona absorbed the emigrants. But this mobility did not essentially alter the hierarchic structure of the community, for those who left were replaced by immigrants from economically less developed towns.

Nevertheless, if we analyse this particular group we find there has been a certain degree of social development, bearing in mind that the comparison supposes different individuals, separated by more than two decades. Firstly there is the change in the work itself. Conditions of work follow patterns different from those of pre-war days. Then, work demanded more muscular effort, men worked harder without counting the hours, toiling from sunrise to sunset, working as long as was necessary to complete a set task the same day. Now there are always fixed hours and a man will leave often a task incomplete rather than work a few extra minutes. At times this attitude is criticized. Previously there existed a well-defined relationship between master and servant, employer and labourer; today the work of the *bracero* is similar to that of a worker in a factory.

We notice also the appearance of a certain restricted type of emigration which could be classified as 'labour emigration'. About thirty men reside in the town but work outside the municipal district. Half have a stable daily job in the city, returning after the day's work. Others enrol themselves in factories in the city or in farms with extensive cultivation, to which they go daily for various months of the year. All spend the night at home. The remainder go from time to time on contract to French farms. None of this existed before 1936.

Thirdly, there has been a considerable change in what are thought of by this group as the 'necessities'. Clothing is, perhaps, the clearest example. There is no distinction in the shape or quality of clothing among young people, no matter what strata they belong to. Raincoats and overcoats, almost unknown in 1936, are now common possessions. No particular garment is characteristic of any particular section of the community. Anything can be worn by anyone.[1] Expenditure on various forms of amusement shows very different patterns from those of 1936 among the *braceros*. Money spent in the bar, at the cinema, on cigarettes and on outings to the city no longer indicates distinctions in social rank, as far as young people are concerned. In those days one went to the city on foot or by cart; today everybody takes the bus; then it was inconceivable to think of buying a radio set, today each house has one.

To sum up: this section of the community has experienced changes in occupation, emigration and immigration, as well as a definite development in its style of living; we are thus dealing with two distinct forms of a group which performs the same functions.

If the incomes are not sufficient to buy the basic foodstuffs, what is the explanation for the external manifestations of a higher standard of living? Possible answers have already been indicated: subsidiary occupations, stable employment in the city, additional income often being provided by the sons, work in France, and so on; but to all these the increase of debts in the shops and payment by instalments in the city shops should be added. Other possible answers will be discussed later. Finally it is important to point out one characteristic common to both configurations of the group: its distance from the centres of political power. Its own power lies in its working potentialities, considerably reduced by mechanization.

The *peones* were defined as proprietors of less than one hectare of cultivable land. The rise in prices of wheat and sugar-beet

---

[1] In 1553 the singularly curious *Reforma, prohibición y limitación de los vestidos y atavíos de personas, assi hombres, como mugeres en el Reino de Aragón* was promulgated. With the exception of religious vestments, this reformatory measure lays down not only for every social layer but even for every occupation (the document covers forty-three) what garments are not to be worn because they are considered too luxurious. From: *Fueros, Observancias y Actas de Corte del Reino de Aragón* (Zaragoza, 1866), T.I., pp. 372–8.

have left them unaffected because their land produces only for family consumption. Therefore their economic conditions are similar to those of the previous group with the difference that their expenditure on vegetables and fruit is appreciably less, as they are able to obtain all these items, or most of them, from their own land. There are other differences. For example nearly all the *braceros* are newcomers to the town, whereas the *peones* belong to it, which nearly always implies owning a house in it and one or more arable strips of land. This property, in spite of its reduced proportions, along with the house, has kept the parents in the town whilst the children may have emigrated.

Another distinctive feature of this group has been the elevation of some members to the next rank, that of *jornaleros*, by the purchase of land previously rented, through the facilities already referred to. Finally some of them, though proprietors of less than one hectare of land are lessees of one or more fields which, added to those already held, provide them with the same income as those of the *jornaleros*, and they then resemble the latter in almost all respects.

The next group up the scale are the *jornaleros*, proprietors of more than one, but less than three, hectares of arable land. The average *jornalero* possesses five *cahíces* of land, which brought in a net revenue of some 1,770 pesetas in 1936. In 1959 he obtained some 29,995 pesetas from the same amount of land. Taking as a base July 1936 = 100 the index number is a round figure of 1,700.

The actual economic resources of this *jornalero* have increased seventeen times, while the cost of living has only risen eleven times. The *jornalero's* income is further augmented by the equivalent of some seventy working days which he is able to put in during the course of the year. With both sources of revenue his economic situation approaches the economic standard that is considered acceptable in the community. Yet psychologically he is not satisfied, for he is still under some compulsion to offer his labour to those in superior economic categories.

The *jornalero* has not felt the need to emigrate. Once his needs of maintenance and clothing have been covered he still has some money with which to emulate the way of life of higher levels in the community. But his situation, through lack of capital, does not permit him greater economic expansion, even if he had the opportunity of buying more land, which in fact he has not. He can do little more than maintain himself at the same level, with few possibilities of moving up to the next. Indeed his children are more likely, if they do not emigrate, to fall back. To avoid this, eight of these families have sent one of their sons to special centres of instruction subsidized by the State to learn a trade.

In these families, therefore, mobility is characterized not just by a higher standard of living but also by a certain degree of prestige derived from the specialization of the son, who does not work in the fields and already lives, or will live later, in the city. This indicates also a change in the attitude of the parents who in pre-war days did not permit their sons to find work outside the town. Secondly, in relation to mobility, some two dozen *jornaleros* attained the rank of *propietarios* in the early days of post-war expansion. Those who did not take advantage of circumstances then now find that the entrance to the higher level is already closed.

Finally, the tendency of this group to approach the peripheries of power must be emphasized. The ambivalent position of its members as small proprietors and temporary labourers affords them second class positions in the Brotherhood, where they are supposed to look after the interests of the small proprietors, the *braceros* and the *peones*. Actually, several *jornaleros* have joined either the committee of cereal farmers or the committee of sugar-beet growers which function within the Brotherhood.

Post-war economic changes have also favoured the *propietarios*. Let us take as an average *propietario* one who possesses 10 *cahíces* of land, from which in 1936 he obtained a net revenue of 3,170 pesetas and in 1959, 56,960 pesetas: the round index number is 1800.

The net income has increased eighteen times since 1936, (the cost of living eleven times), so the *propietario*, once he has met the inevitable expenditures on food and clothing, has a greater net revenue than the *jornalero* to spend on the new post-war 'necessities'. This group, and *a fortiori*, the one which includes the *pudientes*, has developed a varied list of 'necessities', outstanding among which are the expenses incurred by the ostentatious celebration of weddings, christenings and first communions. At a wedding, after the religious ceremony at the parish church, it is obligatory to invite the guests to a banquet at a good restaurant in the city. Normally the guests number more than two hundred. Also the first communions display features not thought of in 1936. As at a wedding, the guests, though fewer in number, are taken in a coach to a banquet at a hotel in the city. Such liberality is more characteristic of the *pudientes*, but the *propietarios* are already beginning to copy them.

In view of the progressively increasing prices of wheat and sugar-beet, the possibility of auxiliary harvests, the positive difference between revenue and expenditure together with the initial occasion of economic expansion after the civil war and a strong determination to take advantage of the circumstances, it is not surprising that the number of *pudientes* has almost doubled because some two dozen *propietarios* have been able to reach the superior category. But, once the opportunity passed, the possibilities, even for this group, of moving up have remained few, for reasons already alluded to.

In 1936 the *propietario* taken as an example in this analysis had a capital of a little more than 6,000 pesetas in implements and mules. Most of this group owned a mule to work the fields and for haulage. The cost of the animal and maintenance was sufficiently compensated by the money obtained from tasks accomplished by it for others. Today they only possess indispensable instruments, almost all of them manual. As the possession of mules and horses supposes a portion of land set aside for grazing or the cultivation of fodder, as well as slow haulage, mules and horses are disappearing. Transportation and ploughing done by tractor is more economical and efficient. Yet neither the number of hectares cultivated nor the resources of the *propietario* justify the purchase of a tractor. This causes the *propietario* to feel dependent on the *pudiente* whose machinery he needs, a dependence which is not found to such an extent in the *propietario* of pre-war days.

The increase of net gains which may represent those of the majority of the *pudientes* can be seen in the following figures. Their net revenue in 1936 was approximately 7,040 pesetas; in 1959 some 133,740 pesetas. The round index number, (July 1936 = 100) is 1900. The average holding of members of this segment of the community is 10 hectares of arable land.

The *pudiente* of 1936 had a capital of no less than 10,000 pesetas, with at least two mules or horses and instruments. He also had a labourer attached to the house—*criado*. In 1936 it was common practice that the cost of the mules and horses and the wage of the *criado* were refunded by the work done by the team for others who needed them for ploughing and transport, and also through work done for others by the mowing machines or other agricultural machines then owned by the *pudiente*. Today the same norm holds good for the tractor. The tractor, along with the ploughs and instruments that go with it, calls for a capital of some 300,000 pesetas. The annual upkeep of the tractor, some 15,000 pesetas, is regained easily by the work done with it for others, and implies besides a considerable source of income which has not been taken into account in the index number. But whereas the *pudiente* of 1936 sent out his resident farm labourer with the team to increase his revenue, the *pudiente* of 1959 drove the tractor himself or sent his son; he no longer had a resident farm labourer.

This partly explains the difference in the crops grown. More wheat is sown than in 1936, even though one *cahíz* of sugar-beet would bring in about 3,000 pesetas more than one *cahíz* of wheat. But sugar-beet involves more labour, and the difficulty of disposing of labour at the opportune moment: cultivation is therefore, to some extent, conditioned by the shortage of hands.

The affluence of the *pudiente* allows all those distinguishing marks which define his group, the most coveted being travel and the higher education in the city he can afford for his children, and set him apart from the *pudiente* families of 1936.

The *ricos-ricos*, those with a minimum of 20 hectares annually, had no parallel in 1936. Those who hold more than 200 hectares are included in this group, though this may seem disproportionate unless we take into account the fact that this segment of the community only cultivates a fourth of its land annually and dry land lying in mountainous territory constitutes the chief part of its property. In 1959 a minimum net revenue for a *rico-rico* was approximately 295,000 pesetas—some have already invested a capital of approximately a million pesetas in machinery which they hire out for additional income.

The volume of transactions rose to a maximum because of the skill and effort of these *ricos-ricos* who could, and wished to, take advantage of the opportunities afforded by the economic situation. Some of them have two tractors, a threshing machine and a combined-harvester, all of which, efficiently managed, considerably increase the revenue obtained from the land. Moreover, some even go to other towns during the wheat *campaña* where they work for several weeks with their threshing machines. With the revenue obtained from all these undertakings they not only reimburse annual expenditure on the wear and tear of the machinery and the cost of using the same on their own lands, but also acquire a substantial net gain. This is the group which is able to afford one of the highest signs of distinction and of economic power, a car.

We have seen how the manual work of the *braceros* and *peones* has been reduced, becoming less fatiguing during these last twenty years, and also how the working day has been shortened. It is the opposite for some *ricos-ricos*; they, along with their sons, or all the brothers together, work all their extensive lands and drive the machinery themselves when working for others. This is an attitude which is sometimes criticized and which has given rise to a new type of family economic unit.

At the height of the corn season for example the *ricos-ricos*, or rather their sons, work from 3 a.m. till 9 p.m. and occasionally plough their lands and transport their wheat by night; as they work by turns the machines are at rest for very few hours a day. Work on their own lands is really heavy. They make every effort to finish it as soon as possible in order to dedicate themselves fully to the harvesting, transport and threshing of other people's harvests to gain an abundant revenue for themselves. This in fact means that their own *cahíces* will normally produce about 100 kilograms less of wheat. On the other hand the sooner the harvest is completed in the town, the greater the opportunity for contracting their machinery in other towns with less mechanical development.

Belmonte de los Caballeros has an average standard of living superior to the national average for agricultural areas; 'necessary' expenditures by each group are higher than in other rural areas. Outings to the city and holidays within or outside Spain, the number of tractors, cars, electric washing machines, television and wireless sets, expenditure on clothing, bars and cinemas etc., are well above the national average. The following table dealing with tractors is a good example.[1]

Number of tractors per 1,000 hectares of cultivated land

1954	1957	1959	
0·5	1·7	2·1	National average
5	10	14·6	Average in the town

If we now bear in mind that of the 2,182 hectares of arable land possessed by the *vecinos* of the town, some 1,000 hectares of dry land (*monte*) are cultivated for only one year out of every two or even four, the figure for 1959 is some 27 tractors per 1,000 hectares.

The use of fertilizers is still more expressive.[2] In 1957-8, 28 kilogrammes per cultivated hectare were used on a national scale compared with more than 500 kilogrammes per cultivated hectare in the town. Again the number of radio sets in the nation was 63 per 1,000[3] in 1959, whereas in the town it was 175; and the number of motor-cycles per 1,000 was 15 as opposed to 45.[4]

Thus the post-war opportunities for economic expansion in this town, situated in a very fertile area, were fully utilized by the dynamic people who were waiting anxiously for agricultural development. Individual and family effort and initiative combined with new opportunities brought about individual mobility, mobility of groups (those at the extremes of the hierarchic scale), the increase in revenues, changes in the style of life, changes in individual and family attitudes and in most of the criteria which define the groups analysed.

III

Economic fluctuations and social phenomena are closely related, as we have seen. The latter amplify the former and are at the same time consequences of them. Till now the economic

---

[1] *Economic Survey of Europe in 1955* (U.N., Geneva, 1956), p. 139. *Economic Survey of Europe in 1959* (U.N., Geneva, 1960), c. VII, p. 13, table 7.

[2] Ibid., c. VII, p. 14, table 9.

[3] *Economic Survey of Europe in 1958* (U.N., Geneva, 1959), c.V, p. 20.

[4] *El Noticiero* (the newspaper), 12 October 1960, p. 22.

fluctuations as causes of social phenomena have been emphasized; it is now time to bring into relief the incidence of extra-
economic aspects in the economic system.

The economy has clearly been characterized by a high degree
of rationalization, if by this we understand the efficient orientation of effective means to achieve economic ends. Nevertheless,
there remain the marks of tradition and of irrational elements,
by which I mean all those which are not essentially economic in
their orientation or end. These irrational or extra-economic
elements condition the selection of means: they diminish the
effects of technically superior methods and hinder rational
economic processes at times, yet in some circumstances they do
unexpectedly accelerate economic development. It is through
them that the social element fully enters the economic field and
becomes of radical importance in a town that for two decades
has intensified its efforts to rationalize its agriculture and
economy.

I have already mentioned that mechanization began, in a
small way, before the civil war, and that one of the major
obstacles it encountered was the shortage of capital and the
difficulties in obtaining it. Thus some *pudientes* found that they
had to form a group to raise the necessary capital to buy a
threshing machine, but at that time the town was divided into
two antagonistic political parties. As the buyers belonged to the
right wing, some of the left wing bought their own so as not to
have to make use of their opponent's machine. The clash of
political ideas in this case definitely accelerated the process
of mechanization. But shortage of capital was not the only
obstacle. Traditional agricultural methods also exercised their
retarding influence. Then the two tractors in the town worked
solely as engines for the two threshing machines and for the
greater part of the year were locked up in a shed, performing
none of the multiple tasks that they do today, such as ploughing
and transport.

One *pudiente* bought a *maquinilla*—the name given to a relatively small mule or horse-drawn implement which removes, by
means of a share, the weeds that grow between the furrows in
the sugarbeet fields and thus saves monotonous hoeing. Its
introduction immediately gave rise to many discussions about
its efficiency. It is easy to use and today any of the farmers can

handle it, but at that time it did not seem so simple and efficient. The animal drawing it frequently damaged the beet and sometimes it did not seem to operate properly. The residents were definitely in favour of the traditional method, and the innovator frustrated by the machine and even more so by the criticism, threw the machine into the canal. Yet a few days later he pulled it out and resumed its use with fresh determination. Today it would be inconceivable to use the hoe for this task, and a good number of people possess *maquinillas*.

The pattern of all innovation in agricultural methods and implements has followed approximately the same lines. A *pudiente* decides to apply new techniques in his fields; the reaction of others is generally negative and disposed to demonstrate the greater efficiency of the traditional methods. They say of the innovator who fails in his experiments that *ha hecho la risa* (he has made a laughing-stock of himself). The fear of incurring laughter may hinder the development of new methods, but at the same time it prompts a scrupulous study of any innovation before it is introduced. If the change proves successful it is quickly adopted, and acceptance implies its immediate and necessary application, for the contrary would mean *hacer el ridículo* (to make a fool of oneself). It is at these points that the economy, attitudes, and values converge and influence each other.

The impulse towards rationalization during the post-war period did not entirely prevent the social, under the forms of customs and ideas, from intruding upon the economic field. This is the reason for certain phenomena of *gaspillage* that are still to be found. It is not necessary to emphasize that the determination of the *peones* and even of some of the *jornaleros* to preserve the tiny strips of land they have inherited is uneconomic. Productivity is low because all tasks have to be done by hand, and the property is usually intended to produce for home consumption only. The owners suffer periodically from unemployment. Even so, sentimental attachments and lack of initiative prevent the rural exodus that a more rational economy would demand.

A certain feeling of personal dignity often limits an increase in the income of a family when it is in fact needed by the household. It is difficult for a *pudiente* looking for a servant girl to be able to find her in the town, where there are several young women without work in families that really need an increased income, for to serve is humiliating, especially since the civil war, and the girls would always prefer to work for somebody unknown in the city. Mowing the alfalfa with a scythe is an energetic, muscular task which is considered degrading. The mower receives 145 pesetas per *cahíz* mowed. The ordinary daily wage, when there are possibilities of working, is only 70 pesetas, but the 145 pesetas are not a sufficient incentive for most unemployed *braceros*. This sense of personal dignity operates at all levels of the community according to definite and distinctive patterns. It does not befit the daughter of every *jornalero* and still less the daughter of a *propietario* to mingle with feminine groups of inferior categories to work in the fields doing tasks which are considered fit for the female sex, even when the girl has little to do at home and her family needs the salary she would gain. The son of a *propietario* would not think of earning daily wages once he has finished work on his father's plots. The whole family would feel humiliated, for people would think that the family was in need of the money.

Transactions with banks have revealed a sequence of tensions and doubts during the past two decades. Those who bought the threshing machine before the war did not apply for credit to a bank. Anybody who needed money would resort to people within the family circle or to intimate friends. The bank was an unknown entity, dangerous and risky to deal with. There were no branches in the town and if any family saved money it was normally guarded with much care in the house.

Some families vacillated for a time despite new opportunities and persisted in their old economic habits. But faced with the alternatives of adapting to the new tendencies or of stagnating —with all that that implied—most families proved capable of revising traditional ideas. Today it is normal to apply to the bank. The volume of transactions of a single branch of a bank in 1959 was almost a million pesetas in the form of letters of exchange and exceeded the 700,000 pesetas put into savings accounts.

Yet the old personal and family reserve in all financial dealings still persists, now in new forms, especially among those defined as *pudientes*. Instead of collecting the proceeds of the sale of wheat or sugar-beet from one of the branches in the town they frequently prefer to go to the city so as to prevent the branch officer finding out how much they realized from the sale and how much they deposited in the bank. If they need to draw out money from their accounts, again they go to the city when they could accomplish the transaction at the branch of their own bank in a few minutes. By these means nobody knows for certain the quantity of money that they possess and thus they avoid the danger of being accredited to an inferior segment. A head of a family applied for credit in order to celebrate the marriage of his daughter according to his rank. People said: 'Who would have thought that a household like that would have needed to borrow money from the bank for a wedding!'

In the summer of 1947 there was a drought, the worst for years. The fields needed water, though at best that would only have saved half the crops. A procession was organized to the hermitage, men carrying the image of the Virgin, the Patroness of the town. As the rains still did not come only then did they begin to dig wells, the tractor engines working day and night. In the *huerta*—irrigated land—there were wells everywhere, and some of them are still usable and indeed in good order, so that if another drought were to recur they would probably resort directly to the wells and tractors instead of marching in another procession.[1] All these examples seem to indicate that after hesitating between traditional forms and more efficient ways of solving problems, it is the latter that prevail.

IV

Is it possible to detect any connexion in time between the ancient configuration of 'classes', as seen in the parish and Council archives, and the different groups that exist today?[2]

Firstly, the possession—or non-possession—of arable lands and agricultural implements was, we found, the fundamental criterion of stratification in the past. This criterion remains in the present structure of the community and one cannot question its force, but today it is not quite so fundamental. University students and pupils of military academies and special schools

---

[1] As they did during a drought in the summer of 1965.
[2] See pp. 62–3 above.

have created a new basis of prestige; they form a social level *sui generis*. Again, the male and female servants of whom the documents speak have disappeared.

Secondly, we saw that within the community it was difficult to move from one category to another. In this respect there have been many changes since the civil war. The constituents of each category are now radically different; the *pudiente* of 1930, for example, probably had more in common with the *pudiente* of the last three centuries than with the *pudiente* of 1959. And also ascent and descent has become possible in the hierarchical system, and there has been a renewal of the components which make up the lowest levels of the community.

Alongside these innovations which followed a more or less slow and peaceful rhythm there appears the violent upheaval of the republican period, which aimed at subverting the hierarchic system in complete opposition to historical continuity. Now that this period has passed and the structural possibilities of further mobility have been almost exhausted, the patterns which dictated the communal hierarchy and ascribed definite functions to each segment have resumed their former course. Landownership has once again become the differentiating principle.

Thirdly, there was a marked emphasis on the economic strata as such in the papers of the archives. In the above-mentioned upheaval, political stratification, in the sense of the political parties, was uppermost, but today the ancient differential principle has again come to the fore. As in the past the *vecinos acomodados*—prosperous residents—represent the continuity of the traditional values in the *pueblo*. They form, after a period of eclipse under the Republican regime, the dynamic group which controls the community, wields the political power and sets the example for correct conduct. These citizens continue to possess the means of production, and are those who have been responsible for technical changes. As in the past too, belonging to the *clase jornalera*—the lower orders—implies a certain aversion to the traditional values, a passive part in the life of the community, absence from the centres of power, and a lower education.

For how long will these characteristics accurately define the strata of the community? The better education received by the sons of some *jornaleros* in the city, preparing them for skilled occupations, will partially weaken the correlation between wealth and education, and the turner in the city and the clerk working in a bank will consider themselves, in fact do consider themselves, superior to their friends in the *pueblo*, though their economic standing may be inferior. Further, as there are still surplus hands to work the plots, it is probable that in the coming years the number of those employed in different skilled occupations, with residence in the city, will rise; so the *jornaleros* (for they provide the greatest number of sons for new occupations) will crystallize in a new configuration, at least in terms of prestige.

But the incidence of new hierarchic configurations has not permanently affected the framework of stratification. It has been very variable in both volume and intensity—slow in the last few centuries, with little change until 1930; violent and sudden from 1931 to 1936, and finally accelerated but without convulsions in the post-war period. The present configuration of strata reproduces, with the changes already mentioned, the main lines of stratification which have developed over the last few centuries.

It will be seen that those structural changes which signified a radical departure from the traditional pattern of the hierarchic system had no lasting effect, whereas those new elements which were either neutral or fitted in or else were gradually introduced, have definitely been incorporated into the system. This means that the recasting of the hierarchy during the last twenty years has been adapted to ancient forms, though the members of the community had not the slightest historical knowledge of them; yet they rejected the recasting of the Republican period which they remembered perfectly. While the ancient, unknown patterns have endured, the recent ones have not exercised any permanent influence. Thus a constant pattern, undergoing a process of accidental variations over a long period, constitutes the infrastructure which upholds the hierarchic system and has remained basically unchanged.

We saw how the clerks, writing up the municipal Minutes, grouped the *medianos contribuyentes*—those of average means—in a general category, without any clearly defined limits. The same difficulty in defining intermediate strata has occurred again and again in these pages. My first attempt revealed seven social layers; setting aside one, six were studied in relation to land-ownership, four in connexion with political power, and in the final pages the categories have practically dissolved into such phrases as 'those of the superior levels' or 'those of the inferior strata', i.e. into two groups; two extreme groups, well-defined as the 'rich' and the 'poor', which imply a middle group without clear outlines. Thus the enumeration of levels in a community is a relative matter depending on the topic considered.

This constitutes what may be called the morphology of the hierarchic system, which can only make sense when we take into account the principles that animate it. Hierarchic forms and external signs always imply an emotional content, a system of evaluations, of which very little has been said so far. This theme will be discussed later.

VII

FAMILY

'Donde la mujer suele estar como en España . . . en su puesto, es decir en su casa, cerca del fogón y consagrada al cuidado de sus hijos, es ella la que casi siempre domina, hasta imprimir el sello de su voluntad a la sociedad entera. El verdadero problema es allí el de la emancipación de los varones, sometidos a un régimen maternal demasiado rígido. La mujer perfectamente abacia en la vida pública es voz cantante y voto decisivo en todo lo demás . . . matriarcado español'   MACHADO

I N the preceding pages brief references have already been made to the family in its broadest sense. Now the sociological content of the word family—*familia*—needs to be considered more precisely. It is an essential theme in the study of the social structure of any community, and particularly important when referring to the family in a small Spanish town, the positive characteristics of which are well known, whilst the negative side, the tensions and conflicts, are rarely mentioned. Yet the latter are just as important and the true character of the domestic community can only be captured by analyzing both. For this reason the emphasis in the pages that follow will be on the family as a centre of tension and conflict.

I

The word family can, of course, refer to anything from conjugal unity to any wider group of people. When a resident says *mi familia*, the real meaning of the word has to be inferred from the context of the conversation. It may be equivalent to the nuclear family, composed initially of spouses, and later of spouses with their offspring. For many purposes the Civil Code[1]

---

[1] Título IV, chap. 1 & 2.

considers the nuclear family as a unique legal personality. The Law of Local Regulations classifies the residents in the community or municipal district as 'heads of families', *vecinos*, and those domiciled in the town.[1] For the purposes of law, and in so far as it interests us here, the heads of families are those who have come of age or who are emanicipated minors, under whose control, for reasons of kinship or personal domestic service, other people dwell together in the same household.[2] The head of the family is its legal representative, and in this capacity he enjoys the rights that the law recognizes as his due; at the same time he must fulfil all the obligations and services attached.[3] He is the point of contact through which the family participates in the benefits and duties of the community. Finally the head of the family as such has the vote to elect a third of the members of the Council. His legal position is thus unique in the community; he possesses *de jure* authority over his wife and children.

This legal superiority of the husband—for if alive he is always the head of the family—is reinforced in many ways. The system of holding property is an example. In the municipal land office the property of both spouses is normally entered under the husband's name; it is always he who is called by the Council to deal with any matter which may arise. The wife refers all final decisions, especially when talking to others, to her husband. To any question asked by someone outside the family she replies, 'it depends on what my husband says'. The husband is the lord and it is he who decides in principle all questions relating to property, plots, improvements, trips, the education and employment of the children, dowries, etc. The woman is conscious of the subordination which from olden times has been associated with her position. It is interesting to see how strictly the principles which according to the moralists of the sixteenth century ought to govern married life have been maintained. Luis de León insists repeatedly that 'to serve the husband appertains to the estate and office of the married woman';[4] that 'she has to obey and serve him in everything';[5] and that it is the duty of the wife 'always to please her husband'.[6] Juan Luis Vives

[1] Art. 42.   [2] Art. 43, 1.   [3] Art. 46.
[4] Luis de León: *La Perfecta Casada*, Colleción Austral, 7a ed., p. 9.
[5] Ibid., p. 76.   [6] Ibid., p. 46.

corroborates this with examples and reiterates that practice, custom, all institutions, all laws divine and human, and Nature herself expressly ordain that the wife is subject to the husband and must obey him.[1] He says to the married woman: 'in conjugal love there has to be a strong compound of worship, reverence, obedience and veneration'.[2] What is more, to him 'wild and imprudent is the woman who does not take orders from her husband'.[3] The husband, 'using his right', can 'heavily' chastise his wife.[4] About women he says: 'as maidens they serve their fathers; when married they serve their husbands; when mothers their sons'.[5] Married women refer to their status today in identical fashion.

Two points must be made clear. The husband derives his authority and position before the law from his automatic status as 'head of a family'; and all the weight of tradition reinforces the position of the husband as the lord of the family, of the house, and of everything that belongs to both spouses. The woman must obey and serve her husband. These are the two general patterns, the ideology which governs the relations between spouses, the tenets which no one questions. But in fact these are the public aspects of this relationship: they are only in force outside the front door. Within the house we find that practice is not the daughter of the theory.

II

In the first place, a strictly defined dichotomy of duties implies a certain partition of authority. The primary responsibility of the husband is to be the breadwinner for his wife and children. 'The man is obliged to work in order to secure'[6] and 'the diligent father of a family' ought to be 'solicitous to gather riches',[7] are two fragments from the sixteenth century which condense the code of behaviour for the husband. The specific activity of the head of the family is centred on work in the fields. Everything relating to the care and cultivation of the plots, such

[1] Juan Luis Vives: *Institutio Foeminae Christianae*, Aguilar vol. I, p. 1085.
[2] Ibid., p. 1085. About obedience of the wife to her husband see also: *De officio mariti*, Aguilar vol. I, pp. 1301 and 1302.
[3] Vives *Institutio Foeminae Christianae*, p. 1086.
[4] *De officio mariti*, vol. I, p. 1338.   [5] Ibid., p. 1340.
[6] Luis de León, op. cit., p. 124.   [7] Vives: op. cit., p. 1335.

as seeds, fertilizers, crops, instruments, and all kinds of transactions, belong unquestionably to the man. At dawn the husband goes to the plots, he returns for lunch, and then labours again until dark. Once he has changed and tidied and until suppertime—9 p.m. in winter and around 11 p.m. in summer—he converses about the day's work with his usual group of friends. He enquires about and discusses the techniques of farming, he may seek help for some undertaking or try to find out the latest measures issued by the Brotherhood of Farmers or the Syndicate of Irrigation. The following day the sunrise sees him going again to the plots. His smallholding is his dominion, the object of his hopes and fears, his daily life.

Within the house, in the domestic sphere, male absenteeism is absolute because—as Vives says—'the thoughts of the husband are by nature intent upon superior matters than with these small cares and household chores';[1] and further, 'it does not become his condition',[2] as domestic duties and care of the family 'are the concern of the woman.'[3] The house, therefore, is the undisputed realm of the woman. The wife looks after the children, and if they are of school age gets them ready for school. She washes up, sweeps the doorstep, goes shopping and cooks. She arranges the rooms in the house and washes and mends the clothes. Never under any circumstance does the husband take any part in this daily routine. If his wife is unable to, either his or her mother or sisters or female relations, or any one of the neighbours, will perform these tasks. If the wife goes to the city she leaves the lunch already prepared for her husband, or he goes to the house of one of his relations—agnate or cognate. At about midday he returns from the plots for lunch; the wife is engaged in putting the finishing touches to the meal. She sets the table and attends to the wants of the children. Meanwhile he waits at the door of the house, chatting to his neighbours or reading the newspaper until summoned to lunch by his wife. He never has any share whatsoever in these 'small cares' and if during lunch he sees that a knife or a glass or wine is needed he will indicate this to his wife but will not fetch it himself, even if she is feeding the children as well as herself. It is inconceivable

---

[1] Ibid., p. 1263. [2] Luis de León, op. cit., p. 35.
[3] Ibid., pp. 35, 54, 67, 73, 75–76, 98, 120, 124; and Vives, op. cit., pp. 1005, 1033, 1106, 1134, 1135, 1278, etc.

that the male should go shopping. Such tasks are feminine by nature.

This rigid dichotomy of labour assumes that the natural, reasonable and befitting status of any adult male is the married one. Life is very difficult for a bachelor who works his plots and keeps house for himself. His meals, the washing and repair of his clothes, and the care of his house all present a serious problem. The bachelor in these conditions is considered an 'unfortunate being' who 'goes about uncared for and ill-kempt'. Eventually he has to resort to one of his sisters or nieces to get his household tasks done. A respected widower of advanced years, without children or brothers and sisters, eats with a different niece every day of the week so that he is well looked after and at the same time he is not a burden to any one of them in particular. Only in these exceptional cases may the man attend to some of these 'small cares' himself.

It falls exclusively to the woman to choose, buy and arrange the furniture, utensils, furnishings and linen, to decide for what purpose each room is to be used, and to carry out any alterations in the house. On one occasion when a new house was being built, the masons undid what the husband had ordered several times because the result was not to the liking of the wife; the husband's directions were always subsequently verified with the wife and every time the husband gave in to her wishes.

The man is entirely unfamiliar with the lay-out of his own house, or at least he has no clear idea of what there is or where things are. Sometimes he cannot change his shirt to go out because his wife is not in and she has forgotten to leave his change of clothes ready; or else he cannot change his clothes because his wife has taken the key of the cupboard with her; or even if the key is in the house he is not sure which clothes to put on, and in any case he will not be able to make up his mind what to wear; or if he can, he still does not know where to find the clothes. He knows he would be involved in the same sort of perplexities if—an absurd hypothesis—he decided to cook for himself. Today the saying of J. Luis Vives is still as strong as ever: 'The kitchen is a more appropriate place for the woman than for the man, in which she is the sole and absolute queen'.[1]

[1] Vives, op. cit., p. 1320.

When she thinks fit they both go to the city to buy a suit for the husband. The choice of the season, day, shop, quality, colour, tailor and cut is also determined by the wife.

The wife is not only responsible for the choice of her own clothes and those of her husband and children but also for the interior and exterior decoration of the house, paints for the facade and rooms, curtains, flowerpots in the balconies, pictures, images of saints, framed photographs, and so on. Her life is centred round the house; it is essential to the activity of the wife, incidental to that of the man. As a result the house bears the hall-mark of feminity, it expresses feminine sensibility and taste.

Since the wife also holds the keys of the cupboards in which the money is kept, she disposes of the family wealth. This is the second characteristic of her estate and office, to keep and administer diligently the earnings of the husband.[1]

The domestic community involves the full sharing in the use and consumption of the goods both spouses have brought in. But what is now important to point out is not so much the communal character of possession but its strongly matriarchal aspect. For any purchase or sale of moderate importance in relation to the plots or agricultural implements—a typical masculine business—if it is not the wife's idea in the first place her consent is required. Again, if she believes any improvement is necessary in the house, even if it is expensive, it will be carried out. It is normally she who goes to collect the wages earned by her husband and sons; otherwise they hand over their whole wage to her themselves. As housewife she pays the rates and taxes, electricity bills, the monthly contributions to the doctor and doctor-assistant, etc. and she is the one who determines how much her family will give to charities and good works. The husband takes no part at all in domestic finances.

In her domestic budget she retains *carte blanche*, the husband being completely ignorant about prices of daily necessities. It would be impossible for him, even assuming, he wanted to, to control the expenditure of his wife. She distributes to the children what she considers a suitable amount every Sunday and every Feast day. It varies according to the age of the

---

[1] Luis de Léon, op. cit., pp. 34, 37, 54, and Vives, op. cit., p. 1032.

children and the importance of the occasion. The single son does not enjoy private means even on the eve of his wedding. All his earnings go straight into the cupboard whose key lies in his mother's pocket. In turn she provides for all his needs. What is more, when the husband wants money to go to the bar or to buy tobacco, she gives it to him, or in some cases he asks for the key and takes what he wants. Finally, she always keeps some petty cash hidden which comes in from the sale of eggs, hens, or rabbits. Vives sums up this dichotomy as follows: 'the lord of the full house is the husband . . . the wife is as the governor';[1] or we could say that the authority belongs *de jure* to the husband, *de facto* to the wife.

The borderline marking this division of labour is uncertain. This is not because the male transgresses the boundaries of the work assigned to his lot; it is the woman who invades the zone of activity in principle considered masculine. Thus at home the woman looks after the farmyard and milks the cows, if there are any, and these are jobs which would be done by the man if he was in the house. Beyond the precincts of the house she goes to the plots, thinning and cleaning the sugar-beet, piling the cotton and maize, gathering the alfalfa, piling the sheaves and lending a hand during the threshing of the corn. Feminine intervention in this masculine occupation is inevitable during any harvest, and in view of the inadequate economic power of the participants. Today, however, the women are giving place to the men in this intermediate zone, due not only to increasing agricultural mechanization but also to the desire of the women to distinguish themselves from those who are compelled to resort to such toil in order to swell the family income. The post-civil war economic affluence has increased the number of females whose activities are strictly confined to the house.

Thus conjugal unity implies a distributive system of authority based on a differentiation of labour according to sex and tradition. Authority, work, routine and residence are divided and separated into subordinate functions which complement each other and are integrated into the conjugal unity. This is one of the principal functions, of basic importance, ascribed to the nuclear family. A childless couple or an aged widower or widow

---

[1] Vives, op. cit., p. 1327.

do not fall into the category of *desgraciado*—unfortunate being.
But a bachelor does, because 'he has nobody to look after him
or his house'; he lacks the feminine complement to accomplish
those tasks befitting the weaker sex and which he needs done.
The connotation of 'unfortunate being' is: 'he does not eat
properly', 'he is badly dressed', 'his house is untidy and dis-
ordered', and so on. The man, wrote Fray Luis,[1] 'cannot assist
in the house, cannot take care of household matters, it does not
become his dignity. . . . while the husband is in the plots, the
wife must serve in the house . . . her own nature ordains that
this duty is a woman's duty . . . . So Nature . . . united them so
that, helping each other according to their respective conditions, those who could not maintain themselves alone, maintain
each other in comfort . . . —a beneficial and sweet harmony'.[2]

Though the woman may at times assume a masculine role,
I have not found any ethnographic material which shows masculine encroachment into female territory. It is always the
woman who crosses the boundary, overstepping the line of her
specific activity. She intervenes, though indirectly, in all and
any activity which concerns the family, so that everything is
permeated by the feminine influence.

During lunch while the mother comes and goes between the
table and the kitchen the father and son talk about the sowing
of the wheat. The husband thinks that, prudently following a
rotation of crops, it would be best to sow all the wheat in the
hills and to use the plots in the *huerta*—irrigated land—for
other crops. The son is of the same opinion. Till now the dialogue has taken place between father and son, the wife remaining silent, but as she thinks the decision taken is incorrect, she
intervenes: 'The crop of the hills is not certain; if you do not
sow wheat in the *huerta* as well, what are we going to do next
year?' Of course in the end wheat is sown in the *huerta* although,
according to the judgment of the father, the plots are not in the
right condition. He is not accustomed to take any important
decision without first consulting his wife. Her judgment is generally imposed in any kind of transaction. A husband ordered

[1] Ibid., p. 35.
[2] Compare with Montesquieu, *De l'Esprit des Lois* (Garnier, Paris, 1956), vol.
I, p. 118: "*Il est contre la raison et contre la nature que les femmes soient maîtresses dans la maison.*"

a cow and paid the retaining fee stipulated by the deal; when his wife saw the animal she thought the bargain a poor one; the husband cancelled the verbal contract, automatically losing the quantity already paid. I could fill many pages with examples corroborating the preponderance of the female criterion in all aspects of family activity, so that the ideal 'beneficial and sweet harmony' of Fray Luis gives way to the everyday state of affairs in which the husband yields his authority in favour of his wife. This concession is never admitted in theory, as it is always the husband who gives orders; or as expressed in popular terms, 'The husband commands in the house, when his wife is not at home'.

III

Solidarity and affection in the nuclear family is something so evident that it does not require illustration. It is enough to keep in mind always that mutual affection reaches its fullest expression in the family with the wife-mother as the fountain from which the affection springs and to which it returns. For the parents no sacrifice is too great. They work as hard as they can, taking the utmost pains to provide a secure future for their children, to leave them a large inheritance, to afford them a higher education, at all costs. Although the domestic budget cannot stretch to new clothes, for special occasions their children will have them; they will buy toys for them at Christmas, although they themselves may have to forgo the necessities of life.

The children grow up under the direct care of the mother until they leave school. The boy then joins his father in the cultivation of the plots. The daughter takes an active part in the running of the house. Both—although the boy only indirectly—continue under the tutelage of the mother until they marry. She controls, or tries to control, the behaviour of her children. The father rarely intervenes in the control of his son, but he intervenes frequently in that of his daughter. When the mother rebukes her children severely she appeals to the authority of the father, whom they fear more. Since they were small the children have been scolded all day long by the mother, so they have grown accustomed to her remonstrances. If the son persists in being disobedient the mother threatens him by saying: 'I'll

tell your father when he comes home'. The father is responsible for maintaining authority, for reprimanding the
children for more serious misdeeds; then he is severe and
punishes the children.

When the boy is about sixteen he begins to show a sporadic
interest in the opposite sex. With a group of friends of his own
age he goes dancing at night—11 p.m. to 3 am.—during the
festivals in the neighbouring towns. These trips require permission which the mother does not like to grant herself, feeling that
it is a matter for her husband. The son, accustomed to seek any
sort of permission from his mother, finds that from this moment
he has to refer all his demands to his father. He in turn follows
the rulings of his wife. The mother exercises her authority over
her son through her husband who reinforces her judgment.
The authority of both governs the conduct of the children until
they are married. The latter possess little initiative of their
own. In the plots they carry out the work as the father orders;
in the house the mother rules everything.

A special deference is due to the father as head of the family
and centre of authority. One external form of demonstrating
this deference consists of not smoking in his presence. The
son smokes in front of his mother and the father knows that once
lunch is finished the son goes to the street to join his friends and
to light a cigarette, but he will not tolerate his son smoking in
front of him until he has completed his military service. The
unmarried son also avoids going to a café or bar when he knows
his father is there, he tries to persuade his friends to go to another
bar. In a group of friends it is almost certain that one or other
of their fathers will be in the bar or café and in these circumstances it is impossible for the sons to feel at ease. They do not
think it is correct to sing, to shout or to let themselves go. Vice-
versa paternal dignity requires that the father does not go to
the bar where his son is already. If he sees his son coming in he
will endeavour to go to another room, or if he is not with guests
he will find an excuse to leave. Young married couples normally
go dancing during the festivals in the town, but when their
children reach the early teens and begin dancing themselves
they oust their parents from the dance floor. In their first
flirtings boys and girls take care that their respective parents
never see them because such a situation would injure the respect

due to parents and cause mutual embarrassment. Moreover
they fear the rebuke which usually follows. At the same time the
parents begin to respect the son who is studying, a respect
which increases as his studies progress because 'he knows more
than they'.

The familiarity of intercourse which is supposed to govern all
relationships between the members of the nuclear family has a
notable exception. The son says nothing, especially to his father,
about problems of the heart; on the contrary, he tends to prevent his parents from knowing anything and he never consults
them in matters of sex. Such a conversation with parents *da
vergüenza* (causes shame). Frequently a couple are considered to
be courting—*novios*—in the town, and their respective parents
are aware of it, but the son will never have mentioned it to his
parents. If the mother disapproves of the match it will be she
who brings up the subject.

A similar code governs the conduct of brothers towards each
other. They systematically avoid any conversation about sex or
any comments about girls. No intimacy is possible in this field
but rather the opposite: reserve, distance, mutual respect. Each
one lives in his own sentimental world in which his friends may
share but never his parents or brothers. Two brothers whose age
difference is slight and who form part of the same circle of
friends, treat each other as complete strangers in the group.
One night the group may decide to go dancing at the festivals of
a neighbouring town; once there each brother goes his own way,
accompanying any other of the group to drink or to invite the
girls to dance. By custom the boys always go in pairs to invite
the girls, but the brothers never act together. Another night, at
dusk the group may go for a stroll in the main street; on this
stroll the brothers never walk side by side, there is always someone between them. Their relations are characterized by the
absence of that familiarity, confidence and friendship which
they enjoy with their friends; a gravity and distance mark the
attitudes they adopt towards each other. In economic matters
and agricultural tasks they are always strongly united. Almost
every day they labour together in the plots at work which requires cooperation; yet the hours elapse without even small talk
between them. This distance between brothers is accentuated
if the age gap is wider. If the father is absent the eldest brother

always takes his place when it is necessary to make any decision in problems arising out of work. His vicarious authority is accepted by the younger brother. If both had planned to go to the festivals in the city on the same date and one of them has to stay behind in the house, it is the eldest who takes priority and goes to the city. If both spend a day in the city each one will go to a different dance-hall or cinema. 'One has a better time with one's friends than with one's brother'. 'One enjoys oneself more and spends more freely with friends than with a brother', they repeat.

Brother and sister, on the other hand, enjoy the closeness and confidence that the brothers lack. She is the one who possesses the least initiative in the house. When at night her brothers go to the cinema or dancing in other towns she is always left at home. Her brothers try to use her as a medium for obtaining whatever they want from their parents—money, clothes, trips, etc.

In this sub-system of interfamily relations, tensions are counteracted and rechannelled into patterns of behaviour. The authority of the father is acknowledged by the deference which the son shows him on the one hand and by the distance he keeps from his son on the other. This authority affects the daughter to a minor degree because of her lesser initiative, as much in her private affairs as in her domestic occupations. The family integration can be endangered not only by the lack of paternal authority and by filial disrespect but in a more radical way by the romantic escapades of the son. It is always the father who reprimands the son for any misconduct in this sense. Moreover the father as head of the family represents the family cohesion. The son disturbs the family cohesion by philandering with the opposite sex. Thus it is not possible to find any familiarity between father and son in their diversions nor any dialogue on problems of the heart. Father and son represent opposite forces and displace each other in both fields.

The vicarious authority, in the strict sense of the elder brother over his younger brother(s), the mutual respect, the distance between them, produces, though to a lesser degree, the same result. The daughter, being most of the time in the house, offers a minor challenge to the family cohesion. Moreover until some years ago her marriage was to some extent prepared by her mother as she thought convenient. The daughter's departure from the sphere of the nuclear family followed patterns which did not challenge paternal authority and which foretold harmonious relations with her husband's family. Towards his sister the brother does not need external norms of respect because they are united by a closer intimacy and are sometimes the confidants of each other's love affairs. The family, therefore, preserves its integration through the regulation of tensions inherent within it. Authority-reverence-affection is an inseparable syndrome, at the same time antagonistic to the syndrome amusements-sex-familiarity of intercourse. The one excludes the other. The former, together with economic solidarity, constitutes the focal point of the family; the latter represents the forces of dispersion.

The third factor contributing to the internal cohesion of the family is the economic solidarity of its members, which can be discussed under three headings. (1) One of the essential constituents of the family is property; a family is equivalent to the possession of a smallholding and a smallholding signifies a family. The son does not marry until his father gives him one or several plots to work. Later on he and his brothers and sisters will inherit all the plots which belonged to their forefathers and will in turn be bequeathed to their descendants. If he does not possess any land he feels he no longer has a part in the town and emigrates. When a father possesses few plots the son goes to the city in search of work. The family loses consistency. A man's right to the land rests upon his being a member of a family. Land and family thus combine to form a tight union which embraces and unites all the members of the family, who strive together to keep and if possible enlarge their holding. (2) Economic solidarity amounts in the second place to the common use and consumption of all the family's goods. Every member contributes to the common patrimony according to his age or sex. It is a collective business, each person contributing to and participating in the benefits; the family is identified with agricultural exploitation or, in other words, with the family economy. (3) Finally, together with the internal cohesion, which is implied by economic solidarity, a parallel external cohesion develops, i.e. a cohesion of the family in opposition to any outside member of it. The consequences of this 'cohesion against' the foreign element are of great importance in the analysis of the relation of the nuclear family with other degrees of kinship.

IV

In the second place family is synonymous with kinship. Kinship is the bond which, in respect to an individual, unites each one of the ancestors, descendants and co-laterals of his family by consanguinity and affinity. Taking 'ego' as a basis in practice its kinship embraces these two zones: (a) from the grandparents to the grandchildren through its line, i.e. five generations on the one hand, and on the other, collaterally till its second cousins and the sons and daughters of uncles and aunts in second degree. (b) Kinship by affinity is more restricted. It includes the family of orientation of the husband or wife. The remaining members who compose kinship of the husband or wife of 'ego' in the sense first defined fall into the category of 'the family of my wife" or 'of my husband'.

The cohesion of kinship in general is weak and flexible. It acquires a certain expression in mutual assistance—the lending of agricultural tools, for instance—which generally though not according to any clearly defined pattern follows the ramifications of kindred. The *rites de passage* are occasions when the fullest implications of kinship are realized. Also people tend to favour their kindred when selling plots or houses; they give them first refusal. The relations of kinship are effectively recognized towards uncles, aunts, and first cousins who are addressed as 'uncle' or 'cousin'; with uncles and cousins in the second degree the ties are weaker and the appellation is frequently omitted. At weddings all the first cousins but not necessarily all the second cousins are invited, although they are notified of the wedding. However a man would join a fight to defend a cousin in second degree.

Deudo is another word which signifies kinship. From the Latin *debitus—debere*—it is equivalent to being a debtor which brings into relief the network of obligations and duties involved by kinship. Nowadays the word has been divested of its initial content and the functions which used to be part of the bonds of kinship have undergone a process of development along other lines so that its cohesive force has been diminished. Familiarity of intercourse can be deeper among families only united by bonds of friendship. Both families express their relationship with the phrase: *nos tratamos como familia* (we treat each other as family). The popular proverb says: 'close friendship makes kinship'. In this case there may be more friendly cooperation between the families concerned than with their respective kin. Between kindred most people have more in common with some of their relations than with others; economic power, temperament, similarity of ideas and personal likings sometimes exert a stronger force than kinship itself, and the same happens through associations with neighbours and friends made in the bar or café. To all this it is necessary to add that the fiercest hatreds and the most violent quarrels occur among members of a family. This prompts a sketch of the flexibility of family affection through another meaning of the word family, a meaning which completely identifies the family with the land, with property, with the economic.

V

The third meaning of the word *familia* refers in a wide sense to a constellation which encloses three nuclear families together with the spouses of all the married members: the families of orientation and procreation of 'ego' and the family of orientation of his or her spouse. This constellation can be symbolized by the following diagram.

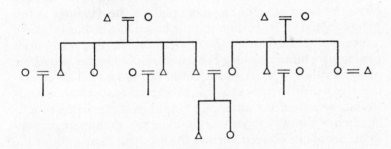

Secondly, and more narrowly, it refers to the family of orientation and of procreation of 'ego', but as 'ego' is married, his or her spouse includes another social cell, i.e. her or his family of orientation, in the nuclear family sphere.

The marriage of the son or daughter alters the unity of affection, the economic unity and in most cases the unit of residence of the family of orientation. If this step in the life of an individual

were a purely personal one it would not be relevant sociologically; but the transition is invested with structural characteristics which automatically incorporate and adjust it first of all to
the system of relationships of kindred, and secondly to the pattern of inheritance. This last in its turn unites the three families
owing to the fact that there is now a bilateral system in the sense
that 'ego' inherits from his own family of orientation and then
from the family of orientation of his or her spouse. To this right
of inheritance corresponds the obligation of both families of
orientation to provide economically for the incipient family of
procreation. What really matters here is that each spouse occupies a key position due to a simultaneous membership of three
families. Through him, or her, the three are interlocked in a
complicated structure of relationships, rights, obligations and
tensions.

The marriage of a son or daughter includes an economic
readjustment in the respective families of orientation of the
spouses. The *donatio propter nuptias* demands that the family of
the husband provides him, if not with legal ownership, at least
with the use of one or several plots or with some other means of
living. The wife must contribute an *ajuar* (furnishings and linen),
with which to set up the new home even if the newly wedded
couple are not going to live by themselves in a house of their
own. The bestowal of one or more plots on the daughter at this
point is optional. By custom it is the husband who has to afford
a means of subsistence for the new family. But frequently if his
parents give him something her parents will offer her something
of equal value *por no ser menos* (not to be outdone). This emula-
tive tournament reaches its height when the marriage has off-
spring, because if the paternal grandparents regale the grandchildren with toys or clothes, the maternal grandparents consider themselves obliged to enter the lists with more gifts for the
grandchildren.

The early symptoms of tension between the three families
stem from the two old families of orientation, both of whom in
turn stir up the family of procreation. Here the main part is
played by the temperament of the respective parents or rather
of the respective mothers, the more or less pronounced tendency
to interfere in the affairs of the new home, the reaction of the
spouses, etc.; but the key to the incipient friction between the

three families is usually economic. There are two focuses of friction: the parents—especially the mothers—of both families of orientation, and the spouses of the family of procreation in relation to their brothers and sisters through whom they affect their parents. The first series of conflicts arises in the first year or even in the first few months of marriage. The second assails the married couple when they attempt to divide the inheritance definitively and legally.

The first phase largely depends on the value that the two original families of orientation attach to the arable land transferred to the son or the goods brought by the wife. The husband's family may think that his wife is *muy gastadora* (very extravagant), that she does not manage her household budget efficiently and that her house could be better ordered and cleaner. If the woman fails to provide any arable land it will be a weapon brandished repeatedly in any family altercation, since whether or not she does so is not regulated by traditional norms. The wife's family of orientation will most probably retaliate: the husband's parents did not provide him with sufficient lands to support his wife, his brothers and sisters obtained the best part in the initial parcellation of the land; he could work harder, spend less money in the bar, etc., because *para lo que le han dado* ... (an untranslatable expression implying that the husband's family are in no position to criticize their daughter-in-law as they failed to provide their son with adequate means).

Thus in this initial period the relationships of the family constellation are the consequences of an economic fact, springing in the last resort from the plots, from the land. The new home involved in these frictions is normally a passive focus because it is not likely that differences are going to emerge between the newly wedded couple in the first months of marriage. Finally the lines of tension originate from the respective mothers of the spouses and passing via the son or daughter through the wife or husband are directed against the other mother. Here we can detect again the preponderance of the mother in the life of the family.

The fathers endeavour to keep outside such dissensions. The respective mothers-in-law exercise their interference through their son or daughter and very rarely do they dispute the matter directly between themselves.

Though relations between the spouses are normally harmonious, one or both tend to look upon the family of the other as a source of inopportune meddling. In many cases these first disagreements are resolved by the birth of grandchildren. By then, too, the parents of the wife have probably given her some land, which is customary when all her brothers and sisters have married. The transfer of land acts as a lubricant and a reinforcement of good relations. Again, the constellation can have a cohesion *sui generis*. The young couple keeps up a certain degree of intercourse with the other two families, which may however have broken off all possible relations with each other, not even exchanging greetings in the street. The relations of the husband with his wife's family and vice-versa have not yet been severed but are cool. If the young couple reckons that the husband's parents have not dealt properly with them in the economic sphere it is possible that the daughter-in-law will not speak to her parents-in-law, renouncing all contact with them. In these circumstances the parents-in-law never go to the son's home; the grandchildren are the ones who visit their grandparents. The son-husband preserves a precarious relationship, if any, with his parents.

A last point in relation to the first of the two focal points of tension. A situation of particular strain arises when 'ego' resides with the parents/parents-in-law. The choice is dictated by the room available in the houses of the families of orientation. Although in the shared home the finances of both families are almost always distinct, there is frequent friction for economic reasons. Both women use the same kitchen and cooker and both families eat at the same table and at the same time. Each wife prepares her own meal, but if the young wife makes use too freely of the salt or oil which belong to the older woman there will soon be trouble. The same happens in the work of the men. The use of even the smallest agricultural tools belonging to the father/father-in-law may provoke the latter into selling them in order to prevent his son/son-in-law from making use of them; otherwise he would find himself in the disagreeable position of having to refuse to lend them, such is the degree of economic separation reached by the two families.

In the diagram of the three families the brothers and sisters of 'ego' are included with their spouses. All are caught up with 'ego' in a well-defined subsystem of relationships. As before I am only going to analyse the zones of friction of the subsystem, beginning by the mildest ones and taking this diagram as a point of departure.

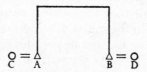

'A', due to special circumstances, i.e. a university education, married 'C' whose family of orientation was of an economic power vastly superior to that of 'A'. His brother 'B' married 'D', whose family was economically on the same level. 'B' did not have a university education. The circle of friends of 'AC' is of superior social standing to that in which 'BD' move; the style of life of the first couple is higher than that of the second couple notwithstanding all 'D's' efforts to compete with 'C'. 'D's' expenditure in first communions, clothes, or jewelry surpasses that which would normally correspond to her 'estate' because it is in this sphere, not in the social one, that she can attempt to emulate 'C'. 'D's' jealousy of 'C' makes for coldness and hostility between 'BD'—'AC' on the few occasions on which they mix socially. Once again the woman appears as the axis of family tension; though what matters here is the difference of economic power and social status. It is this that brings about the rupture, and prevails to some extent over family ties of the first degree.

I have already alluded to some of the norms governing the inheritance which I call 'initial' in the sense that it has these characteristics: (*a*) it is the *donatio propter nuptias* which is a private and not a formal settlement, with no effect before the law; it is a personal arrangement between the father and children. (*b*) The *donatio propter nuptias* is temporary and reversible because it expires the moment the definitive inheritance takes effect, when 'ego' may receive plots or paternal property which till then had been worked by one of his brothers or sisters. (c) The parents distribute the initial inheritance as they wish, and the children must conform to their wishes, because the parents have generously disposed of part of their property and directly control the economy of the remainder. While the parents run the homestead, two lines of tension are possible, on which I have already commented: the interference of the family of orientation of 'ego' in his family of procreation, and the inherent tension in the relations between 'ego' and his/her parents if 'ego' feels that these have been partial to his/her brothers and sisters in the initial distribution of the inheritance. As 'ego' however has not got any customary right on his/her part to claim a bigger or better portion of inheritance, he/she takes care not seriously to offend the parents before the definitive inheritance is drawn up.

The fiercest family conflicts ensue when the legal and definitive inheritance takes effect. Sometimes elderly parents or the surviving parent dispose of their property and transfer it legally to their children. The norm which regulates the inheritance is simple in principle. The property is divided equally between all the children. The practice is more complicated, because it is not always easy to divide equally plots, domestic animals, furniture, chattels, agricultural tools and houses. The parents, or parent, allot a portion to each child according to their own criterion of evaluation, which naturally does not always coincide with the one held by the heirs. If the parents die intestate the same problems arise. From these practical difficulties violent fights spring up between the children, together with the extraordinary efforts made by some of the sons or daughters to persuade the parents, if they are still living, to revoke the will, whether it is already consummated or still in the process of consummation. Here is an example.

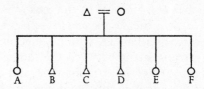

The parents built a house with the manual cooperation of their sons, 'B', 'C', and 'D', two of whom were already married. In return for the help given, the parents promised the house as an inheritance for the sons to the exclusion of the daughters. 'C' who was married, lived with his parents in the newly built house. The mother died a little before 'D' married and he and his wife went to live in his father's house (in which 'C' was not living at that time) to take care of his father. 'D's' wife died and later he contracted a second marriage. The father, of advanced years, found it difficult to get on with 'D's' second wife and demanded that both left the house, but 'D' categorically refused to go. 'A', 'B', 'C', 'E' and 'F' judged it necessary to intervene in the affair—but each from his or her point of view, with an eye fixed on the inheritance of the house. A violent argument followed and the children split up into two fiercely antagonistic bands: one consisting of the brothers with the right to the inheritance of the house, and the other of the sisters with their claim to a share. The daughters took their father to one of their houses to look after him. After a week of better treatment they persuaded him to leave them the half of the house which belonged to him. The other half had belonged to the mother already deceased, who had expressed her desire that the sons should inherit it. Having been persuaded, the old man was furtively escorted to the city by his daughters to make his will. In the face of this *fait accompli* the brothers' reaction was extreme. From words they passed to blows and 'D' beat 'A'. 'A's' sons went to 'D's' house, and when 'D' saw them coming he prepared to meet them with a knife. Fortunately his wife managed to shut him up in a room, and pacified her nephews. Eventually one of the brothers suggested selling the house and dividing the proceeds between all of them; in the end, therefore, nobody got the house. The brother preferred to forgo his share in the house rather than see his sisters enjoy something to which according to 'justice' they had no claim. Later I will comment upon this sense of justice.

An old widow, gravely ill, recommended a friend who went to visit her: 'Don't divide your things before dying; my children's dissatisfaction, not my sickness, is killing me'. The old lady had been submitted to every kind of pressure by her children in an attempt to persuade her to modify her will according to their personal requirements. As a rule when aged parents have made their will they take pains to keep it absolutely secret, so that they may live their last days in peace, respected by their children.

After a major altercation over the inheritance brothers and sisters or parents cease to be on speaking terms. This means absolutely shunning each other always, which in a small community imposes a series of heavy restrictions. Those involved even shrink from physical proximity, choosing a different path in the plots or crossing the street if they see a brother or sister approaching. They take care never to coincide in the bar or cinema. They disentangle themselves from membership of a religious association if there is the danger of meeting one of the *personæ vitandæ* (odious persons to be avoided), because the sight of them is abhorrent. Their names are avoided as true tabus, never mentioned unless to be execrated. They are never invited by their brothers and sisters—or by their sons and daughters—to any kind of *rites de passage*, nor would they accept if they were. If one of the *vitandæ* persons, trying to diminish family tension, sent a present it would be returned. If the *vitanda* sister or brother is seriously ill nobody visits them; if they die no one goes to the funeral. Sometimes, however, such circumstances do provide a starting point for the resumption of relations, and if the parents are the *vitandæ* they are generally visited if gravely ill. Sometimes the duration of the *vitandæ*-relations ends only with the death of one; at other times a *rite de passage* can terminate the family avoidance if only one of the families can climb down sufficiently to issue an invitation which the others can acccept without loss of face. Finally in many cases such *vitandae*-relations lose their vigour gradually after several months or a few years, and the families renew the threads of kinship. Other factors, such as religion or temperament, play their part. This *vitanda*-relationship does not affect the children of the families involved, although their relations may reflect a certain strain during the worst periods of family passion.

In the two examples above the quarrels were centred round the house and the plots, the principal causes of dissension over an inheritance. But there can be other grounds. Three old chairs have occasioned a violent family rupture which finished in the most obstinate *vitanda*-relationship. One insignificant agricultural tool, the yoke, practically unusable since mechanization, has been the cause of a similar conflict. After hours of heated argument one of the heirs to the yoke hacked it in half so that each could inherit 'his' part. This incident was followed by a *vitanda*-relationship of the same intensity as if it had been caused by an inheritance of several hectares of arable land. Of course the dispute over such objects is in certain cases merely the spark which sets fire to a latent antagonism.

Figures can give us an approximate idea of the extent of these *vitandæ*-relations. In 1958 there came to my knowledge sixteen cases which involved directly at least thirty-two brothers and sisters and indirectly, because all were married, sixty-four people. This was only among one age-group, both consorts being in the region of forty, when the definitive inheritance is likely to occur. I know of no case in which this has not provoked real family storms, at least momentarily, because naturally not all of them end in the *vitanda*-relationship described. Common sense on the part of the heirs, the desire to avoid publicity about disagreeable internal affairs, religious sentiments, can lead to a peaceful settlement with mutual concessions.

Conflicts develop because the same objects—houses, plots, tools, furnishings—constitute the focus of the families' interests. Discussion far from being conducted on a purely objective basis involves people not only as possessors of a right to a common inheritance but also in their more intimate, subjective aspects. Their physical defects and personal failings may become the objects of attack, so that although the inheritance has been definitively divided the personal antagonism aroused by these altercations persists. These, the most serious rupture in the life of the community, originate from and acquire their fullest expression of odium within the family circle. The family thus offers two opposing facets: it is the centre of the deepest affection and integration, and the focus of the most virulent hatred and discord.

This supposes, then, two radically different senses of the word family. Competition and conflict in the family, in the sense of the family of constellation, does not affect the cohesion of the nuclear family, the solidarity of which is preserved at all costs. The parents' insistence that their rights to the inheritance be respected by everybody are prompted by consideration for their children's welfare, to whom in due course they will bequeath the inheritance. The *pietas erga liberos* forces the parents to count scrupulously the smallest particle of the inheritance, and repeatedly to weigh up their rights to the same. 'They have

12

stolen a plot from my children', the mothers comment when displeased with the final result of an inheritance. The conflict surges up when one of the children leaves the nuclear family to form another one, when the children achieve economic, legal and social independence. When all the brothers and sisters have formed so many unitary cells through their marriages, breaking up the old family of orientation, so many nuclear families have been consolidated, creating the family constellation of which I spoke. Within this constellation each nuclear family tries to maintain its own cohesion, which means cohesion against the other families within the constellation, because these are the ones which, having a common basis of interest, can affect it more directly. The family tension described is thus limited to the conflict between nuclear family and the family constellation, which in turn reinforces and integrates the former.

VI

The early Middle Ages saw the development, especially in Aragón, of an extensive domestic community composed of parents, married children and their off-spring, and uncles and cousins in first degree. This domestic community was called *germanitas*, a community of co-heirs, and its principal aim was the common exploitation of the land and enjoyment of the parents' patrimony.[1] The post civil war agrarian economy has led to similar results among some *pudientes*. This patrimonial community provides the last meaning of the word family to be analysed. It denotes the parents, their married children and the grandchildren. Here, in the simplest form is a diagram.

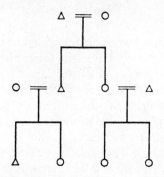

---

[1] L. Valdeavellano: *Historia de España*, vol. I, part II, p. 207 ff (Madrid, 1955).

A *pudiente*, because economic affluence is the *conditio sine qua non* of this type of family, divides his arable land into two or more parts according to the number of children, assigning to each child his respective lot when he marries or shortly after. The legal ownership of the land remains the father's, but the children acquire the use and enjoy the fruits of it. The division of lands may correspond to what each child will eventually inherit, though not necessarily so. The father moreover places all the agricultural instruments he possesses from the smallest hoe to the tractor and harvesting machine at the disposal of his children. Whilst one child, usually though not always the daughter, lives in the same house as the parents, the father provides the others with a house of their own . The economic settlement upon which the solidarity of the family relies is very simple: the agricultural exploitation is a family exploitation and the equipment is domestic. The father, who holds final authority, provides the lands, the house and farmbuildings attached, and the agricultural tools kept there. Usually he does not work himself but supervises and inspects everything. For every farmer this is the ideal status. The children contribute with their work, each child preferably on his own portion of land. The benefits obtained by each child are divided into two equal parts, one for the father, the other for the child. Thus the father takes half the profits, while each child benefits by a fourth of the total.

Such a father enjoys great prestige in the town. First of all this appears to be the best way of treating one's children; secondly his position is envied because his profits increase considerably *viviendo sin trabajar* (living without working); in the morning he is seen reading the newspaper, seated at the door of his house while the others go to work. He relaxes listening to records on his gramophone, he goes to the opening performances of new films in the city and he travels. All these are essential signs of a man of his status. These *pudientes* take a prominent part in the charitable activities organized by the parish and the Council. Their children venerate them because their parents have treated them so generously, saving them from the initial problems of most young families. Moreover the other parents of the children may feel compelled to emulate their opposite numbers in generosity, so that the gifts of both converge to create a state of economic prosperity for the children. Every

Sunday and feast day the *pater familias* presides at his table surrounded by his children and grandchildren. At the same time his children are united by harmonious fraternal relations because their respective interests oblige them to work together in close collaboration. Son and son-in-law use the tractor together in the cultivation of both their lots, they carry out in partnership any task which requires cooperation in any part of the land of the *pater familias*. There is not much place for tension because each one administers his own lot; what they share is the work and the use and care of the tools. Finally this type of family reconciles two opposing psychological problems. The father wields undisputed authority, advising the sons about their work and supervising the arrangements of the plots; but the sons too enjoy wide personal initiative because they operate the modern farm machinery about which their fathers are often technically ignorant.

It seems then that bonds of kinship and family cohesion are specific attributes neither of affection nor of feelings but of property. The *pudientes* most clearly exemplify family cohesion and harmonious relations because of the type of domestic community they can afford. To a great extent the family solidarity is a consequence of the common interests involved in an extensive ownership of land.

To sum up:

(a) The specific spheres of action of the husband and of the wife are so closely modelled on traditional norms and patterns that the moralists of the sixteenth century would observe only slight deviations from their precepts in the family theory of today.

(b) The social and legal authority of the father of the family is more than counter-balanced by the feminine influence, that is of the wife-mother, in all the doings of the family. The woman who in the early part of her life was the least significant element in the house, becomes on her marriage not only the minister of finance but the prime minister as well.

(c) Authority on the one side and familiarity of intercourse on the other govern inter-family relations. To the former corresponds the reverence due to the head of the family; the latter is characterized by a lack of tabus. This duality expresses the institutionalized form with which the nuclear family contends with disruptive forces.

(d) The markedly economic character which has left its impression on all family relationships has been the key point for understanding the integrating and disintegrating forces of the family community in all its different meanings. Economic considerations always underlie questions of social status, tensions, conflicts, *vitandae*-relations and inheritance, and their various repercussions in the family.

(e) The domestic community of the *pudientes* positively corroborates the presence of the economic as an essential ingredient in family relationships, producing a special type of family which has had much to do with the recent mechanization of agricultural methods.

VIII

GENERATIONS

*'La generación es una y misma cosa con la estructura de la
vida humana en cada momento'*
*'Cada generación representa una cierta actitud vital, desde la cual
se siente la existencia de una manera determinada'*
ORTEGA Y GASSET

AGE IS AN important element in the community's system of
relationships. First I will consider the traditional roles
and functions assigned to an individual by the community
according to his age, and then the social conditions under which
new age-groups or generations are formed.

I

The first phase, for the purpose of this chapter, in the history
of an individual covers the period from birth to fourteen years,
the age when most people leave school. This first stage of life
is the least relevant to the prematrimonial relationships and
situs of the individual. In the course of it the child is initiated
into the 'three R's', has to pass an examination in the catechism
so as to be allowed to take first communion, and, what is more
important for the purposes of this chapter, begins to comprehend
the sexual dichotomy imposed by adults on the world of the
young. At the age of six boys and girls go to different schools.
The educational programmes are different, girls spending much
of the time learning the tasks required of their sex. The boys are
taught by a master, the girls by a mistress. Recreation times
bring boys and girls together on the same playgrounds but the
two sexes never mix in any joint games or sports. The same
separation is maintained at Sunday mass and at catechism.
Attempts to transgress the rules of conduct implicit in this

sexual dichotomy meet with punishment by the teacher if committed during school hours; if at other times, it is the parents—
the mother in particular—who apply punishment, although
even then the teacher can and does intervene. The religious
indoctrination preceding first communion, the Sunday catechism, the supervision of schooling exercised by the priest, and
maternal control tend to reinforce the barrier separating boys
from girls.

At fourteen, or earlier according to the standing of the family,
both the boy and girl leave school. He goes into the fields with
his father, she helps her mother in the house. At this age it is
supposed that they have acquired the indispensable education
and that both can now co-operate in the family economy. Their
leisure activities also change significantly. Each one now has his
or her group of companions of roughly the same age, with whom
free time is shared every evening and on Sundays and religious
holidays. In these groups, differentiation of the sexes operates
rigidly. To each belongs a traditional code of conduct which
seems specially designed to impede any approach to the opposite
sex.

When farmwork takes girls and women into the fields they
confine themselves to the tasks described earlier. But there is also
another complementary differentiation. At daybreak the men
and women working for the same employer set out for the fields.
The girls and women go together, keeping apart from the men.
At the lunch break they all forgather round the same fire if it
is wintertime, but in two groups, the women forming one and
the men the other facing them. The homeward journey is the
same. A common work situation is in practice ruled by a rigid
separation.

This is even more marked in other spheres. The young man,
when his work is over, is completely free to join his friends at
the door of the bar, to drink and play cards, stroll along the high
street, go to the cinema, go out again after supper and return
home when the party of friends breaks up. The mother objects
at first but the boy feels himself progressively more independent.
The girl enjoys none of these liberties. She never goes alone to
the café, bar or cinema; when she does go it is in company, and
then only occasionally on Sundays, when she is invited into the
bar with her girl friends by a group of boys or by some older

person or relative. In such cases she will never drink wine. She goes to the cinema with her girl friends, but never after supper. On the whole few feminine groups go for the evening stroll, but at this hour the girls take advantage of shopping errands to chat for a while with their friends; it is their task to prepare supper. It is unthinkable for a girl to go out after supper—which in summer is at 11 p.m.—except during the *fiestas* or, in rare cases, when she goes with a brother to see one of the films that are shown in the town. It is thought unseemly for girls to go bathing and when they do it is never with boys; on the contrary the father of one of them will probably be close at hand to keep the boys from approaching. Nor when visiting the city do they ever go alone to dances, and they do not go to festivals in nearby towns like the boys unless they are staying for the whole festival with relations in the town.

The boys' groups (*cuadrillas*) are made up of friends of about the same age, numbering as a rule between five and ten. The same boys always come together and never mention the affairs of their own *cuadrilla* before strangers. They meet every evening and discuss together what they will do—whether to go to the cinema or the bar, to stroll, to go into the city or to another town, have a snack or second meal together, 'do the rounds' (*rondar*)—and the sum each one should contribute towards the proposed diversion. Comradeship, willingness to fall in with group decisions and generous spending, are essential conditions for every member of a *cuadrilla*. All amusements have one common denominator: they should express manliness—or what is supposed to be manliness. The *rondas*, starting at midnight, with the shouting and hullabaloo in the streets when people are asleep, the extra suppers, smelling of wine or brandy—such things express the manly character proper to young men in such revels. Not infrequently this nocturnal roistering leads the *cuadrilla* to exceed the limits of good conduct: they may raid a chicken-run, for instance, or go out and *rondar* after a second supper without permission from the authorities, an ancient requirement recently reinforced. These and similar transgressions are regarded as normal, 'to be expected of youngsters', and the older people in talking about them look back nostalgically on their own youth. This implies that another of the characteristics of the *cuadrilla* is irresponsibility in regard to certain minor aspects of the traditional code of conduct. 'We were all young once', say the elderly. Such irresponsibility also sometimes demands unity and loyalty among the members of the group. Civil guards posted at street corners once tried to surprise a group doing the rounds without permission. Several of them managed to escape. Those arrested paid their fines but refused to give the names of the others. The latter in turn contributed a sum equivalent to the fines to buy wine. Sometimes the fine is divided into equal parts according to the number of friends, all of them contributing although some have not been fined. In none of these activities does the *cuadrilla*, as such, have much to do with the other sex. Girls are of course the main topic of conversation, but they rarely come into contact with them except at dances during the festivals.

At midnight between the 7th and 8th of December each year there takes place an interesting *rite de passage*. All the young men of twenty are waiting for the first strokes from the church clock to swing the tambourines aloft and start the *ronda* with guitars. They are the *quintos* (conscripts), who in the next draft in a year's time will have to go to barracks to do their military service. The *cuadrilla* formed by the conscripts therefore is based exclusively on the fact of belonging to the same biological generation; it brings together all the males born in the same year. Each of these has to cut himself off from his old *cuadrilla* and form another in company with young men some of whom he may scarcely have had any dealings with or who come from very different economic levels. Membership of the same biological generation overrides all earlier ties or differences in favour of internal cohesion. The first stroke of twelve on that night brings out in the conscript group all the characteristics which make up a *cuadrilla*. Thenceforth they will meet every Saturday, Sunday and feast day for some festive activity, always in a body. Here then we have a socializing agent imposed by tradition, which cuts drastically across everything.

For the first nocturnal *ronda* they will already have prepared several tambourines and guitars which their sisters have decorated with long coloured ribbons. The tambourine is the symbol of the conscripts, only they can play it; they have the right to *rondar* and if they go out they displace any other *cuadrilla* from the street. While waiting for midnight they have already supped together, but more important is the meal on the following day, 8 December, the feast of the Immaculate Conception, to which each one contributes a chicken which their sisters prepare and serve. Between supper on the previous night and the meal the following day they must, in accordance with custom, *rondar* all the streets of the town and make themselves heard on all the street corners, as otherwise they will lay themselves open to the charge—'but you haven't done the rounds', which carries the implication of being soft. 'Call them conscripts?— we didn't know they were there! . . .' Such phrases wound the conscript's manly pride. Their entry into the active life of the community must be resounding.

This is the real significance of this *rite de passage*; it marks the entry into the social life of the town. The first duty of these young men is the preservation of the town's traditions. They enjoy the sole right to decorate the church door with branches on Easter Sunday, the first Sunday in May, and on the feast of the Virgin of the Rosary, the senior brother of whose guild entertains them to cakes and brandy; a sign of the religious character of traditional diversions. It is incumbent on them also to plant a poplar tree in the middle of the square on the night preceding the first of May, to organize a meal at an agreed spot within the municipal district on the day of Our Lady of Caballeros, the patroness of the town, and afterwards to tour the town with a cart decorated with branches.

At times they act as repositories of communal solidarity, as for example when an outsider courts a girl from the town. Before the wedding they can and do demand that the bridegroom treats the boys of the town to brandy. They thus redress the abduction of the girl and the supposed rights of the boys to her.

By right and obligation the conscripts collaborate with the Town Council throughout the year: they escort the festival committee which goes round the town making a house to house collection towards the celebrations. They can on their own account and, employing the same methods, prolong the festivals by one or more days and organize a *corrida de vaquillas* (a 'bull' fight with heifers). This prolongation of the festivals and the bull-fight devolve exclusively upon the conscripts. Apart from such co-operation in festival matters, the Council calls upon them for any special purpose—availability being a characteristic of the group—especially when manpower is needed, for example in preparations for a reception or, the erection of an altar. The conscripts are putting behind them the irresponsibility of their earlier years and are now assuming 'their' role in the community. Along with their rights go their social obligations. For example: if the Council finds difficulty in accommodating a band which is to play during the festivals, each conscript is under an obligation to provide board and lodging for one bandsman. They would of course be the first to come under the orders of the Council in any serious local emergency.

The conscript also automatically receives the initial accolade of his social coming-of-age in regard to certain attitudes towards his parents. He is completely at liberty to take away from his home a string of salami, a chicken, or a rabbit for a second supper; before becoming a conscript he almost always met with objections from his mother. Every Saturday night they all eat together at one or other's home. Naturally no one in the house gets any sleep that night. The son being a conscript the house is at his disposal; the parents have to endure the hubbub patiently in their bedroom. If the son were not a conscript the father would lose his temper and end by throwing them all out. The parents increase the son's pocket money since now there are a great many calls on it. The conscript who wants to go off after supper to a festival dance in the neighbouring towns, or to the city, simply tells his parents, 'Well I'm off'; it is his right that they should say nothing to him, that they should accept the fact without raising any objections, whereas hitherto he has had to ask permission.

Equipped with all these rights and obligations in which he has been initiated for a whole year, the boy leaves the town and does his military service. When he comes home he rejoins his original *cuadrilla*, because the conscript group has broken up; other, younger boys are now going through that stage. They always retain happy memories of their conscript companions and their youthful doings and recall their old group on such occasions as new *rites de passage*: 'so many conscripts of mine are married now', or in more lugubrious circumstances: 'another conscript of mine has died'. But the cohesion and the function of the conscripts' *cuadrilla* have disappeared.

So the young man enters the second sub-period of the second cycle of his life—the cycle which lasts from his leaving school until he marries. *Rondas*, extra suppers, junketing and rowdiness are now for those younger than himself and for the conscripts. Fresh attitudes and preoccupations belong to this age: it is the romantic period, the right time for starting serious relations with the opposite sex. It is very rare to have a sweetheart before doing military service, because parents would object on the grounds that 'boys are too young for such a serious matter', and the son himself sees half-a-dozen years ahead of him before he can get married. Now comes the normal period for commencing relations, which coincides with custom, the biological age regarded as suitable, the parents' opinion, and the economic convenience of the families. But although the young man follows custom in approaching girls at this stage in his life, and in spite of the fact that it is now proper for him to do so, he is in no way free. His own ideas about girls, learned during his *mili*(-tary service) in the city, play no part; on the contrary, he must submit to rigid and irksome canons of behaviour.

II

Until this age a boy has had male but never female friends. There is no place for friendship between a man and a woman, they belong to radically different worlds, and a young man only enters the female world when—a fundamental event in his life—he begins to look seriously for a wife. So the selection of a partner is not effected by way of a group of girl friends with whom he is already on familiar terms; instead the boy finds himself attracted towards one of the girls, chooses her mentally as his sweetheart, and on setting out to court her enters into her group as a first means of approach.

The absence of bonds of friendship between a boy and a girl merits some further consideration, revealing as it does the attitude which is to predominate in the phenomenon of court-ship—an attitude imposed by the community. Access to a girl is difficult. In winter it is almost impossible, but in summer, particularly when the girls' groups go for an evening walk along the high street, there are occasional opportunities, as there are too at the dances held almost every Sunday. But the dances do

little to bring the sexes together; not all the girls attend them
and those who do are usually from the lower and middle strata.
The 'young ladies' (*señoritas*) are therefore automatically ruled
out, and consequently the 'young gentlemen' (*señoritos*) whose
place it is to court them are too. During the *fiestas*, with never
less than seven hours' dancing each day, it is feasible to approach
a girl but not as easy as might be expected. A boy never dances
with the same girl for the whole evening, nor even for most of
the dances; he cannot talk to her day after day during the
fiestas or on several Sundays running, nor invite her group too
frequently to the bar. If he does, then public opinion forecasts
a wedding, everyone believes that they are or will become engaged, and both are tiresomely compromised. Such behaviour
on the boy's part is equal to 'going after her' because 'he loves
her'. Naturally, if he does not intend to marry her, he will not
start such familiarities but content himself with dancing with
all the girls accessible to him without indicating his preferences
in any way. He has to show interest in girls, not just one girl,
unless he has already chosen her privately as his sweetheart. On
the other hand, none of these rules apply to the boy who dances
with a girl from some other town; with her he may dance all
the evening and throughout the whole *fiesta* without the slightest
public disapproval; after all, he is merely proving himself
gallant, a *Don Juan*.

The choice of a wife is a serious matter. Divorce is not permitted; the pressure that the two families will exert has to be
considered; relations cannot be broken off without what is
popularly regarded as just cause, or without losing personal
prestige; a girl who has already had one fiancé will be handi-
capped in her later relations. The boy must assess all the pros
and cons scrupulously: their respective social positions, the virtues or defects of the girl, the likelihood of maternal opposition,
possible repercussions in the girl's family, and so on. Once these
doubts are overcome, the business of making the approach begins.
The stereotyped ways of meeting open to him are: to invite the
group of girls to which she belongs to the bar during the *fiestas*
or on a Sunday and endeavour to make himself congenial to the
group; to join her group during the evening stroll; to ask her to
dance repeatedly and to talk to her, but without clearly indicating his plans in the course of the conversation. She will quickly

enough have realized the boy's intentions and during this brief period, when they never see each other alone, will try to assess the suitability or otherwise of the prospective engagement. If she decides to reciprocate the feelings which the young man expresses for her, her girl friends co-operate. When they go for a stroll she is always on the outside of the party so that he can talk directly to her; her friends chat among themselves without intruding on their conversation, and will in fact seek any excuse to leave them alone together for a few minutes. If this goes on for several Sundays running everyone assumes an engagement.

The second stage in the proceedings begins when by mutual agreement they decide to walk out on their own. When they say goodnight he goes with her as far as the street corner nearest to her home; the corner is the closest he can approach to her house during this period of the relationship. As the weeks go by he goes nearer and nearer to the girl's door, but never right up to it. The respective families meanwhile have followed the progress of the affair step by step. It is at this point that the mothers, if they disapprove, intervene actively to prevent matters going any further. If the affair is broken off it is usually because of maternal interference, though nowadays this is less likely to occur since the boys tend to decide for themselves and have already made up their own minds before taking the first step.

The first two stages have only involved the couple themselves. In the third they have to reckon with a new element: the girl's father as the centre of authority. The affair moves one step further when the boy 'asks for the door' (*pide la puerta*). This means that the boy calls on the girl's father, declares his intentions to be honourable, and asks to be allowed to accompany her to the door of the house, to knock at the door when calling for her, and to talk to her for a few minutes on the doorstep before saying goodnight. The freedom of the door implies that the parents will keep out of the way while the couple are chatting there.

Another visit by the boy to the girl's father marks the beginning of the fourth stage in the courtship. This time it is 'to beg entrance' to the girl's house and to be with her in the kitchen in wintertime or in some other room, generally the dining room, when the heat of the fire is too much. In the first case they stay with the rest of the family and everyone joins in general conversation. When the boy departs the girl goes with him as far as the door, where they prolong their conversation in private. If they are alone in the dining room her mother finds excuses for popping in and out at regular intervals.

The couple are dogged by tabus at this time. They never go arm in arm and their walks are confined to the main street, never out of sight of the neighbours or other couples or groups. The girl never goes to the boy's home. Exclusiveness is absolute on both sides. If, as happens rarely, a girl has a boy who is away on military service she does not dance at the *fiestas*, either at home or in other towns; her only dancing partner is her fiancé. If she should dance—an infrequent occurrence—she does everything possible to prevent her boy from finding out. In the town it sometimes happens that the fiancé suggests her dancing with, for example, a cousin to both of them, or with a visiting friend of the boy to whom he concedes this honour.

The serious light in which courtship is regarded is evidenced by a further series of restrictions which come into force the moment it begins. The boy goes out drinking much less than before, spends less on amusements, shuns the *rondas* and nocturnal roistering, appears more formal and serious in talking about the female sex with his companions, seldom goes out with his old *cuadrilla*, and when on occasion he does join it after supper, he drinks his coffee, chats a while, and when the *cuadrilla* begins to get noisy discreetly goes home. He never goes to dances in other towns, or if after supper he does go to the next town with his friends, while they are dancing he stays in the bar. He is the butt of jokes among his old *cuadrilla*.

At this point in the courtship the respective families begin to get together. Both think about the wedding and the obligations it entails. The fifth stage marks the formalization of the economic arrangements between the two families. A day and hour are appointed for the boy's parents to call on the girl's to 'ask for the wedding' (*pedir boda*). Gifts may possibly be exchanged on this visit, but are not an essential requirement. Once the date of the wedding is agreed, the talk quickly concentrates on the economic resources that the couple can count on, what their respective families will pass on to them or give them, where they will live, etc.; the character of the visit is markedly economic. The couple themselves take no part in it at all. The wedding, which takes place when the groom is about 28 and the bride two or three years younger, marks the end of the second period in the life cycle of the individual. From this time forward he is the 'head of a family' and she is a 'housewife' and on both of them devolve the rights, obligations and attitudes already described. They will imbue their children with the same ideas and attitudes that they themselves received until, having passed through all the stages described, conditioned by the same models, the children in turn reach marriage. Then once again the same cycle will be repeated.

III

Together with the cycle of individual life there unfolds another cycle of wider dimensions—the succession of generations, which in a sense also have their cyclic character and so are linked to the flow of time. A generation in the sociological sense[1] comprises an age-group of men and women who share a common mode of existence or concept of life, who assess the significance of what happens to them at a given moment in terms of a common fund of conventions and aspirations. The distinctive characteristics of a generation are thus three in number: the first and fundamental one is the acceptance and/or partial creation of attitudes and values, the sharing of a common image of the world and of life. The second derives from the first: this sharing implies coincidence in time, being actively or passively concerned in the events which happen to them or which they bring about and/or attempt to regulate. The third is the common fund of aspirations and tasks to be fulfilled. These three characteristics point to two corollaries: in the first place the ideas and attitudes constituting the fundamental nerve of a generation, condition the individual who belongs to it, or, if he belongs to the innovating *élite*, he imposes them, and inasmuch as he is conditioned by or creates them he belongs to the group. Whence the second corollary, that every individual, whatever his biological age, who adheres to that way of life, to that mode of existence, belongs to the same generation. 'Generation' thus has little to do with biological generation; in

---

[1] See bibliography: Ortega y Gasset and J. Marías.

---

this context it is equivalent to social generation. Those who belong to the same generation are called 'coetaneous'; those living at the same time but subject to other ideologies and values are 'contemporaries' of the former. Their respective worlds, although coinciding in time, are different.

A generation is conditioned and formed by (a) the cultural legacy from former generations, (b) the historical situation or situations, and (c) by the new contribution or contributions of the members who compose it. The first clause (a) underlines the dynamic relationship of generations, (b) points to a definite temporal dimension or several in succession and thus implies the idea of variation and change. The content of (c) is the function that the generation performs in the various situations, the perspective from which it interprets them, its sense of duty. With these premises as a frame of reference we may enquire: (1) what is the number of generations in the community; (2) what historical events have modelled them; (3) what are the specific differences between the generations; and (4) what changes have occurred in the system of family relations.

Sixteen biological generations took an active part in the civil war as soldiers. These men were in 1961 aged from 54 to 39 years inclusive, and were born therefore between 1907 and 1922. As all public offices in the town are held by members of this generation we may call it the 'controlling' generation. Those born before 1907 and now aged from 55 to 70 may be called the 'declining generation'. Seventy can be chosen as the upper age limit, first because relatively few have exceeded this age, and second because their function in public life is already slight before they reach it. Individuals whose ages lie between 38 and 20 years form what may be called the 'emerging' generation. I include the 20-year-olds in this category because they were the conscripts of 1961 and beginning to play a part in the life of the community.

It is not only historical and biological factors that appear to support this classification; the action in, and response to, the same historical events of each of these generations have not been identical. But it must be emphasized that this proposed grouping does not necessarily place each individual by reason of his biological age in the corresponding sociological generation;

13

exceptions may arise. What the division does imply is a high degree of correlation between biological age and sociological generation, understanding by the latter the dominant general patterns which regulate the ideology and conduct of its members. Personal exceptions are not taken into account. Finally, individual participation may be coloured by social position, by family, or by political ideology; and the members may belong to either the active or the passive nucleus of their respective generation.

For the 'declining' generation, the town they knew in their adolescence has changed enormously. There was no electric light, no telephone, not even a reservoir of drinking water. Newspapers were unknown. Not many men and very few women learned to read and write. The education acquired during schooldays was minimal. The Minutes of the Council dated 13 July 1901, reports that the schools have been closed for three months because the teachers refuse to take classes unless the Council pays them. Farming methods were purely Roman; there was no machinery of any kind. A stage coach linked the town to the city, but the highway was in such a state that in winter it was an adventure to take the road. No-one thought of visiting other cities. The honeymoon of many who today belong to this generation was confined to going to the city—sometimes on foot—to see a theatre show. When it was over they returned to the town. Very rarely did they see a car and once when a car did pass through the town the boys ran after it throwing stones. Money was rare; most transactions were by barter. The community thus had many facets which suggest a high degree of autarchy. Municipal administration corroborates this self-sufficiency. The competence of the Council extended to spheres in which nowadays it has no power of decision—to the appointment of the doctor, chemist, veterinary surgeon, secretary and schoolmaster, the settling of their contracts, the regulation of the prices of basic foodstuffs such as bread, wine, meat and milk, the division of the population into categories of ratepayers each with its own rights and obligations, the proclamation and public discussion of the decisions taken in session etc.

On the national stage this generation saw the loss of Cuba, the Philippines and Puerto Rico and the war with the United

States, which gave rise on 4 June 1898 to a collection in the
town to aid expenses. There were the beginning of the reign of
Alfonso XIII, the succession of five presidents of the 'Cortes'
and sixty-six ministers in thirty months between December
1902 and July 1905; seven ministries with four presidents from
the summer of 1905 to January 1907; the attempted assassination of the king on his wedding day (31 May 1906) to which the
Council reacted according to the Minute of 2 June, 1906, by
'sincerely deploring the criminal attempt against the King and
Queen'. The conservative party which almost without immediate precedent had kept itself in power for two and a half
years was replaced in the government by a Liberal cabinet
which was in power for four months; the new Liberal president
was assassinated in 1912; power passed from Romanones to
Dato, who declared Spain neutral in the First World War. Dato
was succeeded by Romanones in 1915 and Romanones by
García Prieto the next year, until the latter was forced to resign
in the face of pressure from the Defence Council and the first
named returning to office. In 1917 four governments followed
after four crises; in 1918, three. Seven new governments succeeded each other and in the meantime Abd-el-Krim routed the
Spanish army in Morocco. On 24 September 1921, the Council
sent twenty pesetas to every soldier from the town who was
fighting in Africa—soldiers who today belong to the 'declining'
generation. The Liberal-Conservative party came to power and
was replaced in the same year. In 1923 General Primo de
Rivera brought in the dictatorship which bears his name, putting an end to the change of governments. 'Between May
1902 and September 1923 the King (Alfonso XIII) spent
thirty-three ministries in twenty-one years and three months',
the governments lasting 'an average of seven and half months'.[1]
All this without counting the strikes, assassinations, the 'tragic
week' and regional revolts.

When the dictatorship ended in January 1930, the generation
born at the turn of the century had not only witnessed this extraordinary change of governments and suffered some of the
consequences but had also seen a series of innovations in the
town. Electric lighting had been installed in the houses and

[1] Salvador de Madariaga: *España*, 2nd ed. (Buenos Aires, 1955), p. 414.

streets of the town, they had a reservoir of drinking water and a telephone, and a bus had replaced the old stage coach. These were improvements bequeathed by the preceding generation in authority. The stretch of highway between the town and the city had been converted into one of the best in Spain; motor traffic increased considerably. Money began to pass from hand to hand; in 1901[1] the schoolmaster was paid 1·70 pesetas a day while in 1924[2] the minimum daily wage for a labourer was 5 pesetas. In few of these changes—all operating on a national scale—did they intervene directly, but they did take advantage of the circumstances to improve the efficiency of their farming, introducing machines and, somewhat cautiously, artificial fertilizers. From stoning cars they passed to using them for their increasingly frequent trips to the city, and one or two people possessed their own. One family ventured to spend a few days' holiday in San Sebastián but was sharply criticized by the town. This unnecessary journey was regarded as 'throwing money away'. They knew of the existence of newspapers and wireless sets, because the 'professionals' took or possessed them.

What is more important and characteristic of this generation is that, banding together in an organization of Agricultural Workers, they requested the Town Council, which was still in the hands of the generation preceding theirs, to grant them the premises called *El Granero* (The Granary) for holding their meetings, which 'were becoming necessary in the locality since not only did they tend towards the defence of the farmers but also to the enlightenment of the townspeople by putting them in touch and keeping them up to date with modern life'.[3] The Council agreed to let them have the hall; the repercussions of the opening-up process achieved by this generation have already been described.[4] But much more interesting is the position of the group as such, its receptiveness to innovations from outside, its interest in catching up with the rest of the world. Instead of the Council providing these methods and facilities it is they themselves who prod the Council and force the pace of innovation. It is not asserted in the Minutes that the association had any political character, nor indeed had it. But

---

[1] Council Minute (*Acta*) of 10 September 1901.
[2] Ibid., 12 January 1924.   [3] Ibid., 29 July 1920.   [4] See pp. 136–7.

this attitude of mind of the generation, ripe for change, was soon to face the political welter that arose in 1931.

The commencement of the Republic coincided with the assumption of power, through the Council, by the men of this generation, at that time only beginning to approach the apogee of their mandate. They were between 25 and 40 years of age when this period started and between 30 and 45 when it ended —an age when one has both reached maturity and may still look forward hopefully to a better future. It was the men of this generation who were divided into two bitterly opposed factions. Social progress and welfare—the objects of the whole generation in common—were pursued by different means and from widely different viewpoints, which constituted the integrating principle of each generational unit. For the left-wing the watchword was 'liberty', for the right-wing 'order'. To the Left 'Order' meant being shackled to the *status quo* and so to the abhorred ancient usages; for the Right 'Liberty' meant the destruction of revered tradition.

The Republic was declared in Spain in April 1931, and by 26 September a Minute of the Council reveals the existence of an Employment Exchange, a Republican Casino (club) and a Workers' Union, to which was later to be added an Independent Casino. The Republican Casino and Workers' Union petition the Council to be allowed to examine the Minutes of the Council for the years 1929 and 1930. They further ask for the building of new schools for boys and girls on the property of a *pudiente*. After this petition the regulation of local life is no longer the concern of the Council alone. The two units of the generation intervene directly from their respective platforms and struggle to dominate the Council table where both are represented. National political life and the internal affairs of the town are lived by this generation with an intensity not known before or since in the town's history.

The Minute of 3 October 1931 reports the town meeting called at the Granary to discuss the desirability of building schools; the Minute ends, '. . . and accepting the will of the town it was resolved to set up a Schools Committee'. Some days later[1] the Workers' Union presented at the Town Hall some plans for

---

[1] Council Minute (*Acta*) of 10 October 1931.

regulating relations between employers and workers which the
Council considered itself incompetent to settle, and proposed
'that a meeting be arranged between the latter (the workers)
and the employers in the town to see if the proposals are
accepted or if an understanding can be reached between the
two sides'. Any event in local life has its echoes among the
people, echoes which reach the Minutes. The people want to
know how they are governed and to take their part in the administration of the community. Notice boards are put up at the
street corners so that everyone may re-read the proclamations
of the mayoralty, and the premises known as the Granary are
suitably decorated and lighted for the numerous public meetings
of the inhabitants.[1] The public luncheon given by the Council
on the occasion of the 'secular feasts'[2]—was attended by so
many people that they damaged a stove,[3] and papers for 22 May
1932 refer to a 'large audience' gathered in the Council
Chamber.

Some weeks later the Council meeting ended in insults. Tension was at its height. The secretary writes:[4] 'the resident X
who was among the numerous members of the public crowded
into the Council chamber, its corridors, part of the square and
up against the windows of the Council House, attending the
session, asked leave to speak, and when this was refused by the
Chair the public began to vociferate, hurling disrespectful and
mortifying phrases at the Council'. Then the mayor proposed
a public meeting for another day. 'To these suggestions by his
Worship (Señor) the Mayor, V replied angrily telling him that
they had been on the Council far too long, that the mayor was
in office only because it pleased him, against the will of himself
(V) and his fellows who had more sense of shame than the
Chairman'. In the face of these improprieties the mayor dissolved the meeting and Z affirmed, 'I knew you'd take that way
out'. The audience hung about calling some of the Council
'knaves' and shouting out that they 'didn't know how to run
the town', that 'anybody could govern better', that 'messing
the town about had come to an end, that only five or six councillors had messed about, that these should be dragged out by
the heels . . . since they would never go any other way because

[1] Ibid., 2 January 1932.   [2] Ibid., 5 March 1932.
[3] Ibid., 28 March 1932.   [4] Ibid., 30 July 1932.

they had no shame, that six men between them were going to ruin 300 honest townsfolk', ending up with 'tonight the whole Council must go or die'.

This Minute proves conclusively that the people, or more precisely the 'declining' generation, were passionately and intensely concerned with the problems of the town, all the more so in that the core of the question being debated was not political or a conflict between employers and workers but a discussion of the proposed annexation of the town to the city. Some weeks later the Council limited, 'for reasons of hygiene', the number of those attending the sessions.[1] But in accord with the general tendency for regulations to have more force on paper than in reality we learn that on 13 May 1933 so many people were at the session that 'the three councillors are prevented from seeing each other' and the atmosphere was 'so unbreathable' that it was resolved to hold future sessions in the school hall, if the master permitted. One last example to corroborate the exceptional intensity with which the events of public life were followed during this period: a councillor defending his point of view says that he has risen from bed though ill, to come to this session.[2]

The women did not lag behind. On the morning of 27 September 1933,[3] 'several groups of women affiliated to the U.G.T. (a workers' union) or sympathizers of the same, went round the town adopting a tumultuous and unruly attitude, coercing other women not to work, causing a public scandal by their vulgar language and disturbing public order'. Three days later, when these events were discussed at the Council meeting, the male group in the audience threw the Council into a dilemma with the following ultimatum: either they settle the workers-employers question or they 'get out', and others suggested raiding the shops. The women present hurled themselves into the dispute, defying the men with the challenge, 'let's see who's man enough to stand up to us'.[4]

Through their respective political ideologies both generational units were in direct contact with the city and with national events. Pamphlets, party propaganda, the press and meetings organized by professional politicians set forth the direction to be

---

[1] Ibid., 13 August 1932.   [2] Ibid., 30 September 1933.
[3] Ibid.   [4] Ibid.

followed. The town reacted to any national episode through the two principal factions. Thus the Council protested energetically on 14 May 1932, because 'approval of the said Statute (The Catalan Statute) presented to the Constituent 'Cortes', is not proceeding, believing that national unity will thereby be prejudiced'. In July 1932, the Council sends a telegram to the Ministry of Agriculture in the name of the town's 300 cultivators asking for the interests of the beet-growers to be protected. As is natural, matters that affect the town are to the fore. On taking up his office on 10 March 1936 the mayor congratulates himself in his inaugural address on 'having redeemed the Republic'.

Among these the outstanding question was the division of land. This was the burning topic around which almost all the disputes in the Council were centred and which brought about the split into two hostile factions. Nevertheless it was a theoretical rather than a practical problem, because the Council, according to the Minute of 10 December 1932, invited 'those associates (of the U.G.T.) who have no land (22 of them) and who wish to cultivate on the commons in the municipality, to apply ... indicating the acreage they desire, the district in which it lies, and the boundaries of the plot they wish for'. Schools, street lighting, street cleaning, hygiene, drinking water, etc., were other concerns in which the Council took an unprecedented interest, urged on especially by the Republican Casino. Attacks against any public displays of a religious nature are another of the activities coming from this centre, to be discussed later. On 14 March 1936, the Casino presented a petition at the mayor's office, demanding: (1) the settlement of the workers' unemployment; (2) reduction of the prices of essential foodstuffs; (3) the disarming of the Fascist and Monarchist bands in the locality; (4) the demarcation of the communal holdings. The petition was accepted by the Council in its entirety.

The inaugural address cited above appears to foreshadow the start of a new era, the achievement of the goal struggled for day by day for five years. The Republic, 'of which the honest and hardworking people expect so many benefits', has been redeemed—it is a republican mayor who is taking over. The mayor hopes his efforts will benefit 'especially the needy class',

because 'although poor they are honest', and end unemployment since 'without bread there can be no peace'. Even the
names of the streets reflect the new era, for they were renamed:
'Avenue of the Republic', 'Francisco Largo Caballero', 'Pablo
Iglesias' etc.,[1] all highly expressive. To sum up, there was an
effort to subvert the social hierarchy, to uproot ancient
customs, usages, and values, and forcibly to impose new attitudes on those institutions which could not be immediately
altered.

Almost the whole of the effort to bring about this radical
change sprang from the pugnacity of the republican faction
of the generation. But this faction cannot be understood without
the other against which it struggled. Nor could it have constituted itself, nor reached the high degree of specificity which
it did without the opposition. All members of this generation,
in particular those of the Republican faction, were animated
by the same eagerness to learn from outside influences and by a
sincere desire to change and improve the community. Different
political programmes and different interests drew the generation towards two opposite poles, but each was complementary
and indispensable to the other. The 'declining' generation constituted a sociological generation with its own well-defined
profile. A part of it was opposed to tradition, optimistic, and
aggressively intolerant. Born at the end of the last century, its
adolescence spent in a markedly autarchic, closed atmosphere, in
its youth precipitated into national catastrophe occasioned by the
extraordinary political see-saw, this 'declining' generation sought
to revitalize the town by the 'enlightenment of the townsfolk' and
by its own efforts succeeded in introducing many innovations.
These in turn prepared the way for innovations introduced by
the succeeding generation. The septuagenarian who in his early
days used a candle to light his house today has his television
set. Such things have been made possible by the actions of the
succeeding generation in the economic field. For the succeeding
generation also has its own shape and has also made its own
specific contribution to the community; it constitutes another
sociological generation. But the 'declining' generation, which
felt so politically minded and optimistic in its middle age and

---

[1] Council Minute (*Acta*), 9 May 1936.

whose republican wing was decimated in the first days of the civil war, today hates with a deep-rooted hatred the word 'politics' and all that it involves. It is a word held in absolute discredit. 'No form of government is worthwhile, they all boil down to the same thing; all those who have taken, are taking or will take part in any type of government, have been, are, and will be equally "shameless" (*sinvergüenzas*), humbugs'. 'Liberty' is a word that should be erased from the dictionary. The Republican 'liberty' is still a thorn in the flesh, in particular to those of the right wing.

IV

The 'controlling' generation (*de mando*) covers sixteen biological generations, the men who in 1961 were between 54 and 39 years old. They fought at the front during the war, and all the municipal posts in the town at present are held by the militants of this generation. None of them, on the other hand, were old enough to play any active part in the struggle for power during the republican years, although they found themselves involved in the situation bequeathed by the previous generation and were forced to resolve it in the trenches, fighting against the Republic. Finally they received from the previous generation a positive double legacy: permeability to external influences and the spirit of initiative in agricultural mechanization.

With rifle and knapsack they scattered all over the fields of Spain. Their eyes were opened to other cities and wide horizons. They learned of other crops and other techniques. They discovered that their town, their way of life, their fields and farming methods were neither unique nor the best. 'We learnt a lot in those days', they say. The end of the strife presented them with the old dilemma: the land or the city. Several opted for the latter, remembering the farmers' troubles in the republican period. With their certificates of having fought for the right side they could secure jobs in banks or find employment of other kinds in the city. Others on the strength of the same credentials obtained lands in colonization schemes away from the town on which they settled. The largest contingent of soldiers, however, came back to the town to till the paternal fields.

As we already know, post-war conditions were propitious for the agricultural development of the town. Seasoned in the trenches, these men laboured zealously on the family small-holding. Some of them were not content with their farming but took on also the cares and effort of small businesses, buying and selling straw, alfalfa, draught-animals, cattle, maize, etc. Often, against the advice of their parents—which shows the existence of two different worlds—they sought and obtained loans from the banks, enlarged their own farmland, and bought or leased fields situated in other *términos*, made full use of fertilizers on their fields, introduced the selection of seed, mechanized their work with well-equipped tractors and harvesters, insured their machines and crops. This is not the place to recapitulate all the changes introduced into the town by this generation, but it must be stressed here that this is the generation which has been the agent of them, exploiting the opportunities offered by the national economic-agrarian scheme. Many fathers who at first disagreed with filial innovations (adventures) later joined forces with their sons on realizing the profitable results—results which brought in a new style of living proper to an affluent community. This fresh perspective from which the world and life are viewed today, radically different from that of pre-war days, and into which the old political characterization of the 'de-clining' generation in no way enters, justifies the title of 'genera-tion' given to this group; but leaving this aside I shall point out the changes that have occurred in the system of family relationships.

First, the impact of technical development and its application by this generation to agriculture undermined the model of asymmetrical father-son relationships. Authority, the manage-ment of the domestic economy, used to belong to the father. In the post-war period it has been principally the son who, endeavouring to keep level with the new conditions, has orientated the domestic economy on broader, more technical and lucrative bases. Such re-orientation frequently met with at least tacit paternal disapproval, meaning that in many cases the son had to act on his own account. Furthermore, the mech-anical tools introduced demanded a knowledge of their uses to which the father, by reason of his age, no longer had access. He was not disposed, for example, to learn to drive a tractor. Nor was he either able or inclined to worry about all the mass of papers necessary for obtaining credits, ordering a tractor, or filling up an insurance policy. The son had to assume almost the whole responsibility. Thus the traditional asymmetrical father-son relationship (authority-obedience) began to give way to a more symmetrical, and in some cases new type of relationship, in which the son occupied the former position of the father.

To this change in the sphere of family relationships must be added the beginning of the break-up of the family occasioned by those sons who on returning from the front settled in the city. Such a thing could hardly have occurred before 1936 because of paternal opposition. For the first time the occupations of father and son diverge. The son's identification with the family, his solidarity with it, have lost ground; his evaluations and problems are different, his programme of action extends beyond the family framework. Further, a circumstance which helps to widen the gap, he had got married in the city to a girl whom his parents did not know. The cohesion of the family has diminished.

Whilst a tendency is observable in the western world towards the atomization of the family, in the sense that it is reduced to the conjugal family with its children, we see in the town the appearance of a new type of family with opposite characteristics, which is the effect of an agricultural economy in expansion. This is the type of family found among the *pudientes*.[1] In this case the setting up of a new nuclear family tends not towards the differentiation of the new conjugal unit but, on the contrary, towards integration within a wider framework which encloses two further families. It is true that the solidarity of the group thus constituted is probably founded on things—property, fields, equipment, the co-ordination of labour, etc.—rather than on the persons as such. But what is important is how the conjugal unit returns, in certain circumstances, to the wide domestic group, to a certain *germanitas* of medieval aspect, when precisely similar circumstances produce opposite results in other western nations. The age of the parents and the difference of generation here play a primary part.

Another of the changes in the family is in its size. The average number of brothers and sisters, and of children, among members

---

[1] See pp. 166–8.

of the 'declining' generation was five. The average number of
children born to those in the 'controlling' generation is three or
under; in recent marriages there appears to be a tendency not
to have more than two. They thus 'avoid expense', 'have fewer
obligations' and 'can live better'. Such phrases reveal a mentality very different from that of the previous generation.

The passage of time since the war, the consolidation of new
techniques and living standards and the entry of a new age-
group into the active life of the community have notably
quickened the tempo of change in the structure of the family.
In the third generation, the 'emerging', are grouped all those
between 20 and 38 years of age. As the years passed the newly
introduced farming methods became firmly and efficiently
rooted. This process, with the consequent raising of the standard
of living, brought with it the impossibility of accommodating
all the sons on the paternal farm. The sons of fathers whose
economic position stands on the extremes of the social hierarchy
have found themselves obliged to go beyond the customary
limits in the choice of a profession. The new professions necessitate leaving home and so tend towards emancipation from the
tutelage and authority of the father. Furthermore, the parents'
authority and orientation can count for little with the son whose
profession is beyond their understanding. The father's fund of
experience cannot guide the son who leaves home. In his sphere
of specialization the son enjoys greater authority than his
father, and in any discussion of topics other than agriculture the
father must concede that the son who lives in the city 'knows
more'. For his part, the son with another profession, with a
specialized trade learnt at a technical school, or with a university or military career, acquires a greater degree of individuality.
The traditional moulds of the town cannot shape his conduct,
he has to adjust himself to more cosmopolitan and distinguished
ways of life. He feels a man who has made himself, for which
purpose he has had to remove the shackles of the family. The
parents realize this and consider themselves inferior to the son.
In the 'controlling' generation such cases were sporadic; in the
'emerging' generation they have reached a volume unforeseen
fifteen years ago.

It might be thought that sons whose parents are not in the
extremes of the hierarchy, and who therefore stay in the town,

depend in their work and conduct on the functions we have seen attached to them in accordance with sex and age. To a great extent it is true that they learn the use of some agricultural tools and methods, care of crops, etc., and prepare themselves to take their proper part in the community under parental guidance. But there are signs that the reality is not so simple as it seems to have been hitherto. A striking example of discontinuity between what was and what is or between what is and what according to the old popular values ought to be, is provided by the new tone in courtship. This 'emerging' generation has opposed with the greatest tenacity any maternal interference in the choice of a partner. Disputes between mother and child have been long—sometimes lasting months—and in some cases very violent. Their reverberations have acquired special significance through the final victory of the child. The town would follow every incident in the drama. The contest seems now to have been definitely settled in favour of the young man and if he persists he no longer meets with maternal opposition. This victory for the 'emerging' generation has been followed by another in the same sphere: the custom of 'asking for the door' is becoming a thing of the past—the very recent past, of course. The young men are irritated by so many handicaps that have no meaning for them, and they overcome them in the most direct way, by eliminating them. I have said too that couples never walk arm in arm. That is still true of the walks in the high street. In the city they walk in close embrace, though if they see an acquaintance coming they hasten to walk apart.[1]

Still more spheres of behaviour have been subjected to revision by the 'emerging' generation. The traditional functions assigned to them are resented as imposed and senseless. Indeed, for the last few years the conscripts have not planted the traditional poplar tree which used to celebrate the coming of May and on various occasions they have rejected the demands made on them by the Council, have opposed its plans or the decisions of the mayor. In groups they have protested to the Council against fines for *rondas* or the imposition of work. Other groups of this generation tried to find out how the Council rates are distributed over the municipality and were refused admission to the relevant session by the mayor.

---

[1] In the summer of 1965 engaged couples were walking out hand in hand.

The discontinuity with the past and even with the other two contemporaneous generations which precede them, implicit in the above actions, is not confined solely to the examples given; these are partial aspects of a wider, more complicated whole. The 'emerging' group aspires to the enjoyment of greater freedom. In detail they aim at securing greater independence from their parents (I refer to those still unmarried), to being able to come and go to the city or to other towns without having to give 'any sort of explanation' to their parents. They advocate absolute independence, with no maternal interference of any kind, in sentimental problems. They would like to make more innovations in farming and a greater use of banking facilities. They object to the numerous processions held during the *fiestas* because when the bells announce the start of the evening procession of the Rosary, dancing comes to an end. They oppose the will of their fathers when these suggest working on Sunday mornings. They regard as absurd the duration of military service, and rebel against the national censorship of films. They are less and less tolerant of the Council's communal ordinances and find it unjustifiable that the mayor should impose his judgement without their being allowed to discuss directly those matters which concern them. For its own part the 'declining' generation is severely critical of the new generation, which it accuses of being 'shy of work and fond of spending' (*poco trabajadora y muy gastadora*); 'they never think of saving but only of having a good time', 'they don't know what work is', 'they want to have a lot of money and live well without exerting themselves', 'they buy everything that takes their fancy', etc.

All this seems to justify the supposition that here is not merely a new biological generation making a way for itself but indeed a new sociological generation with a fresh stock of interests, attitudes and ideas, the specific difference of which is their discordance with those that have gone before. Members of this generation have had better schooling than those of the preceding generations; newspapers, radio, the cinema, television and travel put them in touch with the outside world at an age at which the other generations were uninfluenced by such media; some work in factories in the city and even in France, which widens their horizons. The structure of the family cannot provide occupations for many of them; nor do they feel any affinity with the conventions that spring from the social structure of the town. They do not share them because they judge them inadequate for the present day situation; the roles assigned to them are out of tune with the urgency of acquiring a specialized trade. Patterns of action according to age and sex have little appeal to a generation markedly individualistic, which regards itself as superior to its predecessors. Working conditions are much easier than those experienced in their youth by the other generations, field rents are much higher than before, economic affluence allows them to visit the city at any time, and encourages them to look to the city and to forget the old forms of conduct imposed by the community. Consequently the traditional integrating principles of the community are becoming superfluous to those whose work has nothing to do with the land, and a burden to those who remain tied to the soil, because their vital outlook is far from harmonizing with the ideas and attitudes maintained in the community by the weight of tradition.

The general characteristics of the three generations discussed may be summed up in the following three columns, setting out the precise contributions of each.

'Declining' Generation	*'Controlling' Generation*	*'Emerging' Generation*
Held authority	Holds authority	Will shortly hold authority
Initiates technical transformation of agriculture at a time of adverse conditions for the farmer	Completes and consolidates this transformation under conditions very favourable to the farmer	Profits by this transformation
Composed of two antagonistic units	Unity within the generation	Unity within the generation
The two sections attempt to regulate and set their own ideological seal on events in the town during the republican phase	Passive towards these events	The majority are completely unaware of what happened during that period
Did not take any part as soldiers in the war	Anti-republican soldiers during the war	Many born since the war
The generation participates as a whole in the events of local life	Activity by the minority	No active participation. Holds no important positions of authority

Activities political in character. Deprecates 'politics' now	Innovatory activities mainly technical in character. Wants nothing to do with 'politics'	Social functions and roles marked by innovations. Unconcerned about 'politics'

One thing the three generations clearly have in common is a readiness to accept and accentuate the pace of innovation. The first generation is defined principally by a political creed. Its conceptualization of time is bound to, and regulated by, a double political programme. The right-wing unit looks to the past in its efforts to dominate and improve the present. The opposing unit struggles to project the future into the present. The generation is thus split into two units, each defined by a divergent conception of time: the first seeks to modify the present by innovations consistent with a traditional ideology, the richness of whose content—they believe—can supply models adaptable to the present. The position of the second is more radical: they despise the past, do not conform to the present and yearn for the future. Their actions are taken with a view to a future time which they expect to control. The linking of the two antagonistic units struggling for power during the republican period produces a time rich in explosive content, of abrupt alternations between past and future, of innovation, standstill and retrogression.

The innovatory content of the 'controlling' generation shows very different aspects. This age group enters the field at a time of nation wide political crisis. But once the war is over a period of agricultural crisis is followed by one of prosperity. The political dimension of time yields to the technical and economic, whence the importance of this generation. I have analysed elsewhere ecological time and its persistence in social life. The cyclic rhythm of ecological time was considered as a constant. If a generation acquires a new interpretation of ecological time and sets out to make use of it in a technical-agrarian direction, it imposes a distinct and greatly accelerated rhythm on the agricultural calendar. The mechanization of farming with its accelerated rhythm destroys one of the main foundations on which are built and supported the continuity of ideas, customs, labour relations and social functions of a fundamentally agricultural community. Hence this generation, by introducing large-scale mechanization, has radically changed farming methods and, as an indirect result, social life as well. This social transformation has not followed the lines of any political programme, nor been the specific goal of aspirations as it was in the previous generation. The 'controlling' generation has concerned itself with dominating the present, with no political conceptualization whatever; its time is framed by technical and economic models, or in other words, this group has sought to control and subdue time as conceptualized from a technical point of view.

The direct heirs to this current of innovation are the members of the 'emerging' generation. They have not been able to construct a time of their own because they are still making it by ascending stages. They live under the ægis of a time which is not theirs, they must adjust themselves to the structural time imposed on them by the community. This structural time is beset with symbols and functions the content of which they regard as outworn and inoperative in their present situation. In the second place they experience the impact of a new way of life, of the ideas and technical methods which are the contribution of the 'controlling' generation. They must act in two distinct spheres, one of which dates back to the past while the other stresses the present. They for their part look forward to a future in which they can enjoy greater freedom. This distension reveals unbalance, absence of harmony, which they themselves are the first to feel. They reject the conventional standards—or some of them, are non-conformist, and individualistic. The lack of conformity, translated sometimes into individual and sometimes into group opposition, suggests a generational attitude in the making; it manifests itself in a somewhat vague, perhaps unconscious manner, except for occasional explosions which in their turn serve to reinforce it. Their generational time could be formulated as confused, ambivalent, fluctuating between the past which they reject and the future which has yet to take shape in new patterns of conduct.

The articulation of three generations defined in terms of different historical situations, programmes and contributions has served as a framework for the analysis of the changes which have operated on the family structure. Finally we may approach the same events and determine in part their distribution, guided this time by the network afforded by the stratification of the community. Solidarity and family cohesion have been maintained among the *braceros* because in almost every case the whole family migrated to the city. First one of the sons would go, and when he had found a regular job, a flat and a prospect of employment for his brothers and sometimes for his parents, all the family would take the road to the city. Family cohesion may well mean something very different in their new environment, but this is not a problem to be considered here. Some of the *braceros* go to work in France for several months in the year, leaving their families deprived of their head. The separation of members of the nuclear family among the *peones* follows other patterns. The parents live in the town but the son works in the city, where he lives or to which he travels daily, and when he marries he looks for a flat in the city. The daughter is in service in the city and only returns to the town for holidays. Until his military service the son works for wages in the town. From that time on he must look for another occupation.

The disintegration of the elements of the nuclear family runs on different lines among the *jornaleros*. Whilst those in the preceding groups have for the most part obtained occupations looked on as somewhat low, the *jornaleros* have aspired to professions which seem to be more highly regarded, such as the police. Others have sent their sons to technical schools in the city where they have specialized in one of the subjects offered. Both courses mean leaving the family, being away from the town and living in the city. The *propietarios*, as a group, are undoubtedly those who maintain family cohesion without major innovations. Their economic position protects them and does not impel them towards any change. The sons remain with their parents until marriage and are not separated from them by differing professions. The structural roles guide in principal their modes of behaviour. Lastly, the *pudientes* display both the highest degree of family cohesion when they preserve the type of family which they revived, and the most marked disintegration when they send their sons to the university or to one of the military academies. In this latter case, the style of living of the sons educated at the university or the academy, with a prestige-bearing profession, with superior speech, knowledge and manners, is radically different from that of their parents. The social

distance which separates them is wider than in any of the preceding groups.

I began the essay on the family by underlining its economic
character. Now, at the close the same idea arises once more:
family cohesion and solidarity follow very closely the economic
position of the family. But it is also necessary once again to
bring into the study values that are not economic—as in the
case of the *pudientes*—which transcend the limits of an exact
correlation.

*
* *

At the beginning of this chapter I attempted to explain briefly
how two concepts were to guide the development of the theme.
The community has developed its own system of classification
for individuals by sex and age. To each group is assigned a
series of modes of behaviour, and the individual, by the fact of
belonging at a given moment to one or other of these categories,
knows what his conduct must be and at the same time is articu-
lated into the social structure of the community. His relative
position has fixed, well-defined patterns of conduct attached to
it, which guide the individual and which perpetuate in cyclic
form the expected behaviour. The persistence of these patterns
is synonymous with the perpetuation of the social structure.
Hence the qualification of 'structural time' which I give to the
recurrent temporal divisions into which the biological age of an
individual is subdivided.

But the individual does not proceed alone through these
biological classifications. The coetaneous group is always
with him; generations succeed others, and in their turn
meet and struggle with new situations. Each new situation is
seen and experienced from a different angle by the contemporaneous generations and a single event holds very different
significance for each one of them. The antagonism and personal
hatreds, for example, of the republican period have been trans-
cended by the 'controlling' generation and mean nothing to the
'emerging' generation. Markedly distinct situations produce
new generations with partially distinct sensibilities and interpretations of life. This freshness of ideas and attitudes is the
prelude to a change in the social life. A complex historical
situation is the motor that sets the new generation in motion

with a definite programme; situation, generation and programme are comprehended in, and form the content of,
'generational' or 'situational' time. While 'structural time'
implies stability, permanence, enduring qualities, 'generational
time' is accompanied by innovation and change.

IX

LAW: I

'Nos, que valemos tanto como vos, é que juntos valemos más que vos, os facemos Rey para que guardéis nuestros fueros é libertades, é si non, non' LOS NOBLES DE ARAGÓN AL ELEGIR AL REY

'Bravo, mi Señor Don Quijote! La ley no se hizo para ti, ni para nosotros tus creyentes; nuestras premáticas son nuestra voluntad' UNAMUNO

'Cado uno es hijo de su madre, y de su humor, casado con su opinión' GRACIÁN

I

WHEN WE SAY that Belmonte is a *pueblo* we refer in the first place to a well-defined geographical area of seventeen square kilometers. The territorial area or municipal *término* is divided between the *pueblo* proper, or the space occupied by the buildings, and the remainder given over to cultivation or wasteland. There are no inhabited farmsteads; everyone lives in the town and sets out daily to his plots. A geographic community of residence is thus the second characteristic of the *pueblo*, and agricultural occupations (with an almost self-sufficient agricultural economy during the last few centuries) the third. In the centre of the *pueblo* is the parish church, in which the townsmen have placed the images of their patron saints on the main altar. Besides the parish church and outside the town but within the district, there are two hermitages and a small chapel, standing in the middle of the plots. Thus in the fourth place *pueblo* is a parish with special patrons, a priest, a parish church and other sacred places. Fifthly, and fundamentally, *pueblo* is the group of people who live there, or more strictly the *vecinos*. These number less than 1,300. To be a *vecino* is equivalent to enjoying the rights and taking part in the duties attached to the municipality. This supposes a regulating organ—the Town

Council, a sixth essential element in the constitution of the *pueblo* as a political and juridical entity.

The first full description of the composition of the Town Council occurs in a book of the parish of 1619.[1] The council was composed by the *Alcayde* (mayor), *jurado mayor* (first alderman), *jurador menor* (second alderman) and six councillors; the document refers to '*jurado* and council of the said place, forming the governing body and representing this place in the name of everybody . . .'. The representative function of the Council and its democratic character are thus clearly stated. The aldermen were the administrators and justices of the municipality; the councillors formed a corporation which also seems to have dealt with administrative and political matters. During the eighteenth and nineteenth centuries the minutes are much more explicit about the composition and functions of the Council. At times during the nineteenth century the names of the offices change but the attributes and competency are the same.

From about 1750 to 1850 the composition of the municipal Junta and its respective attributes was as follows:

Offices	Attributes
Council:	
Mayor	President of the Council and Government delegate.
First Alderman ⎫ Second Alderman ⎭	Responsible for order, government and municipal justice.
Síndico Procurador General	Defends the *pueblo* against anything he considers oppressive, such as excessive taxation.
First Deputy ⎫ Second Deputy ⎭	Delegates of the people of the *pueblo* whom they represent in the Council.
Corporations:	
Junta of Twenty Commissions	They allot common lands owned by the Council, assess taxes, stipulate terms of contract with 'professionals', examine accounts, upkeep of roads, etc.
Lesser Officials:	
Secretary	
Luminero	Collector of first fruits and tithes.
Alcayde	To look after the jail.
Constable	

The forms of election for the different posts in this period were various. In the last quarter of the year the mayor sum-

---

[1] Book II of the Parish, fols. 319–20v.

moned the Council to proceed with the election of some of the members who would make up the Municipal Corporation for the year to come. Each one desposited one paper with the name of his candidate for the office of mayor, two others for the election of aldermen, and the fourth for the first deputy.[1] Those who obtained an absolute majority of votes were elected; they could not have any kinship with the electors. The mayor and aldermen had to be confirmed in their offices by Royal assent, a clause which was nothing more than a formality. The *Síndico Procurador General* was chosen after a vote by the mayor, the priest and the superintendents of the sodalities of Our Lady of the Rosary, Our Lady of Caballeros and the Infant Jesus. The man elected was confirmed in his office without delay by the provincial authorities.[2] On a Sunday after solemn Mass, when the Council had been in office for a few weeks, the constable called 'under the penalty of five *reales*' all the residents of the town to the Council Hall in order to vote for twenty-four electors, who, in turn, by placing slips of paper in ballot-boxes voted for someone to discharge the duty of second deputy.[3] The members of the Junta of Twenty and the Commissions were chosen by lot from a list made up of names of 'all the persons who have held any post in the administration or government of the town'.[4] Finally all minor officials were named by the Council. All positions except those of the secretary, jailor and constable were held for one year only.

Since 1870 the composition of the Council has been: mayor, deputy mayor, six councillors and a justice of the peace. The method of election, however, became more democratic (until the outbreak of the civil war): all the councillors were chosen by the *pueblo* through a poll. The elected councillors, assembled in the Municipal Hall, chose from among themselves and by an absolute majority of votes the mayor and deputy mayor, and established a hierarchy among themselves.[5] Each one of these

---

[1] Minutes of the Council, 11 October 1800.
[2] Ibid., 25 October 1799.   [3] Ibid., 20 January 1799.   [4] Ibid., 23 June 1804.
[5] The Minutes of 1 February 1875 say that the Council is constituted in agreement with the municipal law of 1870. See also Minutes of 30 June and 1 July 1883. On 3 May 1883 (according to the Minute of 30 June 1883) the number of votes for the election of councillors reached the figure of 204. Several years later the number of votes cast had dropped to 116 (Minute of 1 January 1890).

had his own sphere of duty and at the same time the commissions were permanently sub-divided, each covering a specific
field of duty which still exists. The Council instead of renewing
itself completely every year, renewed half its members, everyone
occupying their positions for two years. During political crises,
pronunciamientos or changes of power, the members of the Council
were dismissed from their posts and replaced by others who
were elected by the outgoing Council. Uniformity of elections,
greater democracy in the method, increasing specification of
functions and a political tinge following the vicissitudes of national events, are the distinguishing features in this second stage
in the municipality. Apart from this the attributes of the municipal Junta continue, practically until the civil war, to be the
same.

This is the picture of government and administration from an
official point of view or *de jure*. In practice the body was enlarged
by convening *pudientes* or *mayores contribuyentes* to arrange the programme for the festivals in the *pueblo*,[1] to discuss the construction of communal works,[2] to give their opinion on national
political crises and to suggest how the Council should act,[3] to
choose the persons for subordinate positions in the Council,[4]
and so on. This sporadic form of contributing to the municipal
administration acquires a precise outline at the end of the last
century when the *mayores contribuyentes* annually chose a certain
number from among themselves to take part in the sessions of
the Council. Those elected were called *compromisarios* and held
the right to vote.[5]

But the people of the *pueblo* also had their various forms of
representation, as can be traced in the Minutes. Thus the Minutes dated April 29 1877 and 19 May 1881, refer to the Council as
having 'nine contributors as associates who represent the three
classes'. But we find other modes of participation as well, much
more direct and personal. When for the purposes of taxation the
townsfolk believed that they had been classified in a group
higher than the one to which they thought they corresponded,
they went to protest to the Council,[6] or they went in groups to

[1] Minutes of the Council, 9 August 1857.
[2] Ibid., 9 February 1862. [3] Ibid., 1 October 1868. [4] Ibid., 12 May 1869.
[5] Ibid., 20 December 1894 & 20 January 1917.
[6] Ibid., 3 August 1887.

the Town Hall to ask that the budget agreed to by the Council
for the celebration of the festivals should be increased,[1] or that
for the day of San Roque 'heifers may be loosed to run through
the public square'.[2] The Council granted their petitions. Further there were traditionally established channels through
which they could make themselves heard. Every year since the
Middle Ages on one September morning at 9 o'clock the bells
rang, inviting the neighbourhood to assemble in the public
square to deliberate and 'vote on the budget and taxes'.[3] By the
beginning of this century the form of voting for estimates had
changed. Once the estimates were agreed upon by the governing body, the next step was the display of the same proposals
'to the public for fifteen days, the exposition being announced
to the neighbourhood by the customary proclamation, in order
that all the taxpayers who so desire can inform themselves of
the administration of public funds and if they have any mis-
givings the secretary of this corporation is given authority
to explain everything within his power about the particular
case'.[4] On 19 March 1910 the chemist of the district who had
contracted his services to the *pueblo* with the Council, sought to
be allowed to go to the city, leaving another in his place. With
this petition before them, the Council 'agreed unanimously to
publish a notice with the object of assembling all the residents
who found it convenient to come to the Town Hall at six in the
evening so that they might know of the matter and could make
any suggestions'.[5] Until the stipulated time for the public to
make complaints had expired, the members of the Council
could not proceed with the ratification of budgets, projects,
elections, etc.[6] All accounts had to be exhibited to 'the public',[7]
as well as lists of elections to municipal offices 'so that they
might be examined by as many who want to see them and submit the objections they think are appropriate, giving account
of which to this corporation in order that they may be resolved . . .'.[8] This last phrase indicates that the objections of the
'public' were seriously examined. The Minutes of January
15th 1921 refer to it expressly: 'Once the objections were

---

[1] Ibid., 11 August 1861.   [2] Ibid., 13 August 1887.
[3] Ibid., 14 September 1870.   [4] Ibid., 15 October 1904.
[5] Ibid., 19 March 1910.   [6] Ibid., 20 January 1917.
[7] Ibid., 20 July 1918.   [8] Ibid., 1 January 1924.

resolved . . . '. In spite of this democratic side of the administration the people went on several occasions in a body to the Town Hall to complain that they did not know how 'specific matters of the administration' were being worked out.[1]

The Council assumed, then, the direct or indirect participation by the *pueblo* in municipal management. It recognized the right of those subordinate to it to be kept informed of the development of the municipal problems discussed in the sessions, a right which was almost equivalent to a form of control. It is to be noted, however, that the *pueblo* did not intervene in the preparation and discussion of schemes and regulations directly around the table in the sessions hall, but only in their approbation or rejection. Nothing came into force until the time for objections had expired. The *pueblo* was informed of proceedings by traditional means: the town crier, a peal of bells, the exhibition of lists and projects. These show that decisions taken by the members of the Council could be opposed. Public opinion thus formed the basis which the Council as an executive instrument had to take into account when planning communal tasks and programmes. On the other hand, as well as this institutionalized participation, the *pueblo* always had recourse to clamorous protests as already noted; there is the Minute of 14 October 1922 a date on which 'owing to the repeated complaints' about the price of meat the Council was forced to intervene. If their protests were not heard, the townsmen, as a last resort, took to disobedience and violence.[2]

The Council structure therefore reveals a wider range than that composed by the administrative and governing body itself, because in part it was the *pueblo* who ruled in the *pueblo*. This combination of oligarchy and democracy which so pleased Aristotle[3] further defines the meaning of the word *pueblo*.

The activities controlled by the municipality included the following. The corporation was responsible for urban management and could call on all the townsmen, according to their age and the rules stated by the Council,[4] for the upkeep and repair

[1] Ibid., 3 December 1927.
[2] Ibid., 24 March 1921.
[3] *Politics* (ed. Loeb); Book IV, VII, 4; V, VI, 3, and VI, II, 4.
[4] Ibid., 10 February 1861.

of roads,[1] bridges[2] and fords,[3] the care of the cemetery,[4] and the
church and hermitage.[5] It was responsible too for instruction
and culture—through the appointment of teachers and the
supervision of schools and education,[6] the arrangement of
both religious and secular programmes for the festivals,[7]
and through the preachers brought to the *pueblo* by the
Council throughout the liturgical year.[8] The determination of
taxable goods and the regulation of municipal impositions,[9]
the administration of the municipal patrimony,[10] and the urban
and rural police composed of the aldermen, constable, jailer and
rural guard,[11] were other responsibilities of the corporation,
together with the regulation of a system of social services. The
socialization of all the agencies related to the spiritual or physical well-being of the community deserves special attention. The
Minutes do not specify whether the vicar was chosen by the
municipal corporation from among several applicants, but they
indicate with sufficient clarity that once a priest had decided to
accept the living he had to discuss the terms and conditions with
the Council. The municipal authorities imposed the hours of
masses which the priest could not alter without giving notice to
the Council the previous day,[12] and determined the first fruits
which were due to him.[13]

The veterinary surgeon, the doctor-assistant, the chemist, the
school-masters, the doctor and the secretary, i.e. all those classified as 'professionals', had to apply for their positions when they
fell vacant in the *pueblo*. Gathered in strength the Council discussed whether to accept or reject the applicant. If he was accepted in principle the matter passed to the respective commission charged with drawing up the terms of the agreement. As
examples I cite some of the oldest contracts that have been preserved. At the beginning of the summer of 1802 a veterinary
surgeon, a doctor-assistant and an apothecary applying for these

[1] Minutes of January and October 1799.
[2] Minutes of the Council, 3 December 1856.
[3] Ibid., 9 June 1861.   [4] Ibid., 15 September 1894.
[5] Ibid., 15 January 1804 & 10 May 1857.
[6] Ibid., 10 March 1872 among others.   [7] Ibid., 9 August 1857.
[8] Ibid., 13 January 1804.   [9] Ibid., 5 October 1851.
[10] The greater part of the Minutes deal with the administration of the municipality.
[11] Minutes of the Council, 1 January 1862 & 12 May 1869.
[12] Ibid., 16 January 1806.   [13] Ibid., 30 September 1806.

posts were admitted for two years starting from St. Michael's Day. Their services had to be paid by the Council according to the price of corn on the said St. Michael's Day. The apothecary had to furnish free all the medicine for every member of the town, both masters and servants; he was absolutely prohibited from receiving any money for it. Nonetheless he could charge for medicine supplied when he dealt with wounds incurred by quarrels or with venereal diseases. The agreement which the doctor signed on 24 June 1804 is given in great detail. He was to take up his post on St. Michael's Day and the Council was to pay him twenty-eight acres of wheat. His duties were: to visit the sick morning and afternoon from 6 to 8 a.m. and 4 to 6 p.m. in the summer, and from 8 to 10 a.m. and 2 to 4 p.m. in the winter; for these purposes the summer began on 1 May and ended on 31 October. He was to make a third visit to the critically ill at night. He was to attend an urgent case at any time, and to attend both masters and servants, prescribing for the sick in their own homes. The final clause prohibits him possessing lands outside the municipal *término* so as to avoid 'any occasion of him not being (in the town) . . . for an emergency case'. Also if he left the district for one day 'he shall have to seek permission from the members of the Council . . . '. This same minute fixed the conditions, obligations and rights of an applicant who had been accepted as the school teacher; the hours for the school were to be 7 to 10 a.m. and 3 to 5 p.m. in the summer and from 8 to 11 a.m. and 2 to 4 p.m. in the winter. Not one of the 'professionals' received any direct pay from the townsfolk. The municipality rewarded their services using part of the money collected through taxes.

Other public services controlled by the Council were the mill, the shop, the bakery and the tavern, which all belonged to the municipality; the Council periodically rented them out at a public auction. The tenant had to pay the agreed sum 'each year on St. John's Day'. It was stipulated to the miller when he could and when he could not charge for his services; in the first case the amount he could charge for grinding the corn was fixed according to the class of grain. Members of the *pueblo* had to be given preference over outsiders.[1] The shopkeeper had to be always stocked with oil, spices, soap, aniseed, pine-kernels,

[1] Ibid., 12 December 1803.

hazelnuts, rice, chocolate, honey, sugar, cheese, spirits, biscuits, sandals, paper, cotton, etc. In the agreement those goods on which he could not overcharge are given in detail, as well as those on which he could make some profit, the amount of which was exactly determined. He was obliged to sell undried codfish 'every fast day'.[1] As for the baker, the sale and varieties of bread are found detailed with the same minuteness.[2] The municipality provided the baker with 'the woman who was the town kneader and baker'. He had to return '100 kilograms of bread well baked for every acre of corn'. He could not charge for the joints of meat brought for roasting by people, but he had to pay if he burnt them. The innkeeper had to provide the town with wine 'until St. Andrew's Day'. They allowed him to make a certain profit from every jugful but this was controlled by the Council. If he bought wine outside the district he had to produce 'a justifiable statement of the price' so that they could assign to him the agreed margin of profit.[3] The weights and measures of oil, wine, spirits and grain were kept in the Town Hall and using these as a yardstick a councillor frequently tested those of the establishments.[4]

The council was also concerned with the regulation of internal local order, and with keeping watch over the life of the community, its customs and correct modes of behaviour. The innkeeper had to close the doors of the tavern at night-fall, 'at the sound of the Angelus';[5] young men were prohibited from walking about at night 'wrapped in blankets' for 'they conceal their faces so as not be recognized';[6] they could not stroll around singing 'after 9 p.m. without permission from the authority',[7] and if they were 'in the streets after 11 p.m. and disturb the peace though only slightly by songs and shouts' they would be fined.[8] The Council endeavoured at all costs to 'avoid the disorders produced in the locality at night by young men with tuneless voices whose only object is to upset the tranquillity of the neighbourhood'.[9] To enforce this every night two councillors patrolled the streets.[10] Their active vigilance forbade 'private

---

[1] Ibid.   [2] Ibid.   [3] Ibid., 6 August 1804.
[4] Ibid., 7 June 1857.   [5] Ibid., 10 May 1857.
[6] Ibid., 26 January 1861.   [7] Ibid., 22 January 1865.
[8] Ibid., 31 August 1879.   [9] Ibid., 14 November 1883.
[10] Ibid., 23 October 1883.

games which are played at night among the labouring class'.[1]
Further in order that this small popular-State or *pueblo*-State
should lack nothing, in 1877 the 'Ordinances of the rural and
urban police drawn up by the Council' were promulgated.
These were nothing but a digest of different edicts enacted previously. In the first section entitled 'internal order of the
population' we read: Article I. 'It is prohibited to form groups
in the porch of the church . . . during the celebration of divine
offices, to stroll around singing, to play ball, or to indulge in
other activities which tend to distract the attention of the faithful, under the fine of five pts'. Article II: 'Those attending at
church are to take care on coming out to leave the exit open,
stepping aside to allow the women and old people to pass'.
These first two articles re-enact a 'law' which had ordered
the same ten years before.[2] Articles III and IV renew that which
had been established forty-five years before.[3] Article III: 'Those
who blaspheme in public or express contempt for sacred things
will be punished by a fine of five to ten pesetas', and Article IV:
'Those who utter obscene, gross or insulting words in public
which contain malicious allusions to the private life of any particular person, lessening his dignity and good reputation,
although they cannot be counted as injuries, will be punished
by the fine of . . . '. Articles V and VI reaffirm the necessity to
break up 'rowdy reunions with *rondas* and other nocturnal
amusements which are clearly going to trouble the neighbourhood with wild and discordant voices out of place in a civilized
country . . . ', and 'to prohibit vulgar songs which offend
modesty and public decency . . .'. Article VII regulates the
change of residence and the method of acquiring *vecino*-ship in
the *pueblo*. Article VIII is directed against charlatans 'who
practise quack methods' and Article IX against games of
hazard and gambling already condemned fifteen years previously.
The Ordinances also fix in detail the rights and duties as regards
irrigation. Besides these 'Ordinances of rural and urban policy'
they set forth a 'Municipal Charter for the economic regime of
the Council', of which however I found nothing more than the
reference. The Minutes refer frequently to a series of measures
which the Council issued periodically. The title of the one for

---

[1] Ibid., 31 January 1862. [2] Ibid., 13 January 1867.
[3] Ibid., 3 May 1832.

13 October 1861 is a 'minute to settle everything suitably for the
vintage season'. Others refer to the reaping season,[1] others to
the fruit season[2]. Using experiences of similar circumstances in
previous years they forestalled and resolved difficulties.

Finally the Council looked after the administration of justice
and means of coercion. The Minutes preserved say nothing
about the functions of the municipal justice in past centuries, the
attributes of the judge, prosecution, defence and witnesses. They
only speak of their existence.[3] Probably the procedure was very
similar to the present one, in that the 'good men' were an
integrated part of local justice, according to the custom of the
Middle Ages. With regard to competence, municipal justice
exceeded the limits to which it is confined today. The Council
used to enforce its orders by fines and by prison sentences. It is
not clear from the Minutes how many fines were imposed nor
how often the prison was used. The only allusion found[4] says
briefly: 'The penalty which the guilty incur cannot be enforced
in the majority of cases as there are no forms'. The Minutes only
refer to the governmental and administrative side of the Corporation. If the municipal Judge or the special commission of
the Council who dealt with justice drew up minutes, as seems
probable, these have not been kept. The aldermen and councillors in turn, the constable and the rural guard were those
members of the body charged with seeing orders enforced.

The extent of municipal autonomy can best be assessed in
relation to the intervention in municipal affairs by national
and provincial bodies. The capital of the province held 'full
authority to nominate persons to fulfil the duties of mayor and
aldermen in the place of Belmonte de los Caballeros . . .'.[5] This
power of nomination, however, was reduced to the confirmation
of the person elected in the *pueblo* and by the *pueblo*. The same
happened with the right which the provincial Audience held,
according to an order of 1762, to sanction the election of the
Síndico Procurador General chosen by the *pueblo* in the manner explained.[6] The Minutes mention two other occasions when the
provincial authority intervened in the activities of the *pueblo*. In

[1] Ibid., 30 June 1861 & 25 May 1867.   [2] Ibid., 12 May 1869.
[3] Ibid., 13 February 1870 for example.   [4] Ibid., 30 November 1877.
[5] Ibid., 24 December 1805.   [6] Ibid., 24 December 1805.

1802[1] the *pueblo* received a mandate from the Council of the provincial capital forbidding the residents to sell the vintage of the district to any place except the capital. Four years later[2] the mayoralty received a writ from the Royal Audience that ordered the first fruits of the corn to be divided, and half of the same to be delivered to the priest. The decree came in response to an appeal made by the same priest to the provincial Court of Justice. Apart from these interventions of a political and judicial nature, I have not found in the Minutes any indication of provincial intervention diminishing the autonomy of the Council.

The constitution and election of the municipal corporation was subordinate to national statutory laws. The secretaries who write the Minutes always emphasize that in the election of 'Justice and Government' which had taken place in the *pueblo*, the instructions enacted in 1772 have been carried out[3]; that the chosen mayor and aldermen have been confirmed in their positions by royal assent[4]; that in 1870 and in 1876 orders were received in the Town Hall which regulated the constitution of the Council;[5] or they comment on municipal laws received for the functioning of the Municipal Junta[6] etc. In national crises the Council had to resign, automatically forming another, chosen by those leaving office from among the élite. Also, it is obvious, government influence made itself felt in the *pueblo* through taxes and levies in the case of war. Finally on 22 May 1806 a Royal Proviso was received by the Council ordering that a townsman should be erased from the books of common state and be elevated to enjoy all the privileges of an *infanzón* (a rank of the lesser nobility of Aragón).

These forms of penetration by the external authority into the *pueblo* were, in reality, far less effective than one would think. Elections were held in the *pueblo* by the residents without any sort of exterior control; those elected were always confirmed in their offices. The methods of electing whether regulated provincially or on a national scale aroused no interest, so little in fact that the Council had to resort to fines to oblige the residents

---

[1] Ibid., 4 January.   [2] Minutes of the Council, 27 October 1806.
[3] Ibid., 1 October 1800 and 6 October 1801.
[4] Ibid., 24 December 1805.
[5] Ibid., 28 September 1874 and 27 November 1876.
[6] Ibid., 1 August 1880.

to cast their vote. To appreciate the repercussions caused in the town by changes in national political creeds and constitutions one ought to remember the isolation of any *pueblo* in the eighteenth and nineteenth centuries, the limited means of communication and of propaganda, and the fact that the members of the Council frequently did not know how to read or write. Further, power passed from hand to hand always within the same strata. As for military service some of the *pudientes* avoided it for their children in normal circumstances by paying a small sum, or even by contracting matrimony at the right moment. Submission to Civil and penal codes in as much as they were outside the sphere of municipal jurisdiction, and the few cases in reality in which the matters were settled out of the *pueblo*, were probably the most effective link between the *pueblo* and the province and nation.

It should not be assumed however that interference by the provincial or national authority was always tolerated in the town. The *pueblo* had its *Síndico Procurador General* whose official task was to oppose the external authorities in everything that he judged to be disadvantageous to the *pueblo*. As late as 1924[1] more than eighty townsmen went to the Town Hall to protest about the inadequate work done by the municipal guard. Under such pressure the Council dismissed him. Some days later the Civil Governor of the province reinstated him in his office, but the Council fiercely resisted such a measure and nominated another person they considered more suitable.

Throughout the eighteenth and nineteenth centuries the town lived its own life in its own backwater. The municipal corporation was a political institution both autonomous and heteronomous, autocephalous and heterocephalous. It was autonomous in the sense that the internal order of the community was regulated by the full Council; heteronomous in as much as the said internal order of the community was to a small extent conditioned by national and provincial laws; autocephalous because the members of the Council were elected by the community; heterocephalous because the persons who occupied certain posts had to be confirmed in them by an authority outside the *pueblo*.

[1] 14 February.

II

The Minutes of the last part of the nineteenth century imply by
their silence that the competence of the municipal corporation
is beginning to diminish. This parallels the process of the
pueblo's gradual incorporation into wider systems. For example,
in the final twenty years of the last century the *luminero*, or col-
lector of tithes, is not mentioned at all. This system of religious-
civil contribution based especially on the donation of corn,
loses its religious character and is reduced to a sum paid in
money to the Council. As the 'professionals' preferred to be
paid in coin, the collecting, weighing and storing of corn in the
town granary ceases and the *luminero* is no longer needed. The
office of jailer remains indefinitely vacant, the post no longer
holding any significance because the provincial authority assumes the responsibility that formerly lay with the *pueblo*. The
more or less voluntary adoption of national models has combined with increasing state interference in municipal affairs to
integrate the *pueblo*, at least in principle, into the national ambit
and to reduce its sphere of competency. The first process has followed a peaceful course, slow but steady; the second occasioned
by national and political crises has been more intermittent and
abrupt. The composition and functions of the present municipal
corporation is the result of the interplay between these two
factors. Here are some examples.

At the beginning of 1892[1] the woman who lodged the school-
masters in her house appealed to the Council 'that they would
increase by ten pesetas the rent for the rooms the teachers occupied'. A little later[2] we read in the Minutes that the schools had
been closed for three months because the masters refused to
teach until the Council paid them the stipulated sum. Two
months afterwards[3] the Council returned to the same problem
—'a question of such vital interest' emphasizes the clerk—and
all its members agreed 'to raise the schools to the category of
competition paying the quantity of 825 pesetas for the teacher'
in place of the 625 pesetas which each had received, 'so that the
schools will be staffed in the only way that everyone wants, that
is by rigorous competition and not by any other form'. There

---

[1] Minutes of the Council of 6 January 1892.   [2] Ibid., 13 July 1901.
[3] Ibid., 10 September 1901.

are various points of interest arising out of this question of the schools. First the Council no longer paid with corn; second, they found themselves in economic difficulties by paying the masters only their lodging and a salary of 625 pesetas. On the other hand, as pupils of that epoch will recall, the school was in fact neglected because of the incapacity of the teachers, whom the people in the end expelled from the town. This implied a blunder on the part of those members of the Council who had chosen these 'professionals' to occupy the position. Thus they decided to fill the vacancies 'by rigorous competition'; that is, they renounced the responsibility of choosing the masters and entrusted it to the national system which, after an examination, awarded the different *pueblos* to the teachers, according to their qualifications. Faced by a 'question of such vital importance', they realized their limitations and voluntarily reduced the sphere of their authority, although in consequence they had to increase the salary of each master to 825 pesetas. This was what 'everyone wants', supply by 'rigorous competition and not by any other form'. In a similar way the appointment of all the remaining 'professionals' which the Council had chosen was being lost to them. The last secretary was nominated by the Council on 27 July 1920 and the last doctor on 23 February 1924. From then on all the 'professionals' were sent to the *pueblo*, after an examination by the responsible national body.

One of the changes brought about in the *pueblo* during the second historical period was, as we have seen, the democratization of elections, in the sense that the *pueblo* chose by ballot all the councillors, who in their turn chose from among themselves the mayor. Elections continued in this manner until 3 October 1923, when the lieutenant of the civil guard of the district presented himself before the Council as 'Bearer of a Royal Decree of the Military Directory dated 30 September ultimo, in virtue of which all councils in the nation shall cease to function immediately'.[1] The municipal Junta, under the presidency of the lieutenant of the civil guard, immediately proceeded to elect a new Council, an election in which the *pueblo* did not take any part. The Council thus formed was obliged to dissolve on 6 April 1924 by a Royal Order of the Ministry of the Interior. In

---

[1] The Minutes refer to the *pronunciamiento* of General Primo de Rivera on 13 September 1923.

1930 and 1931 the Council changed again, but on this last occasion, during the republican period, the election returned to its popular form. Finally in July 1936, at the beginning of the civil war, the scene with the lieutenant of the civil guard was repeated in the Council.

The 'Law of Local Government' approved by a Decree of the Ministry of the Interior in 1955 has regulated the organization and administration of municipalities since that date. 'The Spanish State', says the first article of the preliminary Title, 'is made up of the natural entities formed by municipalities, grouped together territorially in the provinces'. The first article proceeds to recognize the municipality—the *pueblo*—as the smallest political segment in the nation. But the attributes of this smallest political segment are not now the same as during the period previously described. The mayor, whose position must be accepted and who can be compulsorily discharged,[1] is the chief of the municipal administration, president of the Council and the Government delegate.[2] He is nominated by the Civil Governor of the Province,[3] and his appointment is of indefinite duration;[4] he ceases to hold office when ' for reasons of public interest the Ministry of the Interior sees fit'.[5] The mayor appoints a deputy mayor from among the councillors[6]—the office of deputy mayor is also obligatory.[7] If he absents himself from the municipality for more than twenty-four hours he has to make it known to the Civil Governor of the Province.[8] The nomination of the mayor and his deputy, the duration and cessation of their posts, are no longer in the hands of the municipality. Governmental control was unknown in the former period.

The Council is also composed of six councillors who correspond in ratio to the number of inhabitants of the *pueblo*. Two councillors are elected by heads of families; two by the syndicates in the district; and then these four elect the remaining two from among members of economic, cultural and professional bodies in the *pueblo*.[9] The appointment lasts six years, the Council renewing itself by half every three. The mayor and councillors form the full Council which is responsible for the government

[1] *Ley de Régimen Local*, Título III, Ch. 1, Section 1a, Art. 63.
[2] Ibid. Art. 59.   [3] Ibid. Art. 62, 2º.   [4] Ibid., Art. 61.
[5] Ibid., Art. 62, 3.   [6] Ibid., Art. 66.   [7] Ibid., Art. 67, 2º.
[8] Ibid., Art. 68.   [9] Ibid., Art. 86, 1º, 2º 3º.

and administration of the municipality. The mayor as Government delegate has to see that Government laws and measures are carried out; he has to keep order, take care that local services are fulfilled, make sure that taxes imposed by the state are paid, and personally to adopt, in the case of emergencies, any measures he thinks necessary. As president of the Council he summons, presides over, adjourns and closes meetings; he has the casting vote.[1] The mayor always has the secretary of the Council at his side, an outside official with a professional training who reminds the mayor and corporation of the laws and draws up the Minutes.

Urban management, the administration of the municipal patrimony, health and hygiene, supplies, transport, education and culture, charities, and the rural and urban police force continue to be in the municipal competence as of old.[2] But in reality these are words devoid of their former meaning. Urban management no longer means the upkeep of the road that passes through the *pueblo*, for this is now the duty of an agency outside the town. The municipal patrimony has been reduced to the possession of some land of insignificant economic value. Health and hygiene are the concern of the doctor, in whose appointment or dismissal the *pueblo* has no say. The Council's say in the supply and control of provisions in the shops, bakeries, mill and tavern has gone. Inspection of the quality of foodstuffs is no longer the concern of the aldermen but of the doctor and veterinary surgeon. The inspection of schools is a job for the provincial inspector rather than the mayor; and as for the police the civil guard now has more authority than the local force.

In its relationship to the nation the *pueblo* has responded to the demands of a national process of technical-social development by accepting a whole range of innovations. It has facilitated the circulation of money, adopting it as the medium of transactions, entered the more comprehensive national system for the supply of 'professionals' and rural police, and left a free passage for private economy. No law compelled the Council to take these steps at the time and in the circumstances that it took them, but once taken each one meant a reduced sphere of powers for the Council on the one side and a differentiation of

---

[1] *Ley de Régimen Local*, Título IV, Ch. III, Section 1.
[2] Ibid. Ch. I, Section. 1.

responsibilities on the other. Although the responsibility for everything that happens in the *pueblo* falls chiefly on the mayor, it is subdivided into sections. A quasi-voluntary reduction of municipal attributes and an increased differentiation are thus the particular notes which characterize the relations of *pueblo* and nation in the third period described. The municipal corporation could have responded in other ways to the demands and pressures of national development; it could have begun the process of adaptation earlier or have delayed it—there was no external legal pressure. This lack of compulsion is not found in the relation between *pueblo* and the State. The coercive powers of the State have been whittling away municipal power; firstly by diminishing the area of municipal jurisdiction, then by interfering with the democratic forms of electing the corporation, and finally by strictly curtailing and regulating the sphere of activities of local government and administration. The *pueblo* has been won over by the nation, defeated by the State.

III

The Council is the smallest political organ which in its function of governing and administrating the *pueblo* applies laws of a national or provincial character to particular cases, to families and individuals. The mayor is at once the Government delegate and a son of the *pueblo*; the councillors, besides discharging the duties of their offices, represent the interests of the groups by whom they were elected. Both mayor and councillors only hold their offices temporarily; when they leave office they become simply residents again. The autonomy and heteronomy of the institution, as a result of which a man may at the same time be a Government delegate and a resident of the town, a councillor and representative of the interests of others as well as of his own, implies the necessity for some degree of compromise. Similarly the application of abstract norms which originate from the State to particular cases and to oneself, and the adjustment of a traditional internal order to new external laws, imply a certain tempering of the law and the possibility that an individual may find himself at cross-purposes. The ways of combining different commitments and their interpretation by the townsmen is the main theme of the following analysis.

'Council' is a word with different associations for the towns-men; these associations offer various perspectives from which we can consider it. Firstly, there is the word in its old sense: the Council deals with specific problems of the *pueblo*, according to methods that have hardly changed, at least outwardly, in the last few centuries. The programme of the festivals is one example; this is prepared by the Council and the corresponding com-mittee, and in principle the competence of the Council and com-mittee is just the same as it was— although in practice there are some differences. Until 1936 the festivals were public celebrations held in the main square, which is intersected by the national highway; all the residents gathered, and while the young people danced the older ones sat drinking on the terraces of the bars around the dancing; the women seated on chairs watched the dancing, talking among themselves. All took part. Owing to the increasing traffic, the Council was instructed to confine the band in the hall of the old school where only those who are taking part in the dancing, almost entirely the young people, go. The firebull which passed by at midnight, one of the most popular spectacles, no longer runs through the main street, where the traffic police object, but through the narrow side-streets. The pre-war festival sports were of a local character, the lads of the town taking part almost exclusively. Today the cycle race, for example, is run by an organization from the city which has nothing to do with the local committee for festivals; the road police control the traffic, and in the last few years not one boy from the town has taken part. Permission for the amateur bull-fight formerly only a formality is now so complicated that people are discouraged from seeking it. In this way the Council and committee lose effective, though not theoretic, control of part of the festival activities. While the letter of the law has not varied much, the attributes of the Council have been lessened.

With similar limitations, and without the full autonomy of earlier times, the Council or *ad hoc* commission is responsible for local improvements, the cleaning of roads and canals, the per-formance of personal services, the internal order of the commu-nity, etc. The specialization of functions mentioned above is seen in the responsibility for the cleaning of roads and canals: the care of the first has passed to the Brotherhood and the up-keep of the second to the local Junta of Irrigation.

The organization of the internal order of the community is bound up with usages, customs, rights and duties inherent in communal life. Communal life, to be such, has to be regulated to some extent, and the institution that has traditionally regulated it is the Council. 'That is what the Council is for' the residents say and the orders of the Council simply control the forms of good neighbourliness and therefore deserve their support. Not all the residents necessarily obey such ordinances, but all accept as natural and legal the Council's right to expect the collaboration of the townsmen.

The purpose of the former *Síndico Procurador General* was to protect the *pueblo* against anything that might prove a burden to it. He defended the interests of the *pueblo* against the national or provincial authority. Although his office no longer exists there are several recent examples of the same role being performed by the people themselves. In 1920[1] the municipal corporation discussed the 'attitude which the Council have decided to adopt with respect to the taxation—national—of corn', because 'naturally they do not view with pleasure the taxation of corn imposed by the Government, as it is unjust and detrimental for the harvesters'. The members of the Council continue the Minutes, were disposed to support any movement whatever, however extreme, to impede the said taxation. In 1932 the Council 'in the name of 300 farmers of the *pueblo* sent a telegram to the Minister of Agriculture asking him to protect the interests of the sugar-beet growers'.[2] Examples given in chapter II described the reaction of the *pueblo*, through the Council and the Brotherhood to a neighbouring *pueblo* which had claimed that the residents of Belmonte, who held land in their municipal district, should contribute to the erection of a granary. The residents of Belmonte refused to pay the contribution arguing, that they all brought their corn to Belmonte and consequently would not be using the one that was being built. They all went to the neighbouring town to protest to the Council. On their return to the *pueblo* they got together with the Council and the Brotherhood and these bodies agreed to send a commission to Madrid so that the Ministry of Agriculture might solve the problem. The *Síndico Procurador General*, Council, and

---

[1] Minutes of the Council, 28 August.   [2] Ibid., 9 July.

Brotherhood have been—and the last two still are—the channels through which the *pueblo* can seek vindication. The Council guarantees the interests of the townsmen. As *locus* of power and guarantor of their interests against powers outside the town, the Council is considered to deserve unconditional support as the most efficient instrument through which the *pueblo* canalizes its protests. The Council merges into the *pueblo*, is in fact the *pueblo* in action. This fusion is opposed, however, to the fusion of Council and State.

In the third place the Council is where one goes to pay all classes of taxes, duties, fines, to ask for licences etc. There, purchases of any taxable object are declared and there, in the postwar period, they had to declare the yield of their plots, their poultry and the rest of their livestock. The resulting tax was in proportion to what had been declared, and it followed that all residents at one time or another declared less than they in fact possessed or cultivated.

Some figures can give us an idea of the volume of taxation weighing upon the *pueblo*. In 1960 the State received as contribution from lands (291,518 pesetas) and from houses (47,130 pesetas) the total sum of 338,648 pesetas. The provincial Deputation obtained 100,000 pesetas as taxes from flocks and plots, besides a wheel tax of 11,450 pesetas. The municipal land tax, which is kept in the *pueblo*, amounted to 73,606 pesetas and the urban rates to 33,548 pesetas, a total of 107,154 pesetas. The Brotherhood encumbered the residents with a tax of 60,000 pesetas, the Syndicate of Local Irrigation with 59,732 pesetas and the General Syndicate of Irrigation with 300 pesetas for every hectare irrigated (approximately 27,000 pesetas). To this must be added the family quotas paid monthly to the doctor and doctor's assistant. The total gives 703,984 pesetas contributed annually by the town. Taken together with the provincial and national dues for the shops and small industries, cinemas and two small factories, one easily arrives at a sum of one million pesetas as the set contribution paid annually by the *pueblo*.

As the important thing is that 'money should not leave the *pueblo*', a false declaration is considered just and praiseworthy and something to boast about in the bar. 'Those people—the Government or Deputation—do nothing but rob us of our own, why can't we defend ourselves?' Besides, 'he who robs a robber

has a hundred years indulgence'. Frequently they take to the
city chickens, hams, or fruit as gifts to family or friends there.
The introduction of this class of goods into the city is subject to a
provincial tax. The articles are carefully concealed so as not to
attract the attention of the tax-collector. It never occurs to anyone to declare them; to do so would be equivalent to being a
primo (simpleton). The Council may be lenient when declarations are difficult to determine and when the resulting duties are
going outside the municipality, as in the case of alfalfa, for
instance.

On the other hand when the Council deals with a collection of
funds for the municipality through taxes, the municipal guard
verifies the truth of the manifestation in any doubtful case. As
everybody knows approximately what is the economic power of
the others, it is very difficult to evade any class of taxation. If
someone has managed to do so he will be careful to hide it, because if any member of the Corporation finds out he will probably—unless he is on very good terms with the member—be
obliged to pay; nor will he publicize it, for it is not done to boast
about defrauding the municipality, not because *in genere* it is bad
to defraud it, but because as in this case the Council does not
hold any property and has to collect whatever it needs through
taxation, the fraud of one or more residents is a burden on the
rest. Every year the Council needs to collect a minimum of
107,154 pesetas, which is imposed on the residents in proportion
to their means. If any resident avoids paying his due share,
the missing quantity will fall on the others or will cause the list
of taxable objects to be enlarged; in other words, as much taxation is imposed as is necessary to obtain the sum of 107,154
pesetas needed by the municipality. Hence any individual who
manages to avoid part of his responsibility, a responsibility
which is not reckoned as such, maintains a discreet silence in
order to escape the censure of the rest. Thus we deal not with a
juridical sensibility but with a dimension of the communal spirit.

The Council, therefore, is intimately associated with taxation, to such an extent that when the people hear the familiar
sound of the trumpet which precedes the intonated reading of a
Council proclamation by the constable they ask; 'What are
they demanding money for now?'. As we have seen the impositions are either for the State, province, or municipality. As to

the payment of the first, there are no possible subterfuges because the Treasury possesses a list of the lands and houses of every person. It is possible and the attempt is frequently made to dodge the second; it is more difficult and normally one does not try—unless one belongs to the lower sections—to evade the last. If the State contributions and provincial dues are paid it is 'because there is no other remedy'; but 'it would be bad not to put one's shoulder to the wheel' when it concerns municipal taxes. The total sum of the first two taxes 'leaves the *pueblo* and we do not see it again'. 'They—the Government or Deputation—never come to bring anything, only to take something away'. 'With the money they take from us they can now have Avenues and Ministries, but they don't worry much about providing us with more tractors'. 'They only remember us to take away our money' etc.

This attitude indicates a lack of provincial or national solidarity. The residents feel that they only reciprocate the indifference with which the State and province regard the *pueblos*. Of course the contributions demanded by the province and State are 'unjust', and 'it is right' to skimp them when one can. When the communal spirit is effectively felt, as in the case of the municipality, such intentions practically disappear.

In the last aspect of the Council described, it already appears as a mixed organ, a body in which the *pueblo*, province, and State are all combined. This hybrid character of the institution merits a more extensive description. The Council becomes the political cell through which the power of the State makes itself felt in the *pueblo*. The laws which stem from the Government, the frequent innovations of the same, political changes, the military *pronunciamientos*, the passing from a monarchy to a republic and from that to a dictatorship—any national political crisis might be expected to have had its repercussions in the Council. Let us see what these repercussions were against a background.

1812:   a liberal and anticlerical Constitution is promulgated.

1814:   abolition of the same. Establishment of an absolute monarchy. Penalty of death to anyone who speaks favourably of the Constitution. Pamplona rebels against the monarchy.

1815:   Coruña also rebels.

1816:   a plot against the king in Madrid.

1817:   an uprising in Cataluña.

1819:   an uprising in Valencia.

1820:   loss of Florida. The first military *pronunciamiento* by General Riego. Barcelona, Zaragoza, Pamplona, Valencia, Oviedo and Coruña join the General. The king capitulates and swears to abide by the Constitution.

1823:   a French army of 100,000 men enters Spain. They restore absolute monarchy. Bloody reprisals by the king.

1833:   the first Carlist war begins.

1834:   Liberal Statute enacted. Massacre of friars in Madrid.

1835:   another *pronunciamiento*. Massacre of friars in Barcelona, Zaragoza, Valencia and Murcia. Suppression of the greater part of the religious orders.

1836:   Confiscation and sale of church property. The Captain General of Zaragoza writes to the regent to say that this province has declared itself independent. Lesser officials of the army impose the Constitution of 1812 on the Regent María Cristina.

1837:   a moderate liberal Constitution is promulgated.

1839:   *pronunciamiento* by General Espartero.

1840:   the queen regent goes into exile. From September 1833 to August 1840 fourteen ministries.

1842:   General Espartero governs as a dictator. Barcelona rebels, demanding constitutional 'Cortes'.

1843:   another military *pronunciamiento* forces Espartero into exile. Isabel II is declared of age, (she was 13 years old).

1844:   numerous executions for 'offences' (political).

1845:   another Constitution promulgated, but General Narváez governs as a dictator.

1847:   the Carlist wars recommence.

1848:   uprisings in Madrid, Barcelona, Sevilla and Valencia.

1849:   the king-consort manages to become Prime Minister for a day.

1851:   the dictator Narváez sees himself obliged to resign. The right of holding property is restored to the Church. Parliament is dissolved. The new one formed is twice suspended in its functions.

1852:   revision of the last Constitution.

1854:   a *pronunciamiento* by O'Donnell in Madrid is supported
            by Zaragoza. The palace of the queen-mother is
            sacked and she is expelled permanently from the
            country. The press ask for her head. From May 1844
            to June 1854 there were 13 ministries.

1855:   the 'Cortes' make up a Constitution more radical
            than the former ones but it is never promulgated.

1856–68: Rebellions in Zaragoza, Barcelona and Andalucía.
            General Prim tries to force seven *pronunciamientos* in
            four years. War in Morocco, Santo Domingo and
            Perú. A strike of students in Madrid with various
            deaths. Twelve governments succeed each other.

1868:   *pronunciamiento* by the Navy, supported by the Army
            and local Juntas. Isabel II loses the crown and goes
            into exile.

1869:   new Constitution.

1871:   Assassination of Prim. Amadeus of Savoy begins
            his reign in Spain. During his two year reign there
            were six government crises and four general elections.

1872:   Attempted assassination of Amadeus. A Congress of
            the International Workingmen's Association is held
            in Zaragoza. Social agitations by the 'International'.
            The renewal of the Carlist War. The war continues
            in Cuba. Uprisings in Ferrol and Málaga.

1873:   the king leaves Spain. The Republic is proclaimed
            which in less than a year consumes four presidents.
            Cataluña proclaims itself independent. The Navy is
            outside the control of the government. The troops of
            General Pavía lay waste Andalucía. The anarchist
            disciples of Bakunin number some 30,000.

1874:   the *pronunciamiento* of General Pavía dissolves the
            'Cortes'. Zaragoza rebels. Dictatorship of General
            Serrano. The *pronunciamiento* of Martínez Campos
            brings the Bourbon monarchy once more to Spain in
            the person of Alfonso XII.

1876:   another constitution which satisfies neither the
            liberals nor the Church.

1878–79: Two attempts against the king.

1886:   the results of the general elections are published in a newspaper of the government before the ballot has been verified.

1890:   universal suffrage is proclaimed for all men from twenty-four years.

1897:   Assassination of the Prime Minister.

1898:   war against Cuba and the United States; loss of Puerto Rico, Cuba and the Philippines. End of the colonial empire. From November 1885 till May 1902 eleven governments succeeded one another, and from May 1902 till September 1923, thirty-three governments.

1906:   attempted assassination of the king.

1909:   attacks on the garrison of Melilla. 'Tragic Week' in Barcelona.

1920:   Uprising of anarchists in Zaragoza.

1921:   Assassination of the Prime Minister.

1922:   Anarchist conference in Zaragoza.

1923–30: The garrisons of Barcelona and Zaragoza rebel. Dictatorship of General Primo de Rivera.

1931:   Proclamation of the Republic. New Constitution. National anarchist leaders establish their headquarters in Zaragoza.

1933:   nineteen political parties appear in the electoral lists.

1934:   a national general strike. An uprising in Asturias.

1935:   at the end of this year there had been a total of twenty-eight governments since 1931.

1936:   Between February and May: 228 partial strikes, 113 general strikes, ten newspaper offices burnt and sixty-nine political clubs and 170 churches destroyed by fire, besides 269 murders. National Congress of anarchists in Zaragoza.

1936:   July, the beginning of the civil war.

In a little more than a century eight constitutions had been promulgated, there had been thirteen important revolts against the government, some dozens of *pronunciamientos*, absolute and moderate monarchy, democracy and absolutism, a republic and dictatorship, a profusion of political parties, violent anarchy, arbitrary manipulations of power, immorality, intrigue, sectionalism, martial laws, anticlerical violence, strikes (the strike in Spain has a distinctive note of bloodshed and burning of buildings), murders, arson, disastrous national budgets. In short, Spain came close to being a State without law.

The magnitude, not only of this whole sequence of events, but of many of them when considered individually, is such that one would expect that their repercussions would stir up the furthest corners of the nation. But we find reflections rather than agitation in the *pueblo*, and this only in the later part of the period. The Minutes make no mention of any of the national events listed above before 1856 and then only indirectly. On that date the Council is described for the first time as 'constitutional'. The composition and attributes of the Municipal Corporation, however, were just the same as they had been since the eighteenth century, and in all the elections of the members who composed it the Order of 1772 was quoted in order to make it officially clear that they had been carried out in accordance with it. The promulgation of constitutions had no visible effects in the town.

On 18 September 1868 the *pronunciamiento* of the Navy took place causing the exile of Queen Isabel II. The Juntas of Government increased throughout Spain. Thirteen days later one reads in the Minutes of the Council that 'as the city has pronounced itself in favour of freedom and national sovereignty' the mayor summoned 'the gentlemen of the Council and the highest tax-payers' to discuss how the Council ought to proceed. Here the initiative was not imposed by any outer agency. They proceeded—copying the national fashion—'to the nomination of the Junta of Government of this *pueblo*' and chose from among themselves the names of those who were going to constitute it. 'The Council in full resigned its offices and the Junta vested with the facilities the said gentlemen gave it, determined to report to the Junta of Government in the city that they might act as they think best'. Two days later the local Junta was approved and ratified by the Provincial Junta. The 24th of the same month the 'Revolutionary Junta of this town' assembled to name 'an interim Council' fulfilling the orders of the provincial Junta. The interim Council dissolved itself to give way to another on 17 October 1869, when the lieutenant of the civil guard called the Council together 'to inform them of their deposition from their functions . . . agreed to by the Civil Governor of the Province'. From then on the frequent changes in the

membership of the municipal Corporation begins to reflect national political incidents; however the internal order of the
pueblo and the municipal competence of the Council were not
affected. It was only tinged politically in the sense that all who
formed the Council had to take an oath to the 'Constitution
promulgated on the sixth of the present month' (Minutes of the
27 June 1869). The mayor 'took an oath to the Constitution of
the Spanish Nation of 1869' from the schoolmaster, school-
mistress and chemist. This Minute is dated 18 January 1870.
Two days later the Council was replaced and the in-coming
members swore their offices not by the Constitution
promulgated some months previously but by 'the laws the
Nation will make when exercising her sovereignty'.

The modifications in the Council introduced by the Municipal Law of 1870 have already been seen. But as in the former
period, the internal order of the community and the sphere of
municipal administration followed traditional forms; only the
Council, as the Government cell in the town, becomes each time
more susceptible to politics and officially tinged by the political
ideology of the General, party, constitution, or form of government in force. This does not mean that the new councillors were
more addicted to the political ideas of the government than
those leaving office. Neither party had a clear idea of the different political programmes of the governments they represented, assuming that such programmes existed.

Another aspect of governmental interference also begins to be
felt—the subsidies for the maintenance of the Army. On 31
March 1874 the Council deliberated at a special session how to
contribute to assist '150 wounded coming from the army of the
North where they are engaged in great battles which will decide
the fate of the nation'. The impersonal tenor of the Minutes
indicates that the Council was waiting to see which direction the
Carlist war in the north took before committing themselves.
The Minutes do not say whether soldiers from the *pueblo* were
fighting there, as they do, for example, in the Moroccan War.
Nothing more than a contribution was demanded from them,
of no fixed amount. But step by step the town enters the tumul-
tous life of the nation.

During the reign of Amadeus I, the mayor and Council were
called 'popular' in reference to the Constitution. A little later,

however, the adjective disappears because 'the local authority
as a proof of sympathy and loyalty to the institutions which
originate from that form of government' proclaimed the Republic. 'To make the act of Proclamation more public and
solemn they—the members of the Council—were of the opinion
that it ought to be verified in the public square ... The mayor
in solemn and stirring tones read the decree of February 11th
ultimo—1873—in which the two chambers, gathered together
in sovereign assembly, admitted the abdication of Don Amadeus
of Savoy and proclaimed the Republic; having said this he continued clearly and intelligibly and raising his voice as loud as he
could, with the following formula: Let the Republic be now
solemnly proclaimed in Belmonte de los Caballeros! This being
declared there were cries of long live the Republic which were
warmly repeated by the large crowd.'[1] The enthusiastic acclamation of the Republic, if it were anything more than a happening which broke the monotony of daily life, turned into pes-
simism and uncertainty in the face of the Carlist war. The fate
of the nation was decided at the end of the same year by the
pronunciamiento of Martínez Campos, proclaiming Alfonso XII
King of Spain.

In December 1877[2] the mayor declared that 'on the occasion
of the approaching nuptials of H. H. the King (Alfonso XII)
with his distinguished cousin Dª María de las Mercedes
Orleáns, he proposed that the Council, faithfully interpreting
the feelings of those whom it represents, should congratulate the
future royal couple on such an auspicious occasion. The rest of
the councillors expressed unanimously that they received with
goodwill and enthusiasm such an opportune and happy thought,
cordially associating themselves with the congratulations drawn
up by the lord mayor, raising prayers to heaven that the wedding might be a symbol of peace and prosperity for the reigning
dynasty and the Spanish nation: that in the shade of the secular
throne of St. Ferdinand the sciences and industrial arts might
flourish, with the protection of that illustrious king whom the
country salutes gratefully with the just and precious title of the
Peacemaker of Spain, and that, lastly, being chief of a long suffering but loyal and valiant nation, he will endow her with

[1] Minutes of the Council, 4 May 1873.
[2] Ibid., 30 December 1877.

honourable institutions, tightening through this medium the bonds of union between the Throne and the People so attached to the monarchy, because in it are incarnate respect for the religion of our ancestors, for property and family, the glorious national traditions and the memory of the great enterprises realized beneath the banner of the Cross and the Royal Standard, filling the world with such wonders that today appear to us like a dream'. This Minute, approved and signed by the mayor and councillors, is a summary of their frustrations and trials, an expression of the monotony of politics for them, of the desire for peace in an oppressed nation that had suffered for a long time, the absence of stable institutions, the distance between the centres of power and the *pueblo*, and of the hope that the monarchy would restore order. From then on the outgoing Council took an oath from the incoming Council according to the following formula 'Will you swear by God and the Holy Gospels to be faithful to H. M. the king Alfonso XIII . . . ?'[1] They did not swear to any constitution but to the person of the king who, on the date the quotation refers to, had not yet come of age.

Under the dictatorship of Primo de Rivera the mayor and councillors associated themselves with the homage paid to the General (1 March 1924). On 17 January 1925 the *pueblo* and Council made another homage, this time to 'Our sovereigns the King and Queen of the Nation', to express the 'inviolable loyalty of this Council to Their Majesties the King and Queen of Spain'. This did not prevent them on November 3 of the same year conceding to the Dictator the title of *Bachiller* of the Nation, joining in a third homage.

The warm acclamation of the Republic, the inviolable loyalty to 'Their Majesties the King and Queen' at the same time as they paid homage to the Dictator, the sudden change from one form of government to its opposite, the alternation of the same surnames in the Council, all from among the élite, corresponding to the changes of government, appears to corroborate the idea that none of the possible forms of government, with the exception perhaps of the traditional monarchy, meant much to the townsmen. The mayor and Council saw themselves obliged to follow a certain political line according to the situation, whilst

---

[1] Ibid., 1 January 1894.

nobody in the *pueblo* concerned themselves in the least with the particular line followed. Not even the secretary who drew up the Minutes of the proclamation of the Republic appeared to have a clear idea of what it exactly was; he wrote for example that the local authorities attached themselves to and welcomed 'institutions which proceed from that form of government'; a vague and imprecise phrase which could not have clarified the confused ideas which the townsmen had about the Republic. Those of the 'declining' generation confess that they did not know what the Republic was when it was proclaimed in 1931. Very few, and those few belong to the 'emerging' generation, are those who can today distinguish with relative clarity between constitutional monarch, Republic, President, Prime Minister, etc.

The Council in this sense is the ultimate expression of the monarchy (absolute or constitutional); of the republic (federal, regional, unitarian and authoritarian, leftist, extremist, anarchic, in the centre or on the right); of military *pronunciamientos*; of the dictatorship; of whatever political party ruling at a particular time. Each one of the numerous changes of the government has been followed by changes in the Council. It is the symbol of every government. Laws of a political nature, those concerned with public order and administration, frequently varied with each change of government, so that instead of being a stable homogeneous body they became a series of personal decisions; and, as the people who succeeded each other in the Government were usually opponents, the laws diverged. Larra, passing by the Hall of the Parliament, commented:

'*Aquí yace el Estatuto*   'Here lies the Statute,
Vivió y murió en un minuto'   It lived and died in one minute'

This political order, or rather these politics without order, cannot hope to command cooperation, let alone arouse the political conscience of the townsmen. When we consider also the distance between the people and the centres of power, the lack of an ideology among the national élite, the patronage, the red tape and delay, it is easy to understand the reaction of the townsmen to everything that referred to the Government. And as the Council is the symbol of the Government, everything they think about the latter is ascribed also to the former.

Those of the 'declining' generation, those who really have experienced the shambles of government and political parties, strongly recommend the younger people 'never to meddle in politics'; they even disapprove of the commentaries which those of the 'emerging' generation sporadically make upon international politics and political parties. If a son leaves the paternal roof to work in the city the father urges him: 'Above all son, don't you get involved in politics'; 'You can't hope for any good from politics'. Incidentally, if this subject came up in conversation they took the opportunity to advise me 'not to take part in politics in England'. Investigation into what happened in the *pueblo* during the Republic was difficult because those questioned evaded the subject by saying 'Don't let's talk about politics'. Although their political ideas of that period, in spite of propaganda, were very hazy, they remember perfectly well the antagonisms and hatreds that were caused.

Those of an earlier generation already reacted to the vagaries of the political situation in July 1926 in a decisive manner. The councillors, 'basing their views on the long time that they have held office and on what happened to the previous municipal Junta which has died out in changing from the former regime to the present one; and on the fact that it is not possible to conjecture for the moment the date on which the Council will be legally constituted according to the law of the Statute, it being possible that the renewal of the Council could come in a few months or several years . . .', presented their resignation.

The 'controlling' generation also shares this indifference to political matters. There are few to whom it would give pleasure to hold the position of mayor. The outgoing counciilors have to beg for three names in order to put them on the list of candidates for new councillors. Once this difficult problem is solved, because there are many of those who under no circumstances would allow their names to be put forward, they have to seek a couple of dozen people who will cast their vote and choose from among those proposed. Only thus will the law, which requires a ballot, be carried out. Popular indifference towards these elections is general.

The 'emerging' generation reveals a new outlook. A number of this age-group have united to propose their candidate as councillor. Their object was to choose from among themselves a councillor who would be on their side and support the cultural, social and recreational programme which this group, guided by the parish priest, is developing throughout the year. This generation concerns itself with internal problems of a social and cultural nature without touching politics. Though with no clear idea of what happened during the last Republic, they know the unpleasantness of those years for the *pueblo*. However, this generation criticizes the present government bitterly at times, not from a platform of political principles but because of what they reckon to be the small concern of the Government for farming problems. This suggests that if political parties existed, this group might venture into a political alignment.

Lastly, this indifference and scorn for everything that politics involves does not end in what is only political. Contempt for political laws is translated into indocility and insubordination, which is shown towards the administrative laws, whose content they judge unnecessary and ineffective or contrary to the interests of the *pueblo*. From this fourth point of view, the Council is 'useless'—they say.

Finally the Council can be seen in a purely local context. From olden times the corporation regulated, and regulates now through the Local *ad hoc* Junta, the system of irrigation. The control of irrigation in the plots is probably as old as the *pueblo*. The document already quoted of the sale of a vineyard in 1186 describes the *afrontationes* of the same and indicates that one of the parts of the vineyard borders on *illa çequia unde se regat*. The Order of St. John of Jerusalem held some properties in the district in the fifteenth century. At the end of this century they gave the plots in *treudos* to various townsmen. *Treudo* was the perpetual cession of the utilization of the plot to a townsman who was obliged to pay an annual rent and a *laudemio* (sales due) if he transferred the said plot. With the *treudo* they bestowed the 'rights of irrigation and water'; the new owner remained obliged to hold the said plot 'improved and not worsened, well worked and cultivated, trimmed and irrigated at the correct, convenient and necessary times'.[1] They do not

---

[1] Central General Archives, historical section, Order of St. John of Jerusalem. *Lengua de Aragón, Gran Castellanía de Amposta, Treudos* Legacy 530, nos. 7, 8, 10. The dates to which the citation refers are 1503 and 1504, but these grants of *treudos* copy documents of 1495.

indicate which were those 'rights of irrigation and water' or those 'correct, convenient and necessary times', but it proves at least the existence of regulations. These as well as other forms of property already described, the transference of plots from father to son, etc., which in general held no value in the eyes of the law, originate from the environment and occupations of the townsmen.

The concern of the residents for the control of irrigation is well shown in the Minutes. In 1799, 1818 and 1834,[1] the Council and the 'heirs' to a certain part of the district discuss at length and draw up rules to be followed in the irrigation system: they determine who holds prior right, in which parts of the district, and the periods of irrigation; they regulate the drawing of lots for the irrigation ditches and the fines to be paid for infringements. These rules are initiated by the *pueblo*; the people put pressure on the Council so that they will provide expedient measures. In the Minutes corresponding to 2 June 1861, we read: 'Complaints are frequently produced by various residents that in regard to irrigation there has been an intolerable abuse of rights which have hitherto at all times been respected, and that these days they are being broken by certain irresponsible and evil-intentioned persons, using the water at the time when another person happens to be irrigating, thus causing damage and ill feeling and at times putting themselves in a position which may well bring about their own ruin and that of their family . . . '. In 1882[2] in the Town Hall 'an appeal was read out, signed by 'L' and 16 residents' asking that certain problems concerning the waters should be solved 'as soon as possible'. These last two references make clear first, the existence of an ancient regulation, an awareness of the same, and its frequent infringement by residents; second that everyone preferred it to be punctiliously carried out by the established norms, and third that the violation of these norms could cause altercations, quarrels and violence. This description of the situation of a century ago tallies with the state of affairs today. The same problems exist and reactions are similar. From 14 July 1861 till 20 October the same year the Council met five times to deal specifically

---

[1] Minutes of 21 February, 26 October, and 23 February respectively.
[2] Minutes of 14 May.

with the problems of irrigation. Articles 26–32 inclusive of the municipal Ordinances summarize the rights of the irrigators.

The real interest of this fifth perspective is that in this sphere of activities the *pueblo* compels the Council to concern itself seriously with the control of the use of the water; they not only admit the timelinesss of such regulations on the part of the Council, but they ask for 'laws' and demand punishment for their infringement.

X

LAW: II

'*El tratar con sola la ley escrita, es como tratar con un hombre cabezudo por una parte y que no admite razón, y por otra, poderoso para hacer lo que dice, que es trabajoso y fuerte caso*'. '*No es la mejor gobernación la de leyes escritas*'

Luis de León

'*Santo y bueno que se tome uno la justicia por su mano*'. '*El castigo cuando de natural respuesta a la culpa, de rápido reflejo a la ofensa recibida se convierte en aplicación de justicia abstracta se hace algo odioso a todo corazón bien nacido*'

Unamuno

'*Lo primero es el bien; lo segundo la ley*'   Maeztu

CONTINUING the analysis of juridical reality we now pass from the ideas and juridical conscience of the people to the facts, to see when the individual governs his conduct by the juridic order proper and when he acts according to conventions and traditional norms.

I

The irrigation system. Today the irrigation system is controlled by the Syndicate of Irrigation, by the local Junta of Irrigation, and by local conventions. The Syndicate of Irrigation, through its Ordinances, operates in all those towns which benefit from the same canal. It administers the volume of water and repairs and cleans the main canal. This Syndicate is represented in the *pueblo* by the 'water constable', usually an outsider; he is the chief authority concerning irrigation in the town. It is he who can, without witnesses, fine people in the case of infringements, and, if called upon, act as mediator in any disputes that may arise. Each day he reports to the chief guard, who does not live in the *pueblo*, the volume of water passing through the town and the state of the channels. The chief guard informs him when the time for watering begins and ends in the district under his jurisdiction and it is his duty to publish it by proclamation. The Syndicate also sits as a tribunal and punishes the transgressors of the ordinances. It levels a tax called *alfarda*.

The local Junta of Irrigation with president, treasurer and committee is chosen by a ballot. Its duty is to see to the preservation and repair of the larger channels but not of the principal canal. When a channel has to be repaired the Junta sends a member to estimate the general expenses and the number of days work necessary for its restoration. The people who work on it are paid by the day. The income of the Junta accrues from a local tax called *alfardilla*.

The local conventions which regulate irrigation are very extensive and give us examples of the fluidity of the transition from convention to juridical guaranty. There are norms for almost every possibility, and in addition various parts of the district have their own conventions based on traditional methods of using the water of certain channels. All are known in every detail by every man who has left school. New words have been coined, or current words have been endowed with another meaning only known in the *pueblo*, to refer to irrigation matters. *Jembre* for instance, with its variations of *ejembre* or *emjembre*, means a section of the irrigation ditch which does not border on any of the land belonging to the people who irrigate with it. The irrigation ditches are the veins of the channel; their cleaning and care fall to the lot of those who make use of them, and either one of these will clean them and charge the others a certain sum of money, or each will look after a portion of the *ejembre*. Just what arrangement is made depends on the pact between the *herederos*. *Heredero* has a special meaning indicating all those proprietors of fields who irrigate from a channel or important ditch.

The local conventions are either of a general type or refer to the watering time. Here are a few examples of the former: no sluice whatsoever can be opened into the main canals; he whose land borders a channel is obliged to clean it; if the channel bursts through the dyke of one of the *herederos* they must all contribute to its repair; all the *herederos* care for and contribute

to the purchase and maintenance of the watergate. Their contribution depends on the amount of land they irrigate through
it; the irrigator who diverts the water from his plots spilling it
into a path can be fined by the water constable for wasting the
water if it is during a watering time, and by the municipal
guard for swamping the road; if someone irrigating floods the
land of a neighbour because of water overflowing the margin
which separates the plots or by the breaking of the bank, the
one who has caused the harm offers an indemnity to the injured
party. If they are on good terms the settlement is immediate. If
they don't come to an agreement the water constable, who can
impose a fine on the spot for the loss of water, may intervene;
the municipal court can also impose a fine for any loss of harvest.
Two 'good men', according to the old medieval custom,
assess the damages caused and the irrigator usually pays; if anyone fails to clean the part of the channel which borders on his
plots, he is required by the local Junta of Irrigation to do so. If
after a certain interval he has not cleaned it, the Junta do so
'putting it to the account of the laggards', imposing besides a
certain surtax; the irrigator who does not hold primary right,
established when the channel was first constructed, cannot
irrigate without the previous consent of the rest of the *herederos*.

Other norms rule during watering time in the *pueblo*. Once the
time to water has been announced by the sound of the trumpet,
they start watering 'sluice by sluice', that is to say, the person
whose plot is the nearest to the watergate begins. When this one
finishes the owner of the following field irrigates, and so on day
and night, until the last one. If anyone misses his turn, he loses
his right. In small channels, or those with few *herederos*, there is a
certain laxity with this first rule because they 'have an understanding between themselves'. When the watering time has
been in operation further upstream from the *pueblo* for several
days and most of the plots there have been irrigated, water comes
down through the big canal at dusk and during the night; the
watergates of this canal now give water with which to irrigate.
It should be done 'sluice by sluice', but the rotation is less strict
than it is a day or two later when the watering time is in full
force; the *herederos* 'have an understanding', despite the water
constable who resists such laxity. If a man who has missed his
turn finds that the one irrigating is about to finish and that the

owner of the plot further down the ditch, which is next in order for watering, is not present—even though he may have left his canal and the small watergate of his irrigation ditch prepared to receive the water—he can, according to the convention, take the water. When the victim returns he finds someone 'who has missed his turn' irrigating. There is an argument, and if the late-comer closes the watergate of the man who missed his turn there are likely to be blows or the initiation of *vitandae*-relations. Nobody thinks of calling on those who are working in the nearby fields as witnesses, or of referring the case to the water constable as arbiter; nor do they abide by the convention, which in this case gives prior right to the man who is on the spot, even though he had missed his turn. The matter is decided there and then at times by force. The intervention of the water constable in arguments is sought at times, but not in his capacity as guard, for he has no authority to settle a controversy involving local norms. He is consulted only as an expert.

Outside the set watering time the first man to arrive can make use of the water. Where several men are waiting together for another to finish his watering, convention gives preference to the one whose plot is nearest to the watergate of the main canal. This is so even when men have been waiting for a considerable time and a latecomer arrives whose plot is nearer to the canal watergate. Despite the bad feeling it may cause, the latecomer has a prior right. But if the man who is already watering is on good terms with the owner of the plot next to his, he may on occasion, when he sees the approach of a man whose plot is nearer the watergate, simply transfer some of the water down the ditch to his friend who, since his watergate is open and some water, at least, is entering his plot, now holds a prior right over the man approaching. Of course if the latter sees what they are doing there may be trouble, but the dispute is centered not so much on the legitimacy of the *fait accompli* as on the intention of the doers.

When the watering time finishes in the last town downstream to use the water, the water constable there telephones the constable in charge of the fields furthest upstream to inform him that his watering time should begin again. It takes about two hours before there is a noticeable decrease in the water in the *pueblo*.

Legally the watering time is upstream, but as there is for the moment excess water the people in the *pueblo* may take advantage of it. Again the right belongs to the first one to arrive. Anybody who urgently needs to irrigate will hover round the door of the constable's house, watch his movements to see whether he goes to telephone the order through, or whether he goes to a friend's house to tell him to make haste to water. When either symptom reveals itself he jumps on his motor-bike, rushes to the field and opens the watergate.

The casuistry or norms which control special cases embrace—I was told—every known possibility. I only mention one to illustrate how the norms are interpreted. A man opens the watergate of the channel and starts to irrigate the field. The volume of the canal being more than the irrigation ditch can carry, he raises the sluice-gate just enough to obtain what he needs. Whereupon one whose plot is nearer to the watergate comes to irrigate. As he finds the sluice-gate only half open he opens it fully and takes the rest of the water. Let us suppose that after a period of double irrigation the water diminishes considerably and there is only enough in the canal for one person to use. According to the rule, the first man to take the water holds prior right, but as both were irrigating, the second to take the water will argue that the precedent is his, because his plot is nearer the watergate. This situation, frequent enough, implies that although everyone is perfectly familiar with the objectivity of the norm, in applying it to concrete cases each one chooses the arguments to suit his case. If they are alone and on good terms, they will come to an agreement; if their relations are not so good, the more stubborn or the more menacing 'gets his own way' (*sale con la suya*). If, as often happens, others are there, the one whose claim is legitimate will prevail, not because the other gives way in face of the evidence but because the opinion of the rest imposes itself.

Parallel to this proliferation of norms and rules relative to irrigation, only a few of which have been mentioned, there have also been developed in the *pueblo* and by the *pueblo*, forms of ownership, rights and obligations amongst those who own the land, those who enjoy property by half shares, by thirds, by fifths, etc., and governing the varied arrangements between parents and their married children. All these forms, described

in Chapter I, have a validity guaranteed by the common opinion
of the residents. Their 'legality' within the community is
undisputed; altercations and quarrels are provoked only by the
application of the norms to particular cases. This is not so with
the laws issued by the State or by the provincial authority, nor
in some spheres by the Council, when people question the power
of intervention, and indeed the legality of the laws. Thus the
juridical sensibility of the residents operates not in accordance
with what is officially juridical and legal, but in response to
conventions originated for and by the *pueblo*. Ideologically at
least, disobedience is the corollary of the juridical and legal;
full acceptance belongs to the conventions. These, founded on
tradition, are the *suprajuridic*, and the juridic in the strict sense
of the word occupies a small place.

Regulation of contracts. An old woman promised to one of her
tenants that she would leave him the field he was cultivating by
half-shares with her. The lady died without making a will. Some
of her children agreed that the field should go to the tenant so
that her wishes would be fulfilled. The tenant, however, feared
that one of the children would not consent to the transfer of the
field; whereupon he procured a paper in which it was made
clear that the lady had received money in part payment for the
field and had promised to leave him the remainder as a bequest
when she died. Among the witnesses who signed this was a
daughter of the deceased; everyone knew that in fact no money
had been given but they had heard the old woman say that the
field was to go to the tenant. Thus they believed that 'in justice'
the plot should be his. The paper of the tenant prevailed over
the legal settlement of the inheritance. In the *pueblo* everyone
thought that the witnesses and tenant had behaved fairly. Justice
or equity, as they interpret it, comes before, and is above legality.

If through carelessness someone waters the plot of another
and damages the harvest, if the trees on the plot of one person
spread their roots into that of another impairing their yield, if
the flocks eat the grass in a plot etc., the causer of the damage
and the injured party settle their differences between themselves. If the offer of one or the demand of the other is considered unreasonable they may agree to call on the rural guard
or on two 'good men', so that a disinterested party can assess
the damage. Usually such an opinion is accepted. But to call on

a third party implies that there is not complete friendship or mutual trust between the two persons involved.

In the buying and selling of mules, cows, and agricultural implements, in the payment of *medianiles* (the right to make use of the wall of another man's home in building a new house alongside it), or the lending of money, both parties sign a document—*papel*—in which the transaction is given in detail. It is the same when a brother asks another or others for money in part payment of the inheritance which will take place later, or if one on his own account makes improvements in the house in which they all live but which the parents have promised he will inherit, or in the many varied forms of use of lands and property. The document binds the parties in all its clauses and such is its force that informants doubted whether they could offer any examples of one having been violated. Rare is the house in which there are not one or several of these private documents.

A proprietor wants to sell a plot. According to the law, if there is a tenant he has the first offer. If not, the owners of the adjoining fields hold the right of first refusal. If they are not interested or not prepared to pay what is asked, the ground can be offered to anyone. If the vendor really wants the land to go to someone in the family or to a friend, he raises the price of the plot out of all proportion so that nobody wants to buy it. The relative or friend pays before the notary all or part of the sum; if he pays all the vendor later returns the excess to him, and if he pays part, the sum normally coincides with the real price, and the clause that demands that the whole of the sum should be paid is ignored. These operations have been preceded by a private document signed by both in which the true terms of the bargain have been stipulated. This is valid, not the document drawn up and signed in front of the notary. The 'arrangement' saves the legality on one side and kinship or friendship on the other.

Personal judgment, custom and convention are, therefore, the juridical reality, the 'law' governing activities in the *pueblo*. Only when this popular 'legality' fails, when mutual understanding breaks down, do the residents resort to the Law, to the municipal Court of Justice, or if the worst comes to the worst to the lawyers in the city.

The Court of Justice is competent to deal with penal matters, the drawing up of wills, acts of conciliation, and the trial of minor offences. In civil matters its competency embraces acts of conciliation when the execution of whatever is ordered does not exceed 250 pesetas (about 30 shillings). These acts of conciliation are intended to settle conflicts of interests 'without the necessity of a lawsuit but with judicial intervention'.[1] Anybody seeking an act of conciliation must in principle carry out certain essential requirements: he must apply to the Municipal Judge, indicate the name of the defendant, the claims which will be cited, etc. The judge must then convene the two parties. The plaintiff and defendant should each be accompanied by a 'good man' whom they have chosen. The plaintiff puts forward his claim, the defendant replies. Replies and rejoinders follow for as long as is necessary. If no compromise is reached, the 'good men' and the municipal judge try to reconcile them. If they do not succeed, the action is considered as entered and concluded. If the two are reconciled it is the duty of the judge to bring what has been settled into effect. This is the theoretical scheme of an act of conciliation, though in practice it turns out to be rather more simple. One which I attended developed in the following manner: the plaintiff presented himself in the Town Hall one morning and asked the secretary to summon the defendant to appear in two hours time. When he arrived, in addition to the secretary there happened to be one of the councillors there. The plaintiff wanted to turn the defendant out of a field which the latter was renting. The replies and rejoinders lasted about an hour. Nobody but the contestants took part; they had not brought along any 'good men'. In the end, without coming to an agreement, the two left the Town Hall without either the secretary or the councillor having uttered a single word.

The aim in these cases is to make the affair public, so that everyone in the town will know. The plaintiff hopes that public opinion will be favourable to him and place pressure on the defendant to come to terms. In popular language this is 'to wash one's dirty linen in public'. In about half the cases the dispute is settled. If it is not, an appeal can be made to the lawyers and law courts of the city as a last resort.

Juridical indocility. Recently a national law was passed to prohibit walking on roads where there was heavy traffic. For

[1] Juan V. Fuentes: *La competencia y el procedimiento en la justicia municipal* (Barcelona, 1953), pp. 10, 58, and 105.

several days the Press and radio announced it, explaining its
content and expediency. The Civil Governor notified the mayor
that it was his express wish that it should be carried out. The
mayor ordered the law to be published by the town-crier at
every street corner. The people especially the young, continued to make use of the highway for their strolls as if the law
did not exist. The mayor let several days go by, knowing how
difficult it would be to enforce such a law, since people had
always used the road for their evening walks. The second week
after the law had come into force he informed the civil guard of
the advisability of fining one or two persons as an example and
to show that he was serious. The civil guard, consisting entirely
of outsiders, fined an old man, a woman, and one of the men at
that time working on the plots of the mayor. On being informed
the mayor remitted the fines, arguing that these were not the
orders he had given. He had simply proposed that the guards
should fine a 'gang' of young people. This they later did. Those
accosted by the pair of guards began a heated argument: 'Yes,
we are walking in the roadway', they said, 'but why do you not
fine the coaches and lorries which break another law by passing
through the *pueblo* at more than 60 kms. an hour . . . ? Why does
nobody say anything to the lorries which pass so close to us
when we are riding our bicycles? Or is it that justice is not equal
for everybody?' etc. Eventually one of the young men said,
looking at the others: 'Well, do we or don't we pay?'—thus
conceding a doubtful validity to law and authority.

All types of declarations, and the payments of taxes of whatever class, are preceded by a public announcement stating the
time within which they are to be made. As such obligations are
often not discharged by the day stated, the constable has to go
through the streets a second time with his trumpet, announcing
that the stated time has been extended. When this has also expired
the constable sometimes has to go from house to house demanding
what is due from those who have not yet paid. But if the tax
in question is of minor importance and has not been paid by
the poorer residents, the constable usually does not visit them if
they are both hardworking and honest (*honrados*). The declaration
and tax on bicycles falls into this category.

A resident began to build a house, laying a ditch for the
foundations which was not in line with the rest of the recently

laid-out street. The Council intervened, requiring him to rectify
the ditch; but the house was built according to the plan of its
owner with the façade out of line with the rest of the street. The
Council's comment was: 'How can we make him demolish the
house now?'

We have seen that the election of councillors arouses no
interest whatsoever, and in order that the laws may be carried
out it is necessary to persuade some two dozen people to cast
their vote. This, which could only be considered normal in the
election of members of an institution of a political nature or very
much under the control of the Civil Governor, extends also to
any and every association and commission. Nobody wants positions of responsibility.

The Brotherhood of Farmers groups the farmers together to
defend their interests, to repair paths in the municipal district,
secure loans at a very low interest, obtain seed, agricultural
machinery and fertilizers; it is the proper place also to settle the
differences between masters and workers. By its commission it
would appear logical for people to give their support to such an
association, but this is not the case. In the election of president
and committees the number of voters sometimes amounts to no
more than a dozen, so that frequently the outgoing Junta have
to appoint the one to succeed them, having then to convince
those chosen to accept their positions. The president did not
know exactly what were the regulations concerning elections
and was convinced that the Brotherhood was 'useless'. Nobody
goes either to meetings proposed by the Junta of Irrigation to
elect new committees. Nobody wants to hold offices and responsibilities, because it is difficult to give orders when nobody
obeys, and not to be obeyed *hace la risa* (makes one a laughing
stock). If someone compels obedience he turns people against
him, and this is what everybody wants to avoid. Similarly nobody wants to be responsible for the repair of paths and canals,
for there are bound to be differences of opinion about the best
way of going about the job. If the man in charge insists on
doing it his way the rest will argue: 'Who do you think you are
... you are no better than we are'. Attempts to organize this
task have given rise to *vitandae*-relations.

Although almost all, if their own interests are not directly
involved, refuse to cooperate with the Council, the Brotherhood,

or the Junta of Irrigation, in principle they expect these institutions to function adequately and to be a complete protection to the *pueblo*, the farmers and the irrigators. As in practice they cannot be so efficient the residents wash their hands of them, condemning them as 'useless', as 'serving no purpose', and 'hindering everything by unnecessary paperwork'. So it is a vicious circle: they do not function well because there is no cooperation and there is no cooperation because they do not function well; the more suitable people do not wish to direct them because nobody obeys and they do not want to create bad relations with those subordinate to them, and these do not obey because those who give orders 'do not know how to command'. The exercise of authority in the *pueblo* is indeed difficult.

All this leads us to re-state the problem of indocility towards the juridic, not as has been done until now by the indication of the correlation between juridical conscience and forms of sociability, but on deeper and more radical levels. For this purpose I shall use the three historical periods into which I have roughly divided the history of the Council: from about 1750 to 1850, 1850 to 1930, and from then until the present day. The isolation of the *pueblo*, minimum interference from outside, and the autonomy of the Council, characterize the first phase; internal autonomy, political influences on the Council and its growing incorporation in the national life the second; and the control of the Council by the Civil Governor and the loss of most of its functions and competence the third.

II

In January 1799[1] the Council ordered all residents, 'under the penalty of five *reales*', to attend at the Council Hall for the election of a second Deputy. The Minutes, however, refer to 'several residents having come ...', implying that there were not very many. In October of the same year[2] the Council ordered 'the residents of this place' to go out to repair the roads, and threatened anybody who did not help with a fine of 30 *reales*. The size of the fine suggests that this was the only thing that would make the residents comply. The Minutes for 3 November of the same year are even more clear: the mayor 'by

1 Minutes of the Council, 20 January 1799.
2 Ibid., 21 October 1799.

public proclamation called on the residents who had mules, carts, oxen ..., and after a long interval only two persons and no others turned up'. The system of compulsory personal services continued to languish until 1884 (24 March), when faced by the insubordination of the residents the Council decided to modify it, obliging each resident to pay one peseta for a year's service. These references indicate sufficiently the disobedience of the *pueblo* towards its authorities. Nor did the authorities themselves set a very good example. On 5 January 1823 the few councillors who had gone to the Town Hall resolved that members of the Council summoned for the weekly meeting who failed to attend 'without a just motive' should pay a fine of one peseta. This evidently had little effect, for in a session of 1835 the Council voted that 'The person who does not attend the meetings when he has been summoned at the appointed time, taking into account the courtesy wait of a quarter of an hour, must pay four *reales* as a fine'.

In the second half of the nineteenth century—the second historical period—indocility and disobedience are still more marked because of the greater detail in the Minutes. In January 1861[1] the Council shows itself determined to prevent 'the knavish abuses and licence of the previous years'; the text of the Minute is: 'knowing that agricultural tasks do not need to be hurried as is supposed, they—the members of the Council—were of the opinion that none of the residents should work on feast days, so that they might thus assist instead at the divine offices'. Anyone disobeying was to pay 'the fine of twenty *reales*'. The same was repeated four months later[2] and a dozen times since; work on feast days is now prohibited by a national law. None the less they work on such dates just as they always have. Much the same has happened with the prohibition of blasphemy. In 1857[3] young men were forbidden to wander round at night covered in blankets, disturbing the neighbourhood with their shouts, nocturnal brawls and unlawful strolls. The prohibition was repeated on 27 January 1861, 22 December the same year, 22 January 1865, the end of the same year, 6 January 1867, 10 February the same year, 31 August 1879, 14 November 1883 etc. I have alluded several times to the present walking about at

[1] Ibid., 20 January 1861.   [2] Ibid., 26 May 1861.
[3] Ibid., 10 May 1857.

night without permission from the authority. The young men continue to believe today as yesterday that nobody is competent to regulate whether or not they will go serenading at night. The innumerable norms about irrigation repeat the same premises untiringly throughout the last 100 years, a clear confession that insubordination is as constant as the norm. This state of affairs continues to be more or less normal today. The president of the municipal corporation in 1869[1] deplored 'all those persons who wage bitter war or opposition to all the measures laid down'. The session of 11 August 1932 dealt with 'the social element so unfavourable towards the Council that makes itself felt in this locality'. In 1881[2] the Council saw itself obliged to impose new taxes on the municipality. The secretary wrote in the Minutes of that session: 'Every precaution has to be taken because the population of this town is so thoroughly rebellious and could initiate a riot at the slightest provocation'. On 10 December 1932 the members of the Council complained of the difficulty of assessing the municipal taxes fairly owing to faulty declaration by the residents. The secretary wrote that he had 'to make up the omissions of the townsmen', adding 'that if he was inaccurate in any particular case, those who believed themselves ill done by, did not reclaim through the official channels, but instead laid the blame on the writer (the secretary), becoming his enemies'.

The population were wilful and insubordinate, but so were those who made up the Council. In spite of the half-hour wait— it was no longer just a quarter of an hour—which made allowances for those councillors who did not arrive on time, in spite of the fines which they imposed on each other,[3] and in spite of personal and special summons to those councillors who still did not attend,[4] from April 1881 till October 1901 eighty sessions were suspended through the absence of enough councillors to make up the quorum required by law to render such sessions valid. It has already been seen that the present situation in the Brotherhood and Junta of Irrigation is similar.

Throughout the three historical periods, different as they are in their political structure, there is a constant pattern of behaviour towards authority. Everyday actions reveal the absence of

---

[1] Ibid., 13 December 1869.   [2] Ibid., 17 April 1881.
[3] Ibid., 31 July, 1881.   [4] Ibid., 11 July 1885.

any consciousness of juridical obligation. In the chapters which follow we shall see how the *pueblo* was governed theocratically in the century preceding the historical periods described. Even in this phase disobedience and insubordination were prevalent and general. Four distinct historical situations during four centuries reaffirm the indocility of the residents as a distinctive note in all that refers to authority; in other words this indocility, with the ideology it implies, is a constant in the history of the *pueblo*. It cannot, therefore, be explained only by the incompetence of whatever national governing body was in power; beyond that is a more elemental failing.

III

The early history of the *pueblo* reveals a small community whose structure, with internal self-sufficiency and some slight subordination to external authorities, recalls the Greek πόλις. The *polis*, as opposed to the concrete historical situation of the *pueblo* already described, must be seen as an abstraction, a *Gedankenbild* or analytical construction, the 'ideal typus' of Weber. But it signifies, like the *pueblo*, a small town or independent community[1] and the group of persons who compose it.[2] With some variations the territory of the *polis* is usually small. Delos, including Pheneia, possessed some 22 square kilometres[3] an area less than that of the *pueblo* if to its municipal district we add the possessions of the residents outside the municipal boundary. Within its territorial unity was the city (community of residence) with its houses and temples[4]; as in the *pueblo* the inhabitants went daily to cultivate their fields, this being their principal occupation.[5] The population of the *polis* may have

[1] Thucydides in *The Peloponesian War* (Penguin Classics, 1961), p. 106: 'From the time of Cecrops and the first kings down to the time of Theseus the inhabitants of Attica had always lived in independent cities, each with its own town hall and its own government. Only in times of danger did they meet together and consult the King of Athens; for the rest of the time each state looked after its own affairs and made its own decisions.' A description which fits the *pueblo* in the historical phase referred to.

[2] Aristotle's *Politics* (Loeb Classical Library, 1959), III, IV, 7: 'A city is a partnership of free men.' Thucydides, op. cit., p. 482 puts into Nicias' mouth: 'It is men who make the city, and not walls or ships with no men inside them'.

[3] G. Glotz: *La Cité Grecque* (Paris, 1928), p. 30.

[4] Thucydides, op. cit., p. 107.

[5] V. Ehrenberg: *The Greek State* (Oxford, 1960), p. 30.

been slightly larger: Egina, for example, had rather more than 2,000 citizens.[1] Naturally there were no slaves in the *pueblo*, but there was a large number of male servants living in the house of their master and working in his fields, and female servants for domestic tasks. The remaining inhabitants were divided into classes according to their property; the timocratic principle of Aristotle was valid also in the *pueblo*. The rich ones who wield the power were and are called *pudientes*. The Greek word οἱ δυνατοί, employed in the same context, signifies the group of persons who possess power, wealth, rank and influence, and is translated literally by 'those who can', that is to say the powerful ones, the *pudientes*. Aristophanes defines citizens who are the opposite of οἱ δυνατοί as those who have no ground, not even enough to be buried in[2]; the residents of the *pueblo* said and say about one who is very poor: 'he has not enough land to drop dead in'.

The Greek community had its deity or local hero with his temple and chapels and sanctuaries outside the city limits.[3] They celebrated festivals with religious rites of a markedly agricultural character,[4] with amusements, torch processions and sports—very similar to the festivals in the *pueblo*. The hero or local deity corresponding to the patron saints of the *pueblo* was the centre of religious associations as those in the *pueblo* are of the various sodalities.

Vecino and πολίτης have much in common. Both words refer to the rights and obligations of the citizens who live in a community, not only as individuals but as members of a political and social body. In Greek and in Spanish the inhabitants of a community employ the same word to express that they belong to it; son of the *pueblo* or son of the *polis*. In both cases the individual was tied to the land of the community and to enjoy full citizenship he had to pass through special ceremonies. When the *epheboi* came of age legally they made 'the circuit of the

---

[1] Glotz, op. cit., p. 33.

[2] The *Ecclesiazusae*. Praxagora says to the audience: 'no longer shall we see one man harvesting vast tracts of land, while another has not ground enough to be buried in...', *The Complete Greek Drama*. ed., W. J. Oates and E. O'Neill (New York. 1938), p. 1027, vol. II; & T. A. Sinclair, *A History of Greek Political Thought* (London, 1961), p. 116.

[3] M. P. Nilsson: *Greek Folk Religion* (Harper Torchbook, 1961), pp. 18–19.

[4] Nilsson, op. cit., p. 23.

temples', took part in public displays, and did their military service. They then took their place among the citizens.[1] These rites find their equivalent in those of the conscripts of the *pueblo*. The rights of the woman in the *polis* were in certain ways restricted and as in the *pueblo* she fitted into the polity through her father or husband as 'head of the family'.[2]

Agora and main square are essential places in the life of both communities; in them the public assemblies gathered in full. Social life was lived in the *agora*, in the square, in the main street. Square and main street were and continue to be the centre of every activity. Dignity and honour formed the spirit which animated private and social life among the citizens of the *polis* as among the residents of the *pueblo*.[3]

In principle the political constitution of the *pueblo* was democratic; all could achieve positions of authority on the Council and all held the right to vote for the choice of a deputy and to take part in the popular general assembly. In practice this was balanced by a measure of oligarchy, and power was always in the hands of those with more landed property, more knowledge, and the greater ability to govern. It is in fact the form of government preferred by Aristotle, and referred to by Thucydides in his Book II:[4] 'So, in what was nominally a democracy, power was really in the hands of the first citizen', and in Book VIII p. 547: 'a reasonable and moderate blending of the few and the many'. In a Greek oligarchy of this type, the general assembly was summoned by the Council through a herald —in the *pueblo* by means of bells or the constable with his trumpet. The Greeks assembled in the *agora*, either periodically to discuss administrative matters, appointments to offices, or when circumstances required them to deal with legislation and reforms.[5] In the *pueblo* this is paralleled by an assembly which decided on taxes, appointments to offices each year, and dealt with the regulation of irrigation. In both *pueblo* and *polis* the assembly possessed a deliberative voice and in some

[1] Aristotle: *Constitution of Athens* (Hafner Library of Classics, New York, 1950), No. 42.
[2] Ehrenberg, op. cit., pp. 42—43.
[3] C. M. Bowra: *The Greek Experience* (London, 2nd impression 1958), Chapters 1 and 2.
[4] Thucydides, op. cit.
[5] Aristotle: *Politics*, 1298a, 3.

cases the right to sanction; they could sometimes amplify or reform regulations already in force. Before convening the assembly the Greek Council usually—in fact always in the *pueblo*—prepared an agenda of relevant facts and matters to be discussed. Thus in both *polis* and *pueblo* the initiative of the general assembly was controlled by the Council.

The supreme power in the oligarchic *polis* was the Council or *boule*, the members of which were elected by the general assembly. Their number was considerably larger in the Greek community, and when it was too large they chose from among themselves a small committee, the *probouli*. Thus there were two councils. This structure can be compared with the Council proper and the Council together with the full municipal Corporation including the Council of Twenty in the *pueblo*. The Council summoned the assembly, saw to it that the laws were carried out, supervised the moral life of the community and, perhaps more in the *pueblo* than in the *polis*, the Council controlled the administration and governed the life of the community.[1] Although it appears that the Council always had a certain ascendancy over the assembly,[2] this character is clearer and more defined in the *pueblo*. Thus in the *pueblo* the Council was, so to speak, the State.

The numerous matters with which the Council had to deal were divided among committees in both *polis* and *pueblo*. In the former a committee took care of the sanctuaries and festivals, another of the cleaning of the city, a third of town-planning, city improvements and roads. They also had inspectors of the public order, of the market, of weights and measures, men deputed to be in charge of the bakeries, of the prisons and the care of the destitute.[3] All of these committees find their exact homology in the *pueblo*. The function of the Arbitrators is analogous to that of the two 'good men', in bringing contesting parties to an agreement. As in the *pueblo*, if the Arbitrators effected an understanding, the case was finished; if not, the parties could appeal to the tribunals.[4] As there are no facts about municipal jurisdiction during this period in the *pueblo* it is impossible to pursue the

[1] Aristotle: *Constitution of Athens*, p. 71, No. 6. See also note inserted in this paragraph.

[2] Ehrenberg, op. cit., pp. 59–65.

[3] Aristotle, *Constitution of Athens*, pp. 124 et seq.

[4] Ibid., p. 127.

comparison further, apart from pointing out that during the Middle Ages the popular tribunals in the porch of the church or in the squares of the free *pueblos* of Aragón generally decided lawsuits, administered justice and witnessed wills.

Although in a general sense *pueblo* and *polis* have common elements, there are obvious differences of degree and character. The ideas and experience suggested by *polis* are not precisely identical with the ideas and experience which a citizen has today, or had in the past, concerning the *pueblo*. Conceptions of equity, justice, and legality were, for instance, clearly different in the two cases. However, I wish to make use of these differences by comparing the *pueblo* of the three periods which concern us, with the ideal type of *polis* which certain Greek writers held up as a model for political practice.

Pericles in his funeral speech considers that the supremacy of the law over all the Athenians has helped to make the government of Athens a model to be imitated anywhere. 'We', he said, 'keep to the law. This is because it commands our deep respect. We give our obedience to those whom we put in positions of authority and we obey the laws themselves'.[1] For Socrates, he who violates the laws destroys the city; thus the State cannot survive if the decisions of the law have no power. Their force is supreme even if they are unjust. No-one is justified in acting contrary to them.[2] Demarates in conversation with Xerxes defined the Spartans in this manner: 'They are free—yes— but not entirely free; for they have a master and that master is Law, which they fear much more than your subjects fear you. Whatever this master commands, they do; and his command never varies . . . '.[3] According to Plato the citizen not only ought to be familiar with the laws, but he should also understand the reasons behind them, the body of doctrine that sustains them; what is more, he is obliged to respect them outwardly and accept them inwardly.[4] For Aristotle virtue and justice are basically the same thing: 'what is displayed in relation to others is Justice; as being simply a disposition of a certain

[1] Thucydides, op. cit., p. 117.
[2] Criton: *Dialogues of Plato*, selected by J. D. Kaplan (Pocket Library, 1955), pp. 55–57.
[3] Herodotus: *The Histories* (Penguin Classics, 1960), p. 449.
[4] Sinclair, op. cit., pp. 192 & 204.

kind is Virtue'. 'Injustice in the universal sense (is) . . . unjust in general, or illegal'. 'The just' is 'the lawful and the equal or fair'. 'Justice can only exist between those whose mutual relations are regulated by law'.[1] Since it is not possible to dictate laws for every particular case and occasion he suggests an interpretative principle based on equity. 'Equity, though just, is not legal justice, but a rectification of legal justice'. 'This is the essential nature of the equitable: it is a rectification of law where law is defective because of its generality'.[2]

The Law and the city are thus synonomous; the one cannot exist without the other. Law is sovereign and always just. It is not law because it is just, but it is just because it is law. Obedience towards the law, towards authority, is the primordial duty of every citizen. He ought to know the laws and submit to them *ex corde*. For Aristotle the law is supplemented by equity.

The *pueblo*, of course, shows the opposite. Juridic experience is based on a series of unconnected structures, each with their peculiar value. The first and fundamental datum is equity or justice, the conviction that justice—as they understand it—is the supreme value. The interpretation of justice rests on certain desiderata of a personal, traditional and communal type. Equity or justice is above and beyond the law, and it does not aim at reinforcing the law by means of a 'general formula', as Aristotle desired. In the *pueblo*, equity comes before, and is independent of social equity, and justice must be seen to work in a personal and not simply a social context. People hold rights because they are persons and not because the rights are granted by the traditional and communal consensus, by the law or by the State. Personal dignity—as they understand it—is the basis of personal or individual equity. In order to accept the law or authority, neither the laws which proceed from the legislator (legal justice), nor the fact that the laws or conventions are endorsed by common opinion in the *pueblo* and felt to be advantageous by the justice of their content (social equity), are sufficient reason; first the individual must declare his opinion on the equity of the law or convention in a concrete case that concerns

---

[1] Aristotle: *The Nicomachean Ethics* (Loeb Classical Library), V, II, 3 & 8; V, VI, 4.

[2] Ibid., V, X, 3 & 6.

him. So personal equity amounts to a transcendant individualism.[1] What is not *justum* in a particular case cannot in any way be legal, even though it was legally ordained. On the contrary, what is just and equitable in one's own particular case is obligatory even if it is illegal. The Greeks used the word δυσνομία to indicate that the community had laws which were not observed and also to signify that personal opinion judged these laws to be bad ones.[2] This situation of δυσνομία is characteristic of the *pueblo* during the last four centuries.

Secondly, justice or equity requires that kinship, with cordial relations and friendship, should have precedence over the law. Relatives and friends 'come to an agreement', 'have an understanding', make mutual concessions. Equity demands that they should be treated in a special, more human way, and neither convention nor the law should be allowed to intervene. Sociability and equity go hand in hand. A certain degree of intimacy is thus the generator of equity, and the less intimacy there is the further from equity and the closer to conventions.

These conventions, the *suprajuridic*, are a special form of local right or 'law' that regulates relations between people who, without being intimate, know each other personally and have interests in common. In this sense the right is the system of uses, customs and conventions issuing spontaneously from the community. The norms, which do not go beyond the limits of the municipal district, are neither ordained nor sanctioned by any formal code; nonetheless they are authentically juridical owing to the solid consensus of the residents who uphold and re-fashion them. Yet these norms, and here equity comes into the question once more, are applied in concrete cases according to the persons involved, taking into account circumstances, prestige, individual honesty, and so on.

The violation of such norms, on the other hand, calls for a settlement 'man to man', without submission to the slow, costly and impersonal proceedings of the law courts. Justice is some-

---

[1] This individualistic juridical interpretation is also completely within the Spanish tradition. It is enough to remember P. Vitoria, who in *De Jure Belli*, No. 22, said: 'Si subdito constat de injustitia belli non licet militare, etiam ad imperium Principis'. Note that he says *subdito* and not *subditis*. This was written under an absolute monarchy in the sixteenth century.

[2] Sinclair, op. cit., p. 31.

thing to be dealt on the spot, it is essentially direct action. To depend on others or on institutions to achieve justice or equity is to despair of reaching an agreement through any of the preceding juridical structures. Finally, if there is no possibility of a settlement 'man to man', it is necessary to resort to an abstract not a human principle, the law—the Law as opposed to justice or equity.

Only the conventions have a certain relation to the *pueblo* seen not so much as a juridic entity but as a group of persons known to each other and living in the same community. The community as such does not succeed in being a focus of loyalty. Today municipal obligations begin to be felt not because of a greater juridical sensibility, but because public opinion has been angered by the violation of norms or duties which affect everyone. In this sense, and although the *pueblo* is far from coinciding with the *polis*, one can speak of the community as a focus of juridical loyalty. It is a weak loyalty which does not cancel out the other categories of equity and kinship, but presupposes and includes them and is conditioned by them. Such a process has repeated itself in the period during which the community was becoming incorporated in larger unities such as the province and nation. The juridical structures are pre-eminently personal and internal to the life of the community; they do not overstep this barrier and do not in fact include strong loyalties to the province and nation in everyday affairs. The *pueblo* is attached to the province and nation but is not integrated with them.

The essential juridical difference between *pueblo* and *polis* is that the former has not been so powerful a generating centre of juridical sensibility, a productive force of socialization. In this sense the *pueblo* has not really been a *pueblo*, that is a society; and as the *pueblo* is the people, we could conclude that socialization has always gone badly, that to a certain degree some forms of socialization are perhaps lacking, and the individual fails to feel part of something that transcends kinship, friendship and to some extent the *pueblo*. In the last four centuries individuality and particularism have prevailed over the forces of socialization and authority.[1]

---

[1] The nobles' struggle to defend the extensive liberties of the kingdom of Aragon against encroachment by the Crown has been constant throughout its history. On the other hand Zaragoza has always been one of the most active centres of anarchism and was known to anarchists in other regions as 'The Pearl'.

The poetry of García Lorca expresses with lyrical and tragic intensity the conflict between authority and the individual. Spontaneity and liberty which are the essense of individuality are symbolized by the gypsy. The civil guard is the symbol of power, power that withers the freshness and spontaneity of the individual. Lorca's poetry is the drama of the popular contempt for all symbols of power.

XI

RELIGION: I

'Es en el aspecto religioso donde hay que ir a buscar lo más típico y más radical de un pueblo'   UNAMUNO

F ERDINAND the Catholic achieved national unity with the capture of Granada in 1492 and with the incorporation of Navarre into the Spanish State in 1512. At the same time the King and Queen endeavoured to bring about racial homogeneity by expelling the Jews in 1492, and to secure religious unity they obtained a Bull from Pope Sixtus IV (1478) authorizing them to nominate inquisitors in the tribunal of the Inquisition. The Council of the Supreme and General Inquisition was created in 1483 and from the first moment functioned as an instrument of the State, its affairs thus escaping pontifical jurisdiction. The Church became nationalized and religion and nationality were identified with each other. Charles I in his final will insisted on the necessity of eradicating any heretical shoot that appeared in Spain, and Philip II, by a Royal Warrant of 30 July 1564, decreed from Madrid that the 'execution, fulfilment, preservation and defence of that ordained by the holy Council of Trent' were to be considered a law of the State.

In its 22nd session the Council of Trent prescribed that the bishops should visit the churches under their jurisdiction and check their accounts. The prescription of the Council of Trent and the decree of Philip II were duly carried out in Aragón, the Archbishops of the city periodically visiting the *pueblo*. At the end of the pastoral visit the Archbishop's secretary or the secretary of the visiting delegate drew up a record which regulated at the same time the organization and administration of the church and its goods, some of the juridical proceedings of the parishioners, and their civil and moral conduct. The scheme of these records is simple and invariable; almost all the paragraphs begin by an authoritative 'Item we order ...' or 'Item we order beneath the penalty of excommunication. ...' The date with the signature and seal of the archbishop or the visiting delegate close the report of the canonical visit. According to the entries in the Parish Archives, in the last 25 years of the sixteenth century six visits took place; there were 23 visits in the seventeenth century, 9 in the eighteenth and 5 in the nineteenth. The figure given for the eighteenth century is probably inexact because nothing has been preserved in the Parish Archives between 1741 and 1770; one or two more should no doubt be added to the total. With the references preserved in these accounts I intend to reconstruct briefly some aspects of religious life in the *pueblo*.

I

Although from the time of the Catholic Kings the church remained subordinate to the State, the first records of the archiepiscopal visits to the *pueblo* make it clear that at this level the case was the reverse. The Council, so powerful in the free townships of the Kingdom of Aragón until the reign of the Catholic Kings, gave way under the archiepiscopal pressure. It is not the parish that is subordinate to the Council but rather the Council that is subordinate to the parish, to the Archbishop. The latter in his frequent visits to the *pueblo* scrutinizes, corrects and commands in such a way that the communal organization, codes for individual conduct, and every institution come to be distinctly christian and the *pueblo* is primarily a religious rather than a civil community. The rights of the citizen are the consequence of the rights of the parishioner or *feligrés*; nobody can enjoy the former without first enjoying the latter. The parish superimposes itself on the Council and the vicar displaces the mayor.

The right of residence in the *pueblo* passes from the juridic to the religious sphere. In the final instance it is not the Council but the Archbishop or his vicar in the *pueblo* who grants it. The report of the canonical visit carried out in April 1582[1] says: 'Item we order under penalty of excommunication that the

---

[1] Visit of 26 April 1582, Parish Books, vol. I, fols. 51-6.

right of residence in the said place shall not be given to any stranger who comes from a land which has been infected by heresy, nor shall anyone receive him/her as a servant without first giving notice to the vicar who shall examine him/her with great care and diligence in order to ascertain the occasion of his/her arrival, and always he shall take into particular consideration his/her life, speech and behaviour, in such a manner that in all directions the gate shall be shut against the damage which could result from communication with persons who have been contaminated'. Even though strangers or people who were passing through or doing business in the *pueblo* did not have any of the rights of the residents they were obliged to fulfil the religious precepts while they remained in the district. In 1594 the Archbishop gave orders to the vicar[1] in relation to 'outsiders who pass with carts, beasts of burden, being carters and persons who endeavour to earn their bread by peddling, if they arrive at this place on the eve of a feast day he (the vicar) was not to let them leave the next day until they had heard mass and complied with the precepts of the church'. Some years later the same archbishop insisted again:[2] 'Now once again we return to order him (the vicar) ... that he is not to allow anyone, not even persons from other places, to work nor to undertake any labour whatsoever within the boundaries of his parish' on feast days. Not only were outsiders as well as the residents forbidden to work on holidays, or leave the district with their laden mounts on feast days; the archiepiscopal visitor in 1605 also prohibited anybody from passing through the place on feast days with 'carts and other beasts of burden'.[3]

The passer-by who, being taken ill, wanted to seek the care of the municipal hospital had to prove first that he had recently confessed and second that he was poor; thus it was ordained by the visitor in 1586: 'Item we order the Jurymen and council ... that the manager of the hospital cannot receive any poor man who has not first presented himself before the vicar or majordomo, who and each in their turn, shall examine him to see whether he has confessed, whether he brings a testimonial that the woman with him is his wife, and finally whether they are

---

[1] Visit of 28 November 1594, ibid., fols. 71–6.
[2] Visit of 4 February 1599, ibid., fols. 79–8ov.
[3] Visit of 8 May 1605, ibid., vol. II, fols. 204v–6v.

truly poor'.[1] In Fol. 228v, of the Parish Book II comes a record
of a death with the marginal note of 'a poor woman'. The
record says: 'On December 18th 1614 a poor woman died in
the road to Aldeanueva. Her son came to inform me . . . that
she had been frozen to death. The boy said that she was called
Orosia Jiménez and was from the town of Fontefrida and I
mosén Antonio Gil found that the deceased carried with her in a
purse a statement to the following effect: I *mosén* Diego Herrero
prebend of Fontefrida confessor, make it known that Orosia
Jiménez, poor, a widow, belongs to this town of Fontefrida,
Kingdom of Aragón . . . . She is making a journey to Our Lady
of Montserrat with a boy, her son; she is a good christian and
because of her poverty has not got a bull of the crusade.[2] She
has confessed and has communicated by my hand in the said
town on September 29th 1614'. In the following folio of the
same volume the same vicar wrote: 'A poor man. On Holy
Saturday, April 18th 1615, Martín Sar died . . .; he did not
receive any sacrament and they found him dead in a barn. A
note of confession was found on him, which said he had confessed on the 23rd of . . . March 1615'. Thus the certificate of
good religious conduct, of confession and communion was a very
useful and necessary document not only for personal identification but also in order to apply for residence in the *pueblo* and
to have the right to the welfare service of the same.[3]

The mayor and jurymen of the place were subject to the
archiepiscopal authority, and even civic life came to be submitted to ecclesiastical direction. The former had to conform
to the prescriptions dictated by the Archbishop on his latest
canonical visit; mayor, councillors and jurymen were the secular
arm charged with exacting the fulfilment of the church's orders.
The archiepiscopal formulas leave no place for doubts: 'Item
we order the Jurymen and council of the said place that they
redress that which they see to be necessary in the hospital . . .'[4]
'Item because Our Lord is highly offended by public sins as

---

[1] Visit of 10 January 1586, ibid., vol. I, fols. 60–2v.

[2] An Apostolic Bull by which the Popes granted indulgences to those who went
to war against the Infidel or contributed to the costs by donations or alms.

[3] A custom very frequent in several European nations at that time. See H. H.
Gerth and C. W. Mills: *From Max Weber: Essays in Sociology* (London, 1952, 3rd
Imp.), p. 315.

[4] Visit of 10 January 1586, Parish Books, vol. 1, fols. 60–2v.

being so harmful to the societies, we order the vicar to take
pains when there happens to be in this town any woman who
lives immodestly or causes scandal in the *pueblo* or allows sus-
picious persons access to her house, or anyone who lives a bad
life, to correct them privately, and if they do not profit by his
reproof he shall be helped by the Mayor, Justices and Jurymen
and the jailer . . . '.[1] 'Item we order the Jurymen to forbid the
playing of any type of games in the town during the divine
offices, or fighting or blaspheming the name of God or His
saints, beneath the penalty of half a *real* for the first time and one
real for the second and thenceforth they shall be thrown into
prison . . . '.[2] The archiepiscopal 'Item we order' not only
indicates the superiority of the spiritual authority over the civil
in the *pueblo*, singling out whom, why and by what means they
are to be punished; the context of the phrases points to the
identity of sin with civil offences, or at least implies that the
boundary between them tends to be confused. Public sin is
detrimental to the community, therefore it falls to the civil
authority, as the secular arm, to prevent or punish it.

Morals and customs obviously formed part of the specific
concern of the pastoral visits. Christian morals and customs, it
appeared, were not always in accordance with popular practice
—for example the celebration of weddings. The visiting Archbishop sought to curb the frivolity of these weddings: 'Item whereas we have been told grave troubles result from not conducting
marriages with the fitting circumstances and decency and that
many offences have been made under the title of matrimony,
the wives being given to the husbands once the families have
come to an economic agreement and before they have exchanged
the marriage vows in church. Therefore we order under penalty
of major excommunication and of fifty ducats for fiscal costs
and war against the Infidel that, having come to an economic
agreement, the contracting parties shall not take any oaths nor
marry themselves with future promises nor celebrate with
friends or kinsfolk, meals and repasts, nor any other rejoicings
or feasts until, following the admonitions of the Church laid
down and regulated by the Holy Council of Trent, they shall
have been married by the vows made *in facie ecclesiae*, and the

[1] Visit of 4 February 1599, ibid., fols. 79–80v.
[2] Visit of 11 May 1570, ibid., fols. 27v–8v.

others who take part in the oaths, rejoicings, feasts and banquets shall incur the same fine ...'. This was in 1594;[1] however it appears that the pastoral admonitions, major excommunications and the fifty ducat fine did not have the desired effect,, for a century later consummation of the marriage before it had been blessed by the church still persisted: 'Item being informed ... in this place ... of the abuses by which those who are engaged to be married enter the houses of the fiancées before contracting marriage, with frequency and familiarity, sometimes under the eyes of the parents, other times without their noticing, whereof ensue many offences against God under the cape and pretext of future marriage, with loss of their souls, thus beginning the married state in a manner deeply offensive to Our Lord God and exposing the fiancées to the danger of the loss of honour (*honra*) should their fiancés fail them, leave the *pueblo*, or change their minds; to remedy which ... we order that the persons who have arranged to marry ... shall not enter the houses of their fiancées nor they the houses of their fiancés, nor shall they see each other nor communicate with each other in private houses nor shall the parents permit it. The which they shall observe both families under the penalty of excommunication *late sententiae ipso facto incurrenda*, whose absolution we reserve for Ourselves depriving the vicar of the faculty to absolve from this ...; we order the vicar to be vigilant in this matter .... In the same way we require the Jurymen in virtue of Holy Obedience to see to the carrying out of this order and together with the vicar to extract the fines from the disobedient ...'. In the same visit, in order to bring about what he had proposed, he ordered: 'Item in as much as the sacrament of marriage is a living sacrament and ought to be received in a state of grace ... we order the vicar ... not to marry the contracting parties without making certain that they have confessed and communicated and that they know the christian doctrine'.[2] Later it was repeated: 'Item we command the vicar ... not to marry any contracting parties without first examining them and finding them well instructed in the christian doctrine'.[3] Already a hundred years earlier the visitor had ordered the vicar 'before

[1] Visit of 28 November 1594, Parish Books, vol. I, fols. 71–6.
[2] Visit of 17 April 1690, ibid., vol. III, fols. 218–19.
[3] Visit of 22 September 1733, Parish Books, vol. III, fols. 327–28v.

marrying the contracting parties, to examine them to see if they knew the prayers'.[1]

Thus we see from the beginning the christianization of an institution. Couples had earlier contracted what we would call today a civil marriage, followed by banquets and feasts; after some time and as a complement the vicar imparted a nuptial blessing. The economic arrangement came first, the rejoicings came after. Today the economic agreement continues to be essential in the marriage but after several centuries of pressure and excommunications the Church has succeeded in establishing the religious ceremony as the most important part of the marriage, even for those who have not been near the church since the day of their first communion. The civil part of the marriage, which involves signing a document in the vestry after the religious ceremony, is generally of no importance to the newly married couple; they frequently do not know what they are signing, and as it is signed in the vestry they think that they are dealing with the final religious formality. For everybody to marry in church is the only way to marry. No other matrimonial ceremony is valid, nor has it any meaning in the *pueblo*. The institution of matrimony is entirely christianized. On the other hand the prohibition on visits by fiancés to their fiancées has undergone a change in an opposite direction: it is not the christianization of a convention or custom but the socialization of a religious injunction. Prohibition of a religious type has come to be a conventional prohibition of a social type. Social pressure, started by an archiepiscopal order of a moral nature, has succeeded without anathemas and much better than the archbishop in doing what he himself aspired to do.

The church also tried to determine the times and places for certain pastimes. In 1576 the jurymen received orders to prohibit all classes of games played during divine offices; backsliders were to be imprisoned according to the will of the archbishop.[2] The obedience of both players and jurymen must have been very limited because ten years afterwards the visitor renewed the prohibition increasing the fine eight times, although there is no allusion to the previous penalty of prison.[3] It was

[1] Visit of 29 April 1634, ibid., vol. II, fols. 259–60.
[2] Visit of 11 January 1576, ibid., vol. I, fols. 39v–41.
[3] Visit of 10 January 1586, Parish Books, vol. I, fols. 60–2v.

forbidden under penalty of excommunication to run bulls
through the streets 'on feast days two hours before the high mass
and for two hours afterwards'.[1] However the obdurate did not
see in excommunication a sufficient motive for obedience and
continued to play. In 1733 appears the last 'Item we order the
said vicar to watch carefully on feast days to see that they do not
have dances nor play during the divine offices, and if being
threatened with the penalty of excommunication they insist in
their ways to declare them publicly excommunicated'.[2]

Another recurring field of conflict between the archbishops
and the *pueblo* was the subject of work on feast days. The provisions and fines against those who worked on the Lord's day,
written down in the first of the records preserved, are repeated
in all the remaining ones, the only change being an increase in
the size of the fines to be paid. Thus insubordination must have
been the norm. 'Because it has been made clear to us that there
is in this place much laxity with regard to the observation of
feast days, the which gives much offence to our Lord, we order
the vicar to take care that his parishioners keep them as they
are obliged to, punishing those who shall not do so in the
following manner: those who leave the place on a feast day with
carts or laden pack-animals or who do any other servile work, shall
be fined the first time two ducats, the second time four, and the
third time eight; and if with all this they do not mend their ways,
the vicar must inform us . . . in order that some other remedy
may be imposed. Those who set out with carts before the feast
day shall suffer the same penalty . . .'.[3] Five years later the same
archbishop revisited the *pueblo* and could see for himself that
his previous provision had not had the desired effect. He insisted on the same terms and ordered besides that a guard
should be nominated to exact the payment of the fine from the
transgressors: 'Firstly, as there has been much laxity in the
observance of feastdays, especially during summer, in spite of
the last visit when the vicar was charged to take great care to
make his parishioners observe them fully as is fitting; now, once

---

[1] Visit of 21 November 1615, ibid., vol. II, fols. 232–3.
[2] Visit of 22 September 1733, ibid., vol. III, fols. 327–8v. In 1787 allusions
are still being made that 'during divine services people are playing in different
houses . . .' (Visit of 26 June 1787, vol. III, fols. 297v–9v).
[3] Visit of 28 November 1594, Parish Books, vol. I, fols. 71–6.

more, we repeat our orders that he does this, and that he neither
permits those who are from other places to work nor allows
anyone within the boundary of this parish to undertake any
labour . . . and for the exaction and payment of the penalties
which he will impose, he will appoint a guard who shall be a
diligent and careful person who for his work shall be given a
half of the fine, the other part to be spent on religious matters
. . .'.[1] Six years later the visiting Archbishop reacted in a
different way to the impossibility of compelling the parishioners
to abstain from servile work on feast days. He made more explicit the instructions authorizing the vicar to permit his
parishioners to work on Sundays under certain circumstances
and if they paid a certain sum of money for souls in purgatory:
'Item we order all persons whatsoever in the said place not to
irrigate their properties on feast days except in urgent need and
with a licence from the vicar who will be able to give one,
making them pay one *sueldo* and taking this amount for masses
for the souls in purgatory . . .'.[2] None of this made any difference. In 1615 the visitor raised the fine to ten *sueldos*: 'Item we
order the vicar in virtue of Holy Obedience to impose a fine of.
ten *sueldos* on whomsoever person shall work on a feast day . . .
without his licence' etc.[3] Apparently those who chose to work
on days prohibited by the religious code did not even take the
simple precaution of obtaining a permit from the vicar. A
man's own criteria were thus not only above human laws, as we
saw in the last chapter, but above divine laws as well.

One of the objects of so persistently prohibiting servile
occupations on feast days was to oblige parishioners to attend
their parish cults. Archiepiscopal authority regulated even the
smallest details of services, including the position individuals
were to assume during them. In referring to processions, for
example, it is ordained that the 'lay assistants are not to go
altogether in a muddled crowd but one after another';[4] but
still today the men take part in the procession in exactly the
way that was prohibited by the visitor. Among the few notes
referring to women we have the following: 'Item whereas we

[1] Visit of 4 February 1599, ibid., vol. I, fols. 79–80v.
[2] Visit of 8 May 1605, ibid., vol. II, fols. 204v–206v.
[3] Visit of 21 November 1615, ibid., fols. 232–3.
[4] Visit of 26 April 1582, ibid., vol. I, fols. 51–6.

have received complaint that when the divine offices are being
... celebrated there is a very bad custom in the church of the
women being among the benches where the men sit, which
allows for indecency and appears bad ... we order under
penalty of major excommunication that no woman shall sit on
the benches where the men are, but rather behind the benches
where her place is ...'.[1] In other records the times of Sunday
masses are detailed,[2] and also the number, form and order of
processions and the sanctuaries to which they might go in
pilgrimage, as well as the processions which were forbidden.[3]
The number of brotherhoods, their rules and purposes, and the
use of income and subscriptions paid to them[4] was determined,
as well as the condition and forms of conducting funerals,[5]
punctuality and proper behaviour to be observed in the church,[6]
and so on.

In the twenty-second session of the Council of Trent the
bishops were ordered to examine on their visits the state of the
accounts, bequests, foundations, anniversaries, etc. of the
churches. The canonical visits, therefore, had a markedly
economic character. About three-fifths of the records refer to
the checking of the accounts of the tithes and first fruits and of
the income of the brotherhoods, of the wills and pious legacies
of the faithful. They are full of references to the collectors of the
bequests, to the *lumineros* responsible for gathering the tithes and
first fruits, to the executors of wills, notaries or persons who 'gave
witness entitled to faith' of final wishes concerning bequests left
to the church. The managers, priors and stewards of the brotherhoods, the simple faithful with their tardiness in paying the
church part of the fruits of their fields or part of the inheritance
left by the will of their parents for masses or pious works, fill the
pages of the records with their accounts never well presented,

---

[1] Visit of 30 April 1649, ibid., vol. II, fols. 277–8.
[2] Visit of 22 November 1696, ibid., vol. III, fols. 232–4v; visit of 26 June 1787,
ibid., fols. 297v–9v.
[3] Visit of 26 April 1582, ibid., vol. I, fols. 51–6; visit of 21 November 1615,
ibid., vol. II, fols. 232–3; visit of 3 December 1676, ibid., fols. 312–13.
[4] Visit of 26 April 1582, ibid., vol. I, fols. 51–6; visit of 4 February 1599, ibid.,
fols. 79–80ov.; visit of 20 March 1657, ibid., vol. II, fols. 283v–5 etc.
[5] Visit of 26 April 1582, ibid., vol. I, fols. 51–6; visit of 4 October 1607, ibid.,
vol. II, fols. 210–13; visit of 19 June 1673, ibid., fols. 306v–308 etc.
[6] Visit of 26 April 1691, ibid., fols. 317–18.

with their excuses and refusals to pay, and with the excommunications which fall upon them. It is clear that the Visitor
must have spent most of his time clarifying confused written
declarations and verbal replies and verifying them. He tried to
avoid this by charging the vicar 'under penalty of excommunication and of four hundred *sueldos* for fiscal costs and war
against the Infidel' to look through the accounts beforehand,
'to make them as clear and distinct as possible . . . so as not to
detain us on our visits . . . so that we can turn to other matters
. . .'.[1] The examination of the accounts 'has caused us much
inconvenience' grumbled the Visitor on his April visit in 1649.

The parishioners had to pay annually tithes and first fruits
which were collected and administered by the vicar and jurymen;[2] part went to the church and the vicar while the rest was
kept in the municipal granary as the residents' contribution to
the salaries of the doctor and teacher, and for the payment of
medicines. This obligation was thus both religious and civil. In
1609 the visitor ordered the parishioners to 'pay the tithes and
first fruits as they are obliged',[3] which suggests that the 'Item
we order all and every person of whatsoever condition under
penalty of excommunication and ten ducats, to pay the tithes
and first fruits . . .' of two years before[4] had very soon passed
into oblivion, if the excommunications and fines had ever had
any effect at all. There was a renewed insistence on the same
obligation in the visit of 1615,[5] an insistence which was crystallized in 1691 in the following terms: 'Item whereas we are
informed that the residents . . . when they collect their harvest
have introduced a habit of paying neither the tenth nor the
first fruit of the chaff, but *using their own judgment* (my italics)
leaving only a nominal amount . . . and not fulfilling as they
ought the precept of our holy mother the Church by paying
in full the tenths and first fruits. Therefore we order them, under
penalty of major excommunication and of twenty ducats . . . to
pay the tenths and first fruits entirely from the grain and fruits
which they gather, without omitting chaff, neither taking any

[1] Visit of 28 November 1594, ibid., vol. I, fols. 71–6.
[2] Visit of 8 May 1605, ibid., vol. II, fols. 204v–206v.
[3] Visit of 8 April 1609, ibid., fols. 216–17.
[4] Visit of 4 October 1607, ibid., fols. 210–13.
[5] Visit of 21 November 1615, ibid., fols. 232–3.

from the heap so that as from the heap of corn as from the heap of chaff, God may be given of his own'. Later the residents were required to pay exactly the 'tithes and first fruits, as we are told many do not pay all but only the half and that which is the worst and baddest part, bringing the harvest to their homes and not wanting to pay on the threshing floor, on which particular we burden their consciences with the grave and irreparable harm they cause the church'.[1]

At the beginning of the eighteenth century the fulminations began to die down, and appeals to the conscience of the parishioners took their place. Previously however the number of excommunicated people in the *pueblo* must always have been high, and it would appear that the threats and exhortations had never been taken very seriously. Thirteen years after the visit of 1691 the visitor wrote in relation to the problem of the first fruits: 'Item whereas of the inspection we have made of the book of the administration of the first fruits, whereas from the accounts taken, there turns out to be large quantities owing, due to the compliance of the vicar and jurymen who, failing in their obligation, have not compelled the tax-gatherers to make their collection ... we command each one of the debtors to give satisfaction for the sum which is owed within the space of one month, under penalty of excommunication ...'.[2] Apparently the repeated excommunications meant very little, not only to the ordinary faithful but to the jurymen and even to the vicar. It is worth noticing that all the orders rise to a similar crescendo: the passing of time sees a decrease in popular feeling of obligation and religious practices and a corresponding increase in penalties and archiepiscopal excommunications—the latter being the supreme effort to gain control of the community and to restore the flock to the confines of the fold delineated in the sixteenth century by the Council of Trent, the Inquisition, and by fear of the heresies that had divided Europe. Yet contumacy pursued its own course; the anathemas disappeared.

In the record of the visit made in 1582 there appear for the first time in sufficient detail the economic-religious problems which from then on were to be the nightmare of every

[1] Visit of 26 April 1691, ibid., fols. 317–18; visit of 26 June 1787, ibid., vol. IV, fols. 297v–9v.
[2] Visit of 27 October 1704, ibid., vol. III, fols. 249–51v.

archbishop, of the vicar and of the parishioners. Having finished
the inspection of the parish the archbishop drew up in full a programme of reorganization and parochial administration. It was
already ordered from the start that they should make inventories
'for the good government of the ecclesiastical funds', in which
'all the books, accounts and deeds which deal with the goods,
rights and privileges of their church, chapel and altars should
be written down'. Secondly 'another book should be made . . .
in which shall be listed all benefices, chaplaincies, celebrations,
anniversaries, prime masses, alms and pious legacies of whatever
kind they are'. Thirdly: 'Item we order that the collectors of
all alms whatsoever should note down every month in a book
what they have received and what they have spent, very
specifically in a way that shall be clear when they render the
accounts'. It was also laid down that 'the vicar shall not bury
any person without having a valid testimony from the notary
in front of whom the deceased made a will, stating where he
wishes to be buried, and the pious legacies he disposes of'. The
report finishes: 'As they did not know how to give account of
the property of Our Lady of Caballeros and of St. Engracia we
order the vicar under penalty of excommunication that within
eight months he calls before him the tax-collectors of the said
hermitages and in the presence of the jurymen he takes from
them the account of the property of the said hermitages . . .'.[1]
The moderate tone of the orders is interesting. Only the vicar
is threatened with excommunication in the case of disobedience;
probably the Archbishop expected submission on the part of the
parishioners. Nevertheless in 1594, twelve years later, the new
Archbishop found the books of the parish accounts as obscure as
ever. As he was not disposed to tolerate such an abuse, he reinforced the straightforward order of the previous Archbishop
with excommunications and fines for those who became liable:
'Item as we have found on this visit in passing through the
accounts . . . that much harm has been done, and because of the
difficulty there has been in rendering them in a fitting manner,
we order the patron, executors, collectors, managers and
stewards . . . under penalty of excommunication and four
hundred *sueldos* . . .' to have them ready with the greatest

---

[1] Visit of 26 April 1582, ibid., vol. 1, fols. 51–6.

clarity possible.[1] He continued: 'Item as it has befallen many times through the carelessness of the vicar and curate in listing and in ensuring the fulfilment of anniversaries, masses and other memorials which some persons have bequeathed, the heirs come to spend and consume the substance in such a way that when the former try to enforce them they have nothing with which to pay, neither of their own nor of the inheritance.... We order them (the vicars) that from now and henceforth they take great care to hurry the heirs up to carry out the last will and dispositions within the year and before they have spent the inheritance, or to give notice to the judge of pious causes so that they are made to fulfil them, with the warning that they will pay from their own property if they are weak and remiss'.

From now on all the records until the end of the nineteenth century demand clarity in the presentation of accounts, the strict settlement of the same, and the fulfilment of wills and pious legacies by the always reluctant faithful. The disobedient were anathematized and forbidden access to the church. We can follow the authoritative insistence of the prelates, the disobedience of the parishioners, and the personal excommunications made solemnly public at Sunday Mass. In 1607 the visitor ordered as before that 'the said census and duties of anniversaries and whatever other income belonging to the building of the church and hospital and hermitages and other pious works should be put in a book'. He continued: 'And whereas we have found that through the negligence and carelessness of previous vicars ... we could not even know clearly which persons were to pay these duties ... we order under penalty of major excommunication and 20 ducats, the vicar and beneficiary who are at present and who will be in the future, that in company with the notary of the said place and of two persons who had taken more notice of those who have not carried out the anniversaries they were obliged to, shall scrutinize for the last twenty years the five books, tables of anniversaries and wills which have been made in this period and shall clear up all doubts as to the persons who ought to carry out anniversaries; the vicar shall compel these ... to carry out their duties....

[1] Visit of 28 November 1594, ibid., fols. 71–6.

We order the vicar to shut out completely *a divinis* those who have not, by the end of the coming month of February, discharged their anniversaries . . .'. From general cases it descends to individuals: 'Item we order the vicar under penalty of excommunication not to admit Juan de Alba to divine offices until he shows that the will of Ana de Huertas whose executor is the said Alba, has been seen by the Archbishop'. 'Item we order the said vicar to expel from the divine offices Andrés Sánchez and Jerónimo Sánchez heedful that they are excommunicate by us *nominatim*, until they have been absolved by . . . Us and have shown that they have satisfied by judicial decree the obligation by which they have to pay a hundred *libras* to Our Lady of the Rosary'; he mentions further two more persons in the same circumstances, concluding the paragraph: 'And we order the said vicar to publish these our orders at the high mass the first Sunday of the obligatory feast'.[1]

In every one of the records for three hundred consecutive years, that is to say from the seventeenth to almost the end of the nineteenth centuries, we find identical archiepiscopal pressure being brought to bear in an attempt to achieve clarity and the fulfilment of the quoted economic obligations; it is met by an equal carelessness and insubordination on the part of the vicar, jurymen and parishioners. The visitors found that not one of the economic/religious provisions had been carried out as they had ordered. Two years after the last visit quoted, for example, thirteen persons were placed on the list of those who were to stay away from divine service, ten more than in the preceding visit.[2] The number of persons who had not fulfilled their obligations as executors continued to increase until in 1863 there were 63,[3] which means that scarcely any executor had fulfilled his obligation towards the church. But by that date they had not for some time been excommunicated for their disobedience. It was to the judge of pious causes that the religious authority now appealed legally to secure that the heirs or executors of wills should defray the costs of the cults for which they were obliged to pay.[4] On the other hand the failure of the

---

[1] Visit of 4 October 1607, ibid, vol. II, fols. 210–13.
[2] Visit of 8 April 1609, ibid., fols. 216–17.
[3] Registration of Deaths which starts in 1852; 6 December 1863.
[4] Visit of 26 June 1787, Parish Books, vol. IV, fols. 297v–9.

faithful to meet their religious obligations is not altogether surprising, for neither had the gravity of the anathemas succeeded in making the vicars keep a record of the properties of the parishioners, nor of the anniversaries and masses ordered in wills. This is clear from the records. For example, wills 'are written down without order, without any method', the visitor wrote.[1] They are not drawn up in a form which would make it possible to act upon them 'according to our obligation and that of the vicar, the which has caused us much trouble and we have not been able to ascertain anything'. The same happened to the order given to the vicar, and never fulfilled, that he was not to bury any person without being sure of what the deceased had willed and what pious legacies he had left for his soul. Despite all this not one anathema was laid against the vicar after the beginning of the eighteenth century for infringements of an economic character.

From the second half of the sixteenth to the beginning of the eighteenth century the community was essentially christian. Individuals belonged to a theocratic society in which the repertoire of ideas, beliefs and basic assumptions, the solutions for fundamental problems, the outlook on life, laws, institutions, morals and customs were christian. There were in force in this small community a body of laws, ideas and beliefs firmly laid down by the Catholic Monarchs—from Ferdinand and Isabella to Philip II—moulded by their temperaments, the conception of the State and of the Monarchy, and by national and international political circumstances which had very little to do with the town. The result was the total christianization of the *pueblo* and its institutions. But what of the people? What were their ideas and religious feelings, and how did they express them outwardly in a society so markedly theocratic?

II

As before, the reports of each pastoral visit are the only means by which we can try to reconstruct the reactions of the parishioners. Through them we can learn something of their awareness and knowledge of christian doctrine.

In the first record of a visit preserved—1570—we come across an indication that the parishioners' knowledge of christian

---

[1] Visit of 30 April 1649, ibid., vol. 11, fols. 277–8.

doctrine was not all that the Archbishop could have wished. At the conclusion of his visit he wrote: 'Firstly we order the vicar on Sundays and feast days to gather together all the children . . . and to teach them the christian doctrine, and the father and mother who do not send their children, without having a legitimate excuse, will pay six coins each time . . .'.[1] In 1605 neither the teaching of the catechism nor the faithful's knowledge of it had improved and the visitor repeated: 'Firstly we order the vicar of the said church to teach the christian doctrine each Sunday and feast day and to declare the Holy Gospel from the foot of the altar'. He must teach the doctrine 'on feast days, after vespers, in the small square of the church', and he continues 'and not marry nor absolve any person, at least in Lent, should he not be completely satisfied that the person is sufficiently instructed in the same'.[2] The final reference implies that the sacraments of marriage and penance were administered to persons whose knowledge of christian doctrine was slight. Some years later the same visitor insisted afresh: 'We order the vicar . . . to teach the christian doctrine to his parishioners and to declare the Holy Gospel to them every feast day'.[3] This time christian doctrine was to be taught not only to the children, as had been ordered on the previous visit, but also to the parishioners, to whom also the vicar was to explain the Gospel. In 1634 the visitor urged: 'Item we order the vicar to take care on Sundays to declare the Holy Gospel and to teach the christian doctrine in the evening to the parishioners . . .', and a little further down: 'Item we order the said vicar that before marrying the contracting parties he will examine them to see if they know the prayers . . .'.[4] To contract marriage it was enough to know the Our Father, the Hail Mary and some other prayer. In 1645 the visitor put pressure on the vicar, reminding him of his grave responsibility: 'Item we order the said vicar to explain the word of the Gospel and to teach the christian doctrine to his parishioners, delaying absolution to those who do not know it, to whose conscience we solemnly commit the charge'.[5] Weddings

---

[1] Visit of 11 May 1570, ibid., vol. I, fol. 27v.
[2] Visit of 8 May 1605, ibid., fols. 204v–206v.
[3] Visit of 8 April 1609, ibid., fols. 216–17.
[4] Visit of 29 April 1634, ibid., fols. 259–60.
[5] Visit of 28 September 1645, ibid., vol. II, fols. 273–4.

also were to be delayed if the contracting parties were ignorant
of the christian rudiments; thus the vicar was ordered in 1690:
'He . . . shall not marry the contracting parties without making
sure that they have confessed and communicated and that they
know the christian doctrine . . .'.[1]

In spite of archiepiscopal exhortations for more than a
century, Archbishop Rada de la Riva on his visit in 1696 soon
became aware of the faithful's ignorance of the most basic
christian principles and of the confused ideas which reigned
among them. He wrote: 'Firstly we order the vicar that every
Sunday in the year, at the time of the offertory of the High Mass
and early masses he shall explain a mystery of our Holy Faith
or one of the commandments of God's law, or the manner and
form in which the penitents must examine their conscience and
the essential parts of the sacraments of penance, clearly and
briefly so that his parishioners perceive and understand and do
not confuse some points with others . . .'. Knowing that many
parishioners would go to hear the mass said by the chaplain
in which there was no sermon, thus avoiding the sermon of the
solemn mass, the secretary to the visitor continued: 'And whereas
H.E. has ordered the vicar on Sundays and feast days to explain
some mystery of our holy faith at the time of solemn mass, if it
happens that the chaplain celebrates said mass before High Mass
the purpose of H.E. will be frustrated by the people going to hear
the said mass and not attending the high mass to avoid the
sermon, we order that the chaplain is not to celebrate his mass
on Sundays and feast days before high mass . . .'.[2] Succeeding
vicars cannot have carried out their orders, because in 1733 the
vicar is emphatically required not to give Easter communion
nor to marry anyone 'without first examining them and finding
them well instructed in the christian doctrine'. To enforce what
had been ordered so many times the visitor threatened transgressors with excommunication: 'Item we order all those who
shall preach in the church that, under penalty of major excommunication *late sententiae*, they will explain the christian
doctrine up to the Hail Mary of every sermon that is preached
in the church'. At the end of the record the point recurs: 'We
order the vicar every Sunday and feast day to explain briefly

---

[1] Visit of 17 April 1690, ibid., vol. III, fols. 218–19.
[2] Visit of 22 November 1696, ibid., fols. 230v—4v.

and clearly the doctrine and gospel to the faithful, beneath the fine of twenty Jacan pounds'.[1] The same emphasis can be observed in most of the records of visits until 1934.

Thus we see the same pattern of crescendo as in the other regulations. Vicars and chaplains show little respect for archiepiscopal demands; they do not teach the doctrine in a fitting manner, and in general the faithful are ignorant of it. The few ideas they have are confused, and they do not show very much interest in learning christian principles. They receive the sacraments despite their scanty doctrinal knowledge.

Let us imagine any ordinary Sunday about the middle of the seventeenth century as suggested by the denunciations in the visitors' reports. The bells ring out calling the parishioners to solemn mass. Some of them do not go because they are enjoying themselves in a friend's house playing the games which the records condemn but do not specify. Others play outside the church, probably *pelota* (a ballgame), against its walls, which was the custom until 1930, thereby disturbing the devout within. A third group go to work in their plots. A fourth group cannot enter the church for they happen to be excommunicated and banned *a divinis*. Finally others prefer to hear the short mass said by the chaplain and do not feel themselves obliged to listen to the sermon. Inside the church some women are sitting on the benches among the men, distracting them from their devotions. The men for their part smoke in the choir and in the church.[2] At the offertory the vicar reads the list of those persons who have incurred excommunication from that moment or who will incur it within a limited interval if they do not fulfil their duties. At the same time tombs are sold by the stewards of the brotherhoods at a profit. Some curse and blaspheme the name of God. Betrothed couples enjoy married life before receiving the sacrament, which is of secondary importance compared with the economic arrangements, and matrimonial pledges and feasts have already been celebrated. The tax-gatherers, collectors of revenues and administrators of Brotherhoods, never succeed in making a clear return of the accounts because part of the money

---

[1] Visit of 22 September 1733, ibid., vol. III, fols. 237–8v.
[2] The Minutes of 26 April 1691, II, 317–18, say: 'We order the lay people under penalty of excommunication not to smoke tobacco in the choir or in the church'. The same was prohibited for the priests.

sticks to their hands. Executors easily forget their obligations
to arrange masses, anniversaries and novenas for the souls of
those from whom they have inherited and use the money for
more earthly ends. They take care to avoid paying tithes and
first fruits, or pay as little as possible, and that not of the best
quality. Even some of the vicars must have been excommunicated because one infers from the records that in spite of
the penalty of excommunication they did not obey the stipula-
tions of the canonical visits.

Can we then describe these people as christians? Certainly
not if by christianity we understand its dogmas, theological
interpretations, morals and practices of worship. In this sense
the people may have been living in an intensely christian
society, but they were not really christians; the atmosphere was
saturated with religion, but the religious way of life had been
superimposed; the people were a long way from being, or knowing how to be, christians or from wanting to behave as christians.
Thus we shall have to distinguish two different levels. First there is
the official level, to which authority and dogma belong and
from which proceeded the moral code, discipline, and organization governing institutions and customs. This is the level of
established social order, the level which nobody disputed; it was
accepted as given and imposed, as what ought to be. The second
level represents what the people really were, what they believed in
and practiced. Individuals passed easily from one level to the other,
indicating a certain duality or dissension in their christianity.
For, in spite of what has been said, it cannot be literally affirmed
that these people were not christians. They were very much so.

It is clear enough from the records which aspects of religion
were not welcomed by or meant little to the people, but it is
not so easy to trace the positive characteristics of their faith. Yet
there can be no doubt about the religiosity of the residents. In
none of the records is there any allusion to a lack of faith, or to
grave distortions or dogmatic errors. The Inquisition kept a
jealous watch but did not have to worry about the *pueblo*. The
pueblo believed in all that a christian should believe. They did
not have doubts; on the contrary they believed very strongly;
the essence of their christianity was their faith. Everyone received the sacraments; nobody omitted to confess and communicate according to the parish statistics made at Easter every

year. Not one of the records of deaths suggests that anyone died
without the final spiritual comforts, except in cases of sudden
death or fatal accidents. The upkeep of the two hermitages, of
the parish church, besides that of the two priests, the brotherhoods and their members, the tax-gatherers, the collectors of
bequests, the managers and stewards, the frequent processions
and pilgrimages, the repeated donations to the church for
benefices, chaplaincies, celebrations, anniversaries, masses, alms
and other pious legacies seem to suggest an exuberance of faith
and religious feeling. This came to be expressed particularly
through the brotherhoods and processions.

The most important brotherhoods were those of Our Lady of
Caballeros, Our Lady of the Rosary, St. Engracia and the
Infant Jesus. It is impossible to deduce from the records if
women also belonged to these brotherhoods; the priors and
stewards were always men. The members had to pay subscriptions which together with bequests and pious legacies
augmented the revenue of the brotherhoods, which never stood
up to too scrupulous an examination by the visitor. We have
already seen[1] how the tax-gatherers of the most important
brotherhoods did not know how to render an account of their
incomes. In 1594 the penalty for lack of clarity in the rendering
of the accounts rose to 400 ducats, on top of excommunication.[2]
Again in 1713 and in 1772 the visitors insisted on the same
demand.[3]

The celebration of the feasts of Our Lady of Caballeros and of
St Engracia involved going in procession to the respective
hermitages. Processions through the streets in the locality were
organized to celebrate the festivities of Our Lady of the Rosary,
the Name of Jesus, of the patrons and guardian advocates of the
pueblo; they went in procession from the parish to the neighbouring *pueblos* to celebrate the *fiesta* of the patron saints of these
places,[4] and they held processions for any motive whatever 'by
vow and devotion' says a record, setting out to pass through the
streets of the *pueblo* or 'going in procession to some part', that

---

[1] Visit of 26 April 1582, Parish Books, vol. I, fols. 51–6.

[2] Visit of 28 November 1594, ibid., fols. 71–6.

[3] Visit of 20 April 1713, ibid., vol. III, fols. 281–3 and visit of 4 July 1772, ibid.,
vol. IV, fols. 252v–3v.

[4] Visit of 3 December 1676, ibid., vol. II, fols. 312–13.

is to say, to the place decided on by the organizers. They were
so frequent and for such varied motives that in 1615 the visitor
restricted them, forbidding the vicar to take part if they were
not celebrated under certain conditions.[1] The reason for the
prohibition is clear: the processions were a hybrid mixture of
the sacred and profane and frequently more profane than
sacred. In the record of 1582 we read: 'Item, whereas the processions which are made far afield result in improprieties which
are a disservice to God our Lord and very contrary in effect to
that for which they were initiated, we order under penalty of
excommunication, that such processions are not to be made
unless within the same hour the people taking part return to
hear mass in the parish church, and under the said penalty of
ten ducats we order the said vicar and clergy not to accompany
the said processions except in the said manner, and we require
the said vicar and other clerics, jurymen and all the rest of the
pueblo that in place of the said processions and on the days they
were wont to make them, they shall go instead to the nearest
boundary chapel or hermitage of the said place with the most
fervent devotion and send some cleric to say mass in the church
or hermitage where they are accustomed to go in procession and
do other pious works which will please our Lord and so that the
saints shall be honoured and reverenced'.[2] This reveals something of the variety of processions made. Those taking part
either made for the hermitages where mass was celebrated or
else to the outlying chapels, or, according to the censure of the
visitor, it was the custom to go further afield carrying the images
of the saints on their shoulders, to places not specified in this
record. Very probably they ate in the fresh air and there would
take place certain diversions and amusements of which the
Archbishop did not approve. It is clear that frequently the
processions were not very devout, nor was mass celebrated or
the saints honoured in a fitting manner; on the contrary they
gave occasion for lax conduct.

Neither were the processions organized by the brotherhoods
to the hermitages of Our Lady of Caballeros and St Engracia
more edifying, always ending with a feast and the consequent
merrymaking. Already in 1582 the following provision had been

[1] Visit of 21 November 1615, ibid., vol. II, fols. 232–3.
[2] Visit of 26 April 1582, ibid., vol I, fols. 51–6.

written: 'Item, so that the improprieties that are wont to result from the repasts of the brotherhoods shall cease, we order under penalty of excommunication that they shall not eat . . . at the expense of their revenues';[1] but as such banquets continued to be one of the most essential parts of the religious festivities, in 1594 we find a similar command: 'Item it has been made clear to us that the brothers of the brotherhood of Our Lady of Caballeros spend the substance and income which they possess on eating, and thus few suffrages are made for the souls in purgatory, we order them under penalty of major excommunication *late sententiae trina canonica monitione premissa* and of 25 *escudos* . . .' to spend half their income on pious works.[2] Five years later the brothers may have been already excommunicated because they gave no signs of greater sobriety at the patronal banquets: 'Item visiting the brotherhoods which have been founded in this parish we have found that in that of Our Lady of Caballeros there has been, in some years, excessive expenditure on meals while little has been spent on the suffrages for the souls of deceased members. We order the prior and majordomos, under penalty of excommunication and 500 *sueldos* every time that they shall fail in the above written, not to spend on the meal more than the two *sueldos* and six *dineros* that each living brother pays in each year . . .'; the remainder should be spent on 'candles, masses, anniversaries and other pious works'.[3]

Brotherhoods and processions were an essential part of the religious expression of the *pueblo*, in fact they *were* the religion of the *pueblo*. Through them the people expressed their collective devotion to the patrons of the *pueblo*. Religious vitality found its outlet in the public cult, in collective ceremonies; hence the religiosity of the *pueblo* consisted not in ideas but rather in actions. These religious festivals required little concentration. They broke the daily monotony, brought the people together in the square to set out in a procession that required a minimum of organization towards one of the customary places. Picnics, feasting, drinking, noise and merriment were the normal corollary. Very often, according to the rebukes of the Archbishop, they were the essential part of the festival. Thus there was a tendency towards the profane, if indeed the people were

---

[1] Ibid.   [2] Visit of 28 November 1594, ibid. fols. 71–6.
[3] Visit of 4 February 1599, ibid., fols. 79–8ov.

not rather making use of the saints in the procession to bless their profane diversions and make them appear before the strict eye of the visitor who controlled all amusements as religious festivities. This ambivalent character of the collective religious ceremonies, the proliferation and gusto with which they were carried out, makes the cult reversible into *fiesta* and *fiesta* into cult. I have indicated how the visitors prohibited or at least tried to control the processions. The same thing happened with the brotherhoods: they abounded without the knowledge of the bishop. The brotherhood of the Name of Jesus, wrote the visitor on 20 March 1657, 'was not established or founded by the bishop nor by anyone who holds authority'. In 1832 the vicar wanted to create a 'brotherhood of *pudientes* and devout persons from among his parishioners' to keep the vigil before the Holy Sacrament. The fraternity only survived a very short while in spite of the selective character of its membership; this type of association was out of tune with the popular form of religiosity.

It would be a mistake, however, to think that the external, collective religiosity, expressed in particular by religious processions and brotherhoods, was the only essential characteristic of popular religiosity. There were also the soteriological and eschatological aspects. Religion as soteriology was naturally felt on a deeper, more personal level when they felt that death was knocking at their door. The pressure of the ideas dominant in the society in which they lived, religious indoctrination about the existence of a life after death, the consideration of this life as a transitory one in which to obtain the other, had all permeated the popular conscience deeply. The reception of the last sacraments and the donation of property to be used for the soul were the appropriate means. In this way religion was essentially a faith in the life after death and the desire to secure personal salvation. Thus besides receiving the sacraments they used to draw up a will in which they took great care to specify the amount of riches they left for their soul. In the death notices we always read: 'left for his soul', with details of how many masses, anniversaries, novenas and suffrages in general the sick person required afterwards for his soul. Even the poorest people wanted to be sure of a speedy remission of their sins in the other life by means of suffrages celebrated for them after their death. Hence the donations to the church with the intention that they should be rendered into funeral prayers for an early eternal rest. Not to have anything to dispose of in a pious bequest was a misfortune which they tried hard to avoid while still alive. These two records of deaths illustrate this obsessive conviction. The first says: 'On the 1st of March 1599 Juan de Serrano, a poor man died in the hospital ... the clothes which he wore were sold for his shroud and prayers for his soul'. Those who buried him resorted to selling the dead man's clothes so as not to deprive his soul of suffrages. The second says: 'On the 19th March 1601 Joana de Huguet died ... she had not made a will because she had nothing, only for her soul she had kept in reserve ... 20 *escudos* ... for her death, a novena and anniversary funeral'. The woman had been struggling all her life to set aside a certain amount for a matter of such great importance.

Thus although they may in many ways have been hazy about their religion, may have disobeyed the ecclesiastical hierarchy, and practised customs hardly christian, they were at the same time very christian indeed; christians *sui generis* but christians. While external and collective cultual practices were an essential part of their religiosity, it is clear that internal and personal religious feeling and experience were equally essential characteristics.

XII

RELIGION: II

'*Es la existencia humana, limitada, finita y humillada, pero total la que surge en nuestra conciencia con la angustia ante la muerte*'. '*El temor de morir y de condenarse, de ser borrado de la luz definitiva por la mano de Dios*' MACHADO

'*Fundaste este tu pueblo . . . sobre la fe en la inmortalidad personal . . . Senor*'. '*Y cuál ha sido el más entranado resorte de la vida de nuestro pueblo sino el ansia de sobrevivir, que no a otra cosa viene a reducirse lo que dicen ser nuestro culto a la muerte? No, culto a la muerte, no; sino culto a la inmortalidad*' UNAMUNO

I

THE NOTES in the parish books under the heading '*Status Animarum*' seek to determine quantitatively one aspect of the religiosity of the parishioners. At Easter every year the vicar signed a report which almost invariably went thus: 'I the undersigned, make a report, how in the year . . . with regard to the Holy Sacrament of Penance and the Eucharist, the obligation has been fulfilled at the time fixed . . . by our Holy Mother Church, by all the people who are bound by it in this parish of Our Lady of the Assumption. In number they are . . .'. This scheme, copied year after year, furnishes parochial statistics of the fulfilment of the obligation of annual confession and communion. The first statistical report found is dated 1689; from this date to 1740 and from 1771 to 1826 all the parishioners beholden performed their duty. Although written testimony before 1689 and from 1741 to 1770 is lacking one can well assume that from the middle of the sixteenth century until 1826 all the beholden people in the *pueblo* observed the precept of the church. The account of the *Status Animarum*, interrupted in 1826, is renewed in 1896, a year in which 150 men and 45

women had not observed the precept. As it is probable that the
number of dissenters had increased gradually, one can suppose
that abstentions from the Easter Duty began towards the middle
of the last century. In 1863 the visitor complained of families
being slow to notify the priest when one of their relatives was
gravely ill. He said: 'Taking notice that unfortunately there
are many families careless about providing their kinsfolk with
the aid of religion . . .'.[1] The transgression of the Easter Duty
and its impunity (no penalty was imposed on the disobedient
by the archbishop) suggests that a different society was emerging.
In effect the church had lost control of the community, the
Inquisition was finally abolished in 1835, and the Council had
recovered its position of command. This situation is parallel to
the relation between church and state; the former had lost the
control originally conceded by the crown for political purposes.
For one thing the duties committed to the church in the sixteenth century no longer served the same purpose in the nineteenth century.

Already at the end of the eighteenth century the superiority
of the mayor over the vicar begins to be noticeable in religious
and civil matters—in the election to certain positions[2] for example. By the beginning of the nineteenth century interference
in purely religious affairs had reached a point at which the
Council Hall had usurped many of the responsibilities of the
vicarage. The Council had been christianized to that extent.
During the whole of the nineteenth century the *pueblo* was only
visited five times by the succeeding archbishops; and, curtailing
the sphere of their previous authority, in not one of the records
of the visits do they allude to matters which are not entirely
religious. The tone of the records has also changed. The
anathemas have been replaced by fatherly exhortations. Thus
the *pueblo* acquired greater religious freedom, whilst the withdrawal of archiepiscopal authority left the Council with a wider
range of activities. At the same time this period saw the gradual
secularization of the community.

So that the residents might have greater facility in fulfilling
the ordinances of the church, the Council ordered the shopkeeper, as we already know, 'to sell undried codfish all the days

---

[1] Visit of 6 December 1863, Registration of Deaths, fols, 96v–7.
[2] Minutes of the Council, 21 February 1799.

of fasting'.[1] According to the Minutes of 13 January 1804 the Council, the priest not being present, 'decided . . . to give the Lent of this year to . . .'—that is to say, the Council itself chose the preacher who was to occupy the pulpit during specific days in Lent. Two days later they assembled again and agreed (again in the absence of the priest) to instruct the architect of the Council to take suitable steps to repair the roof of the parish church, which was threatening to fall in. In the agreement made with the priest on 16 January 1806, they imposed the time-table of masses by which he had to abide; further, if during harvest and sowing the priest fell sick he was to bring in a substitute to say mass at his own expense. The same year the Minute of 24 September refers to the first friction between the two powers. It concerned the division of the first fruits into two halves, one of which went to the vicar. The Council's delegate divided the collected grain into two more or less equal heaps and, calling the priest, allotted one of them to him. The latter protested about the division and asked that all the corn should be measured exactly. Faced by the Council's refusal to do this, the priest appealed to the City Court and won his case.[2] This struggle and the Council's refusal to agree to an exact division would have been incomprehensible in the former theocratic society.

In 1832 a municipal order was proclaimed by which 'blasphemies, oaths, rude and obscene words, and those persons who while in church did not observe all the decorum and concentration required in such a sacred place' were to be punished.[3] The content of the order is clearly religious; what before had been prescribed by the visitors was now considered to be the concern of the municipal authority. In the session of 16 January 1836 they insisted upon 'the observance in the *pueblo* of the ecclesiastical law which required that priests should have a licence to preach and to hear confession'. Like the visitors, the Council faced the task of persuading the residents not to work on feast days and to assist at the divine offices. At the meeting of 20 January 1861 the mayor said: 'that knowing that the agricultural tasks do not require haste as is supposed, *he was of the opinion* (my italics) that the residents should not work on a feast day so that they might assist at the divine offices . . .'; those

---

[1] Ibid., 12 December 1803.   [2] Ibid., 27 October 1806.
[3] Ibid., 3 May 1832.

who continued with the 'disorder and abuse of former years . . .'
would have to pay 'the fine of 20 *reales* for every occasion'. Four
months later he ordered an edict to be published 'so that not
one resident would dare to work on a feast day'.[1] Orders
identical to those of the archbishop prohibited games in private
houses, groups at the entrance of the church, and regulated the
internal order in the *pueblo*. But after 1861 there did not appear
any municipal regulation referring to purely religious matters.

The competence in religious matters that the Council
assumed at this period is not so intrusive as might first appear.
In reality the sphere of competence is identical; what has
changed is the form, the position of the Council in the regulation of such matters. The Council had been an organ which the
archbishops had endowed with a religious purpose and of which
they had made use to secure aims of a religious character. The
jurymen were directly responsible to the religious authority for
the fulfilment of some of its orders. It behoved them to check
blasphemies, to prohibit and punish work on feast days to put
an end to the games in private houses, to throw backsliders into
prison, be vigilant over public morality, put a stop to scandal or
notorious sin, to see that the faithful assisted at worship and paid
the tenths and first fruits, to repair the hospital, cemetery, parish
church, hermitages, etc. After a time municipal concern in these
matters became normal, one more sphere in the competence of
the Council. The institution had been won by the church.
Henceforward the jurymen and Council passed from the civil
to the religious sphere with the greatest ease. When religious
authority was hardly felt at all in the town, when the archbishop only came every twenty years and his remonstrances
were only directed towards the conscience, the Council continued to intervene as it had since the sixteenth century. Before,
it had functioned as an instrument of the visitor's orders; now it
had come to occupy the first position of command.

This change in the relation of parish and Council, which can
be followed in the municipal documents from the end of the
eighteenth century, continued until about 1850. We have
already seen how the Council then began to reflect national and
political upheavals and to incorporate itself or be incorporated

[1] Ibid., 26 May 1861.

into national life. This coincided, in the first place, with the end
of its purely religious instructions. From then on the Minutes
only referred to economic and administrative problems, and
the election of members to the Council whose dismissal and
renewal followed national political changes. The Council in
other words began a process of specialization; its functions became strictly administrative, political and economic. Religion
only intruded when it was a question of the programme for
the festivals of the patron saints. The Council's role in this was
limited to providing bulls, a band, fireworks and other popular
diversions. Otherwise it actively collaborated with the vicar if
he resorted to the Council, as for example in the preparation
of the reception offered to the Cardinal visitor, to which I have
referred. However, the spheres of competence and activity were
divided; when religion was involved the priest was invited to
discuss the problem with the Council.[1] Relations were harmonious; the members of the Council were *pudientes*, members
of a group which supported the church unconditionally. In the
second place it probably coincided with the first defections from
the Easter Duty, which could well belong to this period. At
least during these years families ceased to worry unduly when
their relatives died without receiving the last Sacraments, which
indicates a change in the religious tone. At the beginning of the
second half of the last century, existing religious laxity, the non-
interference by the Council in religious matters, greater religious freedom, the specialization of the Council in politico-
economic and administrative matters, the increasing participation of the *pueblo* in national life, and the separation of a group
of persons from the parish are phenomena which concur.

In 1896 the parish statistics were resumed and revealed the
following figures: 443 persons had obeyed the precept, 232 (151
men and 81 women) had not carried out their duty. The following diagram represents the variation in the observance of the
Easter Duty from 1897 to 1936; but one has to take into account
that no data have been preserved in the parish archives between 1909 and 1914 and between 1916 and 1923. The
line indicates the total of those who did not comply with the
precept.

---

[1] Ibid., 26 October 1879.

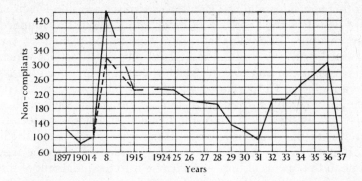

The height reached in 1908 is partially explained by the fact that in 1907 residence was granted to 30 heads of families who had come from other towns. 119 of those not complying the following year, 1908, were not sons of the *pueblo* but outsiders. The dotted line represents non-fulfilment by the actual *vecinos*. Until 1924 smaller waves of outsiders arrived who, in reference to the Easter Rule, began to be assimilated in 1926. In 1931 the number of non-compliant had dropped to 93. From that date until 1936 the number of abstentions from confessions and communion sharply increased. The *pueblo* did not receive any considerable contingent of outsiders during these five years, and the priest continued to be the same, working as before. Leaving aside interpretations of an internal nature the sudden variation can best be explained by political reasons.

In April 1931 the Republic was proclaimed, with its anti-religious and anticlerical character. The republican members of the Council in the *pueblo* intended to copy the model of the recently established lay State, and to laicize the Council. For the festivals in August 1931 they agreed that the full Council should not preside over any of the religious functions according to custom, but would content itself with sending a councillor to represent the corporation. Some months later, 5 March 1932, the Council assembled to discuss the next festivals in honour of the Patroness of the town. The Minutes relate: 'So that the population might enjoy themselves and have some moments of pleasure and happiness, according to the traditional custom of the locality, because of the day of the Virgin of Caballeros, it was agreed to organize *secular* (my italics) festivals for the 28th

of this month, bringing a band of . . . musicians, the which, if
the desire of the residents is such, and without any implied
organization, patronage nor any expense on behalf of the
Council, will be permitted to assist at religious functions which
the faithful can organize, to which the said Council will not go
as an official Corporation, whilst allowing every one of its
members complete freedom so that as individual persons they
may act as they like'. Here the Council appears to dissociate
itself with the religious festivals; it organizes *secular* festivals; it
does not assist as such at the religious functions—for the first
time in the town's history—and leaves it to the judgment of the
faithful whether the band should or should not accompany the
processions and other religious acts as it always had done. On
30 July of the same year and before the August festivals the
Minutes say that 'it was agreed not to authorize the assistance
of the band at the religious acts in the next festivals'. The
distance between the Council and the parish goes on increasing;
the republicans gain ground and the anti-religious temperature
rises in the *pueblo*. In 1931 only 93 people did not confess and
communicate at Easter; in 1932 those who did not observe the
rule were 205. On 10 February 1933 the Republican Club
presented a request to the Council in which among other things
it sought 'that they should order religious symbols to be torn
down from the doors and façades of buildings and they should
not allow public processions of the Catholic cult'. The Council,
said the Minutes of the same day, regarded 'all processions of the
Catholic cult as abolished but if anyone sought permission to
celebrate one, the petition would be transferred to H.E. the
Civil Governor'.

On 12 August 1933 a heated debate took place between one
of the republican councillors and another of the right wing who
represented the Catholic group. They argued fiercely as to
whether the band should play in the square during the celebration of Mass. The crucial question for them was to ascertain
which of them represented the majority in the Council. On 10
March 1934 another uproar broke out in the Council. As the
festival of Our Lady of Caballeros—25 March—coincided with
Holy Week, the celebration was transferred according to custom to Easter Monday. One of the republican councillors
objected categorically, declaring: 'if on other occasions this

festival had been transferred for the convenience and by the impositions of the priests, because it fell in Holy Week, today that prevalency does not exist and I think it fitting that every resident should do as he wants'. In fact, as the councillor claimed, the predominance of the church over the *pueblo* no longer existed, and the process of separation from the church continued. In this year 245 persons did not confess or communicate at the required time, 40 more than in the previous year. The figure rose to 270 in 1935 and to 302 in 1936, when the civil war started.

The republican period is the antithesis of the theocratic period at the end of the sixteenth or beginning of the seventeenth century. At that time monarchic pressure, through the visitors, made the *pueblo* a christian society in which the faithful were as many as the inhabitants; republican pressure separated more than half of the residents from the church. Thus the correlation between State and religion is one of the perspectives from which it is necessary to study Spanish catholicism. After listing the dissenters at Easter 1936, the priest writes: 'not having complied with their obligation 302, in spite of the repeated and exceptional calls made through twice-weekly sermons and in spite of a clever and very zealous preacher from the Order of the Carmelites, spreading the Divine Word in Holy Week. The cause of this lamentable aloofness is the intense anti-religious and immoral propaganda which has been made in this parish by the marxo-communist atheists who like the very plague have smitten the parishes . . .'. During the first days of the civil war the *pueblo* was entered by Franco's forces (the rightists had already assumed control of the town); the war was considered by the nationalists as a crusade to rescue religious values imperilled by the Republic. Religiosity was thus bound to Franco's cause. Not to go to church amounted to sympathizing with or defending the fallen Republic, the red army. After the nationalist troops occupied the *pueblo* the number of those not fulfilling their Easter Duties dropped from 302 in 1936 to 58 in 1937. Of course some of those who would not have complied had fled or had been executed.

A single item such as the fulfilment of Easter duty is necessary but not sufficient for an adequate analysis of the religiosity of the community. I have used it here not only because of its importance but also because it is the only item of historic value preserved; nothing has remained in the parish about the assistance at Sunday Mass, for example. In a community where only one faith exists, where all the institutions and *rites de passage* exude christianity, the possibility of somehow measuring the negative side of religious practice is most important. Not to confess and communicate even once a year in a christian community where everyone knows everyone else and where it is customary to do so, means that a man has decided to swim against the current and has broken his personal ties with the church. The appearance of dissenters around the middle of the last century implies a spiritual change in the community.

Yet religion was something intimate and personal, something as natural as breathing in a community for centuries christian. This makes it impossible to explain religious phenomena today only in terms of the relation between State and religion. During the republican period the wife of one of the most pronounced leftists had a baby. As the left wing claimed to have broken with the church it did not seem proper for the mother to have the child christened. To attack the church, scoff at those worshipping and then to take one's son to be baptized would have been a sign of political weakness. But the mother was not content to let her son go unchristened either. She solved the difficulty by secretly taking the new-born child to be baptized in the city. Similarly, some renowned leftist women used to go to confession in the city. In certain situations, religion came to the surface even in the most extremist republican families.

In this historical analysis certain things have remained constant: (1) The relations of dependence between the variables State and religion, which received their most extreme expression under a monarchy that made religion the foundation of society and under a republic that tried to laicize the nation. The new blossoming of religion under State encouragement since the end of the civil war is another expression of this relation. (2) As historically the State has usually promoted religion as vigorously as possible, the institutions and customs of the community are christianized. Even those who did not observe the Easter Duty, who had no faith and considered themselves emancipated from the church, turned to her as something natural in all the *rites de passage* as indeed they do today. (3) The cult celebrations and collective ceremonies are essential outward characteristics of religiosity in the *pueblo,* and soteriological and eschatological considerations reflect its more intimate personal level. (4) Individualism reveals itself not in disobedience to secular laws but as a religious indocility against divine and religious precepts.

II

Every newborn child is christened a few days after its birth. At seven all the children in the *pueblo* confess and make their first communion or prepare to make it. Later all are confirmed. Marriage is initiated by the nuptial blessing; and a purely civil marriage is not considered. At the hour of their death all receive the Last Sacraments, unless death is sudden and does not allow time for the arrival of the priest, and finally all are buried according to Catholic ritual. In this sense, therefore, all the residents are christians, which is to say Roman Catholics. But there are various grades of religiosity, which can be defined in terms of cultual practices.

Firstly, there are what may be called 'militants': women and to a lesser extent, girls who go to mass and communicate daily—approximately 20—and the women who belong to Catholic Action. There are 29 members of this group, but the majority are included in the first figure. They are married women who collaborate actively under the directions of the priest; they gather in study groups two or three times a month, organize the Christmas charity campaign, see that the gravely ill confess and communicate, and that the neglectful go more frequently to church. They care for the decoration and cleaning of the altars, are in contact with regional catholic organizations, and give the parish priest practical support in his ministerial work. Their husbands are almost all *pudientes.* Then there are about a dozen young men of around 20 years who communicate every week, and another dozen or so married men, almost all of them young, who also communicate weekly. These last have taken part in 'christianity' courses and form the catholic vanguard in the *pueblo* under the parish priest. They hold a weekly study circle, have built and manage a parish cinema, bring lecturers to the *pueblo* to speak on various topics, take part in regional catholic reunions, and so on. They are of a higher cultural level than the average and almost all can be classified as *pudientes* or sons of *pudientes*.

'Observers' are those who attend Mass on Sundays and other days of obligation, who confess and communicate four or five times a year if they are men and approximately once a month if they are women. All are affiliated to one or several sodalities or parish associations; many of the men also belong to one or other of the male societies. Although they contribute generously when sought by the parish priest, the religion of the 'observers' is of a more passive kind than that of the 'militants'. 'Observers' number some 460 persons, 290 being women and 170 men of all ages. Economically the group is formed by *pudientes* and *propietarios*, with some additions from lower categories. Amongst both 'militants' and 'observers' women predominate.

The 'Easter communicants' confess and communicate once a year. They go to church intermittently, almost only on special feasts—the Immaculate Conception and on the feasts of the Rosary, Christmas, Ascension, Corpus Christi, or when missionary friars come to the town to preach for four or five days. The 'Easter Communicants' are for the most part *jornaleros, propietarios* and some *peones*. This group is without doubt the least homogeneous, including those who only go to mass six or seven times a year, those whose assistance at Mass reflects in part the rhythm of work in the fields, and those who without being assiduous go fairly frequently. They are, according to the popular expression, those who go to mass 'when the bells chime'. They probably number about 430.

Some 90 persons remain, the majority men, who may be called 'non-observers' in that they do not even observe the Paschal precept of confession and communion. They go to church very rarely; some may not even go on Christmas Day or at the patronal festivals. However they have all received the sacraments of baptism, penance and communion, and they also receive christian burial and confess and communicate, if there is time, before they die. The mockery and sneers against religion, priests and devout persons come from this group— *braceros* and *peones* for the most part, although there are a few *proprietarios*.

Counts taken in 1958, '60 and '61 of attendance at Sunday or obligatory mass show the following round numbers—omitting the decimals in the percentages: those beholden total approximately 1,050.

	MEN	% of assistance among men beholden	WOMEN	% of assistance among women beholden	TOTAL	%
Fulfilment of obligation during the season of cereal harvest, Summer 1958 (estimated on the base of assistance on two Sundays)	175	33	305	60	480	46
Fulfilment of New Year's day, Feast of the Name of Jesus, 1961	240	44	405	88	690	66
Fulfilmen on a Sunday in the second half of January 1960; without pressure of work	190	35	370	72	560	53

About eighteen Sundays comprise the seasons of cereal and sugar-beet. Assistance at mass on five other liturgical feast days can be equated to that of New Year's Day. On Christmas Day 1961 those assisting at the three masses celebrated in the parish at different hours amounted to more than the total of those beholden, which indicates that some of them heard more than one mass. For these reasons I have preferred to estimate the percentage of assistance of those beholden at Christmas and four more similar feasts (the two patronal feasts, the feast of the Immaculate Conception and of St. Joseph) as 85 per cent, basing this on the fact that an approximate 15 per cent—something like 10 per cent women and 20 per cent men—do not fulfil the precept on the five days referred to according to the parochial data. I estimate that on the remaining Sundays of the year the number of observers does not vary much from on the Sunday in January 1961. The total percentage of observance throughout the year, is therefore about 55 per cent; 39 per cent among the men and some 71 per cent among the women. There will inevitably be some margin of error.

Besides the 29 married women members of Catholic Action
there are 34 subscribers or supporters, who pay a monthly
contribution but do not take an active part or attend the study
circles. 142 women, most of them married, belong to the sodality
of the Heart of Jesus. Many members confess and communicate
on the first Fridays of each month, wearing a scapulary of red
ribbon round their necks which supports on the breast a piece
of material whereon is drawn or embroidered a burning heart.
The feast of the Heart of Jesus is preceded by a novena and
concludes with a solemn mass, a sermon and a procession
through the streets of the *pueblo*, the women carrying the image
of the Heart of Jesus on a stand. The sodality with the largest
number of members, 326 in all, is that of Our Lady of Carmen.
Her festival is one of those which attract the most popular
devotion. Few mothers fail to put the Carmelite scapulary on
their children when but a few months old. The day of the
Patroness is celebrated in the same way as the feast of the Heart
of Jesus, though attendances are larger. The scapulary worn
under the clothes is carried by many parishioners during the
whole year. The Court of Honour consists of 64 married women
who assist at mass on the 12th of every month and alternate in
the adoration of the Virgin of the Pillar. For this they wear the
corresponding scapulary. For one day each month 150 house-
wives have an image of the Holy Family in their homes illu-
minated by small night lights, to which they pray with special
devotion. Of the 29 ladies belonging to Catholic Action, 20
belong to four other sodalities, two to three of them, three to
two more, and finally four to one of them. Not only do they
form the most active group in the parish but they belong as well
to other associations in which, in most cases, they have positions
on the directing committees.

The girls also have their particular groups: 41 compose the
Society of the Daughters of Mary or of the Immaculate Conception; 43 from 16 years upwards form the girls' Catholic
Action; 19 are called 'aspirants', and are aged between 12 and
16; and lastly there are the *benjaminas*, 20 in number, who are
enrolled when they have made their first communion and remain until they are 12 years old. The feast of the members of
the society of the Immaculate Conception has the same characteristics as the festivities of the other two sodalities. 'Aspirants',

benjaminas, and girls of the Catholic Action receive religious instruction in study circles twice a month.

Nineteen boys belong to the masculine Catholic Action; 18 to that of the married men; 98 of all ages, but mostly young men, belong to the brotherhood of the Name of Jesus whose feast is celebrated with great solemnity, communion and a luncheon on New Year's Day. A preacher brought from the city enhances the festival. The first mention of this brotherhood is found in the archiepiscopal visit carried out on 20 March 1654. Today the brotherhood, the festivity and the sermon centre round the exaltation of christian youth. The brotherhood of Our Lady of the Rosary, also of ancient foundation, is composed of 15 married men who with tapers in their hands hear mass from places of pre-eminence and accompany the procession carrying on their shoulders the image of Our Lady of the Rosary and her banner. Membership is limited to 15 and is transferred from fathers to sons among the *pudientes*. On the day of Our Lady of the Rosary at four in the morning a group of men go through the streets of the town singing the *aurora* or songs to the Virgin. On finishing, the brothers go to the house of the majordomo of the brotherhood who invites them to have cakes and brandy. Recently the brotherhood of the Nazarene has been founded in which 48 men, mostly married, are enrolled. They wear ankle-length purple tunics and accompany with tapers the processions of Holy Week, carrying the image of Christ bent beneath the weight of the Cross. Among the men, courses on christianity are also important and form a vital part of parish activity.

Besides the feasts of the Catholic liturgical year there are a succession of cults and devotions peculiar to the community. Novenas to saints and to appellations of Our Lady abound; the seven Sundays before the festival of St. Joseph and the first Fridays in the month are celebrated by a large number of communicants. The septenary of Sorrows in honour of Our Lady of the Seven Sorrows (or *Dolorosa*) is well attended, as is the Way of the Cross on Fridays during Lent. In the month of flowers or month of Mary (May) many women and school-children gather together every evening in the church. At least once a month a Holy Hour is commissioned by some parishioner, and the priest cannot cope with all the petitions for the celebration of masses either for the dead or for private intentions. All *rites de passage* bring kinsfolk and friends together at the church. At the first communions, for example, the parents of the children communicate as well, even if they have not been near the church since their wedding day. At the procession for Corpus Christi the children who have received first communion are clad in white and carry small baskets full of petals which they scatter over the monstrance borne by the priest. It is the correct thing for relations of those making their first communion to take part in all the religious acts in which the children are the principal actors. On All Saints' Day the entire *pueblo* goes up to the cemetery with wreaths and bunches of flowers to lay on the graves of the family dead. Small lamps burn in all the niches and tombs. During Holy Week and after nightfall processions wind through the streets of the *pueblo*. Early in the morning on Good Friday a procession called 'The Meeting' takes place, which dramatizes the meeting of Jesus, burdened with the Cross on the road to Calvary, and his mother. The men with the image of the Nazarene set out in procession and from the opposite direction the women leave the church with the Virgin *Dolorosa*. The two processions meet in a small square and the images of Jesus and his Mother stay face to face. The priest speaks from a balcony and finally they return together to the church. At dusk the same day another procession commemorates the Holy Burial. Boys clad in red Roman tunics carrying long spears and beating drums accompany the tableaux carried by the hooded nazarenes in their long purple tunics. The women carry small lanterns. Mothers lead their children by the hand; elaborately dressed as nazarenes with a tiny cross on their shoulder and a small imitation crown of thorns on their brow, they are a source of pride to their mothers, who have spent time and money on making their costumes. Songs of penitence accompany the procession on its way. The rhythm of the drums, red and purple tunics seen in the half-light of the lanterns, and the slow, expiatory songs give an impressive solemnity to these processions.

The atmosphere of the processions celebrated for the festivals is different. The programme for the processions of 15 August, the day of the Assumption of Our Lady, is as follows. At about four in the morning a group of men go through the streets

Parish Church

San Roque

Our Lady of the Assumption

Processions during the religious festivals of August

singing the *aurora*. At the junction of every street they stop to sing of an episode in the life of the Virgin; they go quietly from corner to corner but the tinkling of a small bell announces their passing. Once the *aurora* is finished the Dawn Rosary leaves the church—at about 5.0 a.m. The faithful go through the streets with banners, singing Hail Marys and reciting the Rosary. At the conclusion of the procession Mass is celebrated. At eleven in the morning the solemn procession leaves the church. It is led by the Parish Cross and by the schoolchildren in two parallel files. The women follow and the men bring up the rear, usually in groups and chatting merrily. The Cross is followed by banners and the image of San Roque borne on the shoulders of young men who are clad in white tunics with red collars, cuffs and belts. Afterwards comes the image of the Virgin represented at the moment of Her Assumption into heaven, also borne on the shoulders of young men dressed in white but with blue in place of the red. Then come the parish priest, escorted by the deacon and subdeacon, and behind them the full Council. During the procession the bells ring continuously. The morning ends with a solemn mass and a sermon by a preacher from outside; there is not room for everybody in the church. At nightfall a peal of bells announces the exit from the church of a fourth procession, or the Rosary, almost identical to the solemn procession in the morning. The only difference is that the boys carry dozens of lanterns, made of coloured glass, on the tips of long wooden poles. The four processions are repeated the following day, the feast of San Roque, and on 25 March when Our Lady is honoured under the appellation of Caballeros.

The religious vitality of the community is, therefore, abundantly clear, and it is a religion that is emotional, imaginative, and extraverted. In the apotheosis of the external cult, the liking for its colour and dramatization, we can see that merging of the profane festival into an occasion of religious solemnity that has played so constant a part in the spiritual history of the community.

III

A bus leaves the *pueblo* every morning for the city at nine o'clock. Once it enters the city it is not allowed to stop until it reaches the bus station, about a mile from the Cathedral of Our

Lady of the Pillar.[1] With unfailing regularity people leave the coach at the entrance to the city, take a trolley-bus that has a stop close to the cathedral, and go to pray before the Virgin of the Pillar. Thus 'the first visit in the city is made to the Virgin of the Pillar'. Very rarely do the women go to the city without entering, if only for a few minutes, 'to see the Virgin'. On taking the coach back to the *pueblo* one sometimes hears the comment: 'I had so many things to do that I didn't even have time to go and see the Virgin'. In the *pueblo* it is thought that not one resident passes the doors of the Cathedral without entering to pray and this includes men who rarely go to church; some men go to see the Virgin as often as the women. Newly married couples consider the visit to the Virgin, more often than not with the bride in her wedding dress, obligatory. In the parish church the Virgin of the Pillar has an altar and the association named the Court of Honour, a novena and a solemn feast. The Virgin of the Pillar is the Patroness of Aragón, intimately connected with its history, and the spiritual centre of the Aragonese; according to the *jota*, the Virgin of the Pillar *is* Aragonese or even better *Zaragozana*.

'*Al otro lado del Ebro*	'On the other side of the Ebro
Hay una zaragozana	There is a Zaragozanese
Y si no sabes quien es	And if you do not know who she is
Virgen del Pilar se llama'.	She is called the Virgin of the Pillar.

This way of thinking about the Virgin allows for that familiarity of treatment which is so typical in Aragón:

'*Cuando voy a Zaragoza*	'When I go to Zaragoza
no voy por ver la ciudad;	I don't go to see the city;
voy por ver una morena	I go to see a brunette
que es la Virgen del Pilar'.	Who is the Virgin of the Pillar'.

Clearly for an Aragonese the protection of the Virgin of the Pillar is the best in the world:

---

[1] According to ancient tradition Our Lady while still alive appeared to St. James (who was then said to be preaching in Spain) on the bank of the Ebro. She was standing on a pillar and revealed that he was to build a cathedral in Her honour on that spot under the appellation of Our Lady of the Pillar.

'*A las orillas del Ebro*   'On the banks of the Ebro
Cantaba un Aragonés: An Aragonese was singing:
No hay Virgen como la nuestra, There is no Virgin like ours,
Las demás son de papel'.   The rest are merely paper'.

This devotion to Our Lady of the Pillar, which even the 'non-observers' share to some extent, is an integrating force on the regional level, or rather its symbol. Even on the national level 'Aragonese' and Our Lady of the Pillar are two ideas hard to separate.

*

* *

The *pueblo* itself is under the protection of San Roque and of two appellations of our Lady: Assumption and Caballeros, from which it takes its name. The hermitage of Our Lady of Caballeros mentioned in the record of the visit in 1575 must even then have been an ancient building. For in 1582 the visiting archbishop ordered that the roof should be retiled. It is believed that the town was constructed around it in the Middle Ages. Thus the hermitage had a double sentimental value: it was the house of Our Lady, patroness of the community, and it occupied the place where according to tradition the *pueblo* was originally founded. It would appear that the tradition has a real foundation, because in the ploughing of the fields surrounding the church indications of ancient buildings have appeared. A few years ago, as in 1582, the edifice was in need of repair. The problem was whether to rebuild it completely or to construct another hermitage nearer the *pueblo* so that visits to the sanctuary could be more frequent. The *pueblo* was divided into two camps, and in the end the priest had to put an end to the arguments that were exciting the whole town, including the 'non-observers', the majority of whom declared themselves vehemently in favour of the reconstruction of the old building; the priest arranged for the shrine to be built in the other place. The Council forthwith formed a commission to collect and administer funds which the residents donated generously. It appears that nobody in the *pueblo* failed to contribute. The hermitage having been erected in a few months, the *pueblo* went in procession to the old one to transfer the image of the Patroness, which for a few days was to be placed in the parish church. Some people did

not join the procession because it seemed unfilial towards a
mother 'to turn her out of her house' where she had been for
centuries; others stayed away because they feared divine
vengeance. While removing the image from the old hermitage
the priest intoned a hymn which was accompanied by sobs and
tears from the women and from some of the men. Nobody was
able to sing except the schoolchildren. The priest carried on
with his intonation but the sobs increased and continued until
the end of the procession. Some days later another procession
took place through the streets of the *pueblo* to carry the image of
the Patroness to the new house. The procession was amazing.
It is said that only the sick and disabled failed to take part and
even these watched from their balconies. Nobody in the *pueblo*
could remember a gathering similar to that one. At every few
yards the women stopped the stand with the image, forcing
those who were carrying it to yield such a prized position. Thus
was the image enthroned in the new hermitage. Devotion binds
the community in this case, as the Virgin of the Pillar brings
out regional loyalties.

But the relationship between the *pueblo* and its religious patrons is complex. They may command very little attention, or
they may function as a powerful disintegrating factor in the
community. The sodality of our Lady of Caballeros, so prosperous and popular in another age, has disappeared; no memory
of it remains today. The same fate has befallen the sodality of
the patroness St. Engracia, also mentioned in the visitors'
records. An Archbishop on visiting this hermitage in 1582
ordered that a window should be put in one of its walls. Processions to the hermitage were frequent. Fr. L. B. Martón wrote
in 1737: 'Approximately half a mile from the *pueblo* there is a
hermitage very devoted to St. Engracia, whom they court with
many attentions. On her day, April 16th, the entire *pueblo*
gather in procession . . . singing most solemn mass with a sermon . . .'; 'during the year they pursue the same cult in all
their necessities'.[1] A century later, 1849, in a description of the
pueblo only one hermitage is mentioned, that of Our Lady of
Caballeros.[2] Saint, procession, mass, sermon and hermitage had

---

[1] '*Origen y Antiguedades del subterráneo y celebérrimo Santuario de Santa María de las
Santas Massas*' etc. . . . (Zaragoza, 1737).
[2] Madoz, *Diccionario*, vol. XIII (Madrid, 1849).

disappeared. All that remains today of that devotion, once so popular, is the rumour that in the old days there was a hermitage in honour of this Saint. Today San Roque, the patron saint of the *pueblo*, is not the object of any particular cult or veneration except on his Day; probably the *pueblo* resorted to his patronage in the last century because of some pestilence (he is the mediator against pestilence). His feast is somewhat eclipsed by that of the day before, the festivity of Our Lady of the Assumption. Neither the Saint nor this Marian invocation are sought by the parishioners in their needs. The Assumption and San Roque are feasts, or profane festivals with a limited religious content, especially among the young people.

During the republican period the leftist party, which included about half the residents, launched its attacks on the established social order. As the social order was in reality identified with religion, the attacks had a double target. The religious festivals, the processions, and the images of the patrons of the community were the symbols of the believers, of those who had imposed the social order. So the leftists sought to impede the setting out of processions with the patrons, threatened to hurl the images into the canal or to smash them up with an axe. The patron saints functioned not as a cohesive force but as a highly disintegrating factor in the community. Religion was so bound up in the existing social order that the economically weak rejected both equally. Together with the religiosity of the *pudientes* and *propietarios* we find the apathy or hostility of *peones* and *braceros*. Even though political circumstances are now highly favourable to all expressions of the Catholic religion, friction between the two still finds outlets and occurs sporadically.

Recently a very fine parish cinema was opened in the *pueblo*, which already had one. Those who belong to the higher strata of the community ceased to frequent the old cinema and many of them bought permanent seats in the new one. Both cinemas show films on the same days, at the same time and of a similar type; the entrance fee is the same. The acoustic conditions, screen, visibility and comfort are superior in the parish cinema. While the more religious, the *pudientes* and *propietarios* tend to go to this one, usually no matter what film is shown, on the whole the other sectors of the community, a few not very religious *propietarios* and those who don't go to church, tend to go to the old cinema. The parish salon is called the 'priest's cinema' and the 'rich people's cinema'. And so in this case religion combined with economic power exercises a negative or disintegrating influence in the community.

*
*   *

On 3 May the bells summon the faithful to the church whence they set out in procession to a boundary cross in the middle of the fields, where the priest blesses the harvest. Some years ago there was a persistent drought and a procession took place to the hermitage to pray for rain. On St. Blaise's day (3 February) and also on St. Valerian's day the women carry maize in small baskets to the church for it to be blessed. Afterwards the maize is given to the few teams of cart-horses which remain. For St. Antony's day on 17 January bonfires are lit in the streets; brushwood is contributed by all those who have animals to guarantee their health. The Brotherhood of farmers celebrate the feast of their patron, St. Isidro, on 15 May. They place a sheaf of wheat in the hands of his image. During the festivals bunches of grapes are hung round the images of the Assumption and San Roque. According to the description of Martón the hermitage of St. Engracia was in that part of the district where the vines grew. A man who has a vague idea of the existence of that hermitage in the remote past told me he had heard his grandfather say that St. Engracia was set in the middle of the vineyards to protect them. It was because the vineyards were not prospering that the people forgot St. Engracia and her hermitage. The real reason for the disappearance of the saint's cult and hermitage is probably more complicated, but this version is logical enough and the masses and Holy hours commissioned for the purposes of obtaining similar favours emphasize the agricultural basis of these functional cults.

Patron saints or invocations of Our Lady are appealed to in all the trials and hazards of life. For a good harvest, for a son's success in examinations, for a safe journey, for an easy confinement, for a cure in the face of some illnesses including incurable ones, for success in business—for all these things they make novenas to the saints, go to the hermitages, offer alms,

commission masses and holy Hours, burn candles on the altars
and wear a costume whose colours symbolize a special invocation of our Lady. They turn to St. Blaise to cure illnesses of
the throat; devotion to St. Agatha is the token of maternity,
mothers turn to her if their milk fails; St. Antony finds things
which are lost and allots sweethearts to the girls. Our Lady of
Carmen comes to the aid of those who find themselves unexpectedly in danger and above all at the hour of death.

*

*   *

At the door of many houses there is a plaque with an image
of the Heart of Jesus, and inside Dutch tiles with the inscription
'God bless this house' or something similar. Sacred pictures,
crucifixes, images of the Heart of Jesus, of the Virgin or of
favourite saints hang on the walls of the rooms. Sometimes
lights or small lamps burn at the foot of the images. Several
images of the Holy Family, whose festival is celebrated with a
novena, pass through 150 houses in the *pueblo*, spending a day
in each of them. Membership of the sodality of the Rosary is
handed down through families. In some houses the family
recites the Rosary together and says grace before meals. Among
the *pudientes* and *propietarios* it is customary when setting up a
new household to enthrone an image of Christ the King in
the house and to hold a ceremony at which the officiating
priest and close relations are present. The *rites de passage*
affect the religiosity of the family group whether considered as
a limited unit or in a wider sense. Thus for example all the
parents, however cut off they may have become from the church,
accompany their children to the communion rail when the
latter make their first communion; the cults celebrated for
deceased members of the family also brings the family group,
understood this time in a wider sense, together in the church.
All these cults reveal a domestic aspect of religiosity.

*

*   *

Five out of the ten altars in the parish church, three of the
four images venerated there, the only painting, and three out
of the six women's associations are consecrated or dedicated to
the cult of Our Lady. Besides the two festivals especially in Her

honour, the feast of the Immaculate Conception is one of the most solemn in the liturgical year. An old parish paper says: 'For a future reminder to posterity and to our successors in the place of Belmonte de los Caballeros . . . in the year of our Lord 1619 on the 15th of the month of September . . . the Mayor, jurymen and councillors of the said place . . . voted, confessed, believed and made a solemn vow to our Lord God . . . and an oath that the common stain of Original Sin which touches and marks all the remaining children of Adam never approached, nor touched, nor marked the most Holy Virgin Mary at the point when God instilled her Soul into her sacred body, but they vowed and swore that She was preserved from all Original Sin'. A little further down we read: 'This oath and vow was taken . . . with great solemnity, applause and concourse of people, the church and altars being all adorned with various, diverse decorations of silks and ornaments, the walls bedecked with richest taffetas, the altars with reliquaries and many beautiful lights . . . with great solemnity and music'. 'Individual persons' the report finishes, made 'great rejoicings' all the eight days that the festivals lasted. The vow was taken in the *pueblos* of the diocese by the will of the Archbishop. Other festivals in honour of Our Lady celebrated with solemnity in the parish are: The Purification, the Septenary which commemorates the Seven Sorrows, the whole month of May or Mary's month, Our Lady of Carmen, of the Rosary, the feast of her Nativity and of the Pillar.

Whether the worship of the Virgin is a conscious or unconscious sublimation of sexuality is a problem whose solution goes beyond the specifically sociological and is hardly relevant to an analysis of the concrete forms of religious expressions and sentiment. The emphasis that has been repeatedly put on the relationship between religion and sexuality, especially virginity, in Spain isolates perhaps only one of the ingredients of the Marian devotion and probably not the most important. It may account for the unconscious substratum which originated and maintains the Marian cult but does not explain its peculiarities in a specific time and place.

From his earliest years every parishioner finds that the Marian cult is prominent in the parish. Small children when they are put to bed, falter phrase by phrase the Hail Mary which their mother repeats to them, and kiss some image or print, or blow a kiss to the Virgin or to the Infant Jesus. When scolded by their mothers they are frequently told: 'The Infant Jesus and the Virgin will not love you if you are naughty' or 'The Infant Jesus and the Virgin will be cross if you do that again'. Every evening in May they are taken from the school to the Rosary and at the foot of the altar they recite poems to Mary. When they grow up, they join, if they have not already been enrolled when they were a few months old, the principal Marian sodality—that of Our Lady of Carmen. We have already seen how the devotion to Mary has a long history maintained for centuries through the invocations of our Lady of Caballeros, the Immaculate Conception, and the Rosary.

The images of Our Lady of Caballeros and of the Rosary, of Carmen and of the Pillar are represented holding their Son in their arms, that is to say, as the Mother of God; Our Lady of Caballeros and of the Pillar symbolize local and regional values; Our Lady of Carmen enjoys a cult numerically and sentimentally more popular owing to the belief that whoever dies wearing her Holy Scapulary will not suffer the pains of Hell; the recitation of the Rosary is the essential idea of the cult of that name. Neither do the Commemoration of the Purification of Mary, her Birth and Seven Sorrows have any relation to the theme of virginity. Further, even supposing that the historic devotion to the Immaculate Conception—which in fact was a wish of the Archbishop—together with the month of flowers, emphasize the erotic element in the devotion to the Virgin, the actual content of the remaining seven Marian invocations have nothing to do with virginity. On the contrary they appear to be more closely linked with Divine Motherhood.

The wife/mother is the centre, the soul of the home. Under her vigilance the children grow up, learning their first Marian prayers, and when they are older she controls them in the background through her husband. Directly or indirectly she is behind every family decision. Her suggestions are imperceptibly turned into orders. Sometimes the mother takes the children's part so that they may obtain something they want from the father; at other times she reinforces paternal authority against the children. Her position tips the scales. The Marian cult in the parish bears the stamp of the woman/mother. This is in a triple sense. Firstly, the cult and devotion to Our Lady issues predominantly from the women. The men take no part in the religious solemnities of the Purification of Mary and her Nativity, of Mary's month, of our Lady of Carmen and of the Court of Honour of the Pillar, and only a restricted part in the septenary of our Lady of Sorrows. The women, on the contrary, form the chief contingent in the religious ceremonies organized for the day of Our Lady of the Rosary, although sponsored by a masculine sodality. Secondly, the Marian cult is characterized by the projection of woman's state to Mary as Mother of God; it is not to God, not to the Holy Sacrament to whom they resort most frequently in their needs, when their husbands or children fall ill or in any emergency whatsoever. In these circumstances they make novenas to our Lady of Caballeros, place tapers on the altars of the Virgin, recite the Rosary or wear in penitence one of the Marian habits, that of the Pillar, for example, or of Our Lady of Carmen. They turn to Mary as woman to woman, so that She being more human and condescending will obtain that which is sought from her Son, who is much more distant. If She hears their supplications She will tip the balance in their favour. They pray to the Son through the Mother as they are sure that the Son can deny nothing to the Mother. They themselves use this last phrase to explain their religious inclination towards Mary. Thirdly, this Marian devotion is also fundamentally emotional. The affectionate and familiar terms in which they speak of the Virgin and Her images are very expressive: 'Poor little Virgin', they say, 'she is very dusty'; or 'I have lit a light on the Virgin's altar as the poor Virgin was in the dark', 'the poor Virgin's cloak is badly ironed', etc. It goes without saying that they take more care with the cleaning and the decoration of the images and altar of our Lady than with the Main Altar. They pick flowers in the fields and even sow them 'for the Virgin'. Such expressions are never applied to images of Jesus or to God; familiarity is not fitting, and one should maintain one's distance and respect. Mary, because of Her special position, is the mediator, the intercessor, the bridge linking man to Divinity, just as the mother intercedes between father and children. When preachers really want to move their audience deeply, for example in the missions held about every five years and in sermons during Lent, they develop with vivid metaphors the theme of the Virgin's sufferings, due to the wickedness and sins of their listeners. The women break into tears and sobs; the men say as they leave the church: 'that is how to preach!'

The emotional element not only gives form to the cult of the Virgin but to religious expression in general. Among the remaining cults practised in the parish those of the Heart of Jesus and of the Infant Jesus stand out. These are essentially feminine: clothes, flowers, decorations, hymns, supplications, play an important part and the men, although they may be in the church, are not very much involved. As in the *pueblo* emotion and feelings are ascribed to the woman and she stamps her feminine sensibility on cultual expressions, it is not surprising that the men refer to religiosity as 'something for women', meaning 'chiefly' to do with women. The woman is expected to be more religious than the man and to fulfil her religious duties more punctiliously. The wife/mother has to elicit blessings for her children and husband by her prayers. She puts pictures and images of her favourite saints in places of honour, and at times she may force the husband not to overlook his religious obligations. If a child is ill she, never the father, will light small lamps or candles before the image of the Virgin or will recite the Rosary or commission a Holy Hour. While her husband is working in the field she attends mass or makes a quick visit to the church. It is her duty, not the father's, to teach the children their first prayers. When one of the family is gravely ill it is always the woman who tells the priest. The religion of the woman is an everyday affair; that of the man is confined to certain practices on certain days. It is fitting for the woman to be noted for her religiosity; it is appropriate for the man to be religious within the traditional norms. A man who heard mass every day was nicknamed the *rezador* (one who is always praying). The feminine associations of religion set a limit to a man's religiosity.

The cult and devotion to our Lady constitutes, therefore, one of the essential characteristics of popular religiosity. It is both a result of the teaching of the Catholic doctrine, and a projection of social feminine values, values which are not necessarily linked with the theme of virginity.

*

*		*

The most intimate personal level of religious experience depends upon the idea of salvation. As we have seen, the cult centres round our Lady of Carmen (a sodality of 326 members), the Heart of Jesus (142), also round confessions and communions on the first Fridays of the month (some 150 persons) and on confessions and communions on the Sundays dedicated to St. Joseph (another 150 persons). The specific tenor of these devotions and the reception of the Sacraments is identical. According to popular belief the Virgin of Carmen has promised that no one who dies wearing her scapulary will suffer the pains of Hell, and that on the Saturday after their death their soul, if in purgatory, will be raised to Heaven. Mothers put the scapulary round their babies' necks almost as soon as they are born and take great care to see that their children and husbands always wear the redeeming token. The Heart of Jesus also assures salvation to those who have confessed and communicated every first Friday in the month for nine months in succession. A similar belief guarantees salvation to votaries of St. Joseph. These devotions, so popular and so deep-rooted in the parish, embracing the majority of parishioners, are all techniques of salvation.

They express the need for an answer to the sufferings, frustrations and tragedies of life and also the desire to survive, the yearning to exist personally for eternity. When death removes any friend or relation it is customary to visit those who were closest to the deceased to console them. Conversation, usually carried on by men themselves elderly, is centred on the briefness of life with all its poverty and misery and attendant sufferings. 'This life is a deception', they say. 'After so much hard work and heavy-going, one dies'. Faced by death they weigh up life and find it hollow. The bitter pain of this reality made Gracián exclaim: 'Oh life, you should never begin, but having once begun you should not finish!'[1], a sentence which exactly sums up popular thought; and before him one of Calderón de la Barca's characters said:

'... *el delito mayor*	'... man's worst crime
del hombre es haber nacido'[2]	is to have been born'.

---

[1] *El Criticón*, Part I, Crisis 1.   [2] *La Vida es Sueño*, Lines 111–12.

This same tragic conception of life prompted Goya's brush when he painted 'It was for this that you were born', 'Bury them and say nothing', 'It will be the same', 'All this and more too', 'The same everywhere', 'Nothing', etc. Goya was Aragonese.

Once born one has no other alternative but to journey through the vale of tears of this life and to end in death. In the words of Jorge Manrique:

'Nuestras vidas son los ríos   'Our lives are the rivers
que van a dar en la mar   Which flow into the sea
que es el morir.   Which is death.
Allí van los señoríos   All dominions go there
derechos a se acabar   directly, to end
e consumir'   and be extinguished'

Recently one of those men who never go to church unless for the celebration of *rites de passage*, died. From the first moment he felt himself to be seriously ill he never stopped calling for the priest. Nobody, not even the most miscreant, dies without receiving the Sacraments unless death is sudden. To receive the Last Sacraments at the hour of death is the best technique of all for securing salvation and everlasting life. The desire to survive after death, to continue existing, makes them at the moment of dying cry out passionately: 'The priest, the priest!' because he alone can satisfy that yearning for personal endurance, for transcendence. This tragic sentiment of life—thus Unamuno names one of his books—when faced by its inherent poverty and the *mysterium tremendum* of death, makes the religion of salvation the fundamental and intimate expression of religious belief in the *pueblo*. It is a religiosity that springs from and reflects vital personal problems, a conception of the world and of life.

From the moment the child starts to speak he is taught by most mothers in the *pueblo* to repeat the names of Jesus and Mary. In the school for children of three to four years he learns the first prayers. The school time-table morning and afternoon is begun and ended by prayers. The catechism is one of the subjects taught in the schools, controlled by the examinations of the parish priest. On Saturdays they recite the Rosary at school. On every feast day of obligation they and their teachers occupy benches reserved for them in the church; it is they who lead the processions. On Fridays during Lent and during the month

312

RELIGION: II

of May they all attend the special services. On fixed dates they all communicate together as well. Before making their first communion those who are going to confess and communicate are taught the catechism with renewed emphasis by the priest and teacher. Those who fail the examination have to wait until the following year to make their communion. Every Sunday after Mass they are also taught the catechism by girls from Catholic Action. The priest preaches for some twenty minutes at every Sunday mass. Every month there is a day of retreat in the parish and every five years a mission. Couples about to be married have to revise the catechism and be examined in it by the priest. Everyone confesses and communicates on their wedding day. The *rites de passage* are or imply religious acts through which each individual passes at important moments of his life. Religious feasts, processions, novenas, Holy Hours, etc., fill the liturgical year. The church bells call the faithful to prayers several times a day. People frequent the church and take part in the services. 'Those who know' (the 'professionals') also attend parish cults; the Council in full presides over them. Press, radio and television encourage religion. Thus continual and intense social pressure leaves very little room for religious indifference. Although this same pressure can at times occasion somewhat violent reactions as previously indicated, at the hour of death, social pressure, family pressure and perhaps more than anything else the early religious experiences of childhood bring it about that nobody dies without disposing their conscience by receiving the Last Sacraments.

The question naturally arises then, what is in reality the religious influence on practical life? Certainly it is very great. Christian values determine life in the community, morals are christian morals. This is not to say however that the daily practices are in complete harmony with religious norms. Moral offences against the sixth commandment, for example, are more or less serious according to age and sex; at times one can boast of them. Nor has the seventh commandment much force in certain circumstances. Indignation and social censure are not only regulated by religious precepts and commands; another code, at times considered superior to the religious code, also comes into play in the appraisement of wrong, in the same way that correct conduct is regulated by other values, as we shall see.

XIII

VIGENCIAS

'*Sería conveniente . . . que el hombre . . . intentase una profunda
investigación de sus creencias últimas. Porque todos . . . creemos
en algo y es este algo, a fin de cuentas, lo que pudiera explicar el
sentido total de nuestra conducta. Sin una pura investigación de
las creencias . . . carecemos de una norma medianamente segura
para juzgar los hechos más esenciales de la historia*'
Machado

'*Vive a la fama y serás inmortal: no hagas caso, no de esa
material vida en la que los brutos te exceden: estima sí la de la
honra y de la fama, entiende esta verdad, que los insignes hombres
nunca mueren*'
Gracián

'*La bárbara ley del honor no es otra cosa que la necesidad de
hacerse respetar, llevada a punto de sacrificar a ella la vida . . .
Como apenas se han socializado estos individuos ni se ha
convertido en jugo de su querer la ley de la comunidad, se
afirman con altivez, porque el que cede es vencido*' Unamuno

THE FULL meaning of social conduct cannot become clear
until the whole range of social beliefs or assumptions has
been examined; these may not at first glance constitute a
coherent system of explicit ideas, but nevertheless they underlie
every line of action and condition the behaviour of individuals.
These basic social assumptions, the collective beliefs in force in
a community, have been termed *vigencias*—from *vigens, vigere*—
by Ortega y Gasset.[1] Their specific nature will be defined in
the pages that follow by scrutinizing the use of certain words and
forms of expression.

[1] J. Ortega y Gasset: *Ideas y Creencias* (Madrid, 1940); *Historia como sistema*
(Madrid, 1941); *Del Imperio Romano* (Madrid, 1960), pp. 98-9. For its systematic
analysis: Julián Marías: *La Estructura Social* (Madrid, 1955), pp. 81-178.

I

Strange though it may seem, the word *honor* is seldom heard. Its place is taken by dozens of words which refer to something closely related but distinct. *Honor* could replace any of them, but would probably sound far too generic. The honorific words or expressions used in the *pueblo* exactly define the aspect of honour to which they refer, whereas although the people know the word *honor* they consider it 'bookish', or too elegant for ordinary use.

There were three degrees of nobility in the Kingdom of Aragón: barons or *ricos-hombres*, knights, and *infanzones*. The nobles were the only ones to receive an *honor* or *honores*, that is, domains, castles, lands or estates. In Aragon, *honor* always meant *honor regalis* or lands of the royal domain, and also strongholds, villages, territorial districts, etc., which the king gave to the nobles and of which they enjoyed the revenues.[1] So the king gave or took *honor* or *honores* to or from the nobles; the nobles possessed and handled *honores*.

Of the commoners in Aragón the *ciudadanos honrados—cives honorati—*were prominent. They were the ones who, while possessing no *honores* in the above sense, answered to this definition: '*habeantur pro civibus honoratis qui ad perpetuum usum, equitaturam propriam seu bestiam de cabalgare teneant, et tenebunt, et de manibus suis laborem non facient, vel faciendam*'[2]. The *Privilegium* adds that it is also necessary *ut honorabiles cives vivant*. The *ciudadanos honrados* of Zaragoza to whom the document refers, in order to remain *honrados*, must behave honourably and have a small income which would allow them to keep a horse for war and to refrain from manual work; serfs and *Moriscos* (Moors who had become Christians) did the manual work in occupations regarded as base. This category of *ciudadanos honrados* occupied a place midway between the nobles who possessed *honores* and the serfs and *Moriscos* who worked with their hands; the citizen was distinguished by his *honra*, by being *honrado*. *Honra* is the key word, constantly heard in the *pueblo*, the word which must be understood as it is the key to the study and interpretation of the

---

[1] Valdeavellano: *Historia de España* (Madrid, 1955); I, 2, C.XIII, pp. 268 ff.

[2] A privilege granted by Peter IV of Aragón to the citizens of Zaragoza. The privilege is dated: '*anno Domini millesimo trecentesimo quadragesimo octavo*'. Found in '*Tratado de la Nobleza de la Corona de Aragón*' written by M. Madramany y Calatayud (Valencia, 1724); pp. 313–15 from the Barcelona edition of 1957.

system of *vigencias*. The ordinary citizen could scarcely make the nobleman his model of behaviour; nobility, the holding of *honores*, was a royal privilege conceded to certain lineages. On the other hand his social position did not coincide with that of those who lived by servile labour. The true distinction of his estate, the name of it in the documents is *honradez*, *honra*, something which does not stem from the royal will nor from one's ancestors, but derive's from one's own virtues and efforts. And these are not sporadic virtues and efforts, to be proved in war against the Moors, in the king's service, but something apparent in normal, everyday life.

Honra, *honradez* (nouns), *honrado* (adjective). In the *pueblo* to say of somebody that he is *un hombre honrado* is the highest praise. The person so qualified possesses all the virtues which the community ascribes in principle to every male who has reached or is near his fortieth year, and is consequently in most cases married and a father. Once we assume that the *honrado* has all the required virtues, the nature of *honradez* begins to appear complex. The word is used almost exclusively as an adjective: they do not so much say that a man has *honra*, but rather that he is *honrado*. It emphasizes a fundamental characteristic of this quality: *Honra* is individual and dwells within the man, who up to a point imparts it to his family; it does not imply the same virtues in a woman as in a man, and the children are never termed *honrados* before they arrive at a mature age. *Honradez* is the most perfect individual attribute that can be applied to a male of a certain age. Further, since *honradez* is an individual attribute which by definition embraces a whole gamut of virtues, it requires in the individual a certain disposition towards the practice of these virtues which may at times not all be in accordance with each other. Finally *honradez* calls for certain actions or the omission of others which are regarded as virtues or faults by the community.

The *honrado* in the *pueblo* is the man who works, gives everybody his due, does not overspend when he should be thrifty, looks after the education and behaviour of his children, shows veneration for his elderly parents, is worthy of any trust placed in him, keeps his word, controls himself in order to avoid all unnecessary arguments and quarrels, makes himself respected, and respects others. A man is not *honrado* if he steals something however insignificant, if he lies, if he gets drunk, has unjust dealings, takes advantage of a public office for his own private interests, picks fights, or shows himself to be a philanderer to the very slightest degree. He must be all of one and none of the other if he is to be regarded as *honrado*.

One component of *honradez* is shame, *vergüenza*. The man who 'is' *honrado* 'has' *vergüenza*. Two men may argue heatedly over priority of rights in irrigation. Faced with the impossibility of coming to an agreement and in order to avoid an endless argument, the one who is within his rights says: 'I give in because I have greater *vergüenza* than you'—which is to say 'I give in because I am more *honrado* than you'. The sentence involves not just giving up his right, but also a certain scorn for the other man, as somebody unworthy. It is only when there is a considerable difference in social rank that one can relinquish one's rights; otherwise *honra* demands that one should reaffirm and maintain them. The man who gave in explains to the others: 'If I were as little *honrado* as he is . . .' or 'if I had as little *vergüenza* as he has, I would not have given in'. In communal works if anybody fails to cooperate, manually or financially, the others say: 'If we had as little *vergüenza* as they we would not have come either'. When a man sends one or both of his aged parents to an old people's home, when he steals, when he persists in violating the rules of irrigation for his own advantage, when he habitually tries to jump the queue with his cart or trailer to unload the sugarbeet, then he is said to have lost his *verguenza*. It is no longer a sufficient incentive to make him do the right thing. Thus the expression condemns both those who commit serious faults and those habitually guilty of minor offences. They are not expected to behave with *honra* in their dealings with other people. *Vergüenza* in this sense has a positive meaning, and to have this kind of selfrespect and consideration for others is essential if one is to qualify as *honrado*.

Honradez and *vergüenza* are correlative terms; the more *honrado* one 'is' the more *vergüenza* one 'has'. The phrase 'to have little *vergüenza*' expresses the first stage in the descending scale of *honradez*. It is employed when, for instance, a group of friends are standing round a bar drinking; they buy and drink as many rounds as there are persons in the group, but if one of them does not pay his round, then he has little *vergüenza*. Or suppose two men are on their way to irrigate their plots, one on foot, the other on a bicycle; though the one on foot may be nearer the sluice—and the first to arrive has prior right if there is no watering turn—the cyclist increases his speed and manages to arrive first. Logically enough the right is his but he also has little *vergüenza*. What is legal is not always just, as we have already seen. *Peones* and *braceros* who work for others have little *vergüenza* if they show scant interest in their work, if they go frequently to drink at a nearby irrigation ditch, if they smoke a lot during their work, if they perform their task deficiently or fail to finish it by refusing to carry on for a few minutes extra. They say that the landowners for whom they work have little *vergüenza* if, when the agreed working time is up, they tell them to load the trailer with uprooted beet and when they do so, do not give them extra money, or when they discount an hour's pay from their wages because rainfall has prevented them from working for an hour. Equity is the parameter of little *vergüenza*.

To have little *vergüenza* implies that a man is still, up to a point, *honrado*. To have none means that he is not *honrado*. On 30 July 1930, there was a very uproarious meeting in the Council. The 'numerous gathering ... began to shout ...' that 'they had more *vergüenza* than the Presidency'; they accused the Council of being so many 'prattlers' and of 'not knowing how to handle the *pueblo*'. They added, continue the Minutes, 'that this mishandling of the *pueblo* was to finish, that it was the work of five or six members of the Council, and what must be done was to seize them by their legs and drag them out ... since otherwise they would not go away because they had no *vergüenza*, six men who were going to be the ruin of three hundred *honrados* residents'. The residents have *vergüenza*, but the Council does not because it fails to govern the *pueblo* as it should, takes advantage of the authority with which it is invested in the interests of its own members. All this is at the expense of the *honrados* residents. Those *pudientes* who for no good reason fail to take part in communal undertakings have no *vergüenza*—in identical circumstances a *bracero* or *peón* is said to have little *vergüenza*. Nor have *pudientes* who do not contribute to the expenses of festivals according to their economic position; nor those who take advantage of their superior physical strength to impose their will on more elderly people in arguments over irrigation; nor those who get drunk, who lie concerning important matters, brawl frequently and steal. 'To have no *vergüenza*' thus implies to lack civic virtues and community spirit. You cannot count on somebody who has no *vergüenza*, you cannot trust a thief or a liar; you should avoid them as much as possible. Someone once stole a bicycle. Apart from having to give it back, he was left without friends, found himself completely isolated, and left the *pueblo*. Very few people would speak to him.

Sinvergüenza—which comes fairly close to the English word 'scoundrel' in significance and means literally 'without shame' —is directly opposed to *honrado*. To call someone a *sinvergüenza* to his face is at least equivalent to establishing *vitandae*-relations, if the expression is uttered with the right intonation and sufficient virulence in a café, on a street corner or in the fields. If a man neglects to treat his aged parents with due respect because the legacy to him is going to be small then he is a *sinvergüenza*; so would be the man who did not give them enough to eat and ill-treated them. When somebody takes advantage of the fact that a family is going through hard times economically and buys their house or land he is branded as a *sinvergüenza*. So also the married man who goes to the city to dance and tries to hide the fact; or provokes young girls or engages in lascivious conversations in the presence of women or girls. Into this category falls any married man who has intercourse with a prostitute, and it is the same with anyone who comments and boasts of what he did on such an occasion. One married man who had intercourse with a prostitute was forced to sleep out of doors for several days because his wife and children refused to admit him into the house. He was a *sinvergüenza*. Any misdemeanour in this sphere of conduct, small though it be, constitutes a grave injury to *honradez*. One wife would not speak to her husband for a month because in a friendly gathering of neighbours he danced with another married woman. Religious 'militants' would regard as *sinvergüenzas* anyone standing in the street or at the door of a café who ignored the priest as he passed in procession to administer the Sacrament to a sick person. In the eyes of the older people, a girl is a *sinvergüenza* if she allows herself to be held tight when dancing, a criterion with which the young men disagree. Thus *sinvergüenza* refers to morality, and particularly though not exclusively to sexual morality.

The expression *es vergonzoso* (it is shameful) reflects on the injustice of certain things which you have no alternative but to put up with. 'It is shameful what is happening to the light', means that all these electric light failures take place for no apparent reason, that nobody knows exactly who is to be blamed and that very little or nothing can be done to put an end to it. In other words 'it is shameful' is the equivalent of 'it is unjust'. The actions of the Government or the provincial authorities are described as 'shameful', and thus unjust, with regard to tractors, fertilizers, or taxes. The members of the 'declining' generation feel that the illmanners and brazen behaviour that prevail today are shameful. This impersonal expression has as its object of reference things which go beyond the community but which directly affect it. It is applied to actions or consequences whose author is unknown, or else when nobody in particular can be considered responsible. Otherwise it is always the individual who gets all the blame.

Thus if a man is to be considered *honrado* he must have *vergüenza*, a knowledge of what his honour dictates. Secondly, *vergüenza* in popular speech is a measure of the absence of *honradez* in the person concerned. Thirdly the concept of *honradez* is based on custom, on equity, and on civic virtues as popularly understood and on the community's evaluation of moral issues. Fourthly the meaning of *honradez* is partly conditioned by ideology, social hierarchy and generation. Fifthly, both the positive excellences that the *honrado* man must have and the negative or shameful ones from which he must be free, tend to promote the virtues of co-existence and co-operation, and the community's cohesion. I have given the name '*vigencias* of cooperation' to the significance underlying the laudatory and defamatory expressions which promote cohesion, the community's functioning.

The *honrado* man must be always on his guard to uphold his *honradez* by cultivating those excellences he is obliged to possess. He must be hardworking, but work has different meanings. In the lower strata of the community it involves heavy physical labour, day in, day out; the *bracero* or *peón* who does not work hard is a *chandro*, lazy and indolent. 'He has been a *chandro* all his life' is an insult which, if seriously delivered in public, forces the insulted man to attack the other. *Vitandae*-relations follow.

The phrase is applied to *peones* and *braceros* because it is under-stood that they are compelled to sweat and toil so that they and their families can improve their economic condition and status. To remain indefinitely among the lower strata says little for the head of the family; either he does not really work or he lacks the ability to take up some other small business or trade. Poverty, they think, is in some measure a sign of personal failure. The *pueblo* cannot always provide work, however, and as being out of work is very badly viewed, such people either emigrate or go to France for a season, or else work for some months of the year in the city. A *chandro* deserves no respect from others, nor any economic aid in time of stress: no shops let him have credit, charity organizations take care of his children but give no heed to the parents. But if a man is hardworking and poor, the Council frees him from some minor municipal taxes. Cinema seats on the first Sunday of each month are one peseta dearer, and this peseta goes to relieve a man with a chronic illness who has always been hardworking but is now unable to work and keep his family. The Council Minutes for 3 November 1894 mention that the municipal tax-gatherer has been dismissed, but at the same time the Council 'bearing in mind that his good name and *honradez* have always been very highly regarded during his years as taxgatherer in this neighbourhood, names his son to be provisional gatherer of municipal taxes in his place...'.

The *pudiente's* industriousness is measured by other standards. He may not be 'hardworking', but he is never a *chandro*. *Pudientes* and *propietarios* must show their industriousness by their ability in organising their landed property, the men who work for them and their economic interests. It is curious that the only time when the word *chandro* is applied to them is when they are slow to apply modern farming techniques. The head of the family should have intelligence and initiative; he must not let himself be deceived, must not fail economically. Recently a resident who ran a workshop for the repair of agricultural machinery failed in his business and had his property seized. The shame of this failure so affected him that, without saying goodbye to anyone, he departed not only from the *pueblo* but from the country. Another resident who owned plots of land and a cinema was also ruined. The day before his property was to be seized and his failure made public he left the *pueblo* and went to South America. Such is the shame felt by the person who fails as a result of his real or supposed incapacity to run a business. To be hardworking as an *honrado* man must, may mean either personal sacrifice and toil and sweat, or self-development and achievement. But the man who fails in his own sphere has nothing left in the *pueblo*: his *honradez* has vanished. One old man was treasurer of the money belonging to a religious brotherhood. Because of his age he left the paying and collecting of the funds in his son's hands; months later he found that his son had embezzled the money. Rather than face so shameful a situation he left the *pueblo* secretly and died soon after alone in Barcelona.

This is another dimension of *vergüenza*. It is felt not only after committing or being involved in a shameful act, whether it is one's own fault or not, but also when a close relative is concerned. In this case people knew perfectly well that the father was an *honrado* man who was not directly responsible for the fraud, but even so they argued 'how could he remain in the *pueblo* and go to the café with his friends? It would have been torture for him'. In such cases the *honrado* man does not allow himself to be treated with pity or sympathy, the only honourable thing to do is to leave the *pueblo*. When that old man went away, without knowing anyone in Barcelona and with very little money, he crowned his reputation for *honradez*.

Work, an essential element in *honradez*, is not an end in itself. By working one seeks to achieve the ideal of life, which is 'to live without working'. The collective representation of happiness is to find oneself in the position of having no economic worries at all. The people jeer at *pudientes* who, besides organizing, work with the *peones* on their land or personally take part in irrigation. *Pudientes* are said to *vivir bien* (meaning to live in a kingly manner with no worries, full liberty and a measure of power) when, without any physical effort on their own part they succeed in organizing the work on their plots satisfactorily. Work is a means to one particular end: money. At the end of the school year there is an exhibition of the pupils' achievements in calligraphy, drawing, needlework etc. This exhibition ends sometimes with a public examination which may be presided over by the Provincial Educational Inspector. Once the inspector asked a six-year old girl: 'tell me, what do we get from the sugar-beet?'. The girl replied without hesitation: 'money'.

Money, or property, provides comfort and material benefits like television, cars, gas or electric cookers, electric washing-machines; it enables one to have a servant or to travel—all these being signs indicating the measure of the head of a family's success in administering his estate. A father's money can find suitable matches for his children, can send them to city schools, and provide the ultimate distinction of a university education. The striving is intense. Inheritances, even where the legacy is negligible, provoke the bitterest and most violent quarrels. It may all be for a few yards of land, for a few thousand pesetas, or for some old articles of furniture or a completely useless yoke, as we have seen. But in these cases love of money comes before brotherly and filial love.

Nor are property and money ends in themselves. The *honrado* man should be magnaminous and generous. His family's *rites de passage* must be of an outstanding splendour. He must spare no expense, or as they say he must *tirar la casa por la ventana*, which means literally to throw the house out of the window. Otherwise he would be 'mean', 'tightfisted', 'not knowing what life is for'. The competition in wedding celebra-tions, for instance, has gone through the following stages. In the years immediately after the civil war, one *pudiente* brought cooks from outside the *pueblo* to prepare the wedding breakfast. Soon after a wedding breakfast took place in the café, which had been hired for the occasion and this banquet was regarded as the more distinguished. Another *pudiente*, wishing to put the others in the shade, took his guests to lunch in a small hotel in the city. Then another reserved the restaurant of a large hotel. Recently a *pudiente* beat all records by not merely treating his guests to a lavish lunch in a first-class hotel, but by engaging an orchestra to play in the *pueblo* during the afternoon and evening, so that there could be a public dance and the wedding an occasion for general festivity. He improved his reputation still more by distributing money among the poorest families of the neighbourhood. Now a similar kind of competition has begun over first communions and baptisms.

The *pudiente*, if he is not to be classed as a man of no *vergüenza*, must make generous contributions to the festival programmes and to the church on all suitable occasions. In the last five years a hermitage has been built, and a parish community centre the cost of which actually topped the million pesetas mark (and much of the work was done gratis), while the normal contributions throughout the liturgical year continued. The *pudiente* like everyone else must vie with his friends in the bar by offering drinks and showing that he is more liberal with his money than they. If several friends insist on paying and offer their money to the barman, the one whose money is taken is honoured, since the barman, knowing them all well, takes the money from the one with the greatest prestige. Every *pudiente* must go to the cinema in the city fairly regularly; he must go to bullfights, have aperitifs in the best bars and go away on holiday during the summer. Those who go abroad for their holidays enjoy very high prestige.

Spending money, even to excess, is more important than possessing it, provided the money is spent on objects the community regards as appropriate. If a man does not have the money to pay for his son's wedding he will resort, with as much stealth as possible, to the help of some relative—if the latter lives in another *pueblo* so much the better—or else borrow money from the bank. It does not matter if he has to go without a decent dinner on a Sunday because he has given all the money to his son to spend treating his friends to cigarettes and liquor in the bar. The important thing is not to become the loser in the battle, to show one's openhandedness, to appear as good as anyone else. This way of thinking of one's superiority, so quick to sting a man to action, governs every aspect of social and public life.

This applies mainly to the *pudientes*. *Braceros* and *peones* obviously cannot compete at this level. Manual labour is the measure of the poor man's *honradez*; hard work it must be too, essential for one's keep and one's good name. The *bracero* or *peón* is expected to improve his economic future by his efforts and by constant sacrifices, and it is essential to save to this end. They themselves, however, regard things differently. They are at pains to show that their economic situation is not after all so precarious as is supposed, and this drives them into lavish expenditure, particularly in summer when wages are doubled. In their *rites de passage*—and any *rite de passage* is a competitive situation—they try not to fall short of the achievements of the groups immediately above them. It weakens the family's economy yet further, but lack of funds is not an impassable barrier in the competitive struggle. You can be lacking in what is necessary, not in what is superfluous. The cinema comes before one's dinner. In the city things can be brought by instalments; the shops in the neighbourhood can sometimes be persuaded to give credit. Money is put away to be used on public occasions, to make a show; competition is much the same as with the richer groups. The point is to stand out among those in an economically similar position to one's own.

There is also a particular tendency among this group to compete on grounds of personal attainments. They boast, for example, of greater physical strength, a greater capacity to eat or drink, or to work; they may claim that they can scythe more grass than anybody else in one day. Challenges and bets are common. For instance a group was talking on a street corner when a man who usually formed part of the group passed with his fishing tackle. One man shouted : 'Anything you fish I can eat raw'. The fisherman caught seven carp, waited until the next day, and when the group was again chatting on the corner went up to them with the seven carp. Showing them to his challenger, he said slowly, emphasizing every word: 'If you are a man, you'll keep your word'. There and then, the other man ate the raw fish. This kind of competition is by no means to the liking of the *pudiente* or the *propietario*, but all groups share alike this drive towards rivalry in some form or other; they are all subject to this one inner demand, this one *vigencia*: to prove through concrete manifestations their manliness, their personal worth.

The *honrado* man has to be *nada menos que todo un hombre*—a favourite expression with Gracián and Unamuno, meaning literally 'nothing less than a whole man'. Manliness demands the defence of one's family, the good name of parents and brothers, and of one's own interests and opinions. For example, at a Brotherhood meeting notice was drawn to the lack of organization in a communal work being carried out at that time. One speaker accused the leader of not working as hard as he ought, thus casting doubts on his *honradez*. The accused man was not himself present, but his son instantly jumped to his feet and struck the accuser. Everybody is expected to act thus when placed in such circumstances—'that is what a man should do'. Whether the accuser spoke the truth or not was immaterial: it was the son's duty—he was a married man—to avenge publicly the public dishonour done to his father, so maintaining his manly worth and his father's good name. It is only afterwards, if the occasion arises—and for the most part it does not, because the quarrel is followed by *vitandae*-relations—that negotiations take place. Even if the man who executes vengeance with his hands learns later that the accuser was in fact right he will not seek to excuse himself on that account or to obtain pardon; he had to act as he did.

During the *pueblo's* annual festival a married couple were dancing at the public dance. The husband got the impression that another man had offensively touched his wife and promptly knocked him down. In fact the other man had got involved by accident and in any case was not entirely to blame as it appears he was slightly drunk, but this did not save him from being knocked down. When quarrels take place bystanders are expected to separate and calm down the two parties. On another occasion Antonio, a married man, made an assault on the virtue of Carmen, a married woman, who resisted him, screaming as loudly as she could to attract her neighbour's attention. Antonio's attempt failed and Carmen's husband, Vicente, on his return home found her in bed suffering from shock; when he learnt what had happened he rushed off to find Antonio. He was seen hurrying grimly along by a man esteemed as one of the most *honrado* in the *pueblo*, a man with considerable authority, none other than the mayor himself, on whose land Vicente happened to be working at the time. Sensing that something serious had happened he stopped Vicente and made him explain everything. Then he forced him to go to the civil guard barracks and report what had occurred; he forbade him to resolve the matter with his own hands as Vicente wished. A trial followed and Antonio was ordered to pay Vicente several thousand pesetas. The latter, though a *bracero*, refused to touch the money, and the parish priest distributed it amongst the needy. Antonio's sister and her husband entreated Vicente and Carmen to forgive him, but met with an absolute refusal, for injuries of this kind cannot be forgiven. Antonio spent several

months without daring to go to the cinema or the café; he goes
to no meetings of any kind and hardly ventures to greet anybody.
He is a *sinvergüenza*.

Such a situation demands a very violent reaction on the part
of the husband. If he did not act accordingly he would not
be 'much of a man'. 'Not to be much of a man' is one of the
most biting and humiliating insults that can be cast at a male.
All women like their husbands to be 'much of a man', and this
expression refers to the manliness that the *honrado* man must
possess; it can also denote his sexual power, but in this sense we
find far more popular and widespread the use of a number of
expressions of sexual character which point directly to this
capacity. The former sense of manliness implies that an essential
ingredient of masculine worth is a hot temper and the power to
sustain resentment.

One other aspect of manliness concerns the way in which a
person asserts his own personality, the energy and tenacity with
which he strives to affirm himself in front of others. In the evenings, once work in the fields is over, groups of friends gather in
bars or at street corners. Conversation is usually about agricultural matters, or about football, bullfighting and the cinema.
In one of these discussions the subject was how to handle a
tractor so as to plough the corners of a field properly. The
speaker—A—was telling one of the others—B—how not to
leave one inch of ground untilled. His explanation was precise
and clear; everybody except B, who handled his tractor in another way, agreed with him. Even someone who knew little of
these matters would have felt that A was right. B argued, however, that his tractor was of a different make, and that in order
to plough the corners thoroughly it was essential to manoeuvre
the tractor as he did. To this A replied that others who had the
same kind of tractor nevertheless followed A's method. B would
not give way and inisisted on his point of view, but in order to
finish the work by his method he had to get down from the
tractor and do it with the hoe. This was observed. Nobody enjoys
being advised or corrected; advice annoys and hurts, because
the person who receives it feels humiliated. Even if he secretly
believes that the other method is going to give him better
results, publicly and in front of his friends he must maintain his
point of view and even alone he must carry on as before. In

this way he appears to show that he has 'his own motive', unknown to others, for using these methods. What must never be
done is to admit that one is in the wrong, that somebody else is
right and therefore cleverer than oneself.

Verbal combat takes place in arguments over bullfighting or
football. The subject provides an arena in which two rivals can
stake all their ability before an audience which enjoys the display
and likes to see which personality will triumph. If one con-
testant is losing ground he sometimes has recourse to almost
nonsensical arguments, or to arguments which have practically
nothing to do with the matter in question, by means of which he
hopes to make the audience believe that he is not completely
wrong, that he is not yet utterly beaten. If it is eventually proved
by facts that exactly the opposite to what he said was true, he
may admit to being partly wrong, but he pulls in fresh evidence
or arguments,—*quisicosas* as they are aptly termed—however
far removed from the matter in hand, to show that he was not
completely in error. It is a desperate struggle in which no
quarter is given or expected, in which the cornered person
takes the defensive and fights to the bitter end. Later on he may
discuss the topic of the argument with others who were not
present, conveniently twisting it to put his own point of view in
a better light.

'*Procure siempre acertalla*	'The man of honour and prom-
el honrado y principal;	inence must always try to be
pero si la acierta mal,	right; but if he be wrong, he
defendella y no enmendella'[1]	must defend what he has said
	or done and never take a word
	back'

For many centuries now it has been usual for historians,
travellers, and writers in general to point out that the chief
characteristic of the Aragonese people is their stubborness.
Even Borrow, who never visited Aragón, quotes one of his inter-
locutors: 'He is an Aragonese, and when one of that nation once
gets an idea into his head it is the most difficult thing in the
world to dislodge it'.[2] The Aragonese continue to be referred to
as 'pig-headed' and a well-known phrase says: 'pig-headed

---

[1] Guillén de Castro: *Las Mocedades del Cid*, lines 661–4.
[2] G. Borrow: *The Bible in Spain* (London, Dent and Son, 1910), p. 126.

like a good Aragonese'. But to describe the Aragonese as simply pig-headed and leave it at that is to remain entirely on the surface. Beneath there can be found a violent individualism. When arguing, discussing or putting forward a point of view, a man is staking his personal dignity, his own worth, his *honra*, which stems ultimately from a manner of feeling himself a man.

So far when dealing with the expression *hombre honrado* I have only spoken about the adjective, but in fact the key word is *hombre*—man. '*Hombre!*' is a word which finds its way into any conversation or argument. *Qué hay, hombre?*—How goes it, man?—is a normal form of greeting. Women call their husbands '*mi hombre*'. *Es un hombre*—he's a man—or 'todo un hombre'—a complete man—are expressions which extol and assert the personality of an individual who knows what measures he must take in any situation in order to prove his personal worth. *Es un cualquiera*—he's just anybody—constitutes a very serious insult. It is even worse to be described as *un poco hombre*—not much of a man. But intensely degrading as this is, *es un nadie*—he is nobody—is the worst thing that can possibly be said and thought about anybody. It reduces the individual to nothingness; it means the end and destruction of *honra*, of the individual. If others hold opinions different from yours, then to yield before what they have to say or, as the popular expression goes, 'to let one's arm be twisted back'—mark the violence of the phrase—signifies that you are not being a true man. You show that you have no ideas of your own, no sense of judgment, that you have not taken up a position from which to view life and go through it, that you are giving up your personality to other people. As we already know, this is not to be surrendered to any laws, civil or religious, although at the hour of death it is precisely this same feeling, in the form of a violent desire to carry on living, that receives its greatest impulse from religion, the only means of achieving everlasting life.

The individual is, so to speak, the real court of appeal. To resort to the formalities of the law with the endless red tape is bound to prevent true justice from being done. A lorry driver ran over and killed a man from the *pueblo*; the dead man's son seized a pitchfork and tried to kill the author of the deed there and then, but was held back by others. Everybody however agreed about this: 'the lorry driver had killed the man and must pay for it; if he was hanged on the spot then everything would be settled and other drivers would have been taught a lesson. Whereas in fact the driver would be tried and would go scot-free; the insurance company would pay all expenses and the dead man would be left to rot in his grave'. Again the owner of a bar in the city, much frequented by people from the *pueblo*, went home drunk every night and ill-treated his wife. She bore this with patience for several years but finally one night she killed him and was sent to prison. People from the *pueblo* said: 'everybody knew that the man was a *sinvergüenza* and that she had tolerated him for too long anyway. Why then imprison her? After all she was right; the law cannot play around with human beings'.

Nobody can be ordered to take part in communal work, pay a contribution, or accept a point of view just like that, without first being consulted. At least this is how common sense demands that you act with your neighbours. A number of people own land outside though close to the municipal boundaries. To go there they use the road which crosses the district. When it was in need of repair the people whose land is within the boundaries and who use the road held a meeting. According to long-established practice, those whose land lay outside were not legally bound to contribute to the repair of the road. One of these willingly consented to pay, but said at the same time: '*A las buenas lo que querais, a las malas nada*'—which implies, since you have invited me in order to consult my opinion, I am prepared to pay anything you say; if you had not invited me, you would not have got anything out of me. As it happens another in the same circumstances was not invited since they forgot about him and he refused point-blank to share the cost of the repairs. He did not pay because '*no le daba la gana*'. *No me da la gana, no me da la real gana* or *no tengo ganas* are expressions which bear some similarity to the English 'I don't feel like it', but are much stronger. They intensify the feeling of individuality the one and only law of which is one's free will. A command has only to be given and straight away people will start saying: 'Well it so happens I don't feel like it', or else, 'it's forbidden is it? Well, I feel like doing it'. *Gana* is a word fraught with a sense of desire, inclination, whim, with more than a hint of defiance; it carries a powerful assertion of the personality. *Mi real gana*—literally, my royal will—is the supreme law, the court beyond which there is no appeal. So it is not to be wondered at that in the *pueblo* they justify the use of this phrase by saying: 'Each one is as God made him' and 'each is a king deep down inside'. It was Ganivet who said[1] that each Spaniard's ideal would be 'to carry a statutory letter with a single provision, brief and imperious: This Spaniard is entitled to do whatever he feels like doing—*le da la gana*'.

Vigencias of co-operation is the name I have given to the first group of excellences and virtues required by *honradez*. This second group of virtues I call 'militant *vigencias*'. They aim at securing success, prestige, fame, in a word individual assertion. But personal worth is mainly measured by economic success and the possibilities of such success are not the same for the different groups in the community. Success, therefore, is conditioned by the relative position of the person who achieves it in the community's stratification. But as soon as any man, within his station in the hierarchy of the community, fulfills what *honradez* demands of him, then he enjoys as much esteem in the community as anybody else. In this sense, nobody is considered superior or more *honrado*. This feeling of equality, regardless of wealth and knowledge, is an essential element of individualism. It comes out with ill-concealed self-satisfaction in conversations: 'If the people who make H-bombs came to work on our fields we would have to teach them'. 'Each one plies his own trade'. 'In my job I'm as good as anybody else in his', 'I'm as *honrado* as anyone else', and 'nobody's more than anybody else', are very common expressions which indicate this sentiment of equality. And the urge to stand out and to assert oneself is something shared by all groups alike.

'*Aunque esta vida de honor*	'Although this life of honour
tampoco no es eternal	is neither eternal
ni verdadera,	nor true,
mas con todo es muy mejor	it is much better
que la otra temporal	than the other temporal
perescedera'.	perishabie life'.

Jorge Manrique distinguishes three lives: between the eternal and the temporal is the 'life of honour', which defines the goal

---

[1] Ganivet: *Idearium español*, Colección Austral (Madrid, 1957), p. 55.

to be sought and the manner in which it is to be achieved. The life of honour permeates the innermost being, and merges into reality itself. When we study the community from this perspective, we can understand it much more fully: institutions, evaluations, and experience assume their true significance. It also helps us to understand Spanish history, the Conquistadors, Don Quixote, *La Celestina*, Gracián's *Criticón*, the plays of Tirso de Molina, Lope de Vega and Calderón, Lorca's poetry and the work of Unamuno and many others; in other words, everything that is regarded as deeply Spanish.

II

Feminine *honradez* demands special qualities in a woman. Several of these have already been mentioned in the chapter on the family; they can be classed as 'domestic *vigencias*'. To look after the house and keep it tidy, to see that the children are well-groomed, and to make sure that all the family are well provided for as regards dress, these are important signs of *honradez* in married women; so also are the management of the money earned by her husband, and in general of everything appertaining to the family. Regular attendance at church is also necessary. Contrary to men, who are required by 'militant *vigencias*' to seek for themselves individual pre-eminence, women must assert themselves by creating an aura of modesty and silence. Woman in fact simply is *honrada* and all her efforts should be concentrated on keeping herself that way. She is very rarely said to be so; in principle it is assumed that all women are. But the one who is not becomes the object of pointed comment and she is said 'to have lost her *honra*'. The linguistic differences in the expressions are striking. To 'be *honrado*' is a phrase applied particularly to the mature man, but to 'lose *honra*' is said of women. The 'losing' indeed refers almost always to a young woman's virginity or a married woman's chastity. The Archbishop learnt on a visit to the *pueblo* in April 1690 that girls' fiancés were going to the girl's houses 'with frequency and familiarity', 'thus beginning the married state in a manner deeply offensive to Our Lord God and exposing the fiancées to the danger of the *loss of honra* (my italics) should their fiancés fail them, leave the *pueblo* or change their minds . . . '. The meaning of the phrase has not changed for several centuries.

During the civil war a girl was left pregnant by a soldier; as she did not marry him and had lost her *honra*, she left the *pueblo* and turned to prostitution. Her family, especially her mother, were shamed in front of everybody, and the shame would last throughout their lifetime. If an expectant girl marries in time she has also lost her *honra* but marriage partially repairs the damage. But at a moment's notice in any argument with other women, she will probably meet with more or less direct allusions to her early slip, calculated to degrade and humble her. It is a burden she will carry all her life. Another woman, already married, broke the marital oath; the adulterer left the *pueblo*. The woman stayed away from all social activities and spoke to nobody. For months on end her mother would not leave the house; later on however she was seen to go to the church, greeting no-one, crestfallen. Everyone pitied her. The unfaithful wife 'had lost all she had to lose', as the popular expression goes.

Even the most insignificant points can endanger the good name of a woman whether she is married or unmarried and whatever her social position. She must stay on the alert all the time, ready for any attempt on her virtue. Victory consists in flight or defence. We have already seen what barriers the community interposes in the relationships between girls and young men, and the steps preliminary to the wedding. Many mothers repeatedly tell their unmarried daughters that they would sooner see them dead than with child. One of the basic responsibilities of a mother is to watch her daughter's moral conduct, to know what she is doing when out of doors, with whom she dances or talks, what the young men say about her. Such familiarities as holding hands, walking arm-in-arm or allowing a young man to put his arm round her are still strictly tabu. If a girl let boys kiss her, the whole *pueblo* would be shocked. It is considered not quite right for girls to smoke, to swim in the irrigation channels, or to go dancing in the city without suitable male escort. When choosing a girl to marry, the men try to recall how she danced; if they had little difficulty in dancing close, she 'loses points' and is less likely to be chosen. A girl who has previously been engaged to someone else, they say, loses 50% of her possibilities, unless it is known that she was not to blame for breaking off the engagement, or the community's standards approve of the break as correct and convenient. If she has been several times engaged she will not find a husband in the *pueblo*: 'As far as we're concerned', they say, 'she can stay and dress up statues in the church'. It need hardly be said that a girl known to have lost her virginity will definitely not marry in the *pueblo*. One girl was ill in bed and people began to whisper that she had attempted to bring about a miscarriage. This sensational story spread like wild-fire and soon reached the ears of the family concerned. The blow to the family was really crippling. They rushed to the priest, to the mayor and to the civil guard. The priest, speaking in church, attacked the unknown slanderers; the mayor summoned the young men one by one to the Town Hall and attempted to find out who had started the rumour; the civil guard did exactly the same in their barracks but without success. The girl in question left the *pueblo*.

Young men who provided information said that when anyone marries he is regarded as enviable if it can be truly said about him: 'Wasn't he fortunate? He began to court her when she first started to dance, and since then nobody else has had anything to do with her'. In fact this is very unusual, since they do not start formal courting until after their national service, when the girls they court have been attending dances already for some years. But it is an ideal, an aspiration, if not a factual reality, showing how exclusivist men are where women are concerned. So if women wish to marry, they must live up to the standards required of them and possess the virtues or *vigencias* imposed upon them by the male sex.

Feminine *honradez* is, therefore, something negative. It must not be destroyed; the women must resist.—What she has to resist is the social pressure or *vigencia* which compels a young man to be, or at least attempt to be, a *Don Juan*. *Donjuanismo* is only possible in a society in which the supreme feminine *vigencia* —backed by a moral code, by religious beliefs, and by the structure of the family—is virginity or chastity. The Don Juan cannot exist without this *vigencia* and vice-versa: the *vigencia* which compels women to safeguard their virginity or chastity in every minute particular requires and is only possible through the existence of the *vigencia* which demands a *donjuanesque* behaviour from young men.

The mother, so jealous in guarding her daughter's modesty, is openly satisfied when she learns that her son is successful with girls and is regarded as a Don Juan; *huele a hombre*—he smells like a man, she says. If girls say about a young man that 'he is a

good lad, but . . . you know . . .', or else 'he is a good lad, but a
square (*tonto*)', it is the same as saying that he is good but shy,
unadventurous in his treatment of them, that he does not try
'to take advantage' of them when dancing, in a word, that he
is no Don Juan. In this feminine reaction we can see the two
vigencias at work; the young man is expected to behave like a
Don Juan. Some girls might think it a little immodest to express
it like that, but as women they must await the masculine challenge. If it does not come they have no way of showing their
feminine virtues. Moreover, to succeed in flirting with a
recognized Don Juan gratifies feminine vanity; he is singling her
out from all the rest and assessing her attractiveness. A young
man would much rather be called '*sinvergüenza*' by the girls
than be described as a nice lad. *Sinvergüenza* becomes a term of
praise, for it denotes that the young man lives up to what is
expected of him; he is gallant, adventurous, a Don Juan. It even
in a sense implies that he is *honrado*. *Sinvergüenza* and *tonto*—
which I have translated as 'square', though it is far more
widespread and of broader meaning—are the two extremes.

What exactly do they mean in the *pueblo* by a Don Juan? A
Don Juan can only be a young man who has done his national
service and is not yet engaged, so that he belongs to the 'emerging' generation. A youth who has not done his national service
is not supposed to walk about the streets looking like a Don
Juan; married or engaged men must certainly not. If they did,
they would be classed as *sinvergüenzas* in the pejorative sense of
the word. Women, whether married or engaged, are also exclusivist. Young men define the Don Juan as one who is a *conquistador*
('lady-killer') of women. They never use the word seducer,
which seems to indicate actual possession of the woman; in this
sense there would be very few Don Juans indeed in the *pueblo*.
The true lady-killer goes about with the air of a Don Juan: he is
well dressed, with impeccable tie, shirt and shoes—these are
their words—and with the three corners of his handkerchief
perfectly arranged in the breast-pocket of his jacket. His gestures
are arrogant. He is self-confident and regards success with girls
as something quite easy; he believes that they are constantly
talking about him, that they never refer to him as *tonto*. He
goes straight up to a group of girls in the main street on Sunday
afternoons and greets them all courteously. He lets them go
first, opens doors for them, pulls up chairs for them—only a

Don Juan can do this sort of thing gracefully in the *pueblo*—and invites them into the bar. His conversation is agreeable, he pays compliments to all of them, remarks at once on their dresses, hair-styles, necklaces, bracelets, and so on. The girls are excited by his presence and his gallantry, feeling unable to cope with him but pleased by his company. They may occasionally invite him to small afternoon parties. Thus the Don Juan achieves his success. Although he has not gained any sexual recompense his pride is gratified by being talked about, by being classed as a Don Juan.

Again, at public dances he is never refused. He dances with the prettiest girls and is an expert at insisting, in a moderate sort of way until he gets what he wants. He may even succeed in holding hands with a girl for a few moments while not dancing, and if he should manage to steal a kiss or any comparable intimacy his success is crowned by the difficulty of the enterprise. Other young men regard him with a trace of envy, but they all like him for his winning ways. His mother will be very pleased to hear about his successes, yet the same woman would reprimand her daughter severely if she had granted a Don Juan similar favours. If the Don Juan manages to seduce a woman—only married women seem ever to have yielded—under no circumstances will he boast about it; on the contrary he hotly denies it, for so *donjuanesque* honour demands if the woman in question is not to lose her *honra*. The woman loses her *honra* if it becomes known, but the Don Juan of course becomes more of a Don Juan than ever. Nobody blames him.

This sense of honour also forbids one 'to take advantage' of ignorant or inexperienced young girls, or of girls when they are by themselves. The true Don Juan proves his ability by winning girls or women 'who know what they are doing' or 'who boast worldly wisdom'. These are worthy opponents. One who takes advantage of other girls is termed a *sinvergüenza*—in the opposite sense to *honrado*. So is the man who in trying to be a Don Juan only succeeds in being awkward, wearisome or coarse. The Don Juan who fails in his attempts, even if these are made with the utmost elegance and ability, ceases to be a Don Juan and becomes a *sinvergüenza*; here the word is one of reproach. To be a Don Juan success is necessary; success makes a Don Juan, failure makes a *sinvergüenza*.

This of course is not in line with Christian morality. Long

sermons are preached against it by the priests, but the *vigencia* of the Don Juan seems to carry more weight than the sermons. However the popular Don Juan does not try to challenge or offend God like the legendary Don Juan. Youth is a gift which soon fades away—as they put it; responsibilities and worries will come later; while you are young you must enjoy yourself. The faults committed—the breaking of the sixth commandment—are slight, unimportant sins, reflecting the weakness of youth; there will be time to return to the right path later ('long indeed is the term you give me', as the play says). It is not a case of their making a tragic choice between temptation and the Christian code, but of transcending this duality in a human way. And when an unmarried young man of the 'emerging' generation is allowed to challenge feminine virtue, to attempt what is forbidden to others, this develops in him that manliness, combativeness, rivalry and eagerness for success which will be demanded of him later on, when full responsibility is his. While he is young these qualities must be shown in nocturnal serenades, in shouting and rowdiness, in driving his motorbike at breakneck speed, and especially in the bullfights during the festivals. For self-respect the young male must always show himself a man and a Don Juan, and not a coward.

To sum up, here is a table of male and female *vigencias*:

		Male	
'Vigencias' of Co-operation'		Married	Young
		Sense of shame	Obedience
		Work	Work
'Vigencias' 'Militant'	POSITIVE	Success	Being a D. Juan
		Superiority	Bravery
		Generosity	Recklessness
		Competitiveness	
		Manliness	
		Individuality	
	NEGATIVE	Having little *vergüenza*	'Square'
		Having no *vergüenza*	'Coward'
		Being a *sinvergüenza*	
		Being just anybody	
		Not being much of a man	
		Being a nobody	

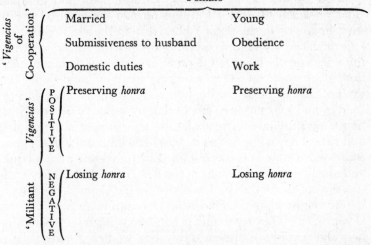

		Female	
'Vigencias' of Co-operation'		Married	Young
		Submissiveness to husband	Obedience
		Domestic duties	Work
'Vigencias' 'Militant'	POSITIVE	Preserving *honra*	Preserving *honra*
	NEGATIVE	Losing *honra*	Losing *honra*

The table shows first that this is a society with a majority of masculine *vigencias*. Secondly, among the masculine *vigencias* there is a majority of those which require positive action, of 'militant *vigencias*'. Thirdly, feminine *vigencias* deal for the most part with sexual behaviour. To conclude then, *vigencias* are evaluative assumptions, and rules of conduct, which orientate the behaviour of the individuals of a community according to status, sex and age.

III

Vigencias not only orientate conduct, but also tend to guarantee its outcome. What is or has been done is important, but equally important is what people believe is being done or has been done. It is public opinion which guarantees adherence to basic *vigencias*. The types of disapproval used by the community are embodied in a series of expressions which warrant that each individual will seek his share of *honradez*. These expressions classify the infringements committed by each individual, judge them, and censure them accordingly. So they point to such behaviour or situations that are especially condemned by the community, and by denoting where the danger lies induces people to behave in what is considered the right manner. In the following list, which is not quite complete, I omit those expressions dealing with *vergüenza* and losing one's *honra*, which have been already considered.

In spring and summer during the afternoon and evening, elderly women sit in small groups outside the door of one of their houses or in the patio sheltered from the sun. While they knit or darn they talk. Everything to do with the *pueblo*, everything that people do or fail to do finds a place in their conversation. They comment on recent engagements, on money spent on the previous or next wedding, on such and such a family's resources and expenditure, on the latest works carried out in a house, on purchases of new clothes, television sets, motorbikes and cars. They whisper about those who have or have not gone away on holiday, on loans obtained by somebody from a bank, and about the state of affairs of the head of a family. They criticize the policies of the 'professionals', of the Council, the mayor, the Brotherhood, of the Provincial Deputation and the Central Government. They try to find grounds to condemn the forwardness and frivolity of present day young women, the disinclination of young men to work; they lash those who are lacking in *honradez*. These gatherings are real court sittings which evaluate, approve (though rarely), upbraid, denigrate, sentence and sometimes absolve; at the same time they are the most effective information bureaux on what is happening in the *pueblo*. Fear of being, as they say, 'food for conversation' in such circles provides a strong incentive for good behaviour.

The phrase 'to undergo *vergüenza*'—*pasar vergüenza*—is the first of the list of concrete verbal terms of censure. People undergo *vergüenza* when they have to speak to people of higher rank than themselves, when they go to the Council (the secretary is a 'professional'), the civil guard barracks, or to the vicarage; they are frightened of choosing the wrong words, of pronouncing them wrongly, and of failing to express themselves properly. They suffer it when they eat in the city in the presence of people they do not know and have to polish their everyday table-manners so that others will not realize that they are from a *pueblo*. A man undergoes *vergüenza* when asking favours, especially concerning money, when he is in debt, or if he is seen in church holding a rosary, or sitting in the front benches in church —he would rather be at the back even if he has to stand. A young man experiences it if he is ignored or avoided in the street in full view of everybody by girls, or on asking a girl's father for permission to speak to her at her door, or on being refused by a girl to whom he has made an offer of marriage. A woman will feel it if she receives an unexpected visit when the house is untidy and the cleaning has not been done. To be in such situations does not mean that any fault has been committed; it is not the others who apply the phrase 'undergo *vergüenza*', but oneself, referring to the situation and the feeling of humiliation, of injured self-esteem. Reasons for undergoing *vergüenza* are lack of foresight, carelessness and uncouthness. The punishment is to feel humiliated.

If a person behaves incorrectly he makes the family, especially his parents, 'undergo *vergüenza*'; the family participates in the shameful situation. Though they are not directly to blame, nevertheless it is possible that they are to a certain extent responsible, since if they had brought up their son better or set him a better example he might have known how to behave better.

The expression takes in other meanings of greater intensity. If a man gets drunk and other people see him in that condition, if he fights, quarrels or causes a breach of the peace which requires intervention by the civil guard, the mayor or the parish priest, if he fails to show due respect for an elderly person, he undergoes *vergüenza* when he realizes what he has done and meets the injured party in the street. Very important is the presence of other people as witnesses; the greater the number of people present, and the higher their social status, the greater the *vergüenza* suffered. The action in itself is not as important as the surroundings in which it takes place. Even though the phrase to undergo *vergüenza* is mostly applied by oneself to oneself, and even though it is an intimate feeling of humiliation, it bears reference to the part played by other people's opinions, embodied in the phrase *qué dirán?*—what will they say?

This phrase is another coercive verbal mechanism. The maxim has two aspects, a positive and a negative one. The former requires everyone to behave in a similar manner. It makes its coercive force felt when it is necessary for everyone to participate in communal undertakings, such as repairing a road. When the August festivals come round they put on new clothes or else the best they have, do up their ties carefully and clean their shoes, and go out into the street where the sun is beating down. A husband who did not want to put on his best clothes for the occasion was asked by his wife 'what are they going to say ... ? They'll think you don't have any'. The suit in question was a winter suit. Sometimes with friends one spends too much money; one has to spend as much as they do and there is no alternative. Otherwise what will they say? They might think that one had no money. One man, the head of a family, had two old mules which he used for his work. What his friends said forced him to buy two younger ones to show that he had the money. When repairing the house, when buying clothes or bride's apparel, as much attention is paid to what other people think and say as to the actual necessity, the extent of one's financial means, and the wishes of the people concerned. Some of the people of the higher economic category, I am told, go to mass on Sundays merely for fear of 'what they will say'; the very same maxim working negatively persuades some of the lower economic strata not to go. Seclusion of girls in their homes for most of the time, their lack of freedom to go into bars by themselves—though in fact they are now beginning to do so— and to go to festivals in other *pueblos*, are customs which survive not because girls never resent them but for fear of what people will say. Elderly men do not sit in the doorway of their houses to enjoy the fresh air in the comfortable rocking chairs which they have inside the house for the same reason. Only the 'professionals' do this and anyone else who behaved in this manner would appear to be getting above himself. When the civil war ended nobody wore overcoats for fear of what people would say— only city people did; nowadays everybody wears one in winter, and they have to wear it in order to avoid becoming a subject for conversation. To swim against the current is to be a laughing-stock.

The phrase 'to be a laughing-stock'—*hacer la risa*—is another coercive verbal mechanism. It implies an infringement of the norm or standard established in the *pueblo*. The person who wears clothes that are out of fashion or in bad taste, or a girl who is out of touch with the latest fashions from the city, these are laughing stocks. Dressing with excessive elegance on a normal Sunday and wearing Sunday clothes on a work day make one the object of the same derision. Other circumstances which make one a laughing-stock include the following: failure to accept innovations in agricultural techniques, putting a seat on a cart so as to drive it more comfortably, to argue about things of which one is ignorant, to speak out publicly and fail to express oneself

properly, etc. 'Making a fool of oneself'—*hacer el ridículo*—is an
expression applied in cases of more serious actions, omissions or
situations. You can 'be a laughing-stock' if you wear an un-
fashionable suit even when you had nothing to do with the
choosing of colour and material, as is customary in the *pueblo*.
The person responsible may be the mother, the sister or the
tailor. But when you 'make a fool of yourself' there are no miti-
gating circumstances, the responsibility rests with you. A man
can make a fool of himself by occupying a seat in one of the city
theatres not in keeping with his economic position, by failing to
spend as much in certain circumstances as those who are his
economic equals, by refusing to go drinking with his friends or
to bullfights, football matches, or any entertainment in order
to save the money. Spending less on a wedding than one can
afford or should spend, and giving insignificant amounts to
works of charity, can also place a man in this situation. If the
difference between what you do and what you ought to do is very
great, as for example if a *pudiente* sits in the gallery at the theatre,
he not only makes a fool of himself but also 'stays that way'.

The expression 'to make a fool of oneself' can carry a subsidiary meaning, denoting that the responsibility of the individual is less. When the person ridiculed is not fully responsible
for what has happened, it is said that 'they have made a fool of
him'. So a witness who refuses to testify at a court hearing makes
a fool of the interested party. If in a crowd of boys and girls, one
of the boys speaks to one of the girls and she takes no notice of
him, she makes a fool of him. Perhaps there is no reason 'to
make a fool of somebody', but it is equally possible that some
motive may exist only known to both of them, in which case the
person made a fool of is to a certain extent responsible for his
ridiculous position. To make a fool of oneself is to lay oneself
open to other people's derision. This injures individuality and
diminishes public esteem.

These maxims classify the infringements of the code of behaviour summed up on the word *honradez*. They spell humiliation
and *vergüenza*, and the corresponding loss of an individual's
honradez. They are an incentive to correct or conformist behaviour, ensuring that everybody comports himself in a manner
standardized according to the ruling *vigencias*, whether 'cooper-
ative' or 'militant'. They also, from another point of view, uphold

tradition and act as a brake on innovations, which explains
why certain practices with no contemporary relevance persist.

*

*   *

'To be worse regarded'—*estar peor visto*—is another frequently
repeated maxim of an evaluative-coercive nature. If we take
group A to mean the higher and group B the lower economic
groups of the community, 'it is worse regarded' if someone
from group A steals, gets drunk, fails to participate in communal undertakings, is too fond of women, does not go to mass on
Sundays etc., than if somebody from group B behaves like this.
As regards sexual immorality, slackness of morals in a married
man is worse regarded than that of unmarried men, and it is
regarded worse in a young married man than in a more elderly
one. Lapses of an erotic nature are regarded worse in girls of
group A than in those of group B; premarital pregnancy is more
common in group B than in group A. Donjuanesque flirting is
regarded worse in married women than in unmarried ones.
Absence from church is worse regarded in women than in men.
If University or High School students get drunk and disturb the
public order, it is regarded worse than if other young men do so;
so also if married men go out serenading. In general terms all
infringements of the popular code of behaviour are regarded
worse in group A than in group B, in elderly people worse than
in younger, in married men worse than in unmarried ones.
Social pressure and criticism are far harder on the former, in
each case, than on the latter; the former are under far stronger
obligation to have a developed sense of responsibility and
vergüenza. Duties, responsibility and *vergüenza* have no single
coercive value, but are conditioned by position, estate, age and
sex. Young men are practically free from all pressure brought to
bear by this maxim; any transgression is 'less badly regarded' if
they are the transgressors.

To understand the maxim 'to be no less'—*por no ser menos*—
we must remember the distinction drawn between social 'situation' and 'position' in dealing with stratification. The expression 'to be no less' is a comparative reflection on people in the
anerest social-economic 'situation'. Within each economic category a man compares himself with those closest to him, with

those who have almost identical economic power. The first question asked by a family—particularly by the women—before a first communion or a wedding, or before buying agricultural tools or modernizing the kitchen, is invariably: 'What did the families G, P, L, or Z do?' The answer is: 'We must do the same in order to be no less', and in practice they tend to do a little more. As many residents admit, there are more tractors in the *pueblo* than is really necessary. Some owners do not possess enough land to make a tractor really profitable; and each year, as the number of tractors increase, it becomes more difficult to find someone else to work for. But if somebody with a certain area of land buys a tractor he forces everyone else in a similar 'situation' to buy one too, even if they have to resort to the bank and run into debt. If families G, P, L, and Z go for their summer holidays to San Sebastián, to the Costa Brava, or to Paris, this is a challenge which forces similar families, in order 'to be no less', to follow suit and go too. All children in group A have raincoats and wellington boots, which are seldom used since rain is rare; but if it looks like rain their mothers make them wear this apparel. Nowadays it is indispensable that girls wear wrist-watches at their first communion, as well as displaying an expensive dress, because 'my daughter must be no less than any other'. In order 'to be no less' one does what one's friends do. Since they all drink brandy, there is no alternative but to drink brandy even if revolted by it, for it is considered a man's drink. When young men go to the city in groups on their motorbikes they must all keep up the same dangerous speed in order 'to be no less'. In this case 'being less' means being a coward. If friends go out into the ring and test their courage in front of the bulls, everyone must, 'in order to be no less', get close to the animal and try to seize its horns. If one of a group of friends does it, he forces the others to try their luck. At work, thinning or mowing perhaps, one man may be supposed to be a better worker than the others; but the rest will not allow themselves to be left behind, 'even if they have to kill themselves working', in order to do the same work and prove that they are no less.

Examples could be multiplied, since to compare oneself with those in the same or very similar economic 'situation' and of the same age is a basic and automatic response. And if you can beat your peers in this competitive tournament you are more than they are—the expression is '*be*', nor '*have*' or '*do*' more. The comparison from that moment on is in your favour. This expression refers mainly to men, to those who are compelled to prove that they have money, courage and manliness.

A word very commonly used is *puntillo*—punctilio. In popular speech it means, first of all, a point of honour, self-respect. Your *puntillo* forces you to accept challenges and prove yourself to be no less than your challengers. The one who flags in the daily struggle to prove himself as good as anybody else is told disdainfully: 'You have no *puntillo*'. The man who lives on his father-in-law has no *puntillo*, nor has the one who gets left behind in his work. *Puntillo* is the magic word which, when appropriately used, is expected to bring out a manly response. It also distinguishes certain niceties in points of honour which may appear excessive in their violence or recklessness. The individual may assert his *honra* under this concept in a trivial or whimsical fashion.

Gracián, who uses the words *honra*, *vergüenza*, *hombre* and *honor* on practically every page of the *Criticón*, says in Crisis XI of Part II: 'They heard that one man was trying to persuade another to forgive his enemy and keep calm; but he replied, and what of my *honra*? Another was advised to leave his mistress and put an end to so many years' scandal, but he said: there would be no *honra* in that now. A blasphemer was told he should not swear and perjure himself, but he replied by asking where would the *honra* be in that. So, also a squanderer, when warned to have an eye to the morrow because his money would not last him four days, answered: my *honra* forbids it. A man of power, when told he should not shield ruffians and murderers also said: my *honra* forbids it. Well you fiends of hell, cried Momus, where does your *honra* lie? . . . Look, see where So-and-so's *honra* lies; and the latter would reply: and where does *his* lie? See him, see that other man, see all of them, wherein does their *honra* lie? . . . What is the matter with that man, asked Andrenio, why does he perspire? Do you not see, asked Momus, that unbreakable point —*punto* (equivalent to *puntillo*)—which he bears on his shoulders? It is that which exhausts him . . . That *puntillo*, pondered Momus, causes many men to perspire and may be to burst asunder, in order to preserve that *punto* into which he entered, or into which he was entered, he spends all his life groaning; his strength is lessened, the burden becomes heavier, expenses become greater, income becomes less and the *punto* must never be absent'. This meaning of *puntillo* refers to certain extreme situations.

If a community's basic *vigencias* impel the individual to compete with and excel all others, and if these *vigencias* are carried to extremes, the individual may well find himself in very disagreeable circumstances. Moreover the small community itself may be endangered. Other maxims of the verbal coercive system demand a certain moderation in these competitive tournaments.

Ese se lo cree or *es un creído* (meaning he thinks a lot of himself), are expressions designed to deflate those who believe themselves superior to anybody else. They are principally used to criticize the 'professionals' and students. Anybody who is always trying to impose his opinion is a *creído;* or anybody who makes dogmatic assertions about agricultural methods, wishing to impress others with his vast knowledge. The person who is always looking for a chance to talk about the journeys he has made and what he has seen is also a *creído*. Then there is the expression *que no se ponga tonto* (meaning something like 'don't let him start giving himself airs'), which has nuances which complement the previous one. It implies that somebody regards himself as superior to others, not because of what he knows, but because of what he possesses: money, land, houses, friends etc. It is also applied to Don Juans when they boast excessively about their successes at the dance; to those who boast that they have obtained a crop unlike any ever obtained before in the *pueblo*; or to whoever keeps repeating that he has utterly defeated an adversary in an argument in the bar. Young men often use the expression when a girl refuses their offer of marriage, if the economic differences between the families are only small. The first phrase— *es un creído*—refers to and criticizes an individual's personal qualities, what he is or thinks he is, whereas the latter phrase refers to transitory states of euphoria.

Money has gone to his head—*subírsele las perras a la cabeza*. This is what they say about a person whose economic category has improved and who has become ostentatious about it. If money has gone to a man's head he is likely to tell to friends in the café that he does not have to cultivate the corners of his land down to the last inch, because his wealth permits him to do well enough without this; or he will announce that he has bought a voucher for the bullfights and passes it around for all to see; or he asserts that his sons will no longer have to work in the fields for his money will ensure that they go to school in the city. When they suffer an economic loss they pretend not to care, their usual comment being: 'Faugh! a few bank-notes and everything's fine', or 'no matter, I've got plenty of money'. This boast is characteristic of some *nouveaux riches* when they happen to be in the café with people of inferior economic power. The same expression is sometimes applied to young men, though more frequent are the phrases *hacer el farol* or *hacer el fanfarrón* (both meaning to be a braggart). They will be used when a young man assumes that because his father has money or lands, all doors are open to him and he can marry whoever he likes; or if he shows off in bars, ordering unusual and more expensive drinks; or when he loses at cards and pretends not to care.

Finally, there is the expression *tenerse a menos*—literally 'to hold oneself in little esteem'. But in Spanish it is used where in English the exact opposite would be said: to hold oneself in too much esteem. *Tenerse a menos de hacer algo* means to feel oneself above doing something which is only suitable for people of inferior category; for example, among members of group A, to gather the alfalfa to the very last handful, or to act similarly with the grain from the threshing-floor, when they can be seen by others. These same people are above taking straw to a factory in the city to sell it, because it is not well regarded for people of their category to act like straw-dealers; they could take it to the city on the trailer as is done with the sugar-beet, but they prefer to sell it at a loss in the *pueblo*. Sons of *pudientes* and even *propietarios* do not work for other people to earn a wage when they get married even if they have received few plots from their fathers; they soon finish their own work, but although their economic situation is nothing like that of their fathers, they will not go out and work for others because to do so would be *llegar a menos*—to behave with little self-esteem.[1] Many women hold themselves in too much esteem to go to the fields, to the public washing-place, or to sweep the doorway of the house; likewise, men of group A hold themselves in too much esteem to enter a

---

[1] This expression has other meanings in a different context on which I do not comment here.

tavern. Others hold themselves in too much esteem to have friends among people of inferior category—I refer to married men—and in group B there are many who hold themselves in too much esteem to mow with a scythe, even though the wage received for doing this work is one of the highest. Everybody knows perfectly well into which category he falls, which is his economic situation, and he behaves accordingly. It is precisely this excessive consciousness of category that the phrase criticizes.

If we bear in mind that one *vigencia* urges people to work and to make efforts to achieve economic success, while another states equality between everybody; that 'point of honour' or *puntillo* emphasizes the importance of preserving one's personal dignity, of not lowering oneself, and that this in turn is the effect of another important *vigencia*, we will see that these form a system, a complex system composed of elements or pressures which are not infrequently contrary to each other. It is precisely this opposition that holds a man back and keeps him from going to extremes. The *vigencia* which compels men to intensify their personality to the utmost, to take part in the struggle and come out victorious in order to distinguish themselves and to stand out, is partially countered by the negative *vigencia* not to be a *creído*, which discredits those who are too zealous in obeying the previous *vigencia*. Those who follow other positive *vigencias* by being vainglorious about their personal successes, about being Don Juans, or by being exceedingly stubborn in their opinions, fall into the category of those who give themselves airs. Economic success is one of the primary obligations of every head of family; the struggle to achieve it can bring about disagreeable consequences for the individual and for the community. An individual may be driven to immoderate spending, may enfuriate his friends by reciting the catalogue of his economic resources. The maxim 'money has gone to his head' balances this *vigencia*, and induces him to exercise moderation. A rigid stratification tends towards a well-defined social distance between members of the community; when those who hold themselves in too much esteem are upbraided by the expression 'money has gone to his head', it lessens that distance just as it strengthens the belief in equality —in its turn the effect of another *vigencia*.

The maxims which counter the basic positive *vigencias* are only partially successful. For the most part they energetically attack a type of conduct that follows from economic success. This is undoubtedly one of the goals that the people seek with the greatest tenacity and sacrifices. But it does not always prevail. When economic success collides with personal dignity—as it is understood in the *pueblo*—it is the latter which prevails. Personal dignity always prevails, in all conflicts of principles or interests. It is not only the essential constituent of *honradez*, but also the principle for interpreting the intimate human structure of the community.

The total system of all the *vigencias*, when analysed, implies an ideal existence, an optimum of good conduct, away from all extremes. The *honrado* man should, in every action, in every situation, come close to this optimum if he is to be termed *honrado*. The test will be to apply to each situation the two *vigencias* which directly affect it, the positive and the negative, the one which commands and the one which limits or forbids. This in turn involves the complementarity of *vigencias*, that is, their mutual exclusiveness, the affirmation of some in terms of others, the affirmation of contrary *vigencias* which complement each other and are integrated in a whole, a system. So, *vigencias* are a coherent system of complementary social pressures, stemming from collective evaluative assumptions, which orientate and demand a specific kind of behaviour from the members of the community. Their analysis and study are essential if we are to understand a society.

CONCLUSION

'Todo hombre necesita ser lo que es para hacer lo que hace'
MACHADO

ABOUT THE middle of the seventeenth century a traveller who passed through the town was surprised at the careful cultivation of the fields. The papers of the Order of St. John of Jerusalem referring to the plots owned by the Order in the *término*, speak of the obligations of each proprietor with regard to the tilling of the soil and the proper methods and seasons for carrying out the tasks. In the document of 1186 there is mention of the irrigation ditches which water the fields. Thus, throughout the history of the town the relation of man to his environment has clearly been a constant factor of importance. The study of the geographical medium as the challenge and man's reaction as the response has proved to be a very fruitful principle, first in the organization and co-ordination of facts and secondly in the understanding of different aspects of the social life of the community.

The extent to which a man is bound to the soil is tellingly expressed in the phrase by which the resident humbly defines himself: *'Soy del campo'* (I am of the country). This fact accounts for a great part of the vocabulary and the metaphors so frequently heard, and for the whole orientation of thought. The topics of conversation reflect the different agricultural seasons and tasks throughout the year. The farming calendar generally determines amusements, visits to bars and taverns, travel, weddings and feasts; it evaluates time and the way it is represented and conceptualized.

The *pueblo* and the *vecinos* are defined mainly in relation to the soil, to the geographical-municipal boundaries or *término*, and the land that is owned. Emigration is a function of the family's agricultural property. To own fields or to increase the number owned is the goal towards which every resident struggles. Ownership of land acts as an integrating force for the residents *vis-a-vis* outsiders; at the same time it translates itself into antagonistic political blocs inside the community, indicating the relationship between property and political ideology.

The stratification of the community is based principally on the amount of land owned. It gives rise to particular relationships of collaboration and subordination. Mobility and social position, prestige and power, the limited sphere of matrimonial opportunities, education, speech, morality, amusements and travel, friendship and style of living, are all ultimately bound up with agricultural property.

Property, too, can be seen as the origin of a conventional and 'legal' system. The different ways of holding property, obligations, rights and sanctions, inheritance, contracts, the complicated irrigation system, red tape and paper work, municipal edicts and fines, are the manifold facets of the relationship between man and his physical environment. The number of plots of land belonging to the head of a family accounts in part for the degree of cohesion within the family, the work done by the women in the fields, and the greater part of the *vitandae*-relationships; the new post-war type of family is a result of the ownership of a certain number of fields by an already elderly head of a family. Property affects religious practices and gives an agricultural basis to functional cults. Finally, it is an essential part of *honradez*, which varies according to groups classified mainly in terms of agricultural property.

There is no aspect of social life, no institution of the community, which does not bear relation to, and is not directly or indirectly conditioned by, the physical environment. Hence the value of ecology as an organizing principle in the study of the community. This ecological principle cannot be understood if one takes account only of the influence of the physical environment on man and social institutions; the relation is fundamentally reversible in the sense that only when we know the influence of man on the environment can we appraise that of the environment on man. This direction in the correlation is sociologically more important than the other because it forms part of a system of ideas, desires and attitudes; differently expressed, the relation man/environment is a particular case within the social system.

*

* *

The members of the community are guided in their conduct by a set of concepts, aspirations and attitudes. These, taken as a whole, manifest the experiences and the feelings, or as I shall call it, the existential attitude of the residents. This existential attitude is essential not only in order to grasp the meaning of each of the social institutions but also their meaning as a whole.

The existential attitude that fundamentally characterizes the members of the community is individualism, this being understood as personal assertion in front of other people and in social relationships, and with regard to institutions. This attitude or manner of being, which in reality is imposed by the 'vigencias', shows itself at a deeper level as a catharsis, a liberation of the individual from social pressures. It forms a superstructure that is not directly determined either by the infrastructure or by social factors; on the contrary, in its different meanings it transcends all the institutional zones and penetrates the infrastructure as well. Thus this existential attitude is a constant in every ecological and social aspect and process. Analysing the community from this perspective we gain the impression of seeing it as a totality.

The generic name of honradez embraces a person's attitude to life and his aspirations, a code of specified conduct for the individual in the community according to status, sex and age. The precise relations with other people, the communal spirit, the correct forms of procedure, morality, the actions and omissions prescribed by this code, inform the whole of life. The personal worth both in its comparative sense and in that of the outstripping of others which honradez demands of every individual reveals the sense of equality in the pueblo, the position of the individual in relation to authority, law and political organizations, his experience and religious response. There is no doubt that guided by this principle we can better understand the whole gamut of family reactions, the position of each member in the family and the ostentation of the rites de passage. The anxiety, the hunger for property, the urge to increase the number of one's fields, the effort put into work, are particular reflections of that competitive spirit which is a driving force behind all aspects of the social system. The rigid stratification of the community and the tenacious effort to rise to a higher economic category are other manifestations of the same imperative. Finally, this existential attitude gives shape to the character, the personality of the individuals in the *pueblo*. A character which is of course an interpretative construction, implying only a unity of direction, a way that characterizes individual actions and reactions.

Ideas, objectives and the existential attitude are factual data as important and necessary for the study of a community as the physical data; indeed, from the sociological point of view they are still more important because human opinions, assumptions, attitudes and objectives make up a world *sui generis*, one of the primary objects of sociology. Social institutions cannot be fully understood except in the light of what the people using and executing them think about them, for social institutions are precisely what men think and make of them. But also, as in the previous case of the relation between man and his physical environment, the relation between man and his social institutions and *vigencias* is symmetrical. These latter internalize themselves in man, create motivations and originate attitudes. In them people feel secure; by them they think and act. The two directions of the relation are thus necessary for the examination of the social system.

Finally it must be pointed out, first that if we make use of the human or personal factor as a category of observation of a social system we observe that what is social is in part non-logical. A large number of *vigencias* can be described as non-logical. Secondly it is important to stress that in a community in which the 'militant' *vigencias* predominate, sociability is partly countered by anti-social forces. The communal life of the residents could be described as an endeavour to form an effective society which is never attained. They themselves realize this. The explanation must be sought in the fact that the greater part of the *vigencias* are anti-social and function as such. The non-logical and anti-social elements are therefore essential constituents of the social.

*

* *

The almost invariable reply to any question of mine to the people of the *pueblo* was couched in the form: 'Before ... [the civil war of 1936–39] it used to be like that'; or 'we used to do that; nowadays it is ...'; or 'we do so-and-so'. These observations point to the wide technical and social changes that have occurred in the community since 1936. The comparison of 'before' (pre-1936) with 'nowadays' is in fact a frequent topic of conversation at gatherings of elderly men and women.

This popular reference to 'before' and 'now' has helped to place the study of social institutions and problems in a wide temporal frame. No important aspect of the study of the community is without this time-perspective of 'before' and 'now'; all the social problems have been studied in relation to at least the period immediately prior to 1936. In other chapters the historical dimension is much deeper, since it goes back to the sixteenth, seventeenth and eighteenth centuries. In these chapters the 'before' and 'nowadays' have been replaced by the historical category of open/closed, referring to the periods of greater or lesser degrees of external influence and of the internal closing up of the town. This dual category of observation under-lines two perspectives for the study of the community. The study of a period of relative isolation enables us to observe and explain social phenomena from the point of view of their internal coherence, consistency and necessity. The results obtained from this study are in turn the supporting points from which we can grasp the process of change. This latter has no direction or mean-ing without the former. For not only do social phenomena change direction and meaning by virtue of their internal necessity, but also they too are affected and conditioned by external agencies, above all in a period during which a com-munity is open to the outside. This is the reason why in several chapters I have stressed the diverse historical situations of the community and its specific physiognomy. Thus, the same social phenomenon, the same institution, are considered in different perspectives and at different moments, and this is the only way of appreciating the sense and direction of their meaning and content. The 'before' and 'nowadays' of the residents, the historical category of open/closed, are no more than methods for perceiving the process, form and change of the community. Both factors are correlated and are interdependent; one has no meaning without the other; linked together they give us a view of the whole.

In these pages I have tried to write a history of an anonymous *pueblo*, or rather, I have made a historical reconstruction of the life and activities of the people of a small Aragonese town insofar as these are the expression of ideas, experiences and sentiments. At none of the specific historical moments considered is the full sense of such life and action present; the integral meaning of the life of the members of the community resides in the whole of them. The life of the community is centred round ideals, attitudes and objectives; these constitute a system with regular and constant characteristics that are repeated and reaffirmed at different historical periods. Only historical analysis can discover these recurrent elements, the structural constant which, throughout the years, and in differing historical situations, maintains a steady and direct relation with every social aspect and process.

In the last three chapters I have tried to capture by means of a historical study these recurrent elements, the structural constant in the community. What has emerged is an existential attitude, a vital sense or sentiment which I have called, to define it in one word, individualism. However, an outlook on life, or the interpretation of the existential attitude, transcends the purely sociological categories of interpretation and introduces a meta-sociological dimension. As the existential attitude is necessary to understand the meaning of the social phenomena, so these require the collaboration of meta-sociological factors in a final interpretative analysis.

*

*   *

The social system of the community can be understood, finally, from another, deeper level: analogy, correlation, opposition and complementarity are part of the logical concepts that provide the key to the final interpretation of a social system.

On the geographical and ecological level one finds several pairs of opposites: *pueblo* is the opposite of everything external, strange and foreign: it is country as opposed to city. Within the geographical and ecological level, but on a distinct plane, binary oppositions continue. The content of the word *pueblo* now bears a differential aspect since it is no longer one of the terms of the opposition or an identity *vis-a-vis*, but rather diversifies into a series of hierarchical correlations such as superior/inferior, with property/without property. These correlative opposites, operating on a distinct plane at the geographical and ecological level, have a common factor or homology: the individualizing element penetrates them, either as personal affirmation and superiority over the rest, or as affirmation subsumed in the whole which forms the *pueblo*.

Complementary relations with the same common element are also found grouped about the sexual dichotomy. The man regards himself as superior to the woman; he works in the fields and lives in the street while she devotes herself to the housework and lives at home—symbols, these, of submission as opposed to the independence represented by the man. On another plane the mutual implication of Don Juan/virginity is evident. As ex-examples of dialectical relations or opposites on different levels there may be cited: elemental family/family constellation, justice/law, the sexual behaviour required by the *vigencias*/ religious sexual morality, equality/stratification, need to work/ aspiration to live without working, thrift/prodigality, *vigencias* of co-operation/militant *vigencias*. In these as in all the binary oppositions mentioned or suggested from time to time there always appears, explicitly or implicitly, the homology to which I have referred above. This in its turn, and from another angle, strengthens the validity of using the existential attitude as a category for the explanation of the social system.

I have noted some examples of opposites based on hierarchy and complementarity, all of them oppositions operating on a sociological plane. But the oppositions also operate on another, deeper level, on the level of concepts or ideals; transposing oppositions to this level makes it easier to see the whole as an integration. This level seems to be made up almost exclusively of masculine concepts and ideals, a logical consequence, indeed, of the greater number of *vigencias* which exert pressure upon the man. Different aspects of reality have their corresponding ideals, complementary and opposed. Faced with the necessity of living and working in the country, they think about and idealize the blessings of city life; being obliged to work, they daydream of a state of perfection wherein they would live without working. To the effective feminine domination, every day and in almost every sphere, they respond with the belief that in principle, theoretically and externally, it is they themselves who are the superior ones, the ones who command. Don Juanism is a masculine idealization, resulting from the severe sexual restrictions to which the community subjects them. The attitude of insubordination, of rebellion, corresponds to the multiplicity and rigidity of customs, conventions and laws. To the *vigencias* which unfailingly determine the right conduct and reactions in each and every situation they reply with a '*No me da la gana*' ('I don't feel like it')—as if they wished to overcome them all and make them disappear for ever.

In this series of oppositions, the examples of which are drawn from different levels, the first element is taken from the reality, from what is, whilst its complementary opposite lies on a mental and ideal level—what they wish were so. To reality they oppose the ideal. This forms an incomplete logical system which sums up their aspirations, what they wish were so but is not. Reality, disagreeable as it may be, has to be reckoned with, while in the sphere of aspirations one must of necessity expect disappointment, which gives a certain tragic character to the opposition. Aspirations offer an escape from reality. The real and the ideal form a dialectic unit in operation.

In the analysis of the *vigencias* it was shown how the social system of the community, by directing and developing the conduct of individuals in accordance with certain rules and patterns, both engendered the prescribed mode of procedure and at the same time provided resistant and antagonistic forces which tended to counterbalance it. While demanding a vigorous personal affirmation in each member of the community they constrain him to behave according to common norms. This is equivalent to saying that his individuality is itself in a sense a product of the *vigencias*, a social imposition. This internalization of the content of the *vigencias* carries with it a certain alienation in the social sphere. But transposed to a conceptual plane it is an incentive to liberation, to the repulse of everything that is obligatory, directing and binding, of everything that is social. The existential attitude in the community could thus be explained as a reaction in the face of strong social pressures, the escape to an ideal level as a mental compensation for them. To put it another way: the oppositions found on the sociological plane of the community and on the logical and mental level in its members could be explained by recourse to a 'theory of complements' or 'system of compensations', that is to say, by recourse to methods or operations tending to synthesize or integrate the real and the ideal, necessity and liberty, man and the community.

GLOSSARY: I

Spanish words and expressions are translated or explained when they first occur. This glossary refers to those which are frequently repeated.

Bachillerato (Bachiller): Educational attainments required before attempting University entrance.

Bracero(s): Those with no landed property, nor any fixed trade in the town.

Caballero(s): second rank of the mediæval aragonese nobility.

Cahíz: equals 38 ares and 140 milliares. The acre equals 40 ares, 47 centiares.

Cortes: Legislative Chambers.

Criado: labourer attached to the house.

Cuadrilla: a group of friends.

Fiesta: festival.

Forastero: outsider; opposed to *vecino.*

Hectárea: equals 2.471 acres.

Huerta: irrigated land.

Infanzón: lowest rank of the mediæval Aragonese nobility.

Jornalero(s): those whose landholdings exceed one hectare but do not exceed three.

Jota: regional song (and dance) of Aragón.

Mosén: priest

Peón(es): those whose landholdings are of less than one hectare.

Propietario(s): those whose landholdings are of more than three hectares but do not exceed five.

Pudiente(s): (a) rich and powerful; (b) those whose landholdings are of more than five hectares but do not exceed fifteen.

Pueblo: (a) town; (b) the people of the town.

Quinto: conscript.

Regadío: irrigable land.

Ricos-hombres: first rank of mediæval Aragonese nobility.

Ricos-ricos: those who own land exceeding fifteen hectares.

Rondar: to go round the streets by night singing and playing guitars.

Señorito: young gentleman.

Término: the land within the jurisdiction of the municipal authorities.

Vecino(s): (a) those born in the town who have come of age or who are independent and who habitually reside in the town, being entered under this description in the council register. (b) those not born in the town but registered in the council as such, after two years residence or by concession following petition, after six months residence.

GLOSSARY: II

In several chapters there appear quotations with the following obsolete monetary units:

dineros
ducados
escudos
libras
libras jaquesas
reales
sueldos

whose translation I have not attempted because of the difficulty in ascertaining their relation to present-day monetary units.

SELECTED BIBLIOGRAPHY

Adkins, A. W. H.: *Merit and Responsibility*, O.U.P. 1960.
Aguado, P.: *Manual de Historia de España*, Vols, II and III, Madrid 1959.
Alleau, R.: *De la nature des symboles*, Paris 1958.
Aristotle: *Constitution of Athens*, New York 1950.
Politics, Loeb Classical Library, 1959.
The Nicomachean Ethics, Loeb Classical Library, 1954.
Bowra, C. M.: *The Greek Experience*, London 1958, 2nd imp.
Bras, G. Le: *Études de Sociologie religieuse*, P.U.F. Vols. I and II, Paris 1955 and 1956.
Buhler, K.: *Teoría del Lenguaje*, Revista de Occidente, Madrid 1961 2^a ed.
Caro Baroja, J.: *Los Pueblos de España*. Barcelona 1946.
Cassirer, E.: *Las Ciencias de la Cultura*, Méjico 1955, 2^a ed.
Essay on Man, New Haven 1956.
Dilthey, W.: *Meaning in History*, London 1961.
Ehrenberg, V.: *The Greek State*, Oxford 1960.
d'Entreves, A. P.: *Natural Law*, London 1960, 5th imp.
Freyer, H.: *Introducción a la Sociología*, Madrid 1951, 3^a ed.
Teoría de la época actual, Méjico 1958.
García Mercadal, J.: (editor): *Viajes de extranjeros por España y Portugal*, Vols. I and II, Madrid 1952 and 1959.
Gerth, HH. and C. Wright Mills: *From Max Weber*, London 1957, 3rd ed.
Gracián, B.: *Obras completas*, Madrid 1960.
Gurvitch, G.: *Sociology of Law*, London 1953 2nd impr.
Le concept des classes sociales, C.D.U. Paris 1954.
La multiplicité de temps sociaux, C.D.U., Paris 1958.
Traité de Sociologie (sous la direction), P.U.F. Vols. I and II, Paris 1958 and 1960.
Halbwachs, M.: *La mémoire collective*, P.U.F., Paris 1950.
Hayek, F. von: *Scientisme et sciences sociales*, Paris 1952.
Jiménez de Aragón: *Cancionero aragonés*, Zaragoza 1925.
Kenny, M.: *A Spanish Tapestry*, London 1961.
León, Fr. Luis de: *La perfecta casada*, Espasa-Calpe 1957.
Lloyd Warner, W. and others: *Social class in America*, Harper Torchbook, 1960.
Machado, A.: *Juan de Mairena*, Losada 1957, 3^a ed., Vols. I and II.

Madariaga, S. de: *España*, Buenos Aires 1955, 6ª ed.
Madramany y Calatayud, M.: *Tratado de la nobleza de la Corona de Aragón*, Valencia 1788, Barcelona 1957.
Mannheim, K.: *Essays on the Sociology of Knowledge*, London 1959, 2nd impr.
Marías, J.: *El método histórico de las generaciones*, Madrid 1949.
La estructura social, Madrid 1955.
Nilsson, M. P.: *Greek Folk Religion*, New York 1940.
Ortega y Gasset, J.: *Le rebelión de las masas*, Espasa-Calpe, 1941, 4ª ed.
España invertebrada, Madrid 1950, 11ª ed.
Ideas y creencias, Madrid 1959, 8ª ed.
En torno a Galileo, Madrid 1959, 2ª ed.
El tema de nuestro tiempo, Madrid 1956, 12ª ed.
Historia como sistema, Madrid 1958, 3ª ed.
Las Atlántidas y del Imperio Romano, Madrid 1960, 3ª ed.
Una interpretación de la Historia Universal, Madrid 1960.
El hombre y la gente, Madrid 1958, 2ª ed.
Parsons, T. and Smelser, N. J.: *Economy and Society*, London 1957.
Pitt-Rivers, J. A.: *The People of the Sierra*, London 1954.
Plato: *Dialogues of Plato*, selected by J. D. Kaplan, The Pocket Library 1955.
Reissman, L.: *Class in American Society*, London 1959.
Ríos, F. de los: *Religión y Estado en la España de siglo XVI*, Méjico 1957.
Savall y Dronda (ed.): *Fueros, Observancias y Actas de Corte del Reino de Aragón*, Zaragoza 1866, Vols. I and II.
Schumpeter, J.: *Imperialism. Social Classes*, New York 1958.
Simmel, G.: *Sociology of Religion*, New York 1959.
Sinclair, T. A.: *A History of Greek Political Thought*, London 1959, 2nd imp.
Unamuno, M. de: *En torno al casticismo*, Espasa-Calpe, 1957, 4ª ed.
Del Sentimiento trágico del la vida, Madrid 1958.
Valdeavellano, L. G. de: *Historia de España*, Madrid 1955, 2ª ed. Vols. I and II.
Vitoria, F. de: *Releciones sobre los indios y el derecho de guerra*, Espasa-Calpe 1946.
Vives, J. L.: *Obras completas*, Madrid Vols. I and II, 1947 and 1948.
Weber, A.: *Sociología de la Historia y de la Cultura*, Buenos Aires, 1960, 2ª ed.
Weber, M.: *Economía y Sociedad*, Méjico 1944 Vols. I and II.
Wright Mills, C.: *White Collar*, New York 1956.
The Power Elite, New York 1959.

INDEX

Abd-el-Krim: 183.

Africa: 183.

Agriculture: agricultural year ...:
24–32, 197; change in mentality
towards: 36, 125, 197; government protection of: 120–1, 122,
124–5 (see also Government);
rationalization of: 122–3, 136, 137;
mechanization of: 24, 28, 35, 69,
70, 71, 72, 81, 117, 118, 121–3,
133, 134, 135, 136–7, 169, 182,
184, 190, 191, 197, 340.

Aldeanueva: 13, 262.

Alfonso I (The Battler): 6.

Alfonso XII: 226, 230.

Alfonso XIII: 182, 231.

Alleau, R.: 94.

Amadeus of Savoy: 226, 229, 230.

Anarchists: 226, 227, 257.

Andalucía: 41, 226.

Animals, domestic: 4, 16, 24, 25,
36, 58, 68, 70, 122, 123, 124, 132,
133, 136–7, 243, 261, 304, 314.

Aragón: 1, 2, 10, 77, 129 166 202,
259, 262, 301, 327–8; towns in
...: 4–5, 84, 254, 260; nobility
in ...: 5, 6, 213, 257, 314;
Cortes of ...: 5; patroness of ...:
14, 300; distribution of land
in ...: 44.

Arcos: 13, 52.

Arguedas: 6.

Aristophanes: 251.

Aristotle: 1, 250, 251, 252, 253, 254,
255.

Asturias: 227.

Athens: 254.

Bakunin: 226.

Bank: 13, 14, 71, 74, 75, 96, 111,
117, 118, 120, 121, 123, 138, 139,
141, 190, 191, 195, 323, 338, 343.

Barcelona: 1, 32, 103, 128, 225, 226,
227, 321.

Barreiros: 5.

Basques: 40.

Belmonte de los Caballeros: ancient
situation: 6; actual situation and
habitat: 5; ancient jurisdiction
over: 5, 6, 18; demographic
variations: 7–8; and outsiders:
10, 12–13, 43.

Boltaña: 6.

Borrow, G.: 327.

Bowra, C. M.: 252.

Boy: schooling: 170–1, 216 (see
also Stratification); amusements:
82, 100–1, 152, 171–5; work: 171.

Bracero(s): 67–8, 69, 70, 71, 73,
74, 75, 76, 77, 79, 86, 89, 124,
126, 127, 128, 129, 130, 131, 134,
138, 199, 294, 303, 317, 319, 320,
323, 325.

Brotherhood, of Farmers and Stockbreeders: 10, 11, 14, 52, 74, 75,
76, 107, 120–1, 131, 146, 220,
221, 222, 246, 249, 304, 324, 338.

Bullfights: 12, 13, 102–3, 174, 220,
266, 288, 323, 326, 327, 336, 341,
343, 346.

Caballeros: 5.

Cádiz: 41.

Calderón de la Barca: 310, 331.

Car: 37, 99, 134, 182, 184, 322,
338.

Cataluña: 225, 226.

Change: in structure of community:
48–50, 119 (see Agriculture; Civil
war; Development; Family;

Sorrows: 297, 298, 306, 307, 308
(see also Religion).
Outsiders: 19, 43, 81, 174, 209, 237,
245, 261, 289 (see also Belmonte).
Oviedo: 225.

Pamplona: 32, 224, 225.
Paris: 343.
Parish: 10, 11-12, 14, 202, 260;
archives of: 7, 55, 139, 260,
284.
Patio: 4.
Patrons (religious): 11-12, 45, 139,
202, 251, 271, 279, 281, 288, 289,
304; as integrating factor: 301-2;
as disintegrating factor: 302-3
(see *Fiestas*).
Pavía: 226.
Peón(es): 68, 69, 70, 71, 73, 74, 75,
81, 104, 108, 124, 126, 129-130,
131, 134, 137, 199, 294, 303, 317,
319, 320, 321, 323.
Pericles: 254.
Perú: 226.
Peter IV: 314.
Pheneia: 250.
Philip II: 5, 259, 274.
Philippines: 227.
Plato: 254.
Politics: ideas and attitudes about:
43, 105-6, 197, 229, 232, 233-4;
propaganda: 43, 233; and religion: 43, 44, 45, 47, 50-1, 303;
political parties: 44-47, 114, 185-
190; and women: 46, 50, 187 (see
also Council).
Position (social): 65, 73, 80, 84, 86,
93, 95, 100, 115, 324, 342-3.
Prestige: 71, 108-9, 115, 118, 123,
141.
Prim: 226.
Primo de Rivera: 39, 41, 183, 216,
227, 231.
Processions: 45, 110, 139, 195, 267-
8, 279-82, 296, 297, 298, 299,
302, 303, 304, 311.
'Professionals': 59-60, 61, 62, 91,
104, 111, 184, 203, 208, 209, 215,

216, 218, 269, 312, 338, 340, 345
(see also Stratification).
Propietario(s): 70-1, 73, 74, 75, 76,
77, 79, 86, 88, 89, 93, 97, 98, 99,
110, 115, 116, 131-2, 138, 199,
294, 303, 304, 305, 320, 346.
Pudiente(s): 58, 71-2, 73, 74, 75,
76, 77, 81, 86, 88, 89, 90, 93, 97,
98, 99, 101, 103, 104, 107, 108,
110, 111, 113, 114, 115, 116, 117,
121, 132-3, 136, 137, 138, 140,
166, 167, 168, 185, 192, 199,
200, 205, 214, 251, 282, 288, 293,
294, 297, 303, 305, 320, 321, 322,
323, 324, 341, 346.
Pueblo: 14, 140, 141, 202-3, 205-7,
211, 213, 214, 215, 217, 221, 222,
231, passim; and polis: 250-5.
Puerto Rico: 182, 227.

Regadío: 8 (see Irrigation).
Religion: (a) historical perspective: christianization of institutions: 260-1, 262, 263-5, 274,
278, 285, 287, 292; and pastimes:
263, 265-6, 287; and work on
feastdays: 31, 32, 60, 113, 248,
261, 266-7, 286-7; cults: 267,
279, 281, 282; administration of
Church: 268, 270-4; tithes and
firstfruits: 268, 269-70, 287; religious ideas: 274-7; beliefs and
practices: 278; brotherhoods: 279,
281; internal aspect: 282-3; behaviour: 263, 268, 287; (b)
changing attitudes: 284-5, 288;
in the Republic: 40, 44, 45, 46-7,
48-9, 110, 289-91, 303; and political power: 291-2; (c) present
day: 11; classification of parishioners: 293-4; local devotions:
296, 297-9, 301-4, 307; regional
devotions: 14, 229-301, 302, 307;
functional cults: 304-5; and
family: 296, 298, 300, 305;
devotion to Our Lady: 305-9 (see
also Our Lady); as personal salvation: 310-11; and amusements: